THE
MOST
REAL
BEING

THE
MOST
REAL
BEING

A Biblical and Philosophical Defense of Divine Determinism

J.A. CRABTREE

Gutenberg College Press

EUGENE, OREGON

First edition published 2004 in the United States of America by
Gutenberg College Press
1883 University Street
Eugene, OR 97403

Typeset in Adobe Garamond
By Treemen Design
Printed and bound in the United States of America.

Oil Painting on page vii by Michael McArtie

Library of Congress Control Number: 2004114013

ISBN 0-9746914-1-0

To Jody,

the most important person

in my life;

and to John David,

who made this

much more than academic.

...that they should seek God,

if perhaps they might grope for him and find him.

Yet he is not far from any one of us,

for **in him we live and move and have our being...**

Acts 17:27–28

THE MOST REAL BEING
Ens Realissimus

The "most real being" (*ens realissimus* or, more typically, *ens realissimum*) is one of several titles that medieval philosophers and theologians used to denote God. The fact that God exists on a higher level of reality than we do—that is, that he is more real than we are—is a critical piece in my resolving how divine determinism and human freedom are compatible. Since the reconciliation of divine determinism and human freedom is a major preoccupation of the book, it seemed apt to refer to this key to their reconciliation in the title. While my concept of God as the Most Real Being is not identical to that of the medieval philosophers, I like the title and have chosen to appropriate it here.

For more information on ordering directly from the publishers,
please visit our web site or contact us via e-mail:

 www.gutenberg.edu
office@gutenberg.edu

CONTENTS

PREFACE

This book is a defense of divine determinism—belief in the unqualified, unrestricted sovereignty of God. Historically, this position has come to be associated with Calvinism and the Reformed tradition. I expect Calvinists to be largely sympathetic with my conclusions. Readers from outside the Reformed tradition will typically be unsympathetic. But it will help both groups to understand the following:

1. I am not a product of the Reformed tradition myself. I have never been a member of any fellowship with historical roots in Calvinism, and none of my spiritual training was particularly Calvinistic.

2. I do not now and never have agreed with the Calvinistic theological system in its entirety. Perhaps I should. Perhaps someday I will. But right now I believe that some of its tenets do not conform to the teaching of the Bible. I greatly respect the Calvinist tradition. It has much to teach us all. But I do not believe it is the last word in theology. Accordingly, this book is not a defense of Calvinism *per se*. It merely defends a particular doctrine that—as it happens—constitutes a fundamental distinctive of Calvinism. It is not a defense of the entire Calvinist system.

3. Even within the Calvinist tradition, the particular view of sovereignty I defend here will not find acceptance with all. Many self-identified Calvinists will consider my view extreme, problematic—perhaps even bizarre. I might be labeled a "hyper-Calvinist"—a four-letter word by anyone's count.

4. Not coming out of a Reformed background, I do not hold my particular view of God's sovereignty out of theological inertia. I became persuaded through biblical study and philosophical reflection. Specifically, I was persuaded by the very line of argument I expound in this book. My eventual persuasion came in spite of strong internal resistance to it. I began my journey with deeply ingrained prejudices against divine determinism—prejudices forged in me through many years of theological enculturation from a non-Reformed perspective.

My purpose in writing this book is two-fold: (1) I want to encourage the sympathetic Reformed reader to give some fresh thought to his exposition and defense of God's sovereignty. Our culture needs a more biblically accurate and more rationally sound defense than it typically receives. (2) I want to challenge the opponent of the Reformed view of sovereignty to reconsider his position. Perhaps the Reformed tradition is right in its doctrine of divine sovereignty. I hope the unsympathetic reader will at least give me the opportunity to make my case. I further hope that, should the reader remain unpersuaded by my arguments, he will respect them enough to answer them, demonstrating how and where they fail. It would be regrettable if a reader dismisses this book as "hyper-Calvinist" after 10 pages, never seriously attempting to rebut its arguments.

Most who reject "hyper-Calvinism" do so on the grounds that its alleged implications are clearly and obviously false. If divine determinism does, in fact, imply that man has no free will, that God rather than man is culpable for evil, that man can do nothing about assuring his own salvation, and that human initiative is futile, then I would readily denounce it as a dangerous heresy. Such an unbiblical view would indeed have false and destructive implications and be deserving of the negative reaction the "hyper-Calvinist" label elicits. But the crux of the issue is whether these alleged objectionable implications are, in fact, necessitated by divine determinism. Many simply assume that they are, with no further thought given to the subject. Few have ever properly examined the question. In this book I reject the tacit cultural assumption that divine determinism entails this specific, identifiable set of false beliefs. One of my key contentions will be that divine determinism does not, in truth, imply any of the objectionable beliefs usually said to follow from it. I would hope, therefore, that my book accomplishes at least this much: to render "hyper-Calvinism" respectable and to secure for it a serious hearing. For far too long it has served as nothing more than a theological insult.

I began this book nearly 19 years ago, in 1985. After completing a rough draft, my work was interrupted by graduate school and a number of other projects. The summer of 1999 was my first opportunity to return to this project in earnest, the summer of 2003 my first opportunity to resume again, and the summer of 2004 my opportunity to finally complete it. In the intervening years it received only brief and infrequent attention. The book is better, I think, for having sat those many years on the shelf. When I first began to consider it, divine determinism was a new and radically different paradigm that required a complete restructuring of my theological foundations. Graduate studies, further time for reflection, opportunities to employ this new paradigm in my bible study, and increased familiarity with it have only served to increase my confidence that divine determinism is true.

In this book I do not interact with the modern theological position sometimes referred to as "openness of God" theology. This theological position did not enter into public awareness until several years after I had finished the rough draft of this work. I decided not to change the structure of my book in order to interact directly with the issues raised by it. Indeed, I have not as yet had time to familiarize myself thoroughly with the position and its arguments. From what little I do know about openness of God theology, it would appear that, in most respects, my views are incompatible with it. But in one important respect my views concur with theirs: we both view the theology of mainstream evangelicalism as incoherent. We both argue that evangelicalism cannot logically believe in divine foreknowledge, even though it purports to do so. If the underlying assumptions of mainstream evangelical theology are taken to their logical conclusions, then one would have to conclude that God's ability to foreknow the future is significantly handicapped. Openness theology embraces that conclusion, believing that God is severely limited in his foreknowledge. I reject it. The Bible teaches God's unimpaired ability to foreknow the future. If modern evangelical theological assumptions are inconsistent with the Bible's teaching in this regard, then the assumptions of modern evangelical theology need to be rejected. Openness theology takes the opposite tack. It accepts the theological assumptions of evangelicalism and simply takes them to their logical conclusion, rejecting what the Bible actually teaches.

There is a second significant omission in this book. While I am familiar with and prepared to interact with Jonathan Edwards' arguments in his book *Freedom of the Will*, I have chosen not to do so here. While I respect Edwards' position and his arguments, his views are not ultimately compatible with my own. Edwards, I would argue, defends divine determinism as an actuality mediated through a sort of natural determinism. Because I take the position that natural determinism, in all of its forms, is philosophically indefensible, being contrary to commonsensical notions of human freedom and responsibility, I must ultimately conclude that Edwards' position is philosophically indefensible. The Arminians with whom Edwards is interacting do, at crucial junctures, raise valid philosophical objections to Edwards' position. The strength of Edwards' work lies not at the level of his philosophical defense, it lies at the level of his clear and unyielding commitment to the teaching of the Bible. While his Arminian opponents are more faithful to sound philosophy, Edwards is more faithful to the Bible's teaching. Edwards has chosen the better of the two, but he has sacrificed rational coherence to do so. My view is that we must achieve both—rational coherence as well as biblical faithfulness. My contention is that the divine determinism I defend in this book does just that.

———————

Let me make a few suggestions to the reader who wants to sample the argument rather than tackle the entire work. Readers who already hold a high view of divine sovereignty as biblical may be able to profitably begin at chapter 9. However, I do introduce concepts and arguments in the initial eight chapters that may, in fact, be indispensable to adequately understanding the arguments in chapter 9 and following. Chapters 1, 4, and 6 may be particularly important. Also, the dialogue in Appendix L is a very concise summary of a substantial part of my argument.

———————

Many have encouraged me to simplify this book. I fully acknowledge that simplicity is desirable. And I have done what I can. But I lack that rare skill needed to make highly complex and intellectually challenging issues simple and readily accessible. Surviving my own intellectual battle with these issues was challenging enough. I fear that the even more challenging task of making my conclusions readily apparent and my arguments simple to follow is beyond my ability. Consequently, some portions of this book may prove to be tough sledding. I apologize. My sincere hope is that the effort will be worth it.

My earnest desire is that we might all come to see and understand God in all his glory, that we might come to see and understand him as the One in whom we live, and move, and have our being, that we might come to know God as the One who authors the entirety of cosmic reality from outside the reality in which we dwell, that we might come to know God as the *ens realissimus*, the most real being.

J. A. "Jack" Crabtree

The Carriage House
Eugene, Oregon
July 2004

ACKNOWLEDGMENTS

It would be impossible to acknowledge all the people whose thoughts and questions and input have shaped and influenced my thinking. I am grateful to all the faculty and students at Gutenberg College and to the larger community surrounding the college. They have created a unique and very spiritually and intellectually stimulating community within which to work. I could not have studied and thought as I have in any other environment. But there are a few whose contribution to this work in particular cannot escape my notice.

I would like to thank the Marjorie M. Schmidt Foundation for helping to make the completion of this manuscript possible. I would especially like to thank Kent Scudder for his personal help in bringing this project to completion. I owe a great deal to Charley Dewberry for getting this book to press; and to Bryan Taylor and Michael McArtie for allowing me to benefit from their talent and creativity. I owe an immense debt of gratitude to Dr. Stan Filarski, whose painstaking critique of an early draft was of immense help to me. Likewise, I am very grateful to Linda Crabtree, Kathryn Wahlstrom, and Gloria Biersdorff for their patient and competent reading of the final draft. I owe special thanks to all the people over the years, too numerable to mention, who have supported me financially and otherwise so that I might carry out my responsibilities at McKenzie Study Center and at Gutenberg College. I owe special thanks to Dale Crabtree, whose generous help and encouragement was instrumental in getting this project off the ground and seeing it to completion. Thanks to Linore Crabtree for a lifetime of support. Particular thanks go to my wife, Jody, for her constant, patient, and loving sacrifice and support. Nothing I do would be possible without her.

While all the above have been personally supportive of me, and while this project would not have been possible without them, none of them can be blamed for the results. Their support has come without specific knowledge of the conclusions I was reaching in the course of my thought and writing. The result is my responsibility alone. I hope it does not come as an unpleasant surprise to any who have placed their confidence in me over these many years. My earnest desire has been to understand and articulate the truth about God. I hope that—by God's grace—I have in some small measure accomplished that.

INTRODUCTION

CHAPTER ONE

DIVINE DETERMINISM:
What is it?

The Free Will–Sovereignty Dilemma

This book explores the relationship of God to his creation. Every Christian familiar with the Bible knows and believes that God is the sovereign king, ruling over his creation. But sovereignty is a highly problematic and controversial concept. When we get specific about what sovereignty means—and what it entails—there is considerable disagreement. One man's sovereign is another man's cosmic wimp. And one man's cosmic wimp is another man's all-powerful, but self-restrained, king.

There are competing theories of God's relationship to his creation. Any theory worth considering must somehow reconcile two realities: (i) the Bible's contention that God is sovereign, and (ii) our commonsensical conviction that man is a free and responsible moral agent. Any serious proposal must do justice to both these facts. Controversy is the inevitable result, for divine sovereignty and human freedom seem utterly irreconcilable, and to reach agreement on how to reconcile the irreconcilable is difficult indeed. By all appearances, to affirm divine sovereignty is to deny, or at least to compromise, human freedom, and to fully affirm human freedom is to compromise divine sovereignty. Which should we do? People cannot agree.

Divine sovereignty, in current theological discussion, has come to mean divine power—the power God has to control reality.[1] The extent of God's sovereignty is the extent of his control. To the extent that things are beyond his control, to that extent he is not sovereign. Hence, if human choice is beyond divine control, then God is not sovereign over human choice and divine sovereignty is limited by human freedom. By this sort of

---

1. So, for example, notice how H. B. Kuhn virtually equates sovereignty with omnipotence in his article on the sovereignty of God. Cf., H. B. Kuhn, "Sovereignty of God," in vol. 5 of *The Zondervan Pictorial Encyclopedia of the Bible*, ed. Merril C. Tenney (Grand Rapids: Zondervan Publishing House, 1975), 468. Whether the concept of sovereignty within modern theological discussion conforms to the biblical concept of sovereignty is an interesting question, but it has no bearing on my point here. If "sovereignty" in the Bible does not mean the power to control, then we could conduct the debate using a different word. The issue is the dilemma between human freedom and the degree of divine control, whatever that control be called.

reasoning, in order to affirm that God's sovereignty is absolute, one must affirm divine control over human choice. But if God controls human choice, then man is not strictly free, for he is not free from God. Divine sovereignty and human freedom appear to be mutually exclusive concepts.

This is the dilemma that has confronted Christians down through the ages. One cannot embrace equally the sovereignty of God and the freedom of man. What's a Christian to do?

THREE SOLUTIONS TO THE FREE WILL–SOVEREIGNTY DILEMMA

Faced with this dilemma, Christians have offered very different solutions. Some, wanting to stay faithful to the Bible while honoring deeply felt intuitions, insist that both divine sovereignty and human freedom are to be affirmed with equal force.[2] They insist that neither concept qualify or limit the other. But we have already seen that—given the prevailing conceptions of sovereignty and free will—this is patently illogical. Its proponents fully acknowledge its illogicality, but they justify it in the name of "mystery." The divine sovereignty–human freedom dilemma is a case of true "paradox."[3]

Proponents of the second solution reject the notion of "paradox." So, seeking to remain faithful to the Bible as they understand it, they refuse to compromise the sovereignty of God. To exempt human choice from God's sovereign control would deny what the Bible teaches—namely, that God rules the earth with unlimited, unqualified sovereignty. Accordingly, some who opt for this solution go so far as to deny the reality of man's free will. Free will is a philosophical fiction, not an authentic biblical concept. Others acknowledge the reality of free will, but they refuse to let this concession affect their theology in any way. They doggedly embrace the clear

---

2. I do not cite any published examples of this or the solutions that follow. These solutions are not so much the domain of particular Christian philosophers, theologians, or schools of thought, but the domain of typical Christians sitting in typical church pews. They represent viewpoints that control the thinking of average individuals in the course of everyday discourse. As such, these proposals need not be so logically unassailable as the notions which we publish in books; for they are only advanced in casual everyday discussions by average Christians. Accordingly, some or all of these ideas have never made it into books. Nevertheless, these are the options that everyday people consider viable.

3. In the context of this solution to the divine sovereignty–human freedom dilemma, "paradox" and "mystery" apparently mean this: something that is true and ought to be believed even though it is utterly irrational to do so.

implications of God's absolute sovereignty, unqualified by the free will of man. While they give a nod to the reality of free will, for all practical purposes they deny it.

The majority of modern Christians are unwaveringly committed to certain foundational assumptions about God and reality that are believed to conflict with absolute sovereignty. They would rather reconsider and redefine the nature and extent of divine sovereignty than reject what is indubitably true. If absolute sovereignty negates human freedom, then so much the worse for absolute sovereignty. Human freedom is so clearly real that one would be a fool to deny it. We are not puppets, controlled and manipulated by God. So we must adjust our concept of divine sovereignty to leave room for undeniably real human freedom.

Neither can we jettison our belief in the perfect goodness of God. If God is in control of everything and is responsible for all that exists, then he is responsible for all the evil that exists in the world. But if God is responsible for evil, how can we affirm that he is good? Surely, to concede that God's sovereignty is limited is more reasonable than to jettison our conviction that God is perfectly good. God is sovereign, but only up to a point. Where the domain of God's sovereignty ends is where the evil in the world begins.

The proponents of this third solution do not agree on where to locate the limits of divine sovereignty. Some would draw the line at evil. God is responsible for the good in the world. He is not responsible for the evil. Others would draw the line at freewill choice. God is responsible for the physical, mechanical creation and all that happens within it. He is not responsible for freewill choices. Others would limit his control in both respects. He is in control of the good and morally neutral things that happen in the physical, mechanical world. But he is not responsible for any evil (Satan is), and he is not responsible for any freewill choices (good or bad).

MY SOLUTION TO THE
FREE WILL–SOVEREIGNTY DILEMMA

This book defends yet a fourth solution to the free will–sovereignty dilemma: DIVINE DETERMINISM. Divine determinism affirms that both terms of the dilemma are true without qualification: God is absolutely sovereign (even over the choices of men), and men truly do have free will and moral accountability. But unlike the second solution above, divine determinism does not appeal to "paradox." On the contrary, I will argue that absolute divine sovereignty and unqualified human accountability are—against all appearance—perfectly compatible. They can be reconciled in a way that is logical, comprehensible, and even commonsensical.

Understandably, divine determinism will ask us to significantly modify how we understand both divine sovereignty and free will. Divine sovereignty and human freedom are irreconcilable under the popular conceptions of each. But under the modified conceptions that I shall propose, they become perfectly compatible.

This solution is not strictly new. Others have affirmed both absolute divine sovereignty and absolute human freedom. And some of these have similarly refused to exalt irrationality under the banner of "mystery." My purpose is to restate and defend this viewpoint afresh. I have found it compelling. I offer it anew for serious consideration. If I contribute anything original at all, it is but two things: (1) a fresh analogy that can help us grasp the rational compatibility of divine sovereignty and human freedom, and (2) a stronger, more confident affirmation that divine sovereignty and human responsibility are intellectually compatible and reconcilable in a way that is not beyond the grasp of human intellect.

Defining Divine Determinism

THE DOCTRINE OF DIVINE DETERMINISM

If divine determinism claimed only that God has determinative control over his creation, then most, if not all, Christians would be divine determinists. Every Christian believes that God controls reality—within limits. But I will use the term more narrowly. By DIVINE DETERMINISM, I mean total, absolute divine control over the whole of reality. Divine determinism is the viewpoint that literally every detail of every aspect of everything that is or occurs in reality is caused and determined by God.[4]

According to divine determinism, God causes everything in the whole

---

4. More familiarly, God's role as the ultimate cause of all things is, I believe, couched in terms of his sovereignty—his absolute sovereignty. I choose to avoid the term 'sovereignty' for two reasons: (1) The term *sovereignty* is understood by different readers in a myriad of different ways. Readers will not necessarily agree on the implications of God's being sovereign. Hence, to describe God as being totally sovereign may or may not convey the viewpoint that I am calling divine determinism. But, if I describe God as the absolute determiner and cause of all things, there can be no confusion as to what I believe is God's relationship to reality. (2) *Sovereignty* is actually a relatively vague metaphorical term that does not communicate with enough philo-

of reality. Everything! Everything that exists, he has created. Everything that happens, he has caused to happen. Rocks, rivers, trees, flowers, birds, moose, or stars—they all owe the entire course of their existence to God. And so do men, angels, demons, and any other intelligent life in the cosmos—even Satan. God determines every thought, word, deed, desire, and choice. He determines the speed and location of every sub-atomic particle in the entire universe. Literally everything that occurs has resulted from his willing it into existence. Nothing can exist and nothing can occur apart from his causing it to be. This includes both good and evil. He has willed the good that is; he has willed the evil that is. He, and he alone, is ultimately responsible (and yet entirely without blame) for the existence of every evil deed.[5] This is the doctrine I am advancing in this book.

Any viewpoint that, in contrast to divine determinism, sets boundaries on the extent of God's determinative control I will label LIMITED DETERMINISM. Different varieties of limited determinism exist.[6] Each would draw slightly different boundaries to mark what God does and does not determine. Some argue that God determines the affairs of the impersonal universe but not the choices of men and angels. Others maintain that God determines the good that occurs but never evil. For the purposes of this book, I will consider all of these different views under the one category of limited determinism. LIMITED DETERMINISM is, of course, a shorthand reference to limited DIVINE determinism[7] in contrast to absolute or unlimited DIVINE determinism.

---

sophical precision to sort out the important issues involved in this discussion. When the Bible speaks of God's sovereignty, it is not with this particular discussion in mind. Its purpose is to exalt God as the ruler, judge, and controller of all history. But questions of how God controls history and to exactly what extent he controls history are generally not the immediate concern. For our more specialized purposes, we need a more precise term.

5. As should eventually become clear, I do not question God's goodness. Though he is responsible for the existence of evil—as he is for everything that exists—he is not culpable for any particular evils that occur. I will argue this in detail in Part Four. I insist, without contradiction, that God is a perfectly good being with a completely unsullied character even though he has created the evil that is in the world. I would hope that those who respond with strong negative emotion to the suggestion that God is the ultimate cause of evil will hear me out. I am no less committed than they to the doctrine of God's moral perfection. If I thought for one second that divine determinism compromises God's moral purity, I would reject it summarily.

6. See appendix A for an understanding of how divine determinism relates to all the various alternative theories regarding the ultimate determinative causes of reality.

7. By LIMITED DETERMINISM I do not mean any form of determinism whatsoever that is limited in its extent. I use LIMITED DETERMINISM to specify DIVINE determinism that is limited in its extent.

THE DOCTRINE OF NATURAL DETERMINISM

At various points throughout this book I will refer to a counter-theory that I call NATURAL DETERMINISM. Natural determinism is the theory that *nature* is responsible for everything that is and everything that occurs.[8] Everything that exists and everything that happens is because of the inevitable outworking of the laws of physics. Therefore, everything happens out of physical and mechanical necessity. This includes not only natural phenomena like rain, wind, earthquakes, and weeds, but human behavior as well. If I order a raspberry milkshake rather than a cup of coffee, I do so because the laws of physics required it. I turned left at the corner rather than right because the physiology of my brain required it. Everything is caused by the physical universe, of which we are a part. Everything moves unyieldingly forward in strict observance of the natural laws. Nothing moves at all except by the mechanical outworking of those laws.[9]

Divine and natural determinism are very different theories. They are not allies; they are in direct opposition to one another. I don't mean in the obvious sense that divine determinism nominates God to be in charge while natural determinism nominates nature. More importantly, they have significantly different implications for human freedom and responsibility. It is in consequence of these very different implications that natural determinism is intellectually flawed while divine determinism is rationally compelling. I shall explain these important differences in due course, but we must be clear that these are significantly different theories having radically different implications. The truly objectionable implications of natural determinism should not be used as our excuse for rejecting divine determinism. Far too often, divine determinism is repudiated because natural determinism is unconvincing. We must permit divine determinism to make its case on its own terms and not be declared guilty by the evidence against natural determinism.

---

8. See appendix A.

9. Two well-known natural determinists would be B. F. Skinner and Carl Sagan. Cf., for example, B. F. Skinner, *Beyond Freedom and Dignity.*

What's a Nice Arminian Like Me Doing in a Place Like This?

I have become a convinced divine determinist only quite recently. Divine determinism is completely foreign to the theological tradition and culture in which I was nurtured. My earliest theological reflections were solidly along limited determinist lines.

The transformation of my thinking has been—especially in its early stages—slow and gradual. It was virtually imperceptible to me. The more my biblical and theological understanding matured, the more intellectually dissatisfied I became with limited determinism. Eventually, as I grappled with the teaching of *Romans*, I was consciously and deliberately compelled to adopt a different theological paradigm. But a gradually dawning awareness that limited determinism was inadequate had plagued me for several years before that.

I presume, of course, that the theological understanding defended in this book is the result of my theological reflections finally coming of age, finally reaching maturity. (And I *do* mean maturity, not perfection.) Whether I am right about that is ultimately something each reader must decide for himself. Embracing divine determinism may be evidence of my theological senility, not my theological maturity. But in any case, I offer my thoughts in good faith. Justifiably or not, I am confident that divine determinism is the only theory that does justice to all the philosophical and biblical data. It alone captures the true nature of God's relationship to his creation.

While it would be too tedious—and perhaps impossible—to reconstruct all the factors that contributed to my dissatisfaction with and eventual rejection of limited determinism, two autobiographical highlights are worth mentioning.

As a university undergraduate, I attended an evangelistic meeting sponsored by a well-known campus ministry. A non-believer in the audience employed the argument from evil as part of his justification for not believing. The argument from evil states that, in view of the nature and extent of the evil that exists in the world, to believe that a good God exists is unreasonable. Confident that I was right, I waxed eloquent about how the emergence of evil was a necessary risk that God took. God did not create humans to be mere robots, I argued. He wanted to create free-will creatures whose love and obedience would be meaningful because it was voluntary rather than a pre-programmed response. So God created man with free will. But in doing so, he necessarily had to risk the possibility of evil. In a free-will creature, the possibility of evil—even its eventual inevitability—goes with the territory. God could not make man free without creating the possibility of rebellion and evil.

When I had finished, a theologically astute staff member questioned me, "Jack, do you think we will have free will in heaven?"

"Sure, I presume so."

"Do you think that in heaven there will be any possibility of our rebelling against God all over again?"

"No, I don't think so."

"So you can conceive of at least one place where God can have the voluntary, freely-given love and obedience of his creatures without its involving the possibility of sin and rebellion?"

"Yes, I guess so."

"Then why couldn't he have created us that way from the beginning? Why couldn't he have created us capable of offering voluntary love and obedience without the possibility of sin—just like you say it will be in heaven? Why couldn't he have created us from the start the way we are going to be in the end?"

That was an uncomfortable conversation. I understood that he had undermined my whole argument (not to mention my pride). My whole solution to the problem of evil had been decimated. I felt rebuked, embarrassed, unsettled, and strangely perplexed. The sting of the rebuke and embarrassment passed. In time, more adequate solutions to the problem of evil presented themselves and my faith became settled on firmer foundations. But I never really got over the perplexity that came upon me that night.

How is it conceivable that in heaven we will be perfectly free to choose and yet, at the same time, it will be impossible for us to choose evil? How am I to imagine a place where being free and being secure in sinless perfection are not mutually exclusive? Nothing in my theory of limited determinism, founded as it was on the absolute autonomy of the human will, could make any sense out of such a possibility. If man's will is autonomous from God, to affirm necessary obedience with no possibility of rebellion is utterly illogical. But somehow, intuitively, it made sense. For that is exactly what lies ahead for the believer: being secure in perfect, voluntary obedience with no possibility of rebellion. According to my limited determinist perspective, this shouldn't make sense. Yet it did. I was perplexed.

Only later, in divine determinism, did I finally find a resolution to my quandary. I didn't give it much conscious attention, but my subconscious presumably cranked away over the years, seeking a solution. Finally, the light went on: *God can control my free will and guarantee its obedience because the human will is not autonomous!* It took me years to reach this simple conclusion. The dogma of human autonomy—a theological legacy handed down from past generations—ran deep and strong in me and was not easily discarded. And once I discarded it, it took still longer to get comfortable with the new perspective. It was such a radically different way of thinking about myself.

The second significant event came from reading *The Meaning of the City* by Jacques Ellul.[10] Ellul traces the Scriptural references to cities in order to establish a biblical perspective on the city as an institution.

He points out that the first city was built by the murderer Cain in an act of distrust and unbelief. Though God had promised protection to the desperately fearful Cain, Cain did not trust God. Instead, he built the first city (a fortified city) to provide protection for himself. From this, Ellul concludes that the city, from its inception, is strictly a product of human sinfulness and unbelief. When man was banished from the garden, he built a city in which to dwell—a place created out of his own restless rebellion. Ellul exposits a series of biblical passages in support of his thesis: the city is an evil institution, seething with man's rebelliousness.

But then we come to the book of *Revelation*. When God is making everything new, we find a very curious fact: the believer's eternal dwelling place is a city! The city being what it is, we would fully expect restoration to the garden to be man's heavenly reward. We would expect the city—born of human rebellion and brimming with evil—to be destroyed. We would hardly expect God to honor man's free rebellious choice to create the city. But that is exactly what we find. Eternity is represented as the New Jerusalem. Granted, the city that shall descend out of heaven will be untouched by human hands, but it will be a city nonetheless.

The implications of this were revolutionary. God's grace is more incredible and mysteriously wonderful than I had ever imagined. God, in his love, will take the natural consequences of a man's choices—even his evil ones—and give them back to him as his *perfect* inheritance. What a radical thought! God's grace is such that even my sinful choices do not and

---

10. Jacques Ellul, *The Meaning of the City* (Grand Rapids: William B. Eerdmans Publishing Company, 1970).

cannot prevent me from gaining the perfect inheritance God has destined for me. In other words, *God's grace cannot be hindered!* It will be victorious even over my rebellion. It does not come as an offer, requiring my cooperation. It comes as my conqueror. If God has determined to show me kindness, then kindness I will get. Nothing—not even I—can stop him. If I rebel against him and refuse to cooperate with his purposes, then—much to my puzzled delight—I eventually discover that the consequences of those rebellious choices were a part of the reward he had in store for me all along. This truth revolutionized my whole theology: *God's grace cannot be hindered!*

Ellul's book was only the beginning of this discovery. Over the next several years I sought to clearly understand the gospel itself through a study of *Romans*. What began as a hopeful suggestion made by Ellul grew into a firm conviction. Every advance in my understanding of the Bible pointed in the same direction: *God's grace cannot be hindered!*

This discovery created serious problems for my view of divine sovereignty. The invincibility of God's grace was in irreconcilable tension with my limited determinist belief in the autonomy of the human will. If the human will is autonomous and beyond divine control, how can God's grace be unhinderable? Given my freedom, surely I could—through foolish and rebellious choices—sabotage the reward God had destined for me. God cannot guarantee the fulfillment of his purposes unless he completely controls the outcome of my choices. On limited determinist assumptions he does not. My choices are mine to make. Logically, if I am truly independent of divine control, I can thwart God's purposes. Yet the Bible teaches the opposite, I discovered—*God's grace cannot be hindered.* I faced a dilemma: either I must deny the clear teaching of Scripture, or I must reconsider how the human will is related to God. But I could not, in good faith, ignore the logical tension that had been created by my discovery. Both cannot be true. Either the human will is not autonomous, or the grace of God can be hindered. Something would have to give.

Ultimately, I had no real choice. My commitment to limited determinism and the notion of human autonomy had to go. The autonomy of the human will had been the non-negotiable foundation of my entire theological system. Now I was forced to discard it and shift to a different foundation—the absolute determinative control of God. My whole theological system had to adjust accordingly. This book is an examination of the kinds of considerations that changed my mind and shaped my theology as I recast it around a new center: God.

Preview of Argument

PART ONE

Our discussion begins with some important introductory concerns. Surveying the most important practical ramifications of divine determinism, chapter 2 demonstrates that whether or not divine determinism is true is not a merely academic question. We seek an answer not to satisfy some esoteric, philosophical curiosity. It is an issue of vital, personal concern.

Chapter 3 briefly argues that reason is the arbiter of truth. Logic (or reason) is foundational to my defense of divine determinism. The validity of my defense hinges on whether logic is a reliable guide to truth. If the reader will not grant to reason and logic the authority to establish truth, then my argument is defeated before it begins. Chapter 3 explains why granting this sort of authority to reason is appropriate. If the reader is already convinced that reason establishes truth—even the truth about God, he can skip chapter 3 without loss.

Finally, chapter 4 explores three concepts that are sufficiently important to the subsequent discussion that they need careful definition. The specifics of my exploration of these concepts are critical to understanding the arguments I advance later.

PART TWO

In part 2, I make my case for divine determinism from the biblical evidence. I argue that divine determinism is logically required by two important biblical doctrines: (1) God as the creator of everything out of nothing, and (2) God as the one who foreknows the future. Since two distinct tenets of the Bible's explicit teaching require it, it is reasonable to conclude that divine determinism underlies all that the Bible teaches.

PART THREE

In part 3, I make a brief argument for divine determinism from a strictly philosophical point of view. Namely, if we are to have a sound logical foundation for the most basic, indubitable assumptions at the foundation of human knowledge and experience, divine determinism is required.

Part 3 is brief—merely indicating the direction that a philosophical defense might take. I have assumed that the reader is a Christian believer who grants authority to the Bible and will, therefore, be convinced by what it teaches. My overall argument, therefore, concentrates on what is biblically required, not on what is philosophically required. My primary purpose in part 3 is to suggest that philosophy and the Bible are in agreement on this point.

PART FOUR

Part 4 is perhaps the most important part of my presentation. There I give attention to the objections popularly raised against divine determinism. I argue that the common objections to divine determinism, though superficially compelling, are, in truth, not rationally compelling at all. They are based on a crucially mistaken assumption.

PART FIVE

Part 5 summarizes the argument and makes some final observations. In light of the fact that compelling biblical and philosophical reasons to embrace divine determinism exist, and in light of the fact that no compelling arguments against it exist, divine determinism ought to be embraced as true. It is the only rationally coherent theory of the creator's relationship to his creation. Hence, it is incumbent upon us, as rational beings, to embrace it.

PART ONE
INTRODUCTORY CONCERNS

CHAPTER TWO

WHAT DIFFERENCE DOES IT MAKE?

To fully appreciate the practical, everyday ramifications of divine determinism, one must first understand exactly what it asserts. And to fully understand what it asserts, one must grasp the arguments in its favor. So, the logical order would be to explore the practical ramifications of divine determinism only after a thorough discussion of its nature and basis as a theory. But another concern motivates me to reverse the order.

Some people will find the more complex and abstract arguments in subsequent chapters difficult, and even tedious. The reader who is not inclined to be patient with such philosophical argumentation will need a reason to persist in this investigation and not abandon it prematurely. He needs to understand what vitally practical and personally relevant issues are at stake. The purpose of this chapter is to highlight just those issues. Our interest is not merely academic. If divine determinism is true, it alters our entire outlook on everyday life.

It may be helpful to read this chapter twice. Now, and then again after finishing the book. Now, in order to understand why persevering in this study may be worth it; again later, because, having gained a thorough grasp of divine determinist theory, you will be better prepared to understand its practical ramifications.

Since my primary purpose in this chapter is to dramatize the vital practical import of divine determinism, this is not an exhaustive treatment. Significant ramifications are very likely omitted. I outline just three of its more important ramifications to illustrate this point: divine determinism is not just an abstract theory; it entails a way to live life. Whether it is the right way to live is a vitally relevant issue.

A Preliminary Concern: Is God Good?

There is a question prior in importance to the question of divine determinism: the question of divine goodness. Nothing beneficial follows from God's control of reality if God is not good. If he is not kind, compassionate, and merciful, God's position as the ultimate determiner of all reality is a curse, not a comfort.

Among believers, the goodness of God is less controversial than the sovereignty of God. Belief in divine goodness is foundational to Christian faith itself. Even the most rudimentary trust in God presupposes that he is good. This is incontrovertibly the Bible's explicit teaching. God is "light, and in Him there is no darkness at all" (I John 1:5). He is "the Father of lights, with whom there is no variation, not even the slightest degree of deviation" (James 1:17). Therefore, throughout the discussions in this book, I shall presuppose the goodness of God. Accordingly, to uphold the absolute control of God over the whole of reality is to uphold the absolute control of a perfectly good and caring benefactor over the whole of reality. That is the divine determinism I defend.

To defend the biblical doctrine of divine goodness is not part of my purpose. But I cannot proceed without acknowledging the controversy that surrounds such a belief. Christian believers are often assailed for an allegedly unjustified commitment to this belief.

We must concede that experience does not always manifest God's goodness with distinct clarity. The extent and nature of the evil and tragedy in the world is truly perplexing—to the believer no less than to the unbeliever. And it does not obviously point to a good and benevolent governor of all creation; indeed it can be a cause for doubt. But the Christian theist's conviction that a good God exists is based on reasons independent of and undiminished by the inexplicable evils we confront. Through observation of and reflection upon the whole of life, reality, history, and personal experience, the Christian comes to believe in the existence of a perfectly good God because it is the only reasonable explanation for all that he has seen. So, when he confronts an evil that is not obviously consistent with the existence of a perfectly good creator, he does not immediately abandon his belief.

Does that mean he is being irrational? Is it irrational to affirm the goodness of God in the face of the evil that we see in the world? No. Admittedly, instances of evil occur in the world wherein it is not apparent that a greater good is being served. But neither is it apparent that a greater good is *not* being served. We have no direct knowledge either way; our perspective is too limited. To insist that we do know would be the height of presumption. The Christian theist refuses to engage in such presumption. For him, inexplicable evil and suffering are not clear evidence against God's goodness. The believer does not presume to know what they mean one way or the other. The one who presumes that he does know is the one who is being irrational—not to mention, arrogant.

The Christian's conviction that God is good is not based on an inductive sample of the joys and sufferings—the goods and evils—of human experience. It is based on an entirely different foundation. Therefore, when a Christian refuses to let the so-called "evidence" of particular evils shake his confidence in the goodness of God, he is not being close-minded or irrational. He is being eminently reasonable. He has a solid rational basis for his conviction that God is pure and uncompromised in his goodness. Accordingly, he believes that God would never permit a senseless, meaningless evil. He may not be able to discern the good purpose underlying every evil, but he nevertheless believes that it is there, for he believes that he has truly come to know the nature of its creator.

At any rate, the goodness of God is not the point at issue in this book. While it is an extremely important matter that is fraught with controversy, my arguments will assume it, not defend it.

Important Practical Implications of Divine Determinism

Divine determinism, you will remember, is the belief that literally everything transpires by the will of God. Not only the impersonal universe, but also the whole realm of personal creatures is totally subject to God's sovereign control. Even free choice is caused and determined by him. Limited determinism is any theory that posits boundaries to the extent of God's determinative control. At the very least, it will exclude freewill choice from being divinely controlled.

The question is: what difference does it make? If divine determinism is true, what difference will that have on the way we live and think about our lives? Does it ultimately matter whether we embrace divine determinism rather than some form of limited determinism?

THE FIRST IMPORTANT DIFFERENCE: A SENSE OF THE PURPOSIVENESS OF EXISTENCE

A burglar breaks into my house, kills my wife and children, and takes ten dollars in cash. A man goes to the top of a tall tower, pulls out a rifle, and shoots to kill anyone in sight. My daughter is there. She dies. A terrorist bombs a plane and kills three hundred innocent people, my son among them. In times like these a question always surfaces, "Why?" It seems so senseless, so absurd, so pointless. Why did it have to happen? And why did it happen to me?

Our questioning is not really from a desire to know the particular meaning of the particular event. More importantly, it is from a desire to be assured that it has any meaning at all. Is it just pointless, without meaning? Is it merely a random occurrence that didn't have to happen? Or does it fit some purpose? Is there some end in view that gives meaning to the event, allowing us to understand and accept it?

The human heart burns with a desire for life to have meaning. If human experience is nothing but a string of random events, then what value does it have? Non-existence would be just as meaningful as existence. Indeed, it would be better, for then there would be no suffering. (Is this not the rationale behind many suicides?) In any case, we simply cannot accept the verdict: my existence is absurd. As some existentialist philosophers point out, to consider human existence meaningless is nauseating.

This nausea is particularly acute when we confront tragedy and suffering. If life is random and pointless, without any rational order—a chaos filled with chance events—then I would look at the brutally bludgeoned corpse of my daughter with a profound sense of regret—a regret so deep that it literally makes me sick, or crazy. *"It did not have to be!!"* And this perspective that it did not have to be can only lead to bitter regret—*"If only..., if only..., if only...!"*

The only antidote to this nauseating regret is the conviction that human experience does have a point. What happened did so precisely because it *did have to be.* It had to happen to accomplish what had to be accomplished. From a brutal murder down to the inconvenience of a crying child at 3:00 a.m., all that happens is necessary and essential, because nothing occurs but what is purposed and purposeful.

Every Christian theology worthy of the name would grant that most of life experience is purposive. It is completely under God's control as he works to accomplish his purposes. But limited determinism places significant limits on God's control. By doing so, it introduces the possibility of randomness and chaos in human experience. Granting the possibility of autonomous choice (including sinful choice), limited determinists must concede that some choices do not advance the purposes of God. These choices threaten to destroy the very thing God wants to do.

God has instructed us to refrain from sexual intimacy outside of marriage. Out of the rebelliousness of sin, a young woman does it anyway. She gets pregnant. How is she to understand her situation? Is there any point to her pregnancy? Is it in accord with the plan and purposes of God? Or is it a foolish, stupid, random disruption of God's plan—a complication brought on solely by her own autonomous choice? Is it a choice that God willed, or a choice that God would rather she have avoided?

Perhaps it is an ugly, pointless stain on the canvas of her life—one that God must now somehow incorporate into a revised, but inferior plan. This is the perspective that limited determinism is logically required to take. As human beings act, there can be no guarantee that their autonomous choices will serve the purposes of God. They can just as easily subvert them. Autonomous choices must often lead to nauseatingly purposeless results, leading only to regret.

Only divine determinism provides an antidote to regret. It alone affirms God's total control of the whole of my existence, including my own choices. It alone implies that nothing I do and nothing that happens will be pointless, that everything that occurs was willed by God to accomplish his good purposes, that literally everything *had to be*. And that being so, regret is banished, for how could one regret God's will being done? No agonizing cries of "what if" can result, if divine determinism is true. For if things had been different, the perfect will of God would not have been done, and that would be truly regrettable!

This is the first important difference between divine determinism and limited determinism: If divine determinism is true, then existence is purposive and profoundly meaningful. If limited determinism is true, I am left with a profound sense of sadness and regret. Taken to its logical conclusion, limited determinism must inevitably result in a heavy sense of futility and absurdity. It leads to the horrifying knowledge that human existence, meaningful as it could be, will always be infected with the meaningless chaos of human foolishness. As a net result, it will always be regrettably absurd.

The personal relevance of this should be clear. To know that one's existence is not pointless—neither in total nor in part—is a profoundly significant reassurance. As I face into adversity, I long to know that I am not just the hapless victim of random chance. As I trudge along week after week in mundane drudgery, I have to know that the excruciating tedium is for a purpose. If I could not know these things, I would surely come unhinged—if I did not drug myself into a stupor to keep myself from thinking about it. The issue is too close, too personal, too important for me to ignore. If divine determinism is true, it answers a very profound need.

THE SECOND IMPORTANT DIFFERENCE:
A SENSE OF SECURITY

Limited determinism logically leads to fear, anxiety, and a sense of vulnerability. Alternatively, divine determinism logically leads to a sense of security, a profound sense that my well-being is protected.

ANXIETY OR SECURITY?

Should we approach life with confidence, or with anxiety? It depends on who God is and on the sort of control he has over our lives. If God is good, if he has my best interests in mind, and if he is in total control, then feeling totally secure is logical and appropriate. But if God is lacking in any of these respects, anxiety is the logically appropriate response. Feeling secure in such a case would be irrational, the result of mere wishful thinking.

As a concrete example, consider the possibility of assault. What if God is not good? Would an evil God be interested in protecting me from assault? Not necessarily. Indeed, if it suited his purposes, an evil God might even promote it. So if God is evil, I do well to fear being assaulted. To tell myself that God would never let that happen to me would be naive and foolish. But if God is good the picture changes. Arguably, violent assault would be repugnant to a good God. He would do everything within his power to prevent it—so long as doing so did not preclude a greater good.

But if God—morally perfect though he is—is interested in the larger cosmic good with no particular concern for what is of most benefit to me personally, can I rest in the security of knowing that he is morally good? No! If God's goodness is not directed toward benefiting me specifically, then it bears no practical relevance to me. Knowing that all things are moving toward the ultimate good for the cosmos does not provide a foundation for my personal security and confidence. Logically, I can only live in fear. I must anxiously anticipate the possibility that he will sacrifice my well-being for the greater good of the universe. It would be naive to try to take comfort in the fact that my sacrifice is serving some larger cosmic good. That would be futile self-deception, for this perspective offers no guarantee that whatever happens is in *my* best interests. On the contrary, if the ultimate good of the cosmos could be served by my being violently assaulted, then a good God unconcerned for my personal well-being would readily allow or even promote such an assault. Evil would come to *me* in order that good might come to the cosmos. To think otherwise would be mistaken. So, if God has no interest in my personal well-being, there is no reason to feel secure.

Finally, if God is perfectly good and if his good intentions are directed specifically toward securing what is good for me, there still remains the question of God's control. Are God's power and authority adequate to control all that happens in reality? Or are they limited to the extent that God may be unable to actualize his good intentions for me? If it is so limited, anxiety and fear are logically appropriate.

All believers agree that God is a perfectly good God.[11] Likewise, all believers agree that God is committed to bringing good to us individually.[12] The point where Christians disagree is this last one: the extent to which God exercises determinative control over reality.

IF MAN BE BEYOND GOD'S CONTROL: ANXIETY

Limited determinists place significant boundaries on the extent of God's control over the events of our lives. God is powerful, they admit. He controls most of what occurs in reality. But his power is limited. Specifically—according to the most popular version of limited determinism—he cannot control the freewill choices of men, Satan, or angels. Whatever portion of reality is shaped by the actions of free-willed creatures is not under God's control. While relatively few would dispute that God controls the impersonal created order, many deny that he controls the

---

11. All Christians agree in theory that God is good, but not necessarily in practice. It is commonplace to affirm the goodness of God. On the other hand, our attitudes and actions often betray the fact that we do not believe that God is good—not as a working conviction. In fact, a true working acceptance of the goodness of God is a mark of a profound spiritual maturity— a level of maturity that relatively few believers have attained. If we were utterly convinced of God's goodness, we would eagerly obey all of God's commands, knowing that his purpose in giving the command is good. But we disobey, showing implicitly our suspicion of God's character, purposes, and motives. But our weak conviction and disobedience do not negate my point here. At the level of doctrinal beliefs, God's goodness is not a matter of serious dispute among believers. While we may not have the maturity to fully believe it in practice, we do not really dispute it either.

12. Two things should be noted here: (1) The same disclaimer needs to be made here that I made with respect to believers' agreement on the goodness of God. While we can agree in theory that God is committed to our individual welfare, too seldom do we believe it in practice. (See the note immediately preceding this one.) (2) The believer's conviction that God is concerned for his own personal well-being does not flow from a conviction that God is committed to the personal well-being of every human individual; rather it flows from a conviction that he is committed to the personal well-being of every human being who is marked by belief in the gospel of Jesus—to that select group Paul calls "the chosen."

actions of free moral agents. Accordingly, much that is directly relevant to my welfare is beyond God's control. Within this paradigm, God will not[13] and does not control the actions of the man wanting to do me harm. The man who would insult me, slander me, steal from me, attack me, or kill me is beyond God's determinative control.

To whatever extent reality is beyond God's control, I am at risk, and personal optimism is unfounded. Christian doctrine affirming God's goodness and compassionate concern for my welfare is irrelevant if God does not control what happens to me. In that case a sense of security has no logical basis.

Consider a specific example. If God does not control the freewill choices of the man who would assault me, I am foolish to think I cannot be harmed. The criminal's actions—like so much random, uncontrolled, unpredictable, and incomprehensible noise in God's otherwise meaningful universe—could sabotage God's well-laid and well-intentioned plans for me. If, beyond God's control, I am chosen by some assailant to be his victim, what can God do? Even if he can bring some semblance of good out of the tragic event, he cannot restore to me the blessings he had originally planned for me before the wicked, free-will assailant sabotaged his plans and stole his intended blessings from me.

Anxiety is the eminently logical result. Fear is virtually required by this view of life and God. Granted, God can be trusted implicitly. But we cannot trust reality, not the part that is out of his control. God is good. But what about the out-of-control randomness? Can I trust the chaos that lies outside his control? I have no reason to think so. It follows that I must live with a profound and inescapable sense of dread, always wondering what purposeless evil might befall me and test God's ability to salvage some sort of good out of tragedy.

In practice, contrary to what logically follows from their theory, limited determinists teach a basically optimistic outlook. Their theory explicitly interprets the evil choices of free moral agents as tragic intrusions into God's plan—intrusions that could potentially sabotage his purposes and destroy the good he has willed—yet they remain optimistic. Their optimism is grounded in God's ability to bring good out of evil. According to their view, God will work all things together for good in the end. God is continually waging war against the forces of evil and sin, seeking to bring

---

13. Rarely would a limited determinist say that God is *unable* to control the choices of a man. The typical position is that while God has the power to control the actions of free moral agents, he chooses not to do so. For the sake of maintaining the dignity and autonomy of humans (and angels), God elects not to intervene in the choices of free moral agents.

good and meaning out of the chaos they produce. He loses some battles, but he will win the war. Perhaps he will have to sew up some wounds. Perhaps he will have to patch up some holes that have been punched in the fabric of his initial purposes. But in the end he will have repaired whatever went wrong. He will have brought a good and wonderful result out of all the bad. Admittedly, it must certainly fall short of what it could have been—what it would have been had there been no sin at all. But good (even if second-best) is much better than bad. And that is what it will be.

Such optimism has a hollow center. A life ripped apart by the evil choices of other people must fall bitterly short of the rewarding experience God initially intended. Who wins, really? God, who has managed to fix reality and make it more-or-less good? Or the vandal, sin, who has managed to permanently scar and deface the smooth, unmarred surface of God's original will? Under such a view, we can proclaim God the victor, but the voice of triumph is somewhat muted.

The implications of such a victory for my own personal existence are somewhat disturbing. I cannot escape ambivalence. I am grateful that God has worked evil for good in my life; but, at the same time, I deeply regret that evil has permanently robbed me of what could have been. My heart cannot help but cry, *"If only it hadn't happened...!"* Such a victory provides no basis for a sense of real protection and security. At best, I can know that whatever happens will result in some sort of good. At the same time, I must live in fear that something beyond God's control will destroy the possibility of my enjoying God's wise and perfect plan for my life—the one he intended for me from the beginning. If this possibility exists—if the voluntary actions of a wayward man could at any moment rob me of the reward God willed for me—how can I avoid anxiety? Fearful insecurity results.

IF GOD BE IN CONTROL: SECURITY

Divine determinism maintains that God controls all that happens to me. Ultimately, all the actions of other people as well as all that transpires within the impersonal created order are determined by him. No tree can fall on me unless God has purposed it. No murderer can murder me if God does not will it. No thief can steal from me if God does not permit. No harm can befall me except as God directs.

On this view of the extent of God's control, the Christian consensus that God is good and has my best interests in mind becomes a powerfully relevant conviction. It becomes the basis for complete and unqualified security. God is perfectly good. In his goodness, he wants only what is in my best interests. And he is totally in control of everything that happens to me. Accordingly, I have absolutely nothing to fear from the world around me!

Whatever happens—no matter how tragic it may appear on the surface—is for my best. It will promote my ultimate happiness and fulfillment. Fear and anxiety, therefore, are banished. They are inappropriate. How can I fear what life will bring when it can bring nothing but the perfect blessing God has destined for me? If God is for me, what evil, of any consequence, can be against me? (See Romans 8:31)

The extent of this confidence is boundless. I need fear nothing. No physical harm, no emotional harm, and no spiritual harm is capable of posing a threat to my ultimate fulfillment.

Do I face poverty? A good and loving God controls the mind and will of every person. He could cause thousands of people to choose simultaneously to give to me. Or God could cause one wealthy person to extend extraordinary generosity toward me. If my income is dependent upon the weather, God controls the weather. If it depends on people buying my product or employing my service, God controls the wills of those people. If God wants my financial needs met, nothing can stop him.

Do I face a life without the fulfillment of marriage? A good and loving God controls the emotions and decisions of the person he wants me to marry. Is it too hard a thing for him to draw that person to me and plant in him (or her) the desire to be committed to me? Then how can I be anxious? If and when God wants me married, I will be married. If God does not want me married, does he not know what will lead to my ultimate fulfillment?

Do I face pain or ill health? Will suffering prevent me from finding fulfillment? No! How can it? The good God who loves me and has my best interests in mind controls my health and everything that happens to me physically. Would he allow any pain or ill health that was not purposed to produce an even greater reward—one that would make all the pain worthwhile? No, of course not.

Granted, pain may threaten my present comfort. Ill health (and indeed any of these "evils" we are discussing) may preclude my short-term happiness. But this does not preclude courage and a sense of security. Inconsolable fear is only appropriate in the face of purposeless suffering. If things are out of control—if I might fall victim to pointless suffering or evil—then I have reason to fear and refuse to be comforted. But purposive "evil" is different. I need not fear it. I can face it with courage and confidence. It is purposed to produce some ultimately good effect; it is conducive to my ultimate happiness.

Of course I do not desire purposive suffering. I would just as soon avoid suffering of any kind. But neither do I fear it, for I welcome the good and rewarding end to which it leads. Indeed, my desire to gain the fruit of such suffering is greater than my desire to avoid its pain. If I must feel its sting in order to receive its benefit, then so be it. At least, to think otherwise would make me a fool. For what God has purposed through that pain and suffering is what is perfect and best for me. So I can welcome the suffering when it comes. Not because I like it, but because I know what will result from it. It is a tool in the hand of my creator to create for me his perfect blessing. I can, therefore, "count it as joy." (See James 1:2)

Divine determinism asserts that a perfectly good and loving God with my very best interests in mind is the one who causes everything that happens to me. This logically results in confidence, courage, fearlessness, contentment, and a sense of security and protection. This is in sharp contrast to the fear and anxiety that logically follow from most forms of limited determinism. Clearly, then, whether divine determinism is true is vitally relevant. Can I live a life of security and contentment? Or must I live a life of fear, regret, and anxious dread? Ultimately the answer lies in whether divine determinism is true.

THE THIRD IMPORTANT DIFFERENCE: HOPE

The third is perhaps the most important difference of all: divine determinism provides a basis for hope; limited determinism leads to despair. Not that limited determinists cannot and do not live in hope. They can and do. But they do so without warrant. Their worldview provides no basis for it. The hope of the divine determinist is solid, because it is valid; the hope of the limited determinist is empty—a groundless optimism.

HOPE OR DESPAIR?

According to the Bible, human existence is fundamentally flawed. We have profoundly self-destructive tendencies. We are so incurably foolish that, left to ourselves, we would ultimately destroy ourselves and everything around us. That is the tragic consequence of human sinfulness. So what does the future hold? Will I ever escape my own self-destruction? Can I ever be rescued from myself? Is there any hope? Or is despair all that remains?

Only a very shallow and unbiblical understanding of the human predicament thinks salvation can result from a change of circumstances— even being transferred to "heaven." Heaven, the place of eternal life, is not a place where *things* will be different. It is a place where *I* will be different. Nothing short of a complete transformation of my very own nature can solve my problem.

This takes us to the very heart of the question: where are there grounds for hope? Who controls me? Do I control my choices and my future, or does God control them? My problem lies in the freewill choices I make. I do evil, foolish, venomous things that inject my environment, my relationships, and my very own soul with the poison of destruction. If these foolish choices are completely and only controlled by me—if they are utterly beyond God's control—then hope for my future is without basis. The duck-billed platypus cannot change his snout. The leopard cannot remove his spots. Neither can the fool shed his foolishness, nor the born rebel cease his rebellion. The sinner cannot choose to be a saint—not if he is left to his own resources. If I, and only I, have control over the choices I make, then there can be no hope for me. I am hopelessly sinful, hopelessly self-destructive, hopelessly blind, and hopelessly lost.

But this is exactly the position to which limited determinism is theoretically committed. It insists that freewill choice is outside the province of God—that the very definition of a "free" will is one outside the scope of his control. He does not and will not control the choices I make. Limited determinism, therefore, is theoretically committed to despair. If no one outside of myself (God, in particular) will ever exert any control over the choices I make, then I am a prisoner of my own moral and spiritual weakness. I cannot free myself, and my autonomy condemns me to be independent of any moral or spiritual resources beyond myself. So where are the moral or spiritual resources that could free me?[14] If everything within

---

14. It does no good to respond, "The resources of the Spirit of God that are at my disposal now that I am a believer." This response misses the whole point. Limited determinism must view the power of the Spirit of God to be something that is put at my disposal to do with as I choose. I can ignore it or avail myself of it, whichever my autonomous will chooses. But what spiritual resources would move my autonomous will to avail myself of the Spirit's power rather than ignore it? Limited determinism is committed to the proposition that the power to choose is our own, unaffected by the Spirit's power. The Spirit of God does not determine the choices of free moral agents; we are left free to choose what we will. So the question still stands: "With what moral or spiritual resources will a sinner who has evidenced nothing but rebellious choices all of his life put an end to his rebellion?"

me has proved itself wicked, with what righteousness will I overcome the inclinations of my own being? The only logical outlook is despair—quiet, profound despair. I am damned to eternal self-destruction.

Nevertheless, many limited determinists do not live in despair. Why not? Here are three contributing reasons:

1. Frequently, limited determinists do not really believe what the Bible teaches regarding human sinfulness. For them, man is not hopelessly sinful—not to the core of his being. Rather, he is basically righteous; but, for a variety of reasons, he has not quite managed to manifest it yet. Accordingly, they are not despairing, for they see no insurmountable problem. Man is not a prisoner of evil. He can cease his sin and self-destruction whenever he chooses. And some, sooner or later, will. The real problem is our environment. We need a different situation—heaven. Put us in heaven and all will be well. We do not need to be changed. The world we live in needs to be changed. While God does not control me—my choices—he does control my environment. So there is every reason to be hopeful. The Bible promises that my world will be made new, and that is exactly what I need. If all this were true, hope—and not despair—would be warranted. But it is not true; it is not compatible with what the Bible teaches. Nevertheless, many Christians hold this odd, unbiblical view.

2. Sometimes limited determinists espouse hope blindly, dogmatically. The Bible teaches it; they believe it. Never mind that, in the context of their own theology, such a hope is completely unwarranted. Never mind that it totally contradicts everything else they believe. They go on in hope anyway, undisturbed by the logical contradiction it entails.

3. Sometimes people who espouse limited determinism are divine determinists in hiding. Intuitively they recognize the philosophical superiority of divine determinism, but—for a variety of reasons—they cannot bring themselves to consciously and explicitly acknowledge it. Their actions and attitudes are controlled by their divine-determinist intuitions, not by their limited-determinist theory. They see the hope that is really there and live in the light of it. But they consciously and explicitly espouse the opposing theory. So they embrace a false theory even while their inner hope is nourished by a true and valid intuition. What they embrace intuitively, they denounce publicly. The inconsistency either goes unnoticed, or it doesn't bother them.

I cannot maintain, therefore, that limited determinists cannot be hopeful. My point is that they have no justification or support for it. If they took their explicit theology to its logical conclusions, their hope would be undermined and destroyed.

Divine determinism, on the other hand, provides a solid foundation for hope. If a good and loving God, who has my best interests in mind, ultimately controls my very choices, then what is to stop him from rescuing me? If God controls me, he can change me. My foolish choices can be changed into wise ones. My rebellious choices can be changed into submissive ones. Therein lies real hope. I can eagerly anticipate a future free from sin and death. The God who controls my will has promised it.

GLORIFICATION: THE CHRISTIAN'S HOPE

The "one hope" that Paul refers to in Ephesians 4:4 is—or, at least, includes—the hope of righteousness, the expectation that one day I will be morally perfect.[15] This is the paramount hope proclaimed by the gospel.

Virtually every Christian perspective acknowledges this hope, but not all value it as they should. All too often we take this hope for granted, or even consciously denigrate it. But, in fact, this hope answers the deepest longing of the believer's heart. The true believer is marked by a profound hunger for personal righteousness. For him, the good news of the gospel comes to this: "You who long for righteousness, rejoice! It is yours!" This is his hope. He lives in confident and eager anticipation of the day when the promise of glorious righteousness will finally be realized in his life.[16]

Will this promise actually be realized, as the believer expects it will? Or will something happen to thwart God's good intentions and prevent its realization? Perhaps the believer will ultimately be humiliated as he sees this hope dashed. Perhaps his confident expectation is nothing more than wishful thinking.

In Romans 5:1-11, Paul asserts categorically that the believer's hope for glorious righteousness will not fail.[17] Then he explains the basis for his confidence. Our hope will not fail, he argues, because God loves us too much to allow it to fail. God has already demonstrated the extent of his love toward us by sending his Son to die on our behalf. If God's love for us extends so far that, in the midst of our damnable rebellion, God acted

---

15. Ephesians 4:4 (NIV) reads, "There is one body and one Spirit—just as you were called to one hope when you were called...."

16. The gospel is captured very succinctly in the fourth Beatitude, Matthew 5:6 (NIV): "Blessed are those who hunger and thirst for righteousness, for they will be filled."

toward us with mercy, then how can it fail to extend far enough to transform our moral natures and grant us the glorious righteousness he promised? If while we were abhorrent enemies, God loved us enough to show us mercy, then certainly now—being no longer enemies, but friends—God loves us enough to grant us our inheritance, the "glory" of moral perfection.

But notice the implicit assumption in Paul's argument. Who does Paul consider responsible for my ultimately becoming a gloriously righteous being some day? Not me, but God. If my glorification lay in my hands, then the depth and extent of God's love for me would have no relevance to whether or not I shall achieve it. But it clearly is relevant for Paul. The very essence of his argument is that God's love for me is so demonstrably far-reaching that my hope of glorification is guaranteed. But this argument is ridiculous if my performance, and not God's, is what is relevant. In other words, God's love can guarantee my glorification only if my glorification is ultimately in his hands. If it were in my hands, God's inclination toward me would have no relevance.

Now what is this glorification Paul has in view? It is that event within the course of my existence wherein I am made pure—that point where I attain perfect righteousness. But what is perfect righteousness, except the point where my choices cease to be evil and begin to be infallibly good? Glorification, then, lies within the nature of my own freewill choices. I am glorious just to the extent that I choose to act gloriously. Now, according to limited determinism, my freewill choices are beyond God's control. I alone control my choices. If limited determinism is true, then, glorification cannot be in God's hands; it would be impossible for God to guarantee it. Whether or not I can ever attain to perfect righteousness is squarely in my own hands. God has no say in the matter.

This creates an irreconcilable tension between the clear implications of limited determinism and Paul's teaching on the certainty of our hope. Paul

---

17. In Rom. 5:5 Paul says, "...and [this] hope will not bring us shame" (my translation). The hope he is referring to is the hope he mentioned in 5:2 when he stated, "...we boast in hope of the glory of God." In my judgment, the hope of the glory of God is the eager expectation (hope) that one day my existence will be made glorious with the glory that God has promised me. What is the nature of the glorious existence that God has promised me? Putting together various clues from the teaching of the New Testament, one thing we can know is this: while my eternal existence will be glorious in many different respects, the most important respect in which it will be glorious is that I will enjoy the glory of perfect moral purity. So when Paul asserts that "this hope will not bring us shame," he is asserting—among other things—that our confident expectation that we will one day be made morally perfect and infallibly righteous is not a vain hope. It will indeed come to pass.

grounds our hope on God's faithful, unfailing love. He assumes throughout that God is the one who will and must bring about our glorification. Limited determinism, on the other hand, is theoretically opposed to viewing God as the author of our glorification. That role is reserved for man himself. Glorification is perfect righteousness, and perfect righteousness can only be achieved by man, as he freely (and autonomously) chooses it for himself. In limited determinism, therefore, the basis for hope asserted by Paul disappears. We cannot ground our hope on the love and faithfulness of God, for God has no control over the outcome.

Can we ground our hope on *our* faithfulness to God? Hardly! It is from our unfaithfulness that we require to be rescued. Can ground our hope on our basic goodness? No. It is our wickedness from which we need to be saved. Can we base our hope on the power of the Holy Spirit within us? No. For again—as limited determinism sees it—the Holy Spirit cannot guarantee our glorification. Glory will be realized only to the extent that I, by my freewill choices, appropriate the power of the Holy Spirit now available to me. The extent of divine power available through the Spirit is irrelevant to the certainty of my hope. It becomes relevant only insofar as I choose to avail myself of it. But that I may never avail myself of it is entirely possible. My hope, therefore, is uncertain. My hope is only as certain as I am faithful to pursue my own glorification. Is that an adequate basis for hope? Can I, on that basis, say with Paul "and this hope does not disappoint"? No. Not unless I have a totally fallacious view of my own loyalty to the purposes of God. Anyone who understands the depths of his own rebellion could never base his hope on his own faithfulness. Limited determinism, therefore, provides no basis for hope. The logically appropriate outlook for limited determinism is despair. Wretched are those who hunger and thirst after righteousness, for they must go eternally unsatisfied. Such is the real implication of limited determinism—if it remains both logically and biblically consistent.[18]

---

18. Glorification is the transformation of the moral nature of a person whereby that person becomes morally flawless and perfectly good at the very core of his moral nature. Sanctification is the transformation of the "heart" of a person whereby that person—while still unrighteous in nature—becomes disposed to love and obey God rather than hate and rebel against God. Sanctification is a process which proceeds here and now in this present age; glorification is an event which awaits us when we leave the present age and enter the age to come. The argument I have made in the preceding text has been made with regard to glorification. A parallel argument could be made with regard to sanctification. Sanctification is guaranteed to God's elect just as surely as glorification is. And sanctification, no less than glorification, involves the nature of a person's freewill choices. Hence, sanctification can be guaranteed by the New Testament only on the assumption that the choices of a sanctified man will ultimately be determined by the God who is sanctifying him. That is, only on the assumption that divine determinism is true.

There is no greater practical import to the doctrine of divine determinism than the certainty of our hope. According to the Bible, nothing in all of human existence is more valuable than personal righteousness. It alone can truly fulfill our humanity and satisfy the longing of our hearts. Accordingly, the question of whether we can be certain of attaining this righteousness is the most personally vital question for all of human existence. Divine determinism provides a firm basis upon which we can have a certain hope. Limited determinism gives us no such basis. It leaves us with two unattractive options: quiet despair or dogmatic, irrational hope. A sound, justified hope is simply not available to the limited determinist. Only divine determinism can provide that.

Living with Meaning, Security, and Hope

Logically, divine determinism results in hope, security, and a sense that the events of life have meaning. Do divine determinists live that way? Do they live confidently and without fear, hopefully and without despair, aware that every event has purpose? No! Not always. What we believe in theory we do not always believe in practice. Being persuaded of divine determinism as a theory does not automatically mean that it will serve as my working understanding of reality, determining my responses in real life situations.

Our inability to trust God implicitly—in the manner that divine determinism theoretically requires—is a function of our sinful imperfection. It is part of the foolishness and ignorance that marks us as sinners. Only by God's grace will we believe in practice what we believe in theory. But while the beneficial implications of divine determinism will only gradually be realized through the process of spiritual maturity, we must nevertheless begin by accepting it in theory. We must acknowledge that no other view provides an adequate intellectual foundation for the hope, security, and sense of meaning that God wants us to have.

Summary

In the debate over the nature and extent of God's sovereign control, much is at stake. It is not merely of academic interest. My conclusions have far-reaching implications for the attitudes I have toward everyday experience. Will my life be anxious, fretful, and full of despair? Will I see life as futile? Or will I be secure and hopeful in the context of a life that is meaningful and purposive? It depends on how I view God and his relationship to created reality. Assuming God is good, the critical question is the extent of his control. Does God determine the whole of reality or not? That is the crucial question at issue in this book.

This chapter does not constitute an argument for divine determinism. The fact that divine determinism has happier and more desirable implications does not prove it true. If, in truth, our lives should be ruled by despair, fear, and futility, then that is how we should live. If divine determinism is not true, it would be irresponsible—mere wishful thinking—to feel secure and hopeful. There is no virtue in that. But if divine determinism is true, many happy implications follow; and those implications are of sufficient benefit to make our inquiry worth the effort. Is divine determinism true? It would be foolish not to care.

CHAPTER THREE
IN DEFENSE OF REASON

A Dialogue

ALEXANDER: You've tricked me somehow, Peter. I can't see anything wrong with your reasoning, but what you are saying is not true. I just know it.

PETER: But, Alexander…if my reasoning is sound, how can you say my conclusion is false?

ALEXANDER: You're a magician, Peter. You always spin fancy logical arguments and make them seem like they're leading to the truth. But I refuse to be bewitched by you and your logic. I'm not going to be swayed from what I know is true no matter how apparently illogical I may seem.

PETER: Let me get this straight, Alexander. Don't reason and logic, rightly done, lead us to truth?

ALEXANDER: Some truth, Peter. Perhaps even most truth. But not all truth. You value reason too highly. You worship it. It's your idol. That's where you go wrong. You think that all truth is accessible to reason. But it's not. Some truth is mysterious and above rationality.

PETER: You mean some truth is not reasonable, not rational, and not logical?

ALEXANDER: Yes. Some truth. Not all truth, mind you. Just some truth.

PETER: But this "mysterious" truth, it's ultimately unreasonable, irrational, and illogical?

ALEXANDER: Yes.

PETER: Then you can't trust your reason to guide you when it comes to this "mysterious" truth?

ALEXANDER: No.

PETER: And I take it that the matter we were discussing just now involves one of these "mysterious" truths?

ALEXANDER: Yep! That's right.

PETER: If you don't trust reason on this matter, what then do you trust? What compels you to the opposite conclusion so strongly that you can remain unpersuaded by the logical arguments I laid out for you?

ALEXANDER: Well, my intuition, of course. I simply know intuitively that you are mistaken. If reason can show me why and how my intuition knows what it knows, fine and good. But sometimes it can't. Then I just have to trust my intuition anyway—even if reason can't prove it.

PETER: And if reason and logic contradict your intuition and prove that it is wrong?

ALEXANDER: Then so much the worse for reason and logic. I would never believe logic over my intuition.

PETER: And how, pray tell, do you know when the matter at hand is a "mysterious" truth rather than just an ordinary rational one? Is that by intuition too?

ALEXANDER: Absolutely!

PETER: Then I'm afraid I'm no match for you, Alexander. I can't possibly win this debate. My only weapon is reason. Since you are able to stay so unmoved by reason, I will never be able to persuade you. I'll have to go try to work my spell on someone weaker and more foolish than you. I don't see how anyone could ever persuade you of anything, Alexander. Your power of conviction is astounding. How secure and comfortable you must feel!

Western culture and the Christian church are in a strange place today. We mistrust reason. We trust feelings and intuitions, but not the conclusions of sound rational argument. When a belief is new and different, in conflict with familiar intuitions, the fact that it follows from a perfectly sound line of reasoning is of little consequence to us. We are not inclined to accept it. And the fact that it is based on something contained in biblical revelation makes little or no difference. If the logical result of any line of reasoning contradicts what we have always "known" to be true, it is false. In and of itself, sound reasoning has little weight with the typical modern Christian. The fact that a doctrine or belief is rationally compelling can never overcome the suspicion that is engendered by its being unfamiliar.

This is the most difficult obstacle that divine determinism faces today. Divine determinism is decidedly not intuitive to modern man. Indeed, his intuitions are decidedly against it. In the light of modern intuitions, divine determinism seems positively weird. Everything we believe about life and reality makes it an alien way of thinking. In the current climate, therefore, to present a soundly reasoned case for divine determinism is not likely to be sufficiently persuasive. A sound rational argument will not be trusted enough to be convincing. When limited determinism feels comfortable and divine determinism feels so strange, we are not about to abandon the former for the latter—even if it could be shown to be more logical. This is tragic, but it is the status quo.[19]

In this defense of divine determinism, my arguments are rational ones. I presuppose that reason and logic are trustworthy guides to truth and that it is foolish to ignore the conclusions to which they lead. But I cannot assume that the modern reader shares my assumptions. If I want my arguments to be persuasive to this day and age, I must first persuade the read-

---

19. Current attitudes toward reason are ultimately pathological. The culture that turns its back on reason turns its back on truth. The culture that turns its back on truth turns its back on God. And the culture that turns its back on God turns its back on life. The early writings of Dr. Francis Schaeffer (notably, *The God Who is There, Escape from Reason,* and *He is There and He is Not Silent*) and the thought of Gordon H. Clark (notably, *Religion, Reason and Revelation*) were important reminders of these truths. In the current climate, we allow our intuitions to rule our beliefs, unchallenged. This must stop. Instead we must learn to allow reason to tutor and discipline our intuitions. If reason does not rule our beliefs, then God does not rule them and we are in rebellion against him. We need to rediscover the biblical perspective wherein obedience to God includes courageously following reason wherever it might lead. In saying this, I am not unappreciative of the contribution made by Michael Polanyi's *Personal Knowledge* to our understanding of human knowing. The "intuitive" or "tacit" dimension is a foundational aspect of all knowledge. Be that as it may, the conscious and willing subjection of our tacit intuitions to conscious rational scrutiny is vital in the quest for truth—especially in the quest for theological truth.

er that reason is a reliable guide to truth. In another age, I could take this view for granted. In the current age I cannot.

This chapter is necessarily incomplete. A thorough discussion of truth and reason would be too great a detour. My purpose here is only to give the reader pause before he totally dismisses my arguments as "too rational."

The Point at Issue

This chapter focuses on what will be a likely objection to the arguments of this book:

"I grant you that your arguments are logically sound. But you forget one thing: some beliefs (particularly beliefs about God and ultimate reality) are perfectly true even while failing to be strictly rational. Indeed, some beliefs about ultimate reality are true even while being contradictory or rationally inconsistent. So when an argument establishes that a belief is rationally superior, it has not necessarily established it as more likely to be true. Sometimes, a true belief can be logically inferior to a false belief."

This objection expresses a view of reason directly contrary to mine. The conclusions I reach in this book rest squarely on two critical assumptions about the role of reason: (1) whatever is logically contradictory or rationally unsound cannot possibly be true, and (2) a belief that is rationally superior is more likely to be true than a rationally inferior one. In other words, I assume from the outset that reason—and reason alone—is the only reliable guide to truth.[20] If I am wrong in this assumption, then the whole book can be immediately disregarded. But, then, so can everything else we claim to know. For if reason is no guide to truth, then truth is not knowable, for all knowledge is ultimately founded on reason.

---

20. I am not, by this, rejecting the absolute authority of the Bible nor discounting its usefulness as an infallible guide to truth. The authority of the Bible is utterly dependent upon the reliability of reason. If reason is not reliable, then biblical authority becomes totally irrelevant; for reason is the avenue through which we attain knowledge and understanding of the Bible—just as it is our avenue for attaining knowledge of anything else.

Understanding Rationality

Critics and proponents of the reliability of reason often talk past each other, for they have very different conceptions of what reason is. Before we can profitably discuss whether reason is a reliable guide to truth, we must be clear about what we mean by 'reason'. When I employ the term 'reason' and related terms, I use them in a significantly broader sense than many do.[21] Therefore, it is important to highlight what is *not* a part of my definition of RATIONAL and what, by my definition, is not excluded from rationality.

RATIONAL, as I define it, does not require a conscious act of reasoning. The product of unconscious thought can be eminently rational. Furthermore, thinking does not have to be characterized by rigor and formal structure (like mathematical reasoning) in order to be rational. Neither must one be able to articulate the thought processes that lead to a belief in order for it to be rational. If RATIONAL were limited in these ways—namely, so that it pertained only to conscious, rigorous reasoning that could be verbalized—then the beliefs discussed below would all be defined as irrational. But, by my definition, the following need *not* be irrational:

1. Intuitive beliefs—Human rationality functions at two levels: the conscious and the subconscious. Most of our beliefs are formulated at a subconscious level. For example, the five-year-old boy learning how to ride a bicycle is not consciously formulating beliefs about the laws of gravity and angular momentum. But, subconsciously, that is exactly what he is doing. His rationality constructs subconscious, RATIONAL beliefs that accurately reflect truths about the physical universe. Intuitively, he grasps laws of physics about which he has no conscious beliefs. Much of our knowledge is intuitive in this way. It would be foolish, therefore, to define rationality in a manner that excluded beliefs formulated through subconscious reasonings. So, *RATIONAL is not limited to beliefs formed through conscious thinking processes.*

Intuitive (subconscious) beliefs may be either rational or irrational. My subconscious is not guaranteed to produce only rational beliefs any more than my conscious reasoning is. The only way an intuition can

---

21. Rather than subject the uninterested reader to a string of tedious definitions here in the main text, I have included as appendix K a brief discussion of my definitions of some key terms pertaining to rationality. The reader who is sufficiently interested can refer to appendix K for more information with regard to my conception of reason and its role in knowing.

be evaluated is by raising it from the level of the subconscious to the conscious. Then, and only then, can we examine whether it and the reasoning behind it conforms to logic. An intuition that remains merely an intuition remains necessarily an unexamined belief.

Consider the respective advantages and disadvantages of conscious and subconscious reasoning. Subconscious reasoning is very fast and efficient. That is its chief advantage. The corresponding disadvantage is that it does not permit validation. It produces beliefs and hunches whose rational justification and derivation are completely invisible to us. Its derivation may be sound. The hunch may be justified. But we cannot know, for we are unaware of the line of reasoning by which it was formulated. This, on the other hand, is the chief advantage of conscious reasoning. Conscious reasoning is relatively transparent and available for evaluation. We can literally slow the reasoning process down and evaluate its logical validity a step at a time. But here, of course, lies its chief disadvantage: conscious reasoning is cumbersome and painfully slow.

2. Inarticulable beliefs—We are not always able to articulate beliefs we clearly hold and utilize. And, even if we can articulate the belief, we may not be able to adequately articulate our reasons for holding it. Why such beliefs exist is understandable. They are intuitive beliefs, and beliefs produced by our subconscious reasoning processes are not readily put into words. Beliefs that can readily be verbalized are those produced by our conscious reasoning processes or those that have been consciously reconstructed from an initial intuition.

As in the case of intuitive beliefs, it would be inappropriate to define 'rational' in such a way that inarticulable beliefs were ruled irrational by definition. Many such intuitions are utterly rational. We must not discount them merely because they are not readily verbalized.

3. Vague beliefs—When we go through a rigorous logical proof of something, we are forced—by the nature of the exercise—to clearly define the belief in question. Furthermore, we are forced to spell out the line of reasoning that leads us to embrace it. But in the absence of such a rigorous logical proof, our beliefs often remain vague. Either the belief's content remains vague, or the reasoning that leads us to embrace it remains vague.

Is a vague belief (which has not been rigorously proved through a process of formal proof) irrational? Not necessarily. Granted, it may be. But many of the vague beliefs we hold are utterly rational—

they conform to the principles of logic. In principle, a rigorous formal proof could be given. But the fact that no proof has ever actually been formulated is not a legitimate indictment against a belief's rational validity. While rational beliefs are formally provable in principle, not all truly rational beliefs have been—or ever will be—formally proved in practice.

Note, then, what can be included within the scope of beliefs that are rational by my definition. Vague beliefs, inarticulable beliefs, and intuitive beliefs all fall within the range of what can be rational.

Many who maintain that reason is not the only access to truth mean merely that "conscious, formal, structured reasoning is not the only avenue to truth." And they are right about that—of course. But claiming that REASON is not the only access to truth is an unfortunate way to express it. REASON, as I have defined it, is the only access to truth. But I do not mean that conscious reasoning is the only access to truth. It is not—it isn't even the primary access. Subconscious reasoning is a vital part of our ability to know. Subjective hunches, intuitions, feelings—all of these things can be valid avenues to knowledge. But these are not irrational avenues to knowledge. To the extent that they lead to knowledge, they are completely and utterly RATIONAL.

My point is simple: when an intuition does lead to truth, it is due to its being a RATIONAL intuition. In principle, such an intuition could be raised to the level of consciousness, clearly defined, and formally and systematically proved. In practice, this can be so difficult as to be practically impossible. But it will always be possible, in theory if not in practice, to give a sound logical proof for every true belief. God could do it, even if we cannot.

Clarification of the Point at Issue

My foundational assumption is that reason is the only reliable guide to truth. Given that, all of the following are implied: (1) whatever is logically contradictory or inconsistent cannot possibly be true, (2) if one belief is logically superior to a second belief, the first belief is more likely than the second to be true, and (3) whatever is *perfectly* logical is necessarily true.

In view of our definition of reason above, we need to keep the following points in mind:

1. Assuming that reason alone is the only reliable guide to truth is not to assume that the only reliable guide to truth consists of consciously constructed, formal proofs. I fully acknowledge that vague intuitions shoved into consciousness by our subconscious powers of reasoning also serve as a valuable access to truth, and they constitute an aspect of human reason.

2. Any belief that is known to be logically inconsistent or contradictory is thereby known to be false. A belief whose logical consistency or inconsistency cannot be determined should not be assumed to be false. Not all true beliefs can be determined to be logically cogent. Some true beliefs have not been clearly shown to be rational. Hence, if a belief—or the reasoning behind it—is too vague for one to discern whether it is rationally valid, it would be a mistake to assume that it is false. For a belief may be rationally valid even when we cannot discern that it is. In other words, not all vague intuitive beliefs are false. Only discernibly irrational beliefs are necessarily false.

3. A consciously reasoned belief is not, by virtue of that fact, logically superior to a vague intuition. A belief's superiority must be judged by the rational cogency of the actual reasoning that supports it. It makes no difference at what level that reasoning has occurred—conscious or subconscious. The only way to compare the rational cogency of two beliefs is to raise them both to the level of consciousness, articulate the reasoning that underlies them, and evaluate that. Without doing so, there is no basis for just evaluation.

So here is the bottom line. If two beliefs are both raised to a level of conscious reasoning so that they can be compared at that level, and one of the beliefs is more logically cogent than the other, the one that is more log-

---

22. By 'sound reasoning' I mean reasoning as it ought to be done—as God would do it. It is the opposite of fallacious reasoning. Fallacious reasoning is reasoning which is flawed and leads to error rather than truth because it is illogical and irrational at some critical point. Much human reasoning is fallacious. For this reason—among others—an inerrant, absolutely authoritative Bible is valuable to us. It is not likely that humans would arrive at all truth simply by reasoning from the data of experience; we are too prone to reason fallaciously. An inerrant, authoritative interpretation of reality can serve as a check on our own wayward reasoning. The teaching contained in Scripture is more reliable than the actual reasonings of foolish, fallen humans. But this is not to say that the teaching of Scripture is more reliable than SOUND reasoning from experience. The Scripture and sound reasoning from experience are equally reliable, equally authoritative, equally inerrant, and equally essential.

ically cogent is necessarily the one that is more likely true. And a belief that is perfectly logically consistent is necessarily true.

But this is exactly the point to which many might object. In their view, to assume that reason will necessarily lead us to truth is wrong—especially when the truth in question concerns God or other ultimate issues. From the critic's perspective, for a true belief to be less rationally cogent than some false belief is entirely possible. But I must show that this perspective is unbiblical. In the biblical view, sound reasoning (with 'sound' being a very important qualifier) is an infallible guide to truth.[22]

The Biblical View of Reason

I base my belief in the reliability of reason on two facts: (1) it is the teaching of Scripture, and (2) it is philosophically required.[23] In this chapter, I deal only with the first of these. I will show that the assumption that reason is the only reliable guide to truth underlies all that the Bible teaches.

John 1:1–5 is the most helpful passage in this regard:

In the beginning was the *logos*. Now the *logos* was with God, indeed God was the LOGOS. This *logos* was in the beginning with God. All things came into existence through this *logos*, and not one thing that has ever come into existence came into existence apart from it. Included in this *logos* was Life, and Life was the light of men. Now this light shines in the darkness, and the darkness has not extinguished it. (original translation)[24]

---

23. Virtually every ancient Greek philosophy gave the same answer to the question of how knowledge is possible: *The rational structure of the cosmos and the structures of the human mind derive from the same primal rationality. Since this is so, the rationality of the cosmos is discernible to the rationality of the human mind. They correspond; for they have the same source.* No one in the entire history of philosophy ever improved on the essence of this answer. The Bible's answer is essentially the same. The Bible nominates a different candidate for the primal rationality that functioned as the source of all things. But it explains the possibility of knowledge in fundamentally the same way.

24. A thorough defense of this translation and the interpretation underlying it would be too involved to tackle here. Two considerations are most decisive in my thinking: (1) The argument of John's prologue is that God's rational purpose for man from the very beginning was that man have life, that this life be the very essence of human fulfillment, and that this life remains a possibility because of who Jesus is and what he has done for us. In other words, John is suggesting that the gospel story he is about to tell is a story of how the possibility of human fulfillment (i.e., life) has been preserved by God through his Son, Jesus. In the light of this understanding of the

As you will note, I translate John 1:1 differently from most of the standard English translations. The standard English translations all follow the King James Version in translating *logos* with 'word'. The NIV, for example, renders John 1:1, "In the beginning was *the Word*, and *the Word* was with God, and *the Word* was God" (my emphasis). I consider this translation off the mark. My personal translation of John 1:1–2, if I were to translate *logos* into English, would run like this:

> In the beginning was the rationally ordered and purposive script of the whole of cosmic history. Now this pre-existent script was with God, indeed God was the primal rationality who authored this script. This pre-existent script was in the beginning with God. All things came into existence in conformity with this script, and not one thing that has ever come into existence came into existence apart from it. Included in the script was Life, and the way to Life was the light of men. Now this light shines in the darkness, and the darkness has not extinguished it.

THE MEANING OF *LOGOS*

If you were to consult a beginner's text on New Testament Greek, its vocabulary list would give 'word' as the English translation of *logos*.[25] Consistent with this, all the major English translations of the Bible translate *logos* in John 1 into 'word'. On the other hand, if you were to consult a classical Greek lexicon, its entry would show a much wider range of possible usages for *logos*. Among them would be things like 'argument,' 'rational discourse,' 'thinking,' 'reasoning,' 'rational reflection,' 'account,' 'argument,' 'story,' and most notably, 'reason'.[26] In the Greek of the

---

prologue, LOGOS as the divine principle of purposive rationality contributes to this meaning; *logos* meaning the WORD would not. (2) Understanding LOGOS as the primal purposive rationality involves a straightforward understanding of the word *logos* in its Greek milieu. The suggestion that designating God as the WORD is a reference to the Genesis creation account where God speaks the creation into existence has always seemed forced to me. The fact that God speaks and creation occurs does not directly suggest that God *himself* should be designated the WORD. On the other hand, the fact that God is the ultimate, self-existent rational mind that has created and designed all of reality does directly suggest that God *himself* should be designated the MIND—that is, the LOGOS—particularly in the cultural milieu of John's time.

25. See J. Gresham Machen, *New Testament Greek for Beginners* (Toronto: Macmillan Company, 1923), 23 and 262; and see Eric G. Jay, *New Testament Greek: An Introductory Grammar* (London: S.P.C.K., 1958), 32.

ancient world, reason, intelligence, mind, etc., are clearly within the field of meaning of the word *logos.*

In John 1, John uses *logos* to convey two different, but related meanings. On the one hand, it can be used to denote a story or narrative—a script. On the other hand, it can denote the rational faculty. In my initial rendering above, I render the Greek word *logos,* simply transliterating the Greek term, when John means to denote the pre-existent script that God purposed for cosmic history. I render it LOGOS where John means to denote the rational mind that devised that script. It is the latter usage that concerns us here. In the latter usage (LOGOS), John uses the Greek term *logos* not to denote reason in the abstract, but to denote the concrete reason that lies behind all that exists—that purposive, intelligent reason that planned and ordered all things. He means Reason with a capital R.

Virtually all ancient Greek philosophy held that a primal rationality was the source of all rationality and created the structure and purpose of everything that exists. Stoicism was a very popular philosophy in the world of John's day. Stoics held that the world (i.e., the cosmos) came into being by the design of an intelligent, purposive force. The cosmos is rationally ordered and purposive precisely because a rational creative force gave it its form and existence. They had a name for this rational force. It was called the Logos.[27] (Stoicism maintained that the Logos was an impersonal force. They did not believe in a personal creator God. Therein lay an important difference between Stoic philosophy and the biblical worldview.) But the general concept was not confined to the Stoics. Hence, it provided a concept that John could effectively employ in the prologue to his gospel.[28]

It was widely accepted in the world of John's day that the order and purpose of the cosmos was to be explained by reference to a primal rationality widely referred to as the Logos. John accepts the attribution of cos-

---

26. See *A Greek-English Lexicon, compiled by Henry George Liddell and Robert Scott,* 9th ed. (Oxford Press, 1940), s.v. "λογος". Although many New Testament usages are legitimately translated 'word', it is debatable whether the usage of *logos* to mean word is a root, foundational meaning or a derived meaning. It seems likely to me that *logos,* when used to mean "word"—as well as *lego* used to mean "speak"—comes from the fact that a word—whether written or uttered—is the symbolic representation of a CONCEPT—a product of RATIONAL thought. If so, then the word's more primitive and basic meaning is the one mentioned here—reason or rationality.

27. F. E. Peters, *Greek Philosophical Terms: A Historical Lexicon* (New York: New York University Press, 1967), 110–112.

28. While Stoicism was a popular and widely influential philosophy in the first century, the concept of the LOGOS as the primal rationality that gave rise to the rational structure of all of reality was shared by virtually the whole ancient Greek world—though it was not always identified by the name 'logos'. It was not a uniquely Stoic concept; it was pan-Hellenic.

mic order and purpose to this Logos. But he does not accept the Greek (particularly the Stoic) conception of the Logos. The Logos is not an impersonal force. It is one and the same with the personal God who revealed himself to Abraham, Isaac, and Jacob.

> In the beginning was the *logos*. Now the *logos* was with God, indeed *God* was the LOGOS. This *logos* was in the beginning with God. All things came into existence through this *logos*, and not one thing that has ever come into existence came into existence apart from it.

But John's primary purpose in the prologue is not to challenge the Greeks' inadequate understanding of the Logos. That is secondary. His primary purpose is to highlight the pre-existence of divine Reason and to thereby highlight the rationality of the created order. The pre-existent God is himself rational. He is the primal reason who, in the beginning, was the source of all reason. He is the self-existent rational being who imparts rationality to all other rational beings and who created the whole cosmos in conformity to the dictates of reason, an attribute of his own being.

Why is John intent on highlighting the pre-existence of Reason and the rationality of the created order? Because he wants to focus on one aspect of that created order: namely, he wants to focus on man and stress the fact that man was made *with a purpose*. Specifically, man was designed to experience Life—what elsewhere is called Eternal Life. Life, by the design of the rational creator who created the whole cosmos, is the ultimate good of mankind. This goal, if achieved, would fulfill the very purpose for which man was created.

> All things came into existence through this *logos*, and not one thing that has ever come into existence came into existence apart from it. Included in this *logos* was Life (as the ultimate good of mankind), and (the way to) Life was the light (the ultimate wisdom) of men.

This, then, sets the stage for one of the most succinct statements of the gospel in the entire Bible:

> Now this light shines in the darkness, and the darkness has not extinguished it.

Death is mankind's problem. We do not have the Life purposed for us by the LOGOS, and we do not know how to gain this Life, our ultimate fulfillment. Instead, we are in darkness. Are we forever abandoned to the darkness of ignorance and death that now surrounds us? Has the darkness so completely enveloped mankind that no hope remains? "No!" John says. A ray of hope continues to shine, penetrating the darkness. Threatening though the darkness is, it has not extinguished the light. The possibility of Life for man remains. He can still achieve the Life for which he was created. That is the significance of the gospel. That is the meaning of the story about Jesus that John is about to recount.

My exposition above is meant to illuminate the point at issue. What is the LOGOS in John 1? The most reasonable interpretation is that John uses *logos* to designate the most ultimate rationality in all of reality, God.

THE SIGNIFICANCE OF GOD AS THE LOGOS

Some very important implications for our view of reason arise from an understanding of John 1:1–3. John highlights two important facts: (1) God is the LOGOS, i.e., the Primal Reason, and (2) the entire created order has been created by this LOGOS, God himself. What follows? Very simply, that the entire created order is rational and conforms to the dictates of reason.[29] God created it to function in conformity to the principles of reason and logic. But not only is the impersonal created order rational (making physical science possible), all other aspects of the created order are rational as well. Even those aspects of reality that come into existence through the choices of free moral agents ultimately conform to rational orderliness. Every part of reality and everything that happens originates from the creator God in conformity to his rational design and his rational purposes.[30] So, not only is God rational, all of created reality is rational as well.

---

29. John does not explicitly highlight this inference; to address the philosophical problem of the possibility of knowledge was not his purpose in writing. Nevertheless, by identifying the God of Abraham, Isaac, and Jacob with the LOGOS, John is clearly acceding to the concept of the LOGOS current in the intellectual culture of his day. But the contemporary concept of the LOGOS was, in part, developed to answer the philosophical problem of knowledge. Therefore, by identifying the God of Israel with the LOGOS, John is implicitly acknowledging the point I want to make explicit. The philosophical problem of knowledge is answered in the biblical conception of the rational creator God.

30. In chapter 6 I discuss the relationship between the Creator and freewill choices. I maintain that freewill choices are products of creation just as surely as rocks, trees, mountains, and quarks. For now, it is sufficient to note that if John had only the impersonal created order in mind when he says "…and not one thing that has come into existence came into existence apart from it (the *logos*)…", then only the laws of physics would be knowable by human reason. Knowledge of an individual person or of human nature would not be knowable through common sense and normal human intelligence. It would be impossible to discover any rational or logical patterns that

Significant implications for the Bible's view of reason, truth, and knowledge follow from this:

1. *Created reality is knowable.*

Man, reasoning from life experience, can acquire valid knowledge of what exists in the created cosmos. The faculty of reason (*logos*) that God (the LOGOS) created in man constructs beliefs according to those same laws that define and order the universe—i.e., the laws of reason and logic. God created the cosmos to be rational. Therefore, a built-in match exists between rationally sound (*logikos*) beliefs and the truth about how things really are.

God purposed for us to know, so he made our minds such that we truly could know. He made our minds to correspond to reality. Specifically, he designed our minds so that the beliefs that constitute genuine knowledge of reality—because they give us true information about the way things actually are—are the very beliefs we judge to be rationally valid.

The essence of "the problem of knowledge" that has interested philosophers for millennia is this: how can we know that those beliefs we judge to be true do, in fact, give us accurate information about reality as it actually is? John offers the only really adequate solution to this aspect of the problem of knowledge: because God designed our minds to judge in conformity with the way he created the cosmos to be. The built-in rationality that shapes our beliefs about the cosmos is the same rationality that has shaped the cosmos itself.

Many thinkers have agreed that human knowledge and the reality external to man conform to a common standard—namely, the standard of reason itself. As we have seen, this alone solves the problem of knowledge. I can know that my true beliefs conform to the world as it truly is precisely because my beliefs and the world are equally rational according to one and the same rationality. Human reason can comprehend the intrinsic rational structure of the actual world; hence, man can know the truth about the world.

The ancient Greeks believed this. Most secular naturalists would affirm this. Various philosophies throughout history have offered this solution to the problem of knowledge. But no one—other than the biblical theist—can adequately answer the ensuing question: how can I explain that there

---

would constitute a true understanding of history, sociology, psychology, or anything else in the humanities or social sciences. Though such skepticism is in vogue among secular thinkers, it is contradictory to everything common sense tells us and to everything on which our everyday lives are based. Such radical skepticism is not livable in practice; and there is no greater refutation of a belief than our inability to live it.

is a correspondence? Why is it that human intelligence and the cosmos operate according to the same ordering principles of reason? Secular naturalism and other philosophies dogmatically assert that this is so. But they have no intellectually satisfying explanation for why it should be so.[31] Only the Bible offers that: namely, because created reality and the human mind were created by the same self-existent creator God who is himself intrinsically rational and whose purpose in creating human intelligence was so that man could know the truth about reality.

2. *Irrational beliefs about created reality are false beliefs.*

The rationality of the created order has a very important implication: any belief about created reality that does not conform to reason or logic (i.e., that is an irrational belief) cannot possibly be true. Everything that has come into existence, according to John, has come into existence according to the dictates of the rational purposes of God. ("...All things came into existence in conformity with this *logos,* and not one thing that has ever come into existence came into existence apart from it....") Therefore, if some belief does not conform to the dictates of reason, it cannot be a true belief.

3. *God is knowable.*

Man, reasoning from life experience and God's revelation of himself, can know the truth about God. The reason (*logos*) that God (the LOGOS) has created in man constructs beliefs about God and ultimate reality that conform to principles that are intrinsic to God's very essence. A built-in match exists between our rationally sound (*logikos*) beliefs and the truth about who God is. God made our minds not only to match the reality of the created order, but also to match the reality of who he is. God purposed for man to know himself as well as his creation. So he made our minds to function in such a way that we truly could know him. Our rationally valid beliefs about God—the transcendent One—are indeed *knowledge* of him.

---

31. According to Socrates, true beliefs that, while true, are not accompanied by an explanation for why and how they are true do not rise to the level of knowledge; they are merely true opinion. The witch doctor who cures a diseased eye by putting cow dung on it does not have true knowledge of the cure. The modern doctor who has learned that a certain chemical (which the cow dung contains) heals a particular eye disorder for a particular reason is the one who has true knowledge. The secular naturalist, like the witch doctor, may have the right cure for the problem of knowledge, but he has no true knowledge of that cure if he cannot explain why it is so. Only biblical theism can do that.

4. *God and ultimate truth do not transcend reason.*

The Bible, then, is at odds with the popular belief that God and ultimate truth transcend reason. Nothing can transcend the self-existent God who existed before the cosmos. He is the ultimate transcendent reality. Yet John states explicitly that—before the birth of the cosmos—there was LOGOS, REASON. How can that be? Only if, as John says, God is that pre-existent Reason. God cannot transcend reason, for that would be to transcend himself. Reason, like goodness or holiness, is an attribute of his very being, and God does not transcend his own attributes.

The more popular notion posits a serious limitation on the ability of human reason to know God. This is unbiblical. True, we are seriously limited in what we can know about God. We can only know of God what he reveals to us. He is, after all, transcendent. He is not a part of the data of everyday experience. But this limitation on our knowledge of God is not what the popular notion has in mind. The popular notion would suggest that reason itself fails us when it comes to knowing God. But reason itself does not fail us. Reason is unfailingly reliable with respect to a knowledge of God. It is the extent of our experience that limits us. Reason cannot operate without data, and the data we have on God is not (and never can be) complete. Hence, we can never acquire a complete and exhaustive knowledge of who he is. Human knowledge of God will always be limited. But not because reason was involved! What little we can know about God is valid precisely because it does conform to reason. No irrational belief about God could possibly be true, for God is LOGOS itself.

5. *Reason is not merely a part of the created order, nor is it functional only within the created order. It transcends the created order and can function to give us knowledge of God himself.*

This follows directly from (3) and (4).

6. *Irrational beliefs about God are false beliefs.*

It should be clear from the discussion above that any belief about God and transcendent truth that does not conform to reason or logic (*i.e.,* that is an irrational belief) cannot possibly be true. This conclusion should be highlighted for the purposes of this book. John states that God is intrinsically rational. Indeed, God is himself the origin of all rationality.[32]

---

32. This is not explicit in John's statement, but it is clearly implied. For John, as for the ancient Hebrews, nothing existed in the beginning but God. Everything else was created by him. Hence, any other manifestation of rationality had to be created by him.

Therefore, if some belief about God does not conform to the dictates of reason, it cannot conform to a true understanding of who God really is.

7. *To be irrational is to be in rebellion against God; to opt for irrationality is to opt for something that is wrong—something contrary to God's very nature.*
This is yet a further implication of God's being the LOGOS. Evil and wickedness constitute rebellion against God, for God is himself intrinsically good, and to be evil is to refuse to emulate who God is. Likewise, irrationality constitutes rebellion against God, for God is intrinsically rational, and to be irrational is to refuse to emulate who God is.

OBJECTION TO THESE INFERENCES

One might object: "All that you have been arguing assumes that man's reason is, for the most part, the same as God's reason. But that is not so. God's logic is not like our logic. God's ways are not our ways. God's reason is not our reason. We cannot assume that God's rationality is the same as our rationality."

No one can argue with the contention that God's ways are not man's ways. That much is clear. But to concede that does not require that the divine *logos* be different from the human *logos*. God's ways being different from ours is attributable to a host of other differences between God and man. God is holy; we are wicked. God is the transcendent creator; we are finite creatures. God is wise and knowing; we are foolish and ignorant. We have a perspective narrowed by the present moment; God has a perspective as broad as the future itself. There are numerous reasons why God's ways are not our ways. But the claim that human rationality is different from divine rationality is not one of them.

In discussing the issue of divine rationality as it relates to human rationality, an inadequate conception of what rationality is contributes to the confusion. Reason must not be confused with an actual piece of thinking and its conclusion. That is, REASON differs from REASONING.[33] There is no question that, due to our limited perspective, our thinking (reasoning) arrives at very different conclusions from God's thinking (reasoning). But not because God employs different rules of logic. Rather, he applies the same rules of logic to a different set of facts, values, and assumptions. Fallen, weak human beings hold wrong-headed assumptions, have a perverse set of values, and lack many of the relevant facts. Inevitably

---

33. See appendix K for my definitions of these terms.

we will come to conclusions that differ from God's. But the difference is not due to a different rationality. It is attributable to a different and inferior application of the same rationality.

We, as human beings, are all equipped with the same rationality. Yet we arrive at significantly different conclusions. Why? Because we start from different assumptions, we have different perceptions of the facts, we have different hierarchies of values, and we have different personal agendas. It is clearly *not* because we are equipped with different kinds of reason. Neither is the difference between God's way of thinking and our way of thinking due to different kinds of reason. We share the same *logos*.

When God asked Abraham to offer his son Isaac on the altar, was he asking him to do something that was totally illogical? Something that made no sense by the standards of human logic, that only made sense in the light of an alien divine logic? No! God was not asking Abraham to reject ordinary human reason as an avenue to truth and obedience. He was not being asked to reject human logic in favor of some mysterious divine logic. Rather, he was being asked to trust that he (God) was in a better position to determine what ordinary human reason would entail. God and Abraham shared the same standards of logic, the same principles of rationality. But God knew more facts, and he understood more clearly how his purposes were to be achieved. Hence, he had a superior perspective from which to judge what ordinary human reason dictated.

Not uncommonly, Abraham's faith is described as if it were a crazy, dramatic abandonment of reason, replaced by a blind, irrational obedience to God. But nothing in the Bible justifies such an interpretation. Abraham's faith was eminently rational; he made a logical choice. Granted, what God was requiring did not appear to be a rational act. But that is where Abraham's faith lay: he trusted that God would never require of him something that was rationally inappropriate. Abraham's conviction was that, if he knew what God knew, the divine command would be manifestly reasonable. But, not knowing what God knew, it was understandable that it appeared crazy and absurd. He trusted that it was a rational act, against all appearances, because he knew he did not possess all the facts.

This is the New Testament's perspective on Abraham's action. The apostles do not present Abraham's faith as a courageous abandonment of reason.[34] On the contrary, they presume that Abraham's faith and obedience were utterly rational—justified on utterly rational grounds. Abraham knew the God who had promised him an inheritance through Isaac. He was capable of fulfilling that promise—even if Isaac died. If need be, God could raise Isaac from the dead.[35] One way or the other, God would fulfill his promise. In the light of who God is, such faith is utterly reasonable.

Death cannot thwart the unfailing purposes of the creator.

Nevertheless, many feel that we diminish God when we affirm that we share the same *logos* with him. God must have a different, exalted *logos* if he is to be worthy of his status. But this is not the Bible's perspective—most notably, it is not the perspective of the gospel of John.

As noted earlier, *logos* was a common word in the Greek language of John's day. The meaning of *logos* is informed by the phenomena of everyday human experience. *Logos* denotes ordinary human reason and its expression in language. From his choice of *logos* to denote God, we can reasonably infer that, for John, there is no gap between human reason and divine reason. To describe an attribute of the nature of God, he uses a term whose content is wholly defined in terms of ordinary human reason. Why? Arguably, because he believes that divine rationality can be accurately portrayed in terms of human rationality. If John believed, as many do, that God's mind works according to some alien principles of logic (where, for example, logical contradictions can be true), how could he have picked *logos* to describe the mind of God? If God's logic so totally violates what we mean by *logos*, how can that particular word be used to describe it? Surely another word would have been required—even if John had to invent it.[36] To suggest that he grants the title of LOGOS to that which is alien to *logos* is an unlikely understanding of what he means. Far more likely, he calls God the LOGOS precisely because he believes that there is one and only one form of *logos* in all of reality—namely, that which is intrinsic to the divine nature. The rationality that structures creation is simply a reflection of the rationality that exists in God himself. Far from being at odds with divine logic, human rationality is completely congruent with it.

To drive a wedge between the logic of God and the logic of man is an attractive strategy for exalting God and affirming his majesty. But it is

---

34. Some would argue that this is exactly what Kierkegaard is suggesting in *Fear and Trembling*—namely, that Abraham's faith consisted in his courageous abandonment of reason. I think this is a complete misunderstanding of Kierkegaard. But if it is not, then Kierkegaard's suggestion is without any support from the New Testament.

35. See Hebrews 11:19. See also Romans 4:21 with regard to the nature of Abraham's faith.

36. If John believed there was a gap between human reason and the divine Reason, then I would have expected something more like the following as the prologue to his gospel: "In the beginning was the Irrational Mystery (or, Inexplicable Super-Rationality). Now the Irrational Mystery (Inexplicable Super-Rationality) was with God, indeed God was the Irrational Mystery (Inexplicable Super-Rationality). This Irrational Mystery (Inexplicable Super-Rationality) was in the beginning with God. All things came into existence through this Irrational Mystery (Inexplicable Super-Rationality), and not one thing that has ever come into existence came into existence apart from it."

wrong-headed and unbiblical. Many differences exist between God and man; reason is not one of them. In order that we might know him and his handiwork, God has equipped us with a mind that operates according to the same logical principles that are intrinsic to his very being. Any view that denies this is at odds with common sense, with sound philosophy, and with the teaching of the Bible.

CONSIDERING THE CONSEQUENCES

But before we leave this objection, let's consider the alternative. What if God's logic were different from our own? Two devastating results would follow:

1. *Knowledge of God would be impossible.*

If the principles that give structure to the very being of God are incongruent with the principles that give birth to our beliefs, then the beliefs we form about God will be fallacious—radically out of sync with the reality of who God is. We can infer from the creation and from our experience that God exists and that he is good. But this is based on human logic. If God does exist and is good, we have a happy coincidence. But, what if the logic innate within God's nature differs from the logic of our minds? Where is the guarantee that our theological beliefs, constructed to conform to human logic, will be true? For all we know, it is just as true to say that "God does not exist" and that "God is evil." If human reason does not apply to God, beliefs contrary to human reason may nonetheless be true.

Only divine logic could produce assuredly true beliefs about God. But, on the assumption that God's logic differs from our own, we are incapable of reasoning in accordance with divine logic. Consequently, we could never know anything about him. At least, we could never know that the beliefs we have formed about him are true. We know what our narrow human logic tells us about God. But we could never know whether it depicts him accurately.

2. *No knowledge of anything would be possible.*

Whatever rationality makes up the divine being, John says that everything that has come into existence has come into existence in conformity to that rationality. Accordingly—if human logic is not congruent with divine logic—no knowledge of anything would be possible. The principles of reason that shape our beliefs would not conform to the ordering principles that have shaped objective reality. Consequently, our beliefs would create a magnificent fiction—internally consistent and rational by human standards, but bearing no resemblance to the actual world that lies beyond the reach of my thoughts and perceptions.[37] If human reason does not represent the structure of reality as it actually is, then human beings have no real knowledge of it, for human knowledge is based on human reason.

Here is the bottom line: unless we are prepared to say (against all common sense and against all that we do, in fact, believe) that no knowledge of God and no knowledge of reality is possible, it is absurd to suggest that divine logic and human logic are two different things.

The Sunday School Calculus: A Denial of Reason

In practice, we deny the validity of reason in many different ways. One particularly subtle denial plays an important role in the debate over divine determinism. I call it the "Sunday School Calculus." We find it in both beginning and advanced levels.

On one occasion, trying to teach my daughter that heaven will be a very desirable place, I asked her, "What is the funnest thing you can think of?" (I was teaching her theology, not grammar.) I expected her to say, "Disneyland!" My next move was going to be, "Well heaven will be more fun than Disneyland." But, having mastered Beginning Sunday School Calculus, she sabotaged my pedagogical strategy. Quickly and confidently, she answered, "God. God is the funnest thing!" Beginning Sunday School Calculus says, "Take any adjective whatsoever, add 'est' (or its syntactical equivalent), and you have discovered a valid attribute of God."

This same beginning calculus resulted in my son's confident assertion that God was the stinkiest thing in the world. (We had just driven past a pulp mill.) His older sister—having mastered the Advanced Sunday School Calculus by then—argued that, to the contrary, God was the best-smelling thing in the world. Advanced Sunday School Calculus instructs you, "Take any adjective that defines a positive attribute (and it must be a positive attribute), add 'est' (or its syntactical equivalent), and you have discovered a valid attribute of God."

---

37. The student of philosophy will recognize the specter of Kant here. If God's logic were different from our own, we could have knowledge only of the phenomenal world, the world of our experience. We could never know if we have knowledge of the world as it is in itself, independent of our experience of it.

What does any of this have to do with the issues we are discussing? An axiom of the Sunday School Calculus holds that *all things are possible with God*—literally, *all* things. At first blush, this axiom seems sound enough. But, in actual practice, it is frequently used as a subtle camouflage for rejecting reason. It can be construed in such a way that it denies the rationality of God.

From a biblical point of view, *not all things* are *possible with God.* God cannot do evil. It is contrary to his very nature. Likewise, God cannot do what is logically impossible. That, too, is contrary to his nature. God is rational; rationality is intrinsic to his very being. Indeed, he is the source of reason itself. Therefore, everything he does will be rational and logical.

One tempting counter to the ensuing arguments for divine determinism will be to assert, in effect, that God can do what is logically impossible.[38] As you shall see, if God can create something to be uncreated, can cause something to be uncaused, or can cause something to be self-causing, my arguments for divine determinism are inconclusive. I am confident that God can do none of these. They are logical impossibilities—things that a rational God could not do. But one schooled in the Sunday School Calculus—committed to the lesson that "all things [even logically impossible things] are possible with God"—will refuse to grant me this assumption.

"All things are possible with God" sounds like a pious and noble defense of God's supremacy. But, in fact, it is a denial of the God of the Bible. God is no more irrational and illogical than he is evil. *He cannot violate logic any more than he can violate goodness.* This is fundamental to my argument. If God is not logical and rational and if human reason is not a credible guide to truth, then my defense of divine determinism is hopelessly flawed from its inception. But if God is rational and if human rationality is a reliable avenue to truth, then my reliance upon rational argument in defending divine determinism is a strength, not a defect.

---

38. Can God create a rock so large that he cannot lift it? This presents an insoluble dilemma to the Sunday School Calculus. If one says "no," he denies God's omnipotence by conceding that there is something he cannot create. If one says "yes," he denies God's omnipotence by conceding that there is something he cannot lift. But from the standpoint of the biblical worldview, the answer is simple. No! God cannot create a rock so large he cannot lift it. A rock so large that an omnipotent God could not lift it is a logically impossible entity. And God cannot create something that logically cannot exist (like a square circle), for God is bound by logic because he *is* logic. This is not a denial of the biblical concept of omnipotence, for the Bible (unlike the Sunday School Calculus) never claims that God can do what is logically impossible. Omnipotence is the attribute of being powerful (or transcendent) enough to do anything that is logically possible and morally good. Anything else would violate his nature, and that he cannot do. It is not possible, for example, for God not to exist. But this is no counter-example to his omnipotence.

Summary and Conclusion

It will soon become apparent that my arguments for divine determinism are rational arguments. We live in a day of strong anti-rational sentiments. Many will dismiss my arguments because they are too rational. But, in this chapter, I have maintained that, not only is rational argument valid, but reason and logic are the indispensable tools of a sound theological method.

It makes as much sense to accuse an argument of being too logical as it does to accuse God of being too good, my wife of being too faithful, or my dog of being too canine. The goal of intellectual inquiry is to construct beliefs that are perfectly rational, perfectly logical. The more rational the argument, the better!

So I am not embarrassed by the importance logic and reason play in my defense of divine determinism, for I am convinced of three important propositions: (1) reason is the only tool God has given us for arriving at truth,[39] (2) reason is entirely reliable, and (3) reason is adequate to the task of leading us to truth. To reject reason is a self-defeating intellectual suicide—a renunciation of the God-given intelligence that has served us well all of our lives.

Like college freshmen in an introductory philosophy course, discovering the power of skepticism for the first time, we can wax skeptical toward reason. But skepticism is nothing but a clever sleight of hand. It creates the illusion that it is rational to doubt the reliability of rationality—a sort of philosophical carnival act. But reason cannot be seriously doubted by serious thinkers. How can one, on the basis of reason, seriously doubt reason?

To doubt the validity of reason is to doubt the possibility of knowledge itself—including the knowledge of one's own existence. It is to call into question all knowledge and all truth. It is to call into question the foundations of intelligence itself. Going even further, to deny the validity of reason is spiritual and intellectual suicide of the first degree. It is to reject the very tool that makes knowledge of truth possible.

Furthermore, the denial of reason can only occur in a theoretical discussion (if even there). Sitting in his office, his feet on the desk, the professor can afford to argue that reason is unreliable. But seeing an oncoming car as he prepares to cross a street, that same professor does not step in front of the oncoming car, reasoning that—since reason cannot be known to accurately represent objective reality—he need not allow reason to con-

---

39. However, see note 22 above.

trol his actions. Determining that it is better not to step out in front of the car, he trusts human logic implicitly. While we can deny reason in theory, we cannot deny it in practice. But if we cannot deny it in practice, what is the point of denying it at all? Our beliefs are valuable to the extent that they help us understand and navigate in the real world. If the unreliability of reason is not a proposition we can practice, in what meaningful sense do we believe it?

The Bible assumes the importance of sound reason to the task of understanding. Further, it explicitly claims that rationality is linked to the very nature of God himself. God is the LOGOS, reason itself. Reason, then, is not a provisional tool given to humans for use while they are "down here." It defines the nature of all existence, even God's. It will remain into eternity as one of the parameters that define all true existence. Accordingly, my ultimate defense of reason is a theological one. To deny the validity of reason is ultimately to deny God. Or, at least, to worship a false god—one whose nature does not include rationality as an attribute.

In the arguments that follow, I hope to demonstrate that divine determinism follows by logical necessity from the concept of God clearly taught in the Bible. If I am correct—if I have not made any errors in reasoning—then divine determinism is true. According to the Bible's view of reason, what is logically necessary is true. It would be irresponsible rebellion against the very nature of God himself to dismiss my arguments without refuting them on the grounds that they are too dependent on human logic.

CHAPTER FOUR

THREE CRITICAL CONCEPTS

Three important concepts need clarification before I can proceed with my case for divine determinism. In this chapter I discuss divine transcendence, common sense, free will, and other important related concepts.

Transcendence

What does it mean for God to be transcendent? In many respects, the doctrine of divine determinism hinges on whether God transcends reality. More specifically, it hinges on the exact nature of his transcendence. A clear grasp of divine transcendence and its implications is critical to the defense of divine determinism.

My contention is that to be transcendent is to exist in complete independence from that which is transcended. To say that God transcends the cosmos is to say that God's existence is completely independent of cosmic existence. His being does not depend upon the existence of the universe in any way. He did not begin with the universe; he will not end with the universe. The Bible teaches, in effect, "Before the beginning of anything at all, God was there."

God exists on an entirely higher level than created reality. Created reality depends upon God for its existence. If he does not will and cause it to exist, it will not exist. But divine existence does not depend upon created reality in the same way. He exists whether there is a created order or not. He is self-existent—that is, he contains the explanation for why he exists within the very nature of the sort of being that he is. While we can affirm the statement "the universe exists" just as validly as "God exists," we must not be deceived. They do not mean the same thing. The universe was created; God is self-existent.

Humans exist on the same level of reality as the created cosmos. We are simply a part of created reality. Accordingly, we do not live on the same level as God. If you took an Acme Super-Deluxe Metaphysical Eraser and erased the whole of created reality, we would be gone, but God would still exist.

A more typical conception of divine transcendence exists: namely, that God transcends not the created realm, but the *physical* realm. It is conceived as a synonym for spiritual. Under this typical conception, transcendence means that God exists in the same realm as angels, Satan, and demons. It means that God's existence is not dependent upon material reality, that he exists without material substance. Under this conception, God is no more transcendent than other spiritual beings—angels, Satan, or demons—for they all transcend the material realm. God is more powerful, in possession of greater authority, but—under this conception—he exists on the same level of reality as they.

The biblical conception of transcendence is more radical than this. Specifically, God transcends the spiritual—the heavenly—realm just as surely as he does the physical realm. God is not made of the same spiritual stuff as angels. He is not made at all! He is the creator, not the created. He is the creator of both realms—the physical and the spiritual. Both exist only because God—who existed before either of them—willed them into existence.

Understanding this biblical conception of transcendence is critical to understanding my defense of divine determinism. Divine transcendence refers to God's existing behind, beyond, above, and below everything in all of reality, including heaven and the spiritual realm. (See Diagram 4.1) God does not live at the top of the hierarchy of created being. He exists outside the hierarchy altogether. He lives outside as its maker, not inside as its king.

As so defined, transcendence is something that will never describe me. No human will ever transcend created reality. I will always be a creature. I could never be otherwise. No matter what different sort of existence God might grant me in the age to come, it will necessarily be a created existence, derived from and dependent upon him, the creator. God is unique in his transcendence. He is the one and only author of all things. He alone exists above and beyond created reality. Only he is "outside the box."

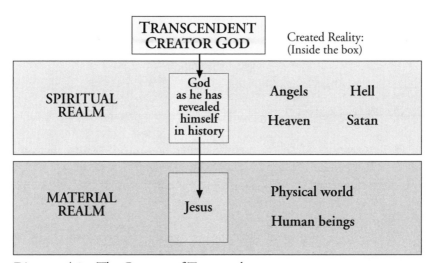

Diagram 4.1   The Concept of Transcendence

THE AUTHOR METAPHOR:
UNDERSTANDING TRANSCENDENCE

I claimed above that we humans will never transcend created reality. Can we, therefore, never understand what it means to be transcendent? Must transcendence remain an empty, abstract concept for us? No! As a matter of fact we can experience transcendence. Granted, we can never transcend the created cosmos. But we can transcend something.

Consider, for example, the relationship that would exist between you and the imaginary world of a novel you were writing. You, the author, are its transcendent creator. You are not a part of that world; you exist above and outside it. Every fictional character in that novel "moves, and lives, and has his being" in you. (See Acts 17:28) Everything that exists and everything that happens does so only at the determination of your will. To the extent that you understand the power, the absolute control, the absolute distance, and the complete otherness that defines your relationship to that fictional world, you understand transcendence.

God's transcendence of our reality is exactly analogous to this relationship between an author and the work of his imagination.[40] God is the author of our reality; we are characters in the story he is telling. In his fun-

---

40. As will become clear in part 4, the power of this author analogy to explicate the nature of divine transcendence is an extremely important tenet of this book.

damental essence, he is not a part of this reality; he is the one who lies behind it as its creator. Only when we understand God in this light—as the author of all reality—do we understand his transcendence.

THE TRANSCENDENT GOD
AND THE GOD OF THE BIBLE

As noted earlier, God is transcendent, not because he sits atop the hierarchy of beings, but because he exists outside and apart from the hierarchy of beings altogether. God lives outside that hierarchy as its maker, not inside as its king. He is not merely God, the Most Powerful. He is God, the Wholly Other.

Yet the Bible clearly and unabashedly presents God as the almighty king ruling over his creation. If he is the completely transcendent author we have been describing, how can the Bible describe him as the almighty king *within* reality?

The answer lies in an understanding of God's prerogatives as author of all reality. The author of a novel can always write himself into his own story in two ways: (1) he can give himself a distinct identity with a part to play within the story of the novel, or (2) he can create an actual being within the fictional reality of his novel that he, the author, identifies as himself. God, the author of our reality, has done both.

TRANSCENDENCE AND YAHWEH

Suppose I am writing a mystery. I want to play the role of secret informant within my story. I do not want to create a fictional character to be the informant. Rather, from my position outside that fictional reality, I want to *be* the informant myself. How could I do that? Simply by revealing myself to the relevant characters within my novel and disclosing what I want them to know.

I could make myself manifest to them however and whenever I wanted. There is no limit to how I might reveal myself. I could speak out of a bunch of flowers, a lamp, or an ashtray. I could whisper secrets to them from out of a curtain. I could broadcast what I know in a loud, deafening voice from the sky. Any means whatsoever is at my disposal.

Nor is there any limit to what I would know. I would know every word of every secret conversation that each of my characters have had. I would know their every hidden thought. Hence, there would be no limit to the knowledge I would have to disclose.

The first sense in which God has written himself into our reality is exactly analogous to this. God has given himself a role to play within cosmic history, and he has given himself a distinct identity to make known to us. As the transcendent author of all created reality, he could easily have remained invisible in the background—creator of everything, explicitly manifest in nothing. But God has not chosen to remain invisible. He has chosen to make himself known as a distinct, identifiable being, and to play a part in the history of the cosmos. He has acted and he has spoken. In the form of a burning bush, as a deafening voice emanating from a quaking mountain, and as a still small voice, he has spoken. In many different shapes, in many different voices, and in many different situations, he has spoken. He exists nowhere in the reality we inhabit; yet he can manifest himself anywhere within it, at any time, and in any form.

The transcendent God has given himself a name—Yahweh. And as Yahweh, he has given himself a part to play. As Yahweh, he has revealed to us who he is, what he expects, and what role he plays in our lives and our destiny. As Yahweh, he is the almighty king over all. He is the lawgiver. He is the judge. He is the one who has adopted Israel to be his people. He is the one who controls the course of history. He expects us to fear him, to love him, and to obey him. He has warned us: how we relate to him defines the nature of our destiny. In brief, God (Yahweh) has given himself a definable character with a set of definable roles within the drama of cosmic history, and he has spoken and acted within history to make that character known to us.

We must not lose sight of a vital distinction between Yahweh insofar as he plays a role in cosmic history and Yahweh the transcendent author. Yahweh-the-God-of-Israel commands Israel to obey, expects them to obey, and promises that he will punish them if they do not. Yahweh the transcendent author of all reality decides whether, at this particular juncture, the people of Israel will or will not obey their God. And it is Yahweh, the transcendent author of all reality, who creates in their hearts the inclination or disinclination to do so. In the first case, Yahweh is an actor within the drama. He is Yahweh the lawgiver. In the second case, he is the ultimate author of all that is. The latter is who Yahweh is, in and of himself; the former is who he is in his role in cosmic history. With respect to his nature and being, Yahweh is the transcendent author of all reality. But with respect to the part he is playing in the cosmic drama, Yahweh is Judge of all mankind, the exalted King over all creation. God's part is performed within the warp and woof of our reality; God's being lies above, beyond, and apart from it. Yahweh is never a being within created reality, existing as a permanent, distinct being on our level of existence. Rather—even as he plays out his role as Judge and exalted King—Yahweh is the transcendent God himself, revealing himself to humankind in his self-determined role. While he plays the particular part that he has assigned to himself, his being lies outside our reality, sufficient unto itself.

We can illustrate this distinction this way: If you took the aforementioned Acme Super-Deluxe Metaphysical Eraser and erased created reality, you would erase Yahweh the Almighty King. But Yahweh himself would remain. If created reality ceased to be, Yahweh's role within it would cease to have any meaning; indeed, it would cease to exist. What could it possibly mean to be the Almighty King over the entire universe if there were no universe? But the self-existent, transcendent Yahweh exists whether he has a role in cosmic history or not. Our eraser could never touch Yahweh-the-transcendent-author.

JESUS AND TRANSCENDENCE

As I stated above, there is a second way an author can write himself into a story he is creating. He can create a character within the story to be identical to himself.

I am writing that aforementioned mystery. I decide that I want to be the detective, and not the informant, within the story. It would be absurd, of course, to think that I—a human being—could literally be absorbed into the reality being created in my novel. It would be absurd to think that I—a flesh and blood human being—could be a fictional character within it. But I could create a character to be me. This character would exist alongside all the other characters, but my intention would be for that particular fictional character—the detective—to be me.

While this fictional character is me, he would be different from me in a very important sense. His existence is tied to the fictional world I have created. He does not transcend it; he is a part of it. On the other hand, as the author, I transcend that imaginary reality, and my existence is in no way linked to it.

By creating a being in my novel that I identify as myself, I both transcend the reality I am creating and, simultaneously, exist and function within it. I function within it through the character I have made identical to myself; I transcend it as the human author that I am.

The second sense in which God has written himself into cosmic history is exactly analogous to this. God, the transcendent author, has created a being within created reality to be identical to himself—a being who accurately reflects who he, the transcendent God, is. To be specific, he created Jesus.[41]

Jesus is a being within the same realm of existence we inhabit. He exists in exactly the same sense that we do. He has exactly the same kind of being that we have. His existence is as fully dependent on the will of his creator as ours is. In other words, Jesus is fully and unmistakably human. But, at the same time, Jesus is uniquely God himself. The transcendent author of all reality created a man to be him. For all eternity, that man Jesus—the transcendent creator's representation of himself in human form—will be the eternal king of all the universe.

THE SOVEREIGNTY OF GOD

Traditionally, the power and authority that God has over his creation has been designated by the term 'sovereignty'. This term is too vague for our purposes. 'Sovereignty' designates God's kingship over the cosmos. It describes God as the one who sits at the apex of the hierarchy of being. It is a fitting description of the King and Judge of all the earth. But it does not go far enough. To call Yahweh sovereign does not, in and of itself, necessitate his transcendence. It does not imply that he is a revelation of the transcendent author of all reality who exists wholly apart from the cosmos.[42] To conceive of a God who is sovereign while not being transcendent is entirely possible.[43] The term 'sovereignty', therefore, is inadequate to affirm all that the Bible teaches about God. God is not just infinitely more powerful than anything else in the cosmos. He is the very cause of its existence. He is the ground of its very being. It is in him that all things live and move and have their very being. (*cf.* Acts 17:28)

This work, therefore, is not merely a defense of the absolute sovereign-

---

41. This is why Paul can write of Jesus, "And he is the image of the invisible God." (*cf.* Colossians 1:15)

42. I believe that to describe God as "wholly other" or as the "Wholly Other" can be helpful and accurate. But I do not agree with Karl Barth's view. While I can accept Barth's title for God, I do not accept his view that God's otherness makes him unknowable. Hopefully, I will make it clear that, while God is wholly other, he is fully capable of making himself truly known to us.

43. This, I would argue, is how the Babylonians conceived of Marduk, for example. The Babylonians did not understand Marduk to be transcendent as I am defining that. Marduk was just as much a part of reality as the Babylonians themselves were. But Marduk was the most powerful force within our reality. He was literally at the apex of the hierarchy of being. As such, he had to be heeded. See appendix J for a more extensive discussion of ancient polytheism and its concept of a god.

ty of God; rather, it is a defense of his absolute transcendence—of his being the ground of all that exists and occurs. It is an affirmation that God determines all that is and all that happens. This is my thesis: *to reject divine determinism is to deny the transcendence of God.* Or, at the very least, it is to conceive of his transcendence as only a transcendence of the material world, not of reality itself.

Common Sense

DEFINITIONS AND A CONVENTION

'Common sense' can be used to mean very different things. One popular notion of common sense could be defined:

> **COMMON SENSE** *is that set of beliefs widely (if not universally) embraced by mankind everywhere.*

This is not how I shall use the term. While my arguments presuppose the reliability of common sense, they are not based on the reliability of popularly-held belief. Therefore, I must distinguish common-sense-as-popularly-defined from common-sense-as-I-mean-it. Here is the convention I shall use: When I am referring to the popular notion of common sense defined just above, I refer to it as 'kommon sense'. I will reserve 'common sense'—which I define below—for the concept upon which the arguments of this book are based. My convention, therefore, is this:

> **KOMMON SENSE** *is that set of beliefs widely (if not universally) embraced by mankind everywhere.*

> **COMMON SENSE** *is that set of beliefs that any intelligent being could and should recognize as true, simply on the basis of his own personal mundane experience.*

A commonsensical belief will typically be a common belief. If one forms a belief through intelligent, intellectually honest, and responsible reasoning from the shared experience of all human beings, then he will, in all probability, hold that belief in common with every other intelligent, honest, responsible human being. But sometimes, beliefs that are eminently commonsensical are very unpopular in a particular culture. In theory, a commonsensical belief could be universally rejected by a culture. A commonsensical belief ought to have universal acceptance, but when it does not, it is nonetheless commonsensical. If a belief is commonsensical, it is so regardless of its popularity.

An appeal to common sense, therefore, is not an appeal to majority opinion. It is not based on the notion that the most popular idea is the truth, nor that the masses cannot be wrong. Rather, it assumes that vast areas of truth are accessible to every human being everywhere, and that— so long as other belief-shaping forces do not subvert the process—there will be wide agreement within such areas of truth. Some of these truths are readily accessible because they can be learned by induction from the everyday, mundane realities of universal experience. Others are readily accessible because they exist as intuitive assumptions foundational to the very existence of intelligence itself—commodities that no human being is without. But what characterizes every commonsensical belief is that no intellectually honest and responsible human being is without the requisite data from which he could know that it is true.

A commonsense belief, then, can be distinguished from a scientific belief, from a scholarly conclusion, and from a rigorously and systematically proven belief.

You do not need scientific research in a laboratory or space ship to establish the truth of a commonsense belief. It is drawn from man's universal experience of mundane existence. You do not need a microscope or telescope to check it out. The necessary observations come as a matter of course in everyday, ordinary experience. Neither do you need scholarship and research in libraries to substantiate a commonsense belief. Not scholarship, but ordinary, practical living is the genesis of commonsense beliefs. Furthermore, you do not need rigorous, systematic proofs using logic, mathematics, or philosophy to establish a commonsense belief. More typically, a commonsensical belief is the immediate, intuitive output of our reason, formed as a direct response to everyday experience.[44] Some intuitions are not derived from experience by induction so much as they are the built-in assumptions that constitute the foundation of human intelligence itself. These are so foundational that to deny them would be self-

---

44. I call your attention to our prior discussion of the intrinsic rationality and provability of correct intuitions in chapter 3. I am not saying here that commonsense beliefs *cannot* be rigorously proved. They are provable in principle, of course. Rather, I am only suggesting that we do not typically accept them on the basis that they have been rigorously proved. We accept them as direct and immediate outputs of our rationality, that is, as intuitive beliefs. Furthermore, the proofs for many such beliefs would be so involved and so complex that most ordinary mortals would, in practice, be incapable of constructing an adequate proof. But as we saw in chapter 3, that is not a mark against the rationality of such a belief.

defeating, and perhaps silly. To deny them would be to deny the validity of knowledge itself. Such intuitions are included in common sense.

THE SIGNIFICANCE OF MISTAKING KOMMONSENSICAL FOR COMMONSENSICAL

Whether we base an argument on common sense or kommon sense makes all the difference. An argument from kommon sense (universal acceptance) is totally fallacious; an argument from common sense (rational self-evidence) is valid. Since kommon sense is merely what is universally accepted, an argument from kommon sense is nothing more than a thinly veiled argument from unanimous opinion. But unanimous consent is not the arbiter of truth. Kommon sense proves nothing!

Arguments from common sense can be dangerous, therefore, since common sense is so easily confused with kommon sense. Popular acceptance of a belief is so easily mistaken for the rational soundness of that belief. We must not be misled by an argument that purports to appeal to common sense but that, in actuality, is appealing to popular opinion (kommon sense).

KOMMON SENSE, COMMON SENSE, AND SELF-EVIDENCE

Immersed in a particular culture as I am, two very different kinds of belief strike me as self-evident. Some beliefs strike me as self-evident precisely because they are *rationally* self-evident. Others strike me as self-evident because everyone around me takes their truth for granted; in other words, because they are cultural assumptions automatically accepted by everyone within my culture. Both kinds of belief qualify as kommonsensical. Regarding either sort, virtually everyone in my culture accepts them. But while both are kommonsensical, both are *not* commonsensical. Only beliefs that are rationally self-evident qualify as commonsensical, and not every widely-held belief is rationally self-evident. Some cultural assumptions, while widely-accepted, are not the least bit compelling to sound, unbiased reasoning. Some such beliefs are shaped by cultural prejudice, not sound reason.

There can be exceptions, but most commonsensical beliefs will enjoy near-universal acceptance. If a belief is commonsensical, it will typically be kommonsensical as well. But the opposite is not necessarily true. A popularly-accepted (kommonsensical) belief may very well not be rationally self-evident (commonsensical). A belief's having near-universal acceptance, therefore, does not necessarily mean that it is a valid rational belief. A belief that is contrary to common sense can readily gain widespread cultural acceptance.

The antebellum South's widespread acceptance of the black man's inherent inferiority provides an excellent example. While the inferiority of the black man seemed self-evident to a significant portion of Southern culture, there was nothing rationally self-evident about it. It was a cultural prejudice, uncritically accepted, *not* the sound conclusion of responsible reasoning from experience.

If I forget that something can be self-evident because it is kommonsensical without being commonsensical, I will mistakenly assume that 'commonsensical' means nothing more than 'self-evident'. This mistake, in turn, can easily lead me to mistake a merely kommonsensical belief (one that is self-evident due to its being a widely accepted cultural prejudice) for a commonsensical belief (one that is self-evident due to its being manifestly rational). And that mistake, in turn, can easily lead me to accept a fallacious argument from kommon sense as valid—as if it were an argument from common sense. This sort of confusion can lead to one's embracing any number of rationally unsound and manifestly false beliefs in the name of common sense.

There is yet another source of confusion. Commonsensical beliefs, contrary to our expectations, are not necessarily self-evident. A commonsensical belief that is also kommonsensical will, of course, be self-evident. But a commonsensical belief that is not also kommonsensical will typically not strike us as self-evident. Belief that there exists an ultimate objective truth is no longer kommonsensical within our culture. Hence, it is no longer self-evident. But such a belief is, I would argue, commonsensical. The immediate, non-critical acceptance of a belief is more often a function of its near-universal cultural acceptance than it is of its rational self-evidence. That is, *self-evidence is more directly the result of kommon sense than of common sense.* Hence—if we mistake being commonsensical with being self-evident—a commonsensical belief can appear not to be commonsensical. If our culture rejects some truly commonsensical belief (thereby rendering it not self-evident to us), it may not seem commonsensical to us (for it is not self-evident). Therefore, when I describe a belief as commonsensical in this book, I do not mean that it is immediately self-evident. It may not be. While in ordinary speech we often use 'commonsensical' and 'self-evident' synonymously, I do not employ them as synonyms in this book.

Free Will

When we speak of the human will, what do we mean? In popular the-ological discussion, one gets the distinct impression that the will of man is an actual organ of the body—not unlike the heart or liver. Not much sophistication is needed to realize that this cannot be right.

'Free will' is typically employed to describe a rather vague—but ulti-mately commonsensical—notion. Although vague, it is quite serviceable and should be adequate for the purposes of this book. The will of man can be described as follows:

> *An individual's will is that reality, whatever its form, that gives rise to his voluntary decisions and that explains why he voluntarily acts or thinks in one way rather than another. In other words, an individual's will is the reality that gives rise to his free choices.*

Our philosophical curiosity wants to know exactly what form of reali-ty the will has. Otherwise, we are not satisfied that we truly understand it. Is it a spiritual organ of some kind? A non-material counterpart to the heart or kidney?

I do not choose to satisfy our philosophical curiosity here. Such a level of understanding is not needed to make my arguments.[45] The vaguer con-cept of will typically employed in ordinary language should be adequate for my purposes. Therefore, I shall use 'will' as defined above.[46]

FREE TO CHOOSE

The definition of the will offered above is dependent upon another problematic concept—that of being "free to choose." We must be clear what we mean by that.

Some things we do are out of physical necessity. I don't choose to pump blood with my heart. It just happens. The laws of physics are in control. My body is so constructed that my heart beats automatically—a result of the autonomic nervous system.

---

45. I do not believe it is possible to reach that level of understanding of the human will that is wanted by our philosophical curiosity without first coming to terms with the arguments pre-sented in this book. Consequently, if I did intend to formulate a rigorous definition of the human will, it would have to come at the end of the book, not the beginning.

46. However, in chapter 9 I will analyze our commonsense notion of free will even further than is represented by this definition.

Can my decision to leave the house and go to the grocery store to buy a jar of pickles be explained in the same way? Is it—like the beating of my heart—the necessary outcome of physical laws? Common sense says "No!"[47] Some of my actions and some of my thoughts are not attributable to the inexorable outworking of the laws of nature. They cannot be explained in terms of biology or physics, for they are "free" from (independent of) physical causes that automatically lead to their results. When the physical cosmos does not dictate the choice I make, we say that I was "free to choose." A FREE CHOICE, then, is one that is not a function of the mechanical outworking of the laws of physics; and a VOLUNTARY action is one that is independent of the material universe.

Further, a freewill choice happens neither out of physical nor logical necessity. It is neither mechanically inevitable nor logically required. It is not the mechanical outworking of inexorable physical laws, and neither is it logically impossible that it not occur. "Freedom to choose," therefore, means that a person has before him more than one option that do not violate the laws of logic nor the physical universe. In the case of actions where an individual is not "free to choose," one and only one option exists. Under normal circumstances, a healthy heart does not have the option to stop beating. It beats out of physical necessity. Likewise, there is no other option but for me to be me rather than not-me. I am me and not not-me out of logical necessity. For me to be not-me is logically impossible. Therefore, being me (and not not-me) is not the result of "free choice."

A ROBOT AND TWO BOOKS

Suppose we have a room with two identical books lying on a table. A robot comes into the room and, in accordance with its programmed instructions, picks up the book on the left. Now you enter the room and pick up the book on the left. Is there any difference in these two events?

Absolutely! The robot is completely controlled by its engineering and programming—hence, by physical laws. The robot's physical environment and its programming ultimately determine the result. In picking up the

---

47. Some philosophers would answer "yes." For example, B.F. Skinner, in *Beyond Freedom and Dignity*, would answer "yes." But most of us reject such theories; and we do so precisely because they are contrary to common sense. We do not deem it possible, with logical consistency, to live, act, and think in accord with them. And I cannot bring myself to authentically believe, in practice, what the theory requires in principle. Most of us cannot take seriously the suggestion that my choice to go to the grocery store is no different, in principle, from the automatic beating of my heart.

book on the left, it does not make a "free" choice, for its action is the inevitable mechanical result of what it was made to be. Given the particular hardware and software that constitutes the robot, it was physically impossible for the robot to pick up the right-hand book instead.

When it comes to you, on the other hand, the situation is different. It is just as possible for you to pick up the right-hand book as the left-hand book. You do not act out of physical necessity; both options are open to you. To pick up the book on the right will no more violate the laws of physics than to pick up the one on the left. You are "free." Hence, you make what we typically label a "freewill choice."

THE POINT AT ISSUE—HOW FREE IS OUR WILL?

From a biblical perspective, there can be no question but that freewill choices do occur. The Bible rejects natural or physical determinism.[48] Some of our choices clearly cannot be the result of physical or logical necessity. Disagreement among Bible students arises with respect to this question: do choices exist that are *absolutely* undetermined? Granted, a freewill choice is not determined by the laws of physics. But could it be determined by something else? Could it be determined by God, for example? The divine determinist says "Yes, my freewill choices are determined by God." The limited determinist says, "No, God does not determine my freewill choices. If he did, they wouldn't be free."

Consider the book-choosing example above. The divine determinist views it like this: While you did not choose the left-hand book out of either physical or logical necessity, you did choose it out of *theological* necessity. The will of God—which controls everything—necessitated that you pick up the book on the left. Since that is what God willed, that is what you had to do. Freewill choices are free with respect to the physical cosmos, but they are not free with respect to the will and purpose of God.

The limited determinist, on the other hand, views it differently: You did not choose the left-hand book out of any sort of necessity of any kind—so neither did you choose it out of theological necessity. Your choice was "free," and no choice can be "free" unless it is totally and absolutely undetermined. If an action is free, then it must not be necessitated by anyone nor by anything outside your own will—including God. Freewill choices, therefore, are not free only with respect to the physical cosmos. They are free with respect to the will and purpose of God as well.

---

48. See chapter 1 for a definition of natural (or physical) determinism.

Herein lies an important ambiguity in the common phrase "free will." Everyone can agree on one aspect of its meaning: free will refers to the experience of making choices that are free from logical and physical necessity. But others insist that free will must describe something more far-reaching than that. For them, free will refers to the experience of making choices that are free from *any and every* sort of necessity—free from theological necessity just as surely as from logical and physical necessity.

If the latter is an accurate and meaningful definition of free will, then obviously divine determinism and free will are mutually exclusive concepts. Free will—so defined—is precluded if divine determinism is true. *But divine determinism does not preclude free will* if, by 'free will', we mean only a will that is free from logical and physical necessity.

The point at issue between divine determinism and limited determinism, therefore, will often come down to this: What exactly is the nature of our free will? Is it free only from the physical cosmos—remaining subject to the determinative control of God, or is it free from God as well?

I will argue for the former. Therefore, when I argue for the reality of free will in the pages to come, I do not support a human will that is free and independent of God's control. I mean, rather, a will that is free of the physical cosmos, a will whose choices are free of physical necessity.

I will analyze our commonsensical notion of free will further in chapter 9. Until then, the important thing to note is this: My notion of free will is different from the more typical notion of free will that exists among Christians today. Namely, modern Christians typically understand by "free will" a will that is autonomous from God. But my understanding of "free will" is a will that—while utterly dependent upon the will of God—is autonomous (FREE) from the physical cosmos.

PART TWO
THE BIBLICAL CASE FOR DIVINE DETERMINISM

CHAPTER FIVE

DOES THE BIBLE TEACH DIVINE DETERMINISM?

Why Ask the Question?

I do not begin this exploration of whether the Bible teaches divine determinism out of idle curiosity. Personally, I grant absolute authority to the Scriptures. I assume, beyond question, that what the Bible teaches is true. Accordingly, studying the Bible is a vital part of my philosophical method. As I see it, to learn what the Bible teaches on a given subject is to learn the truth on that subject. Accordingly, if the Bible teaches divine determinism, divine determinism is true.

This chapter, therefore, explores whether the Bible teaches divine determinism under the assumption that the Bible has absolute, infallible authority over us. To present an argument in defense of biblical infallibility is outside the scope of this work. Therefore, I must ask the reader who is not already convinced of it to temporarily grant me my assumption regarding biblical infallibility for the sake of the arguments that follow in this chapter.

Anyone who has tried to settle a doctrinal debate by quoting a verse of the Bible knows that a belief in biblical infallibility does not settle the question of truth. It merely shifts the debate to another front. What the Bible teaches is indeed true, but there remains the question of how we are to understand what it actually teaches. What it "teaches" one person is rejected as contrary to the Bible's teaching by another. To learn from the Bible requires that we interpret it, yet the Bible is prone to variant interpretations.

Orientation to This Chapter

Variant interpretations of the Bible present a problem. How can we employ the Bible to discover the truth when everyone interprets it differently? Whose interpretation captures the infallible revelation encoded in it? In this chapter I shall briefly explore this problem and its solution in relation to the doctrine of divine determinism.

The first section will take a cursory glance at certain aspects of my theory of biblical interpretation. I begin the first section by exploring the role our prior assumptions play in the formation of all further beliefs. How we understand an experience and what we learn from that experience is shaped decisively by the beliefs we already hold as we enter into the experience—that is, by our pre-understanding. Bible study is no exception. Pre-understanding, in large part, determines how we will interpret a biblical text. The typical procedure we call "proof-texting" fails precisely because it ignores the crucial role of pre-understanding. But the powerful influence of our pre-understanding can nonetheless be overcome. In other words, the Bible can actually teach us truth rather than merely reflect our prior convictions.

The second section of this chapter concerns itself with the relevance of these theoretical observations to the specific issue of divine determinism. I apply my interpretive theory to the question of whether the Bible teaches divine determinism and outline the line of the reasoning by which I conclude that it does.

How Do We Know What the Bible Teaches? *Theoretical Concerns*

THE PERSONAL FACTOR IN BIBLICAL INTERPRETATION: THE BIBLE AS A MIRROR OF OUR OWN BELIEFS

When we seek to understand the Bible's teaching, we must face squarely the personal factor in biblical interpretation. That the Bible "teaches" a person what he already believes is a very real phenomenon. More often than not, whatever beliefs I hold when I begin my study of a biblical text find "confirmation" in that text—whether they are actually upheld by that biblical text or not. In fact, due to the influence of previously held beliefs, the infallible Bible can "teach" me things that are not even true.

How can this be? Obviously, something is amiss. How are we to understand what happens in a situation where I understand the Bible to teach a particular doctrine and where that doctrine is false? It cannot be that the infallible Bible is actually teaching that doctrine. So how did I go so wrong?

It is not always and necessarily the case that my understanding of a biblical text reflects what its author actually intended. Its author did not put that meaning in the text—I did. By shaping (even distorting) the meaning of the text to make it conform to what I already believe, I turn the text into a mirror of my own understanding rather than allow it to stand in judgment over me as the objective revelation of truth. Accordingly, I can quite readily believe that the false doctrines I embrace are actually "taught" by the Bible.

This phenomenon is not confined to irresponsible interpreters who exhibit a careless disregard for truth or a stubborn pride that refuses to acknowledge error. It also affects responsible interpreters who are sincerely seeking truth with integrity. This is not a controversial claim. I am saying nothing more than that misinterpretation is both a theoretical possibility and a concrete reality.

THE WAY KNOWING WORKS

This should not surprise us. It is a straightforward result of the way God designed the learning process. We inevitably seek to make sense out of anything we encounter in terms of the way we already understand the world. Why not? I very reasonably assume that the way I currently understand the world is most likely the correct way to understand it. For, if it were not the correct way, why would I embrace it? It would be strange indeed to hold a view of reality that I am pretty confident is not the truth! Accordingly, by interpreting my experience in the light of my current view of reality, I assume that I am maximizing my chances for arriving at a correct understanding of current experience. To interpret my experience in the light of some other view of reality (one that I was less confident was true) would be absurd. Consequently, this is the process employed by every human being: experience-by-experience, we try to make sense out of the realities of life in terms of that view of reality we currently embrace as true.

The process of formulating our beliefs is conservative. That is, it tends to minimize the alterations that we make in our belief system. If at all possible, I understand my experience in such a way that my current view of reality is confirmed by my experience, not overturned. Experience will overturn my present worldview only if it confronts me with something that absolutely resists being explained in terms of my current worldview.

And so I proceed, indefinitely—until such time as my view of reality cannot make adequate sense of my latest experience. When that happens, I have a choice. I can exercise integrity, concluding that my worldview simply is not true, or I can be intellectually dishonest, stubbornly insisting on the adequacy of my worldview anyway. If I opt for integrity, then I must change my worldview—adjusting it as needed to make sense out of this new inexplicable experience. Or, if necessary, I will discard it and adopt an entirely new worldview. But if I opt for intellectual dishonesty, I must somehow insulate myself from the incriminating fact of this inexplicable reality. I may dogmatically and arbitrarily insist that, contrary to appearances, it is consistent with my worldview after all—accepting an unsound or inadequate explanation for how that can be so. Or, I may simply refuse to think about it. Growth toward true understanding occurs only when the realities of life and experience show up the inadequacies of my current understanding and thereby force me to alter it.

For our purposes, the main point is this: all of us have a current working understanding of truth by which we seek to make sense out of life and experience. We always seek to interpret our experience such that our interpretation is coherent with and upholds this understanding. This is as it should be. It is the way God designed human reason to operate. Reason always starts with certain assumptions about what is true and proceeds from there. Without assumptions, inefficiency would paralyze our reasoning. If every time we sought to understand something, we were required to justify our most basic, foundational assumptions, growth in knowledge would be brought to a halt. Deduction of the simplest and most rudimentary belief would require so much time and energy that there would be nothing left to proceed any further. Practicality, therefore, dictates that reason must establish some assumptions and proceed from there, using them as the base upon which to construct further understanding. This is how understanding operates in every area of life. Understanding the Bible is no exception.

PRE-UNDERSTANDING
IN BIBLICAL INTERPRETATION

When we come to the Bible, we have a set of assumptions that we "know" to be true. While there is much we do not know, these things we know. We take them for granted; accept them as given. This set of assumptions that we accept as given prior to our confrontation with the biblical text is what some philosophers and theologians call our PRE-UNDERSTANDING. My pre-understanding is that understanding of reality (including, but not limited to, my theological understanding) in the light of which I try to make sense out of what I am reading in the biblical text.

Pre-understanding plays a prominent role in directing and shaping my interpretation of a biblical text. So long as my pre-understanding seems to

work—that is, so long as I can continue to construct plausible interpretations of the biblical text that are coherent with my pre-understanding—I
will continue to allow it to guide my biblical interpretation. So long as my
pre-understanding appears to be a reliable guide to reading the biblical
text, I will continue to embrace the reading of the biblical text that it com-
mends. Consequently, my pre-understanding strongly influences—even
controls—the way I understand the Bible. The Bible, in turn, will always
seem to support and promote a worldview that is congruent with my own.
Since I interpret its text in the light of my pre-understanding, the Bible
will inevitably confirm my pre-understanding, for my understanding of
what the Bible is saying is deliberately constructed to be compatible with
my pre-understanding in the first place.

THE DIVINE DETERMINISM DEBATE AS AN EXAMPLE

Take divine determinism as an example. Suppose Dietrich Determinist
and Freddie Freewiller are debating whether God is the cause of absolutely everything that happens.

Before he ever owned a Bible, Dietrich Determinist was convinced that
God is the ultimate cause of everything that happens. Divine determinism
is a part of his pre-understanding. But then so is his belief in the free will
of man. He firmly believes in human freedom and moral accountability,
but he believes that human freedom and accountability do not exclude the
reality of divine control over human choice.

Freddie Freewiller, on the other hand, has three very different assumptions contained in his pre-understanding: (1) God is perfectly good and
could never cause evil, (2) God cannot cause the choices of free moral
agents if their choices are to be truly free, and (3) man has a free will.
Everything he reads in the Bible is filtered through the grid of these three
assumptions.

The debate begins with Dietrich focusing on Paul's description of God
in Ephesians 1:11 as the one "who works all things after the counsel of His
will." Dietrich understands this clause in the light of his determinist pre-
understanding. Obviously, since it is true that literally everything that happens is caused by God, Paul must simply be referring to that fact in
Ephesians 1:11. When Paul says all things, he means literally all things. All
things happen by the will of God. From where Dietrich sits, this verse
ought to end the debate.

Freddie, on the other hand, is looking at this clause in the light of a
very different set of assumptions. To him Paul obviously cannot be saying

that literally everything happens by the will of God—for that would not be true. He already knows that evil and the choices of free-will agents are outside the scope of divine control. If Paul were saying that these happen by the will of God, he would be wrong. Obviously he cannot be saying that. Paul must be speaking figuratively (hyperbolically) when he says that God works "all things" after the counsel of his will. By the "one who works all things according to his will," Paul is merely describing God as the one who, in his wisdom and might, is working to accomplish his overall goals in cosmic history. Paul surely does not mean that every particular of reality is subject to God's will. Accordingly, this verse has posed no real problem to Freddie's limited determinist perspective. It could only pose a problem if it were grossly misinterpreted along the lines of how Dietrich has interpreted it.

Now Freddie Freewiller tries to end the debate. He focuses on a constant thread throughout the Scriptures: God commanding man to live in accord with divine standards. "Love God." "Trust God." "Love your neighbor." "Submit to one another." "Do this." "Do that." Rightly so, Freddie looks at these commands in the light of his pre-understanding. Human choices are determined either by God (in which case man does not freely make them) or by man (in which case they are not subject to divine control). But this steady stream of commands obviously assumes that man determines the choices he makes. Otherwise, it would make no sense to appeal to him to be obedient. If he does not determine his own actions, why command him at all? So, Freddie reasons, if Scripture assumes that the individual man himself determines human choice, then it follows correspondingly that God does not. If anything can end the debate, this can. How can Dietrich ignore so prominent a feature of biblical revelation as the Bible's moral commandments?

Dietrich Determinist, however, sees the commandments of Scripture in an entirely different light. Unlike Freddie, he does not understand human freedom and divine control to be mutually exclusive. For Dietrich, no less than for Freddie, human choices are determined by man himself. Man chooses freely and is accountable for the choices he makes. But, at the same time, man's free choices are subject to divine control. Man will always freely choose in accordance with the divine will. What sounds like double-talk to Freddie makes perfectly good sense to Dietrich. It is a very vital part of his pre-understanding. Freddie's evidence against divine determinism, therefore, is utterly unconvincing to Dietrich. Freddie's evidence proves only that man makes freewill choices, a conclusion that Dietrich has never challenged. The point at issue is whether man's freedom to choose rules out God's sovereign control. Freddie's appeal to biblical commandments does not prove to Dietrich that it does. Only in the light of Freddie's prior assumption that human freedom and divine control are mutually exclusive can the commandments even appear to be evidence. But in the light of Dietrich's assumptions, the commandments prove nothing. The debate goes on.

The thing to note in all of this is the powerful influence on biblical interpretation that is exerted by the pre-understanding. Neither Freddie nor Dietrich were being unreasonable or illogical. Both of them, given their respective starting points, reached intelligent and responsible conclusions regarding the meaning and implications of the biblical text. They came to opposite conclusions because they started from opposite assumptions. Each ultimately saw in the text what they had brought to the text to begin with. It acted like a mirror, reflecting their respective assumptions. It is not so much the case that the Bible has taught Dietrich and Freddie what to believe as it is that they (that is, their pre-understandings) have taught the Bible what to say back to them.

WHY PROOF-TEXTING FAILS

The above example illustrates the futility of proof-texting. Typically, PROOF-TEXTING is the method used by Bible-believing Christians when they are trying to persuade another of their point of view. Proof-texting involves citing a particular verse or text that one is confident presents decisive evidence of the biblicality (and, hence, the truthfulness) of his point of view. This is the method Dietrich and Freddie were employing in the example above.

In their case, as in every similar case, proof-texting is virtually useless, for it has serious limitations. Namely, it proves a particular point of view only to those who already adhere to that view, only to those who already have that point of view as a part of their pre-understanding. To anyone who does not have that point of view as a part of their pre-understanding, the proof text will inevitably be unconvincing.

The interpretation one gives to any given proof text is so decisively shaped by his own pre-understanding that two people with significantly different pre-understandings must inevitably reach a different understanding of the meaning of the proof text. It would be virtually impossible for them to reach the same understanding of the proof text. Accordingly, what the proof text "proves" to the one who is using it as evidence it does not "prove" to his theological opponent, for his theological opponent gives it a radically different interpretation.

So, the divine determinist's proof texts are only convincing proofs to other divine determinists, and the limited determinist's proof texts only convince other limited determinists. The tongues-speaking charismatic's proof texts are valid only to other charismatics. The adherent of believers' baptism cites texts that convince fellow-adherents of believers' baptism, but they are not the least bit convincing to the adherent of infant baptism. This reality renders proof-texting of very limited value. It is virtually useless in a debate across differing pre-understandings.

THE VICIOUS CIRCLE

Does this important role played by our pre-understanding mean that we are prisoners of our current point of view? If the only way the Bible can teach us is through the mediation of our pre-understanding, then how could the Bible ever correct any false pre-understanding we might have? Biblical revelation cannot circumvent our pre-understanding and speak to us directly. So, it could appear that our original pre-understanding must be the permanent paradigm within which all our subsequent beliefs must fit.

Can we never escape imprisonment within our own pre-understanding? At first glance it would appear not. Biblical interpretation looks like one very vicious circle. My interpretation of the Bible is dictated by my pre-understanding. But I justify believing that pre-understanding on the grounds that it conforms to what the Bible teaches me. What the Bible has taught me, of course, was determined, in the first place, by the pre-understanding I had when I came to the Bible. That pre-understanding, of course, was justified by what the Bible taught me. What the Bible taught me, of course, was determined by my pre-understanding .... ad infinitum.

We have this vicious circle operating in the debate over divine determinism. On the one hand, the divine determinist will find texts that (seen in the light of his pre-understanding) clearly "teach" divine determinism. On the other hand, the limited determinist will find texts that (illuminated by his pre-understanding) "teach" limited determinism.

Philosophers label this circular interdependence between one's interpretation of the biblical text and one's pre-understanding the HERMENEUTICAL CIRCLE. As we saw earlier, the hermeneutical circle is alive and well in any debate over divine determinism. Each side of the doctrinal divide circumnavigates his own hermeneutical circle—justifying his doctrinal position by an appeal to what the Bible teaches while, at the same time, deliberately reading his Bible in a manner purposed to ensure support for his prior doctrinal position. This hermeneutical circle appears to be inescapable. But it is not. Due to the inherent tensions that will and must exist within a false pre-understanding, there is a way out.

ESCAPING THE HERMENEUTICAL CIRCLE

I accept as axiomatic that *a true understanding of reality will be perfectly coherent and self-consistent* and, even more importantly, that *a false understanding of reality will be at some point incoherent and self-contradictory.* This is a necessary implication of the biblical view of God as Logos and the cosmos as a rational creation.[49]

Now my pre-understanding—the set of prior assumptions I bring with me to the biblical text—includes every belief I have about anything. If my pre-understanding is true in every detail, then it will be perfectly coherent and self-consistent. In such an event, the hermeneutical circle would indeed be vicious, but in a benevolent sort of way. My perfectly true prior assumptions about reality will dictate my interpretation of the biblical text which will, in turn, confirm my perfectly true understanding of reality. But if—as we are assuming—my pre-understanding is unfailingly true to begin with, then neither it nor my interpretation of the Bible that has been shaped by it will ever come into conflict with sound reason nor with the objective meaning of the biblical text. That, of course, is not a problem.

But if my prior understanding of reality is false in any detail, then there must exist an inner tension, an internal incoherence, among some of the beliefs that make up my pre-understanding. This incoherence makes my pre-understanding vulnerable and ultimately implausible.[50]

How is a false pre-understanding vulnerable? Granted, a false pre-understanding will be incoherent and contradictory. That makes it vulnerable to sound logic. But, given the hermeneutical circle, how could it ever be vulnerable to biblical revelation? How could my reading of the bib-

---

49. See chapter 3.

50. Such rational incoherence is not immediately obvious to me. If it were, I would not allow it to remain. Assuming I am committed to intellectual integrity, I would modify my understanding to fix any incoherence that becomes apparent. But the fact is—even assuming intellectual integrity—I inevitably live with various internal contradictions in my view of reality. Why? Because my understanding of reality is not perfect. Some of my beliefs are false, and false beliefs inevitably create incoherence in one's worldview. But this incoherence is fundamentally invisible to me; I am not yet aware of it. (Or, incoherence in my worldview can exist for still another reason: lack of intellectual integrity. Lack of intellectual integrity leads to a high tolerance for internal incoherence; and that, in turn, leads to my allowing incoherence to continue to exist.)

lical text, controlled as it is by my pre-understanding, ever expose my pre-understanding as incoherent and false?

Very simply, the rational incoherence intrinsic to a false view of reality creates the potential for irreconcilable conflict within the pre-understanding itself. Such conflict is necessarily there in a false view of reality, though it may lie unnoticed for years. What is needed, if the hermeneutical circle is to be broken, is a catalyst to force the contradiction out into the open where it is visible. Any experience can be such a catalyst. It does not have to be the biblical text. But, for the believer, it often is. Such a catalyst text (if one exists) is a text that somehow forces me to make a choice between two conflicting beliefs that are causing rational disharmony in my pre-understanding. The catalyst text exposes the previously well-concealed contradiction and thereby forces a decision between the two conflicting assumptions.

Instinctively, I seek to interpret a text in such a way as to satisfy my pre-understanding. But a catalyst text (or, as I will call it from now on, a CONFUTER TEXT—that is, a text that confutes one's pre-understanding) has some feature that precludes this. It is a text where no possible interpretation can satisfy both (or all) aspects of my pre-understanding. Therefore, my inherent desire to interpret the text in the light of my pre-understanding is frustrated. I find myself confronted with a logical impossibility. I cannot accept two different interpretations, yet no single interpretation can satisfy every facet of my pre-understanding. (It is precisely because my prior beliefs are in irreconcilable conflict that I cannot satisfy all of those beliefs with one interpretation.) The only option open to me— if I maintain my intellectual integrity—is to modify my understanding of reality. One or more of my prior beliefs is false. I must decide which is false and must either reject it or modify it—adjusting my pre-understanding in whatever way is necessary in order to make a single interpretation of the confuter text possible. The net result: the text has changed the way I view the world. It has exposed the rational incoherence of my pre-understanding and forced me to fix it. If I fix it intelligently, it will lead me one step closer to an accurate understanding of reality—an understanding that conforms to biblical teaching.

THE GREAT ESCAPE: AN EXAMPLE

Consider a relatively straightforward example of the above:

Early in my theological experience, my understanding of apostolic authority looked roughly like this: *The apostles were infallible. Hence, any-*

PART 2 | CHAPTER 5: DOES THE BIBLE TEACH
DIVINE DETERMINISM?

87

*thing an apostle might claim about the gospel, the nature of the gospel, or any-
thing related to the gospel should be accepted as true by virtue of his authority.* As I understood it then, the nature of apostolic authority was such that
it was impossible, even in principle, for anything an apostle said about the
faith to be wrong. At the same time, I believed that the apostles were ordinary, fallible human beings.

As a matter of fact, my working understanding of apostolic authority
at that time was latently inconsistent and false. On the one hand, my view
of apostolic authority entailed the personal infallibility of the individual
apostles. On the other hand, it entailed that they were in every respect
ordinary, fallible human beings.

The tension between these two beliefs never surfaced. Not until one
day I gave due consideration to what proved to be a confuter text—
Galatians 1:8, "But even though we, or an angel from heaven, should
preach to you a gospel contrary to that which you received, let him be
accursed." Two things are quite clear from this statement by Paul, understood in its literary context: (1) Paul is making a statement that assumes
that it would be theoretically possible for him to teach some version of the
gospel that was damnably wrong, and (2) the touchstone of whether something he might say about the gospel is true is not whether it comes out of
his mouth, but rather, whether it conforms to what had in fact been
revealed to Paul by Jesus—a message and revelation that he, Paul, had
already conveyed to the Galatians. Putting these two observations together, Paul did not understand his authority as an apostle to lie in him personally. He understood it to lie in the authority of the revealed truth that
had been entrusted to him. He had been granted an infallible, authoritative understanding of God's purposes in human history. The authority of
Paul's teaching derived from the fact that he had been granted such an
understanding. To the extent that his teaching accurately and faithfully
conveyed the gospel message that had been revealed to him, it possessed
the authority of the infallible revelation itself. Theoretically, however, Paul
could teach something that did not conform to the infallible revelation he
had been granted. If that were to happen, Paul says, the Galatians should
no longer believe him.

Galatians 1:8 makes clear how Paul conceived of his own authority: the
locus of his apostolic authority lay in the infallible understanding of the
gospel revealed to him, not in the person of Paul himself. No plausible
interpretation of Galatians 1:8 would suggest the latter. For an apostle
whose authority lay in his very person—that is, whose authority extended
to every statement that passed his lips—how could he ever be disregarded?
Yet that is exactly what Paul recommends to the Galatians: disregard me if

I should ever depart from what I have already taught you. Paul allows for the theoretical possibility of an apostolic mistake with respect to the gospel.

How can that be? Only if I was willing to adjust my understanding of the nature of apostolic authority could I make sense of the notion of an apostolic mistake in the teaching of the gospel. By recognizing that the locus of apostolic authority lay in the authority of the message entrusted to them and not in them as individuals, it became clear how an infallible authority could inhabit ordinary, fallible human beings. Namely, since their minds had been illumined to understand clearly and flawlessly the gospel of Jesus Christ, to that extent they were infallible. For such an understanding came to them through an infallible revelation from God. At the same time, being fallible human beings, the theoretical possibility always existed that they could fail or falter in conveying that infallible, revealed truth to others.

My original, faulty pre-understanding of the nature of apostolic authority did not generate a hermeneutical circle from which I could not escape. I was not trapped in my ignorance. The biblical text eventually exposed the logical incoherence of my pre-understanding and forced me to modify my view of apostolic authority. The Bible taught me! And as is often the case, it was a confuter text that exposed and forced me to correct the false view of apostolic authority contained in my pre-understanding.

Applying the Theory—
Does the Bible Teach Divine Determinism?

I turn now to the primary questions with which this chapter is concerned. Does the Bible teach divine determinism? And how would we determine whether it does?

THE INADEQUACY OF PROOF-TEXTING TO PROVE DIVINE DETERMINISM

The popularly accepted method for answering such a question is proof-texting, a procedure we briefly discussed earlier. As I will immediately show, proof-texting cannot adequately establish divine determinism.

PART 2 | CHAPTER 5: DOES THE BIBLE TEACH
DIVINE DETERMINISM?

89

PROOF TEXTS FOR DIVINE DETERMINISM

There are numerous texts that provide compelling evidence for divine
determinism to anyone who already embraces it as true. If divine determinism is in fact true, it is most probable that these texts reflect the biblical authors' belief in it; in some cases by explicitly stating the doctrine, in
others by implicitly assuming it. We have already seen one such verse:

> ...having been predestined according to His purpose who works all
> things after the counsel of His will...
>
> Ephesians 1:11

If divine determinism is true, then this verse is most naturally interpreted as an explicit statement that literally everything that happens is the
"working" of God in accordance with "the counsel of His will."

Limited determinists are reluctant to interpret Ephesians 1:11 quite
this straightforwardly. Primarily, because such an interpretation has implications that are unacceptable to them—namely, (1) that God would be the
author of evil, and (2) that God would be the author of the freewill choices of human beings. But again, if divine determinism is in fact true,
numerous texts provide evidence that God is ultimately responsible for the
evil that occurs as well as the freewill choices of human beings. On the
assumption that divine determinism is true, these texts are best interpreted as charging God with ultimate responsibility for both.

Some explicitly proclaim, in general terms, God's responsibility for evil,
tragedy, and calamity:

> ...If a calamity [Hebrew = ra'ah = evil] occurs in a city has not the
> Lord done it?
>
> Amos 3: 6

> ...That men may know from the rising to the setting of the sun that
> there is no one besides Me. I am the Lord, and there is no other, the
> One forming light and creating darkness, causing well-being and
> creating calamity [Hebrew = ra'ah = evil]; I am the Lord who does
> all these.
>
> Isaiah 45:6–7

Others pinpoint some specific evils (and most notably, some specific,
evil freewill choices) for which God is explicitly claiming to be responsible.

For instance, the crucifixion of the innocent Jesus, the most spectacularly evil choice of all, is held to be God's responsibility.

> ...this Man, delivered up by the predetermined plan and fore-knowledge of God, you nailed to a cross by the hands of godless men and put to death.
>
> Acts 2:23

> For truly in this city there were gathered together against Thy holy Servant Jesus, whom Thou didst anoint, both Herod and Pontius Pilate, along with the Gentiles and the peoples of Israel, to do what-ever Thy hand and Thy purpose predestined to occur.
>
> Acts 4:27–28

Other evil acts are credited to God as well. For example, the invasion of Palestine by the Chaldeans.

> For behold, I am raising up the Chaldeans,...then they will sweep through like the wind and pass on. But they will be held guilty, they whose strength is their god.
>
> Habakkuk 1:6–11

and Pharaoh's decision to resist God and rebel against him

> Thus I will harden Pharaoh's heart, and he will chase after them ...
>
> Exodus 14:4

and Israel's stubborn rebellion against God

> Why, O Lord, dost Thou cause us to stray from Thy ways, And harden our heart from fearing Thee? Return for the sake of Thy servants, the tribes of Thy heritage.
>
> Isaiah 63:17

In fact, decisions by people in general are credited to God as being determined by him. The Scriptures mention several specific instances of it:

> The king's heart is like channels of water in the hand of the Lord; He turns it wherever He wishes.
>
> Proverbs 21:1

...for the Lord had caused them to rejoice, and had turned the heart
of the king of Assyria toward them to encourage them in the work
of the house of God, the God of Israel.

Ezra 6:22

...and the king granted him all he requested because the hand of the
Lord his God was upon him.

Ezra 7:6

And complex events of history are explicitly claimed to be his doing—

...For I am God, and there is no other; I am God, and there is no
one like Me, declaring the end from the beginning and from ancient
times things which have not been done, saying, 'My purpose will be
established, and I will accomplish all My good pleasure' ...Truly I
have spoken; truly I will bring it to pass. I have planned it, surely I
will do it.

Isaiah 46:9–11

There are others, but these represent a healthy sample of the kinds of
texts that divine determinism could offer as evidence, as proof texts, of the
truth of their position.

THE FAILURE OF THE DIVINE DETERMINIST PROOF TEXTS

But as we have already seen, such a procedure has serious limitations.
It only proves divine determinism to the divine determinist! What a verse
or passage means to any given individual will be shaped by his or her pre-
understanding. Therefore, though the divine determinist can easily find a
whole host of proof texts that are convincing to himself, none of them will
be persuasive to the person who is not ready to be persuaded. The unpersuaded, in the light of their own respective pre-understandings, will interpret each of these proof texts quite differently—so that, to them, the texts
prove nothing.

How exactly the limited determinist circumvents these proofs texts is
not important. There will be as many different interpretations of these different proof texts as there are different unpersuaded interpreters. The
important point is this: each limited determinist will indeed have an alternative, plausible interpretation of each and every one of these proof
texts—one that no longer entails divine determinism.

PROOF TEXTS FOR LIMITED DETERMINISM

The limited determinist can just as readily compile his own list of proof texts. As the divine determinist would grant, biblical evidence exists for the unadulterated goodness of God and for individual moral accountability for freewill choices. According to the limited determinist's pre-understanding, the implications of this are clear: if God is good, then he cannot cause evil; and if man is accountable for his choices, then they cannot be caused by God. So, from the limited determinist's perspective, a proof text that establishes the moral perfection of God is tantamount to a proof text that establishes that God does not cause evil. (For example, "…God is light and in him there is no darkness at all."—I John 1:5) Likewise, a proof text that establishes that man is responsible for his choices is tantamount to a proof text that God does not cause the choices of men. (For example,"…that whoever believes in him should not perish, but have eternal life"—John 3:16) In both cases, God's determinative control is proved to be limited.[51]

But once again, these limitations on God's control are proved only to the person already persuaded of limited determinism. These proof texts are unconvincing to the divine determinist, who is not already persuaded of limitations on divine control. He believes just as earnestly in the unadulterated goodness of God and in man's moral accountability. What is not proved to him is something else: that these two facts necessarily imply that God cannot cause evil and freewill choices. The limited determinist's proof texts do not satisfy him in this regard.

PROOF-TEXTING IS INCONCLUSIVE

The inescapable reality of the hermeneutical circle means that one cannot settle the debate about divine determinism through proof texts. It is virtually certain that one can find verses in the Bible "proving" his viewpoint, whether he is a divine determinist or a limited determinist. The verses are there, ready and waiting to be shaped by his pre-understanding

---

51. There is nothing wrong with this line of reasoning by the opponent of divine determinism—treating certain logical implications of the Bible's explicit teaching as facets of its authoritative teaching itself. This is a valid method. If the opponent of divine determinism is correct in his assertion that human moral accountability necessarily implies that God cannot be the cause of human choices, then he is correct in seeing biblical support for human accountability as decisive, authoritative proof against divine determinism. I will utilize this same line of reasoning at various points throughout this work.

into convincing evidence for his position. But as we have already seen, they are convincing only to the already persuaded. To the unpersuaded they offer no evidence at all. The divine determinist can find numerous biblical texts that show his position to be true. But so can the limited determinist.

Proof-texting, as popularly understood, brings us to an impasse. What the Bible actually teaches on the subject of God's sovereignty cannot be decided on this basis. It must be decided on a completely different basis.

THE WAY TO PROVE DIVINE DETERMINISM: CHOOSING THE RIGHT PRE-UNDERSTANDING

The divine determinist and the limited determinist interpret the Bible differently. Both approaches to the Bible are plausible, reasonable, intelligent, and logical, relative to their own respective sets of assumptions. But both are not valid, for both sets of assumptions are not valid. How am I to decide which is right?

The correct interpretation of a biblical text is the one that interprets it to mean what its author intended it to mean and to imply what its author intended it to imply. The correct interpretation will be an interpretation that is informed by the same set of assumptions that guided the biblical author as he wrote his text. To put it another way, the correct interpretation of a biblical text is one that is based on a correct pre-understanding— that is, on a pre-understanding that conforms substantially to the pre-understanding of the biblical author.[52]

To resolve the impasse in the proof-text battle over divine determinism, we must first establish which pre-understanding informed the biblical authors. Did the biblical authors write from a set of assumptions shared with divine determinists? Or from a set of assumptions shared with limited determinists? As they wrote, did the biblical authors begin with the assumption that divine determinism is a completely untenable position (as limited determinists assume)? Or did they begin with the assumption that divine determinism is true?

---

52. Some are skeptical of the possibility of knowing an author's intent and the pre-understanding which underlies his written text. This skepticism is not justified. Sound hermeneutical theory recognizes the fact that language works—and communication is possible—because an author's intent is objectified in his words. To defend this claim and to explore exactly how one does discern an author's intent from his words is beyond the scope of this work. For a discussion of this issue, I recommend *The Language of God* by Ron Julian, J.A. Crabtree, and David Crabtree.

Establishing which is the correct pre-understanding (the one that corresponds to that of the biblical authors) is the place where our discussion must begin. Before we can know how to understand the implications of the proof texts listed above, we somehow need to determine what are correct prior assumptions with respect to divine determinism. Settling that question will automatically answer whether the Bible teaches divine determinism, for then we will have a host of evidential texts along with a correct orientation with respect to how to interpret them.

But how can we discover which is the correct pre-understanding? We discussed earlier the dynamic by which the hermeneutical circle can be broken. If we are to find a way out of the impasse to which the proof-texting dual leads, we must discover a "confuter text" that will expose the particular pre-understanding that is false. We must find an aspect of the Bible's teaching that can bring to light the not-yet-visible inconsistencies in the incorrect pre-understanding. We need to locate some element of the Bible's teaching that forces an either/or choice between some inviolable element of biblical truth and the fallacious pre-understanding regarding divine determinism.

WHAT THE BIBLE TEACHES

I maintain that such "confuter texts" do exist—namely, those texts that teach divine creation *ex nihilo* and those texts that explain the fact and nature of divine foreknowledge. Creation *ex nihilo* is the doctrine that God created all of reality out of absolutely nothing.[53] Divine foreknowledge refers to God's ability to know and predict the future in advance.

One cannot maintain that God is the creator of everything out of nothing and at the same time, with rational consistency, deny divine determinism—unless one is willing to deny some other basic tenet of common sense. So, if we accept the biblical teaching about God's creatorship, we are forced, by logical necessity, to accept divine determinism. Similarly, if we

---

53. The Bible's teaching is that, starting from absolutely nothing (except himself), God created the entire created order and every particular in it. He created not only the stuff of reality, but the structure of reality. The doctrine of creation from out of nothing denies that there was any pre-existent stuff, structure, or reality of any kind from which God fashioned the cosmos. Before the creation, literally nothing existed other than God himself. There is a Latin phrase that is often used to refer to this biblical doctrine of creation—*creatio ex nihilo* (meaning, creation out of nothing). Throughout the book, I may occasionally use this Latin phrase or a Latin-English hybrid, CREATION *EX NIHILO*, to refer to this biblical doctrine of creation out of absolutely nothing.

accept the biblical teaching about God's foreknowledge, we are forced to embrace divine determinism.

Those who accept the biblical view of God's creatorship and fore-knowledge and yet insist that divine determinism cannot be true are embracing a rationally inconsistent worldview. Their pre-understanding is fraught with logical tension. Ultimately, the inconsistency of their world-view must be resolved. Apart from the possibility of denying basic, indis-putable assumptions about language, reason, and truth, one has only two possible options for resolving the inevitable conflict: (1) he can reverse his prior denial of divine determinism, or (2) he can reject the doctrines of creation *ex nihilo* and divine foreknowledge. Any Christian who is anxious to submit to the authority of Scripture and to uphold the objectivity of verbal communication cannot possibly reject these latter two doctrines. They are too clearly taught by Scripture and (in the case of divine creation) too philosophically essential to be denied.[54] The only reasonable response is to acknowledge the truth of divine determinism.

In this sense, then, the Bible teaches us that a pre-understanding that accepts divine determinism is the one that coheres with the biblical world-view. Hence, divine determinism is the pre-understanding that will lead to a true and accurate understanding of biblical revelation as a whole. Conversely, a pre-understanding that denies divine determinism is ration-ally incompatible with the biblical worldview and, hence, can only lead to false and distorted interpretations of the biblical text.

In saying this, of course, I am presuming to be right in my insistence that divine determinism is logically required by God's creatorship and foreknowledge. But I have not made any case for such a claim. That task still remains. The next two chapters are devoted to demonstrating what I have simply presumed above—namely, that divine determinism is a logi-cally necessary ramification of God's creatorship and foreknowledge. If my presumption that these two doctrines logically require divine determinism is correct, then we cannot escape the conclusion that the Bible teaches divine determinism. It clearly teaches creation *ex nihilo* and divine fore-knowledge. If divine determinism is the only way one can, with rational

---

54. By 'philosophically essential' here I am suggesting that a philosophical proof of God's exis-tence, and more specifically, of God's role as creator of the cosmos is possible. In general, I believe some of the classical proofs of God's existence are on the right track and are based on rationally sound intuitions. Most of them are attempts at formulating formal proofs that reflect deep rational intuitions. Unfortunately, they are probably unsuccessful at capturing completely the rational intuitions and sound reasoning that underlie them. Nevertheless, the sub-conscious intuitive reasoning that these formal proofs are attempting to capture has persuaded millions of people over the centuries.

consistency, account for these two truths, then it must be the view of reality that underlies all that the Bible says. To think otherwise would be to charge biblical revelation with being logically incoherent, and for someone like me, who accepts the traditional view of biblical authority, that would be untenable. Divine determinism, therefore, is appropriately the pre-understanding through which we interpret every biblical text. As a result, the correct interpretation of the Bible turns out to be the one that yields a long list of proof texts supporting divine determinism.

Summary

Does the Bible teach divine determinism? Yes, I think it does. But one will never be convinced through a series of proof texts. Proof-texting is compelling only to one who is already persuaded. To one who needs to be persuaded, it is a futile exercise. Ultimately, one will become convinced only when he grasps the necessary logical implications of God's being (i) the creator, and (ii) the one who knows the future. Only then can he see the rational necessity of divine determinism and the inconsistency of any other view of God's nature and power.

CHAPTER SIX

DOES GOD'S CREATORSHIP IMPLY DIVINE DETERMINISM?

In this chapter I shall attempt to defend the following thesis: if God has created the cosmos through an act of absolute creation *ex nihilo*, as traditionally accepted, then it necessarily follows that everything that is and everything that occurs has been determined by God. It is outside the scope of my purpose to offer a thorough defense of the traditional doctrine of creation. So the result of my arguments will be hypothetical: if the traditional view of divine creation is true, then divine determinism necessarily follows from the fact that God is the creator. But it will remain logically open to the reader to reject the traditional view of divine creation and thereby reject divine determinism. What the arguments of this chapter seek to demonstrate is that one cannot embrace the traditional doctrine of absolute creation *ex nihilo* and at the same time reject the doctrine of divine determinism. To do so would be rationally inconsistent.

Understanding the Biblical Doctrine of Creation

CREATION AS AN EXPLANATION OF THE ORIGIN OF THE UNIVERSE

Various answers are given to the question of cosmic origins. Theism offers a distinctive answer—namely, creation by a divine creator.[55] The universe as we know it resulted from a creative act by a powerful, transcendent, pre-existent God.

The universe is not itself eternal—as theories of cosmic evolution typically assert—with the intrinsic potential to transform and organize itself. Neither is it the subjective creation of the individual or collective human

---

55. The fact that divine creation is the Bible's teaching with regard to cosmic origins is virtually indisputable. Genesis 1:1–2:25 is the primary biblical text teaching divine creation. But there are a dozen or more explicit references to God's creation of the cosmos. See, for example, John 1:1–5, Colossians 1:15–17, Acts 14:15, Acts 17:22–31, Hebrews 11:3, and Revelation 4:11.

mind—as some strains of New Age thought might assert. Rather, it is the objective handiwork of the powerful, transcendent God.

So, as philosophies go, the bare claim that "God created the heavens and the earth" is a distinctive answer to the question of origins. But it is not, in and of itself, a very specific answer. It is altogether too imprecise to answer a number of vexing questions.

To advance my argument for divine determinism, I need to explore two such important questions: (1) the scope of God's creative activity, and (2) the nature of the consequent, ongoing relation between God and his creation.

THE SCOPE OF DIVINE CREATION

Most biblical theists agree that God created everything that exists. He created the rocks, the trees, the animals, the elements, the stars, and so on. But how far should this list extend? Granted, God created every THING, but what constitutes a "thing"? God created the earth, that giant mass of matter we all call home. But did he also create its gravity? Is gravity a created "thing"? God made the sub-atomic particle; it is arguably a "thing." But what about the physical laws that rule its existence? Are they created "things" as well?

When all is said and done, there are various sorts of realities that, in one way or another, impinge upon our existence. Of all these different sorts of realities, which of them are the product of divine creation, and which of them have their origin somewhere else? Until we have answered this, we have not thoroughly understood the scope of divine creation.

THE CATEGORIES OF REALITY

One way or another, we confront very different kinds of realities in human experience. All of them could plausibly be construed as having real existence. I propose five such realities that I believe exhaust the field of all possibly real existents:

1. *Mechanically-determined entities*—that is, impersonal entities, composed of matter and energy, that operate out of physical or mechanical necessity in accordance with the laws of physics. This category, in my judgment, would include all animals and all material objects.

2. *Free moral agents*—that is, entities (persons) who do not operate exclusively out of physical or mechanical necessity. These are creatures who are capable of operating out of what is commonly called free will. Apart from God himself, human beings and angelic beings are very possibly the only free moral agents in all of reality.

3. *Abstract, ideal realities*—that is, concepts or ideas that either describe or constitute the rational structure of the cosmos. This category would include the laws of physics, the laws of human ethics, the principles of aesthetics in art, etc. These realities dictate the very real, objective relationships that exist between the concrete, tangible creatures[56] in the cosmos, but they are not themselves tangible or concrete things.

4. *Events*—that is, occurrences within the real cosmos.

5. *Eternal, necessary realities*—that is, God and the various eternal aspects of the divine nature. The eternal, self-existent God himself would be included in this category. But so too would various aspects of his nature that are co-eternal with Him—for example, the principles of holiness, rationality, and personhood that make up the divine being of God.

DIFFERENT VIEWS WITH RESPECT TO THE SCOPE OF DIVINE CREATION [57]

We can immediately eliminate *eternal, necessary realities* (category #5) from the list of created things. Clearly God is not created. He did not create himself. Neither did God create any aspect of his own intrinsically nec-

---

56. By "concrete" and "tangible" here I mean to indicate creations that are not abstract. I do not necessarily mean material as opposed to immaterial or spiritual. Hence, these abstract ideas could form the objectively real relationships between angels or between an angel and the physical cosmos just as surely as they do form the objectively real relationships between material beings.

57. My purpose here is to present important logically-possible alternatives, not to survey actual, known positions. As a matter of fact, I am not aware of any serious theoretical discussion of the scope of divine creation. To my knowledge, therefore, there are no well-articulated theoretical viewpoints on the subject. The actual viewpoints that people hold on this subject tend to be revealed in their tacit, not-articulated, intuitive mental picture of creation and the inferences they make from it. At this level, it is possible that all of these alternatives are embraced somewhere by someone.

essary and eternal nature. By definition, if it is necessary and eternal, then it has not been created. So whatever the scope of divine creation, it clearly cannot include this fifth category of realities. This category of existent being should be viewed as incontrovertibly outside the scope of divine creation in the discussion that follows.

Given this disclaimer, there are two different logical possibilities with regard to the scope of divine creation: either divine creation is absolute in scope, or it is not absolute in scope. Hence, one believes either in ABSOLUTE DIVINE CREATION or in NON-ABSOLUTE DIVINE CREATION.

The former—ABSOLUTE DIVINE CREATION—is the view that God has created absolutely everything that exists (except Himself and other eternal, necessary realities). That is, God has created absolutely everything that exists in each of the first four categories of reality listed above. God has created or creates every physical, material entity, every free moral agent, every abstract, ideal reality, and every event that occurs throughout time. Nothing that exists is outside the scope of his creative activity.

The latter view—NON-ABSOLUTE DIVINE CREATION—may be non-absolute for a number of different reasons: (1) one might believe that certain categories of reality are outside the scope of divine creation, (2) one might believe that certain species of existents are outside the scope of divine creation, or (3) one might believe that certain particular, individual existents are outside the scope of divine creation.

Let us consider each of these three forms of NON-ABSOLUTE DIVINE CREATION respectively:

1. The first form of NON-ABSOLUTE DIVINE CREATION believes that certain categories of reality (the ones listed in the previous section) are outside the scope of divine creation.[58] So, for example, someone may be hesitant to acknowledge abstract, ideal realities (category #3) as products of God's creative activity. God created only the concrete, tangible realities; not the abstract ones. Or, more likely, one might be hesitant to acknowledge events (category #4) as products of God's creative activity. There are two primary reasons why one might prefer to see events as outside the scope of divine creation:

---

58. We have already conceded that ABSOLUTE CREATION makes exception for category #5 being necessarily outside the scope of divine creation. To espouse NON-ABSOLUTE CREATION, therefore, one must place one or more of the *first four* categories of reality outside the scope of divine creation.

a) One may understandably prefer to view the actors or participants in cosmic events as the true creators of those events. God does not directly cause or determine what occurs in reality. Rather, the behavior and actions of the participants directly determine the course of events. Events are created by the created participants themselves. God does not create them.

b) Events do not, properly speaking, have existence in the same sense that things do. Let me illustrate. Did the Battle of Gettysburg "exist" in the same sense that Abraham Lincoln "existed"? Did the occurrence of the battle have the same ontological status as the men who fought in the battle? Perhaps events do not "exist," but rather, "occur." Perhaps to speak of an event's existing is simply a sloppy way of speaking of an event's occurring. If so, then events may not have existence in the same way that people, things, and even abstract realities do. And if not, then it makes no sense to speak of their being created by God, for they do not even have existence.

2. The second form of NON-ABSOLUTE DIVINE CREATION believes that certain species of existents are outside the scope of divine creation. Within each and every category of reality are various species of realities that are subsumed under the category. The first category includes the species micro-organisms as well as the species comets, for example. It includes the species rivers as well as the species trees. Category #2 (free moral agents) includes the species of human beings as well as the species of angels. While a person may not believe a whole category of reality is outside the scope of divine creation, he may believe that whole species of beings in that category lie outside the scope of divine creation. Some people may hesitate to believe that God created disease-causing organisms. While God created biological organisms like dogs, cats, and monkeys, he did not create germs and viruses. In the category of free moral agents (category #2), a person may believe that God created human beings, but deny that God created angels. In the category of ideal abstractions, a person may be more than willing to believe that God is the creator of goodness, but he may refuse to believe that God created evil. Some people are very reluctant to believe that God created abstract realities like pain and suffering and poverty. With respect to category #4 (events), a person may believe, generally, that God creates the events of our lives. But yet he may deny that God is the creator of any event insofar as it is the result of freewill choices. Or, he may deny that God is the creator of any event insofar as it results in evil.

3. The third form of NON-ABSOLUTE DIVINE CREATION believes that certain particular beings or existents are outside the scope of divine creation. Even though, in general terms, it can be said that every category of being and every species within each category is created by God, this view wants to allow for individual exceptions in the case of individual, particular existents. These are examples of what a person might believe:

a) While germs and viruses, generally, are created by God, the ebola virus is not his creation. It is so devastatingly evil that God could not have created it.

b) While free moral agents generally—both human and angelic—are created by God, the particular individual Satan is not created by God.

c) While hurricanes in general are created by God, the particular hurricane that destroyed my city was not created by God.

THE BIBLE'S TEACHING WITH RESPECT TO THE SCOPE OF DIVINE CREATION

The Traditional Understanding of Divine Creation

The traditional interpretation of the Bible is that God created everything that exists from nothing. Starting with absolutely nothing, God, by his creative power, brought into existence all that exists. This doctrine has come to be called creation *ex nihilo* (*ex nihilo* being Latin for "out of nothing").

Emphasis can be placed on any of several important possible ramifications of this traditional doctrine. All of the following are important ramifications of the doctrine of creation *ex nihilo*:

1. Nothing (other than God himself) existed before the original creation. *Everything that exists was created by God.* [This highlights the all-inclusiveness and absoluteness in the scope of God's creatorship.]

2. God, and God alone, existed before creation. He is the one and only being worthy of the designation "God." *He and he alone is an eternal, necessary, self-existent being* (that is, one who has always existed and who needs no further explanation for why he exists other than the fact that he necessarily must exist). He and he alone transcends the created order. [This highlights the uniqueness of God with respect to self-existence. And, on the other hand, it emphasizes the utter contingency of everything else but God. Nothing in the cosmos had to be what it is. Nothing in the cosmos had to *be* at all.]

3. Everything that has been created *has been created out of nothing.* The creation of the world was not merely the restructuring and reorganizing of some pre-existent stuff. Rather, it was the creation of that which did not previously exist in any sense or in any form. [This highlights the nothingness before creation.]

If we could know that the traditional doctrine of creation *ex nihilo* did, indeed, synthesize the biblical teaching with regard to creation, then there could be no question with regard to the scope of divine creation. The view we have called ABSOLUTE DIVINE CREATION would reflect the biblical view, for such a view is necessarily entailed by each of the three formulations of creation *ex nihilo* above.[59] If, before the beginning, there was absolutely nothing (but God), then nothing that exists now is uncreated. God's creative act was an act of ABSOLUTE DIVINE CREATION.

To be perfectly precise about the traditional view, therefore, I shall call it ABSOLUTE DIVINE CREATION *EX NIHILO*. Someone may be willing to grant that whatever God created he created from nothing (*ex nihilo*), but they may want to exempt certain aspects of the created order from the scope of God's creative activity. In other words, they may prefer one of the forms of NON-ABSOLUTE DIVINE CREATION discussed above. So to be perfectly clear, the traditional interpretation of the Bible is that the Bible teaches ABSOLUTE DIVINE CREATION *EX NIHILO*.

---

59. The suggestion here is that if creation *ex nihilo* is true, then it follows that absolute creation is true. The converse is not true, however. If absolute creation is true, it does not follow that absolute creation *ex nihilo* is true. In the Babylonian creation myth, the almighty Marduk may very well have fashioned absolutely everything that exists in the created cosmos out of the carcass of a slain sea-monster-god, but he was not creating the cosmos out of nothing. He was starting from the stuff present in the carcass of the sea-monster-god. Hence, Marduk— arguably— engaged in an act of Absolute Creation; but it was not an act of creation *ex nihilo*. Accordingly, from the fact of absolute creation it does not necessarily follow that creation has been *ex nihilo*.

What Does the Bible Actually Teach with Regard to Divine Creation?

Does absolute divine creation *ex nihilo* accurately reflect the teaching of the Bible? It is the traditional interpretation of the Bible's teaching, but is that traditional interpretation accurate? Or, is the traditional doctrine of absolute divine creation *ex nihilo* a theological or philosophical view that has been imposed on the text of the Bible?

It is troubling to some that the Bible never explicitly asserts absolute divine creation *ex nihilo* in just those terms. That is, the Bible never explicitly asserts that God created *out of nothing* everything that exists. It frequently asserts that God created everything that is. But it never explicitly asserts that he created it from *nothing*. Does that mean that this doctrine has been imposed on the Bible, that the Bible does not really teach it? That is the question we must address now. To do so, I will address the two parts of the doctrine respectively: (1) Does the Bible actually teach absolute divine creation? And (2) Does the Bible actually teach divine creation *ex nihilo*?

Does The Bible Actually Teach Absolute Divine Creation?

It is clear, I think, that absolute divine creation is the *prima facie* teaching[60] of the Bible—that is to say, on the face of it, it would certainly seem that the Bible espouses absolute divine creation. A number of passages are intended to stress and highlight the all-inclusive scope of God's creative act:

Paul, speaking to the residents of Lystra, says,

…and we bring you good news, that you should turn from these vain things to a living God, who made the heaven and the earth and the sea and *all that is in them.*

Acts 14:15 (ESV, emphasis mine)

Speaking to the Athenians at Mars Hill, he says,

…What therefore you worship as unknown this I proclaim to you. The God who made the world and *everything* in it, being Lord of heaven and earth, does not live in temples made by man, nor is he

---

60. By *prima facie* teaching of the Bible I mean the teaching of the Bible on the face of it, at first view, as it would initially appear, before further, deeper investigation.

served by human hands, as though he needed anything, since he himself gives to *all mankind* life and breath and *everything.* And he made
from one man *every* nation of mankind to live on all the face of the
earth, having determined allotted periods and the boundaries of their
dwelling place.

> Acts 17: 23–26 (ESV, emphasis mine)

In Revelation, the elders praise God saying,

Worthy are you, our Lord and God, to receive glory and honor
and power, for you created *all things,* and *by your will they existed and
were created.*

> Rev 4:11 (ESV, emphasis mine)

Ecclesiastes reads,

As you do not know the way the spirit comes to the bones in the
womb of a woman with child, so you do not know the work of God
who makes everything.

> Ecc 11:5 (ESV, emphasis mine)

John begins his gospel,

In the beginning was the logos. Now the logos was with God—
indeed God was the Logos. The logos was in the beginning with God.
*All things came into existence in conformity with it; indeed not one thing
that has come into being came to be apart from it.* Among these things
was life, and life was the light of men.

> John 1: 1-4 (my translation and emphasis)

Paul writes to the Colossians,

He (Jesus) is the image of the invisible God, the firstborn over all
creation. *For with a view to him all things were created:* things in
heaven and on earth, visible and invisible, whether thrones or powers
or rulers or authorities; *all things were created with a view to him and
for him.* He is before all things, and in him all things have been
constituted.

> Colossians 1:15–17 (my translation and emphasis)

Paul and John are suggesting as strongly as they can that absolutely nothing exists that God did not create. Everything has been brought into existence in conformity to God's pre-existent *logos*, says John. Everything has been created to serve God's purposes for Jesus, Paul insists in Colossians.

These are not isolated, marginal comments within the biblical text. These are explicit assertions of what clearly appears to be a background assumption that underlies every assertion the Bible makes. On the surface, there can be little question: the Bible teaches that God is the creator of absolutely everything that is.

But a conclusion that we reach from a *prima facie* reading of the Bible is not sufficient for our purposes. One who is inclined to reject the doctrine of absolute divine creation can legitimately argue that the above passages are merely generalizing. When the biblical authors say that God created all things, they don't mean absolutely and literally all. They mean "all" as a generalization.

If I tell someone that they are late *all the time*, I do not mean that literally. I mean that they are, generally speaking, late. There are exceptions. But the rule is, they are late. The biblical authors could be speaking in the same sort of way. God created all things in heaven and on earth. But that does not mean that there are no exceptions. It means that, generally speaking, there is nothing that exists that God did not create. But there may be individual, isolated exceptions to the general rule of divine creation.

Clearly this has to be allowed as a viable interpretation, for we all tacitly understand the biblical authors to be making at least one exception. We don't for a moment think that they mean God created himself. Nor do we think for one moment that God created his own nature and attributes. There are certain eternal realities that are obviously intended to be exceptions to the all-inclusive claims of the biblical authors with respect to divine creation. But if we will readily grant that these eternal realities were intended to be exceptions to the general statement, why can't there be other obvious exceptions?

My theological or philosophical assumptions will dictate what I believe must certainly be excepted from the scope of divine creation. Some will want to exempt all evil. When it says God created all things, it certainly does not mean to say that God created evil. Others will want to exempt the freewill choices of human beings. When it says God created all things, it certainly does not mean to say that God created the freewill choices of human beings. Others may want to exempt still other realities: pain, suffering, disease, or whatever else one's philosophical assumptions dictate.

Clearly, then, if I have philosophical reasons for wanting certain things to fall outside the scope of divine creation, then it is logically available to me to insist that "all things"—in the biblical assertions of creation—does not mean literally and absolutely all things. To say that God created all things is merely a generalization. The biblical writers fully expected their readers to understand that there are certain obvious exceptions. Accordingly, in spite of the *prima facie* evidence in support of it, the biblical data does not clearly and incontrovertibly support absolute divine creation.

One could, at this point, collect more biblical assertions as evidential support for the doctrine of absolute divine creation. One could, for example, find biblical assertions that claim divine creation for every category of reality outlined above.[61] But, in the end, this would not be sufficient to prove the traditional doctrine. There could always be one or more species of existents within any given category of reality that the biblical authors knew to be an exception. Or, if not species of existents, there could always be particular, individual existents that were an exception.[62] One would always face the possibility that the all-inclusive language of biblical assertions is only a generalization and not an absolute statement. In the end, therefore, it would be impossible to find a set of biblical assertions that is sufficiently exhaustive to prove decisively and incontrovertibly—from those assertions alone—that there are absolutely no exceptions to the scope of divine creation.

Does The Bible Actually Teach Divine Creation *Ex Nihilo*?

It is clear, I think, that divine creation *ex nihilo* is the *prima facie* teaching of the Bible—that is to say, on the face of it, it would certainly seem that the Bible espouses creation *ex nihilo*.

The primary biblical account of creation is found in Genesis 1–2. The account of creation recounted there describes God as commanding reality to come to be in a particular way and its coming to be as he commanded. God does not take some pre-existent substance and fashion it into the heavens and the earth and all that is in them. He just says "Let it be," and

---

61. See section above titled "The Categories of Reality." So, for example, Gen. 1–2, Jonah 1:9, and Isa. 42:5 assert the divine creation of existents belonging to category #1; Acts 17:22–31, Gen. 1–2 assert the creation of human beings (which belong to category #2); Psalm 33:6, Psalm 148:1–6, and (arguably) Col. 1:15–17 assert the creation of angels (which also belong to category #2); Isa. 45:7, John 1:1–5, and Genesis 1–2 (arguably) assert the creation of abstract realities (category #3); and Hebrews 1:2 and 11:3, arguably, and possibly Isa. 45:7 assert the creation of events (category #4).

62. See the section above titled "Different Views with Respect to the Scope of Divine Creation." I discuss there the sorts of exceptions to absolute creation that one could propose.

it is so. It seems clear, on the face of it, that the Genesis narrative is a poetic way of describing creation *out of nothing*. The Genesis account is striking and distinctive in this regard in the context of the other ancient Near-Eastern "creation" accounts. Only in Genesis is God described as having the ability to simply will creation to be, and it is. Only the God of Genesis speaks, and it is. The other creation accounts describe a god or gods fashioning the world out of some pre-existing materials. On the surface, at least, it would seem quite apparent that part of the meaning of the Genesis creation account is that God is a being who is capable of creating all that is, starting with absolutely nothing.

But, once again, the conclusion that we reach from a *prima facie* reading of the Bible is not sufficient for our purposes. One who is inclined to reject the doctrine of divine creation *ex nihilo* can legitimately appeal to the vagueness of Genesis 1–2 and any other relevant texts. When biblical assertions are made to the effect that God created the cosmos, they were not constructed to address the issue of the exact nature of divine creation. They were constructed with entirely different issues in mind. Accordingly, they were not constructed with the sort of precision needed to answer our question. Certainly, they assume a particular view of divine creation in the background. But they are not devised in order to highlight and bring into the foreground the exact theory of divine creation that the biblical authors embrace.

Prima facie, it seems likely that in the background of the biblical authors' assertions is the doctrine of creation *ex nihilo*. The creation account in Genesis—an account with which they were familiar and a teaching about creation to which their understanding presumably conforms—is, in my judgment, pretty compelling as a statement of creation *ex nihilo*. The burden of proof is on the reader who would deny that it is an expression of creation *ex nihilo*. It may be, therefore, that the biblical assertions, in this regard, ought to pretty much settle the question. But, be that as it may, if one is inclined to be skeptical, the biblical assertions are not sufficiently precise to offer clear, incontrovertible proof that the Bible teaches divine creation *ex nihilo*.

Given the nature of those assertions, no set of biblical assertions with regard to divine creation of the world will suffice to prove the traditional doctrine of creation *ex nihilo* to one who is inclined to reject it. In the end, therefore, it would be impossible to find a set of biblical assertions that would prove decisively and incontrovertibly—from those assertions alone—that the divine creation of the world was absolutely and unexceptionally *ex nihilo*.

Summary: Does The Bible Actually Teach Absolute Divine Creation *Ex Nihilo*?

We have seen that, while the *prima facie* evidence of the Bible certainly supports the traditional doctrine of absolute divine creation *ex nihilo*, the doctrine cannot be finally and incontrovertibly established on the basis of explicit biblical assertions alone.

Does this mean that we can never know with certainty what the Bible teaches with respect to the scope of divine creation? No, it does not mean that. Ultimately, I should be able to resolve the question of what the Bible teaches with respect to the scope of divine creation when I resolve the issue of divine determinism itself. The two questions are inextricably bound together. I cannot answer one without answering the other. But if I am ultimately able to answer the one, I will therein be able to answer the other.

That means, however, that I cannot produce a straightforward argument for divine determinism from divine creation. I will argue in the remainder of this chapter that the traditional view of divine creation (absolute divine creation *ex nihilo*) necessarily entails divine determinism. If we could establish the truth of absolute divine creation *ex nihilo* without first establishing divine determinism, then we could conclude that divine determinism must be true because absolute divine creation *ex nihilo* is true. But that will not be the conclusion of this chapter, for, as I suggested, we could never discover the right sort of evidence to establish that absolute divine creation *ex nihilo* is the incontrovertible teaching of the Bible independently of addressing the truth and biblicality of divine determinism. So the conclusion of this chapter will be hypothetical in nature: *if it is true that the Bible teaches absolute divine creation* ex nihilo, *then the Bible necessarily teaches divine determinism*. It must leave open to the reader the possibility of rejecting the doctrine of absolute creation *ex nihilo*. Having said that, it is no light and trivial matter to reject the doctrine of absolute creation *ex nihilo*, for to do so without a good basis founded on an intellectually honest and responsible reading of the Bible, would be a failure of spiritual and intellectual integrity. *Prima facie*, the Bible does teach absolute divine creation *ex nihilo*. One needs to have a compelling reason to reject it as the teaching of the Bible.

In the remainder of this chapter, I will assume the truth of the traditional doctrine of absolute divine creation *ex nihilo*. What needs now to be explored is what such a doctrine would imply with respect to God's ongoing relationship to his creation. It will be my contention that it rationally requires that God be the determiner of everything that is and of everything that occurs. Accordingly, if the traditional doctrine of absolute creation *ex nihilo* is true, then divine determinism is true.

THE NATURE OF THE RELATIONSHIP BETWEEN GOD AND HIS CREATION

Having explored the scope of divine creation, we must now turn to a second important question: what exactly is the nature of the on-going relationship that exists between God and the created order?

We need a model for understanding what the God-reality relationship looks like. In constructing this model, we must fulfill two criteria which have emerged from our earlier discussion: (1) our model must picture God in a way that is compatible with a traditional Judaeo-Christian concept of God,[63] and (2) our model must present the God-universe relationship in such a way that it is compatible with the presumed biblical doctrine of absolute divine creation *ex nihilo* defined in the earlier discussion. There are only two models that can meet both of these criteria.

THE COSMIC AUTHOR MODEL

Imagine a novelist sitting at his keyboard composing a novel. Suppose that this novelist has envisioned the entire story perfectly and exhaustively from beginning to end in one glance. Suppose further that he is capable of anticipating exactly what next to write in this novel so as to advance flawlessly toward the plot he has comprehensively envisioned in one glance. Suppose, as a consequence, that he never makes any false starts. As he writes, the story unfolds perfectly—exactly as he wills it—as the spontaneous output of his imagination.[64]

As this author creates his story, nothing that exists or occurs in the world of his story exists or occurs apart from his will. If the author wills that it rain, it rains. If he wills that it snow, it snows. If he wills that a char-

---

63. This requirement follows from the composition of my intended audience. It is not my purpose to defend traditional Judaeo-Christian theism to the atheist, monist, or non-traditional theist. Rather, my purpose is to defend divine determinism to the already persuaded theist. Therefore, while one could devise other models of God's relationship to the universe, if they are not compatible with traditional theism, they are not relevant to the purposes of this work.

64. We are clearly imagining a super-human novelist here; no real human author would be capable of such a feat.

acter deliberate over a tough moral decision, the character deliberates. If he wills that that character make an evil choice, he makes an evil choice. Every detail of everything that transpires in his story is shaped by the will of the author.

This is the first model by which one might picture God's *ex nihilo* creatorship of our world in a manner consistent with the Judaeo-Christian conception of God. Under this model, God's relationship to the cosmos we live in is analogous to an author's relationship to a novel he is writing as he creates it line-by-line in his imagination.[65] According to this model, then, the unfolding of the events of each day, in all their details, are the ongoing creation of the story of the cosmos in God's creative imagination. Reality is not like a novel already written, sitting on the shelf. It is a novel being written. Each day is the production of the next scene in God's creative imagination, created perfectly in accordance with the unchangeable purpose and the fixed and detailed plot that God has already determined in his mind.

THE COSMIC INVENTOR MODEL

Imagine a human inventor, a genius, who created a whole world: "Robo-world." First, he created a huge building with thick, totally-impenetrable walls, floor, and ceiling. Then he invented computer-controlled equipment capable of counteracting any and every effect of the outside world—including the physical laws like gravity. The net result is that our inventor has made a building that—inside—is completely devoid of any physical laws. Then—with more computer-controlled equipment—he created an entirely new physical environment exactly to his specifications. As a final result, everything inside the building is totally controlled by this inventor's computers. Nothing outside the control of his computers can have any effect on the environment or events inside Robo-world.

Next this inventor invented scores of robots and programmed them all to move, act, communicate, and learn. He programmed each with detailed instructions concerning how to respond and how to act in any specific set of circumstances. Furthermore, he equipped each robot to make it possible to control its movements and actions directly by remote control whenever he wanted to do so. Therefore, when it is not being

---

65. The analogy is inadequate in one very important respect. Whereas a human author can only work on one character, one scene, and one plot line at a time, God works on limitless characters, limitless scenes, and limitless plot lines simultaneously.

controlled by its own internal programming, each robot is controlled by the inventor's direct command by way of a remote control override of its internal programming.

Having invented all his equipment, he set all the robots and a variety of inert props in exactly that initial state he wanted; and with the push of a button, he started Robo-world in motion.

In a sense, Robo-world can be said to have been created *ex nihilo*. Strictly speaking, of course, our imaginary inventor had some help. God created the matter, the energy, and the laws of physics that the inventor is exploiting. But, apart from this slight head-start, our genius inventor created everything else in Robo-world, building on the foundation God had laid for him.

The relationship of Robo-world to its inventor provides an analogy for understanding our second viable model of God's relationship to his *ex nihilo* creation. Under this model, the cosmos is like a grand-scale Robo-world. God has created all kinds of different creatures who all operate in exactly the way he has "programmed" them to act. Everything that happens results from the interaction of these various creatures. Nothing exists in this grand Robo-world that he did not invent. Therefore, every moment of God's Robo-world functions in keeping with the design and programming that God built into it.

DIFFERING PERSPECTIVES WITHIN THE COSMIC INVENTOR MODEL

The basic cosmic inventor model can take several different specific forms, depending upon the amount of direct involvement one believes God has in the cosmos:

THE PARK FOUNTAIN MODEL *{The Deistic Model}*—God, the cosmic inventor, invented the cosmos, set it in motion, and now is occupied exclusively with watching it, enjoying his handiwork. He does virtually nothing in the way of having direct control over its affairs. Reality is to God much like a park fountain is to most people. It is an interesting thing to watch; and, indeed, that's what it's for.

THE TOY TRAIN MODEL *{The Deist-Interventionist Model}*— A boy who sets up an electric train does so primarily to enjoy watching it chug around the tracks. But not exclusively. At times he will do more than watch. He will intervene, changing the conditions of the track in order to see something different. He will devise train wrecks and other interesting occurrances. By analogy, under this model, God does not merely watch the cosmos. He also intervenes on occasion, to accomplish some specific purpose. In this model, God might sometimes exercise direct control over certain portions of his creation.

THE AIR TRAFFIC CONTROLLER MODEL *{The Semi-Automatic Providentialist Model}*—Generally speaking, an air traffic controller controls the flight patterns of the airplanes under his jurisdiction. He is constantly monitoring their flights and, as necessary, ordering minor adjustments in their flight paths. He doesn't control every aspect of an airplane's flight, of course. The pilots control most of that. But, insofar as the pilot guides his plane in response to the air traffic controller's instructions, it is the air traffic controller, through his constant intervention, who is ultimately determining the flight path of all the airplanes in his air space. This is a third model for God's relationship to the cosmos. God intervenes on more than rare occasions. Rather, like the air traffic controller, his intervention is the guiding principle that determines the general, overall course of the cosmos. A cosmos that otherwise would proceed upon its course automatically is being constantly redirected by the intervention of the creator.

THE VIDEO GAME MODEL *{The Total Providentialist Model}*—There are various video games in which the "characters" are totally controlled by a human manning the joy stick. These electronic characters do not make a move apart from the direction of the player. Our final model is analogous to this. God (through some sort of analog to remote-control command signals) intervenes constantly with concrete and specific directions that control our lives. Like electronic characters in a video game, our every move is directed by him.

Although these different models range widely with regard to the perceived level of direct intervention by God, they are all basically the same model. They differ only by degree. Each of these models see created reality as essentially capable of an existence independent of God. And each sees reality as intrinsically susceptible to direct control by God—should he will it. The difference lies in the extent to which God is believed to assume direct control.

THE ALL-IMPORTANT DIFFERENCE BETWEEN THE COSMIC AUTHOR AND INVENTOR MODELS

There is an important fundamental difference between the Cosmic Author Model and the Cosmic Inventor Model: namely, the perspective each takes on the nature of ongoing cosmic existence. Under both models, the *original* fact and "shape" of cosmic existence is under the willful control of the creator. But under the Cosmic Author Model, the *ongoing* fact and "shape" of cosmic existence is also under the willful control of the creator. If the cosmic author chooses not to create the next line of the cosmic narrative, the cosmos would simply cease to exist, for under the Cosmic Author Model, the ongoing existence of the cosmos is utterly contingent on the will of the creator. This is not the case under the Cosmic Inventor Model. Under it, once set in motion by the creator, the cosmos has an autonomy from the creator that allows it to go chugging right along with or without him. Its creator could die and turn to dust and the cosmos would continue to exist and function. Cosmic existence is contingent upon the will of the creator in the sense that the cosmos would not be here if the creator had not willed it to be. But, under the Cosmic Inventor Model, the ongoing existence of the cosmos is *not* contingent on the will of the creator.

The Concept of a Controlling Nature

The point of this chapter is to present an argument for divine determinism on the assumption of absolute divine creation *ex nihilo*. But the implications of divine creation *ex nihilo* for the nature of God's determinative control of the cosmos are not transparent. Some aspects of the question are highly complex. Our discussion will be greatly simplified if we employ a key concept—the concept of a CONTROLLING NATURE. So, before I construct my argument for divine determinism, I digress to define and discuss this important concept.

DEFINITION OF CONTROLLING NATURE

Every creature who acts, wills, thinks, chooses, or moves does so in accordance with a certain set of laws that determine that it will act in one way rather than another. This set of laws (whatever they may be and whatever form they may take) is the CONTROLLING NATURE of that creature.

Every participant in cosmic events has a controlling nature that dictates how it will act. It makes no difference whether that participant is a human being or a stone. Though each model would involve a significantly different notion, the concept of a controlling nature is just as meaningful under the Cosmic Author Model as it is under the Cosmic Inventor Model.

To understand 'controlling nature' in the context of the Cosmic Author Model, we need to observe something about an analogous situation—the human author. When a human author writes a story, he creates various characters who will play some role in the narrative. Right from the start, he has a concept of their nature, character, personality, and the various other circumstances of their lives. These concepts may initially be somewhat vague and ill-defined, but they are there guiding the author's writing nonetheless. As the writing of the story progresses and one creative decision after another presents itself, the author makes these creative decisions with reference to his initial concept of each of the characters. He does not want any of his characters to act "out of character." So, in a very real sense, his initial conceptualization of the story's characters controls or determines to a significant extent the creative decisions that the author can make in the ongoing development of those characters.

Under the Cosmic Author Model, something similar can be said about God. God's initial conceptualization of each of his creatures controls or determines the creative decisions God can make in his ongoing creation of them. An important difference exists between God and his human counterpart. Whereas the human author's initial conception of his characters is vague and incomplete, God's initial conception of his creatures is, presumably, perfect, clear, and complete. God's initial conception of a human creature includes a grasp of literally every detail of everything that will happen to that creature. So, for example, God's initial conception of Adam includes the notions that (1) he will be the first human being, (2) he will be married to Eve, (3) he will have a specific number of sons and daughters, and (4) he will rebel against God. Indeed, it would include literally every other detail of his life. The divine author—because he has a perfect grasp of the whole plot of cosmic history and a complete understanding of all the interrelationships that exist between his "characters"—cannot fail to grasp the whole history of a creature from the moment he first conceptualizes it. This complete and perfect conception of his creatures functions for God the same way the vague and imperfect conception of his characters does for a human author: it is the blueprint that directs the creative decisions that he will make in his ongoing creation. It follows that while the human author's conceptions of his characters provide him with only a general outline, that they direct him only partially, God's conceptions of his creatures direct him completely and perfectly. God's perfect and complete conceptions of his creatures is definitive. These original conceptions of his creatures do, in effect, determine every aspect of their existence. God's original conceptions of his creations, therefore, are their controlling natures. *Under the Cosmic Author Model, the controlling nature of a creature is the perfectly complete concept of it in the mind of God—the concept that dictates and determines its ongoing creation by God.*

Under the Cosmic Author Model, the whole of reality is determined by the controlling natures of each and every creature. And this is to say, the whole of reality is determined by God, for it is God who determines the controlling natures of every creature that exists. In other words, the whole of cosmic history is determined by God, the creator, in accordance with the controlling natures of things, which he has freely determined.[66]

Under the Cosmic Inventor Model, on the other hand, the controlling nature of a creature is not necessarily a divine conception or blueprint that God employs in his ongoing determination of that creature. It could be something altogether different from that.[67] Instead, it could be something with an autonomous existence that literally controls the creature through some sort of mechanical causation[68] in accordance with its divinely created design.[69]

---

66. The reader who is familiar with the philosopher Leibniz will notice some distinct resemblances to Leibniz on several points. By no means do I follow Leibniz in all respects. But his implicit belief in the rationality of God, his belief in the rational interconnectedness of the universe, and his corresponding belief in divine determinism are, I believe, essentially correct. According to Leibniz, for God to create the cosmos means that he had to create it as a rationally coherent whole. Therefore, to create it at all meant that he must determine every little detail of its existence. I think Leibniz was right about that.

67. I say "could be" here, for—as we shall see—the controlling nature of a thing could still essentially be a blueprint in God's mind under the Cosmic Inventor Model just as surely as under the Cosmic Author Model. Under those versions of the Cosmic Inventor Model where God's intervention in the direction of cosmic events is high, it would be "blueprints" in the divine mind that would determine the nature of God's intervention. So, for example, if we conceive of events as the result of divinely-sent remote-control signals to which God's creatures are designed to respond, blueprints would dictate the commands God sends via remote control. In such a model, these blueprints would be the controlling natures of things. Only insofar as a version of the Cosmic Inventor Model views a creature as functioning autonomously from God must the concept of "controlling nature" take on a very different form and consist of something significantly different from a blueprint.

68. By "mechanical causation," I do not necessarily mean *physical* causation. I mean it to include spiritual, non-material causation—if such exists. By spiritual, non-material causation I would mean causation that functions in a manner analogous to physical causation but in the absence of physical matter and energy.

Any conception of the cosmos that understands cosmic events as the direct creation of God or as the direct result of his causative influence leads clearly and directly to divine determinism. Questions arise when we conceive of a cosmos where the controlling natures of things function autonomously from God.[70] Does this view of the cosmos also lead to divine determinism, or does such a conception of the cosmos make room for the possibility that cosmic events are outside the scope of God's control?

This being the question, I make two assumptions for the purpose of the ensuing discussion: (1) I assume that every actor in the cosmic drama (from angel to rock) has a controlling nature as I am defining it, and (2) I assume that every creature's controlling nature controls its every action autonomously—in independence of the divine will—by a sort of mechanical causation.

As I have already suggested, the concept of a controlling nature could be employed under any conception of the cosmos. But under some conceptions of the cosmos, it is superfluous; instead of being helpful, it complicates the discussion unnecessarily. But in the context of the two assumptions listed above, the "controlling nature" is a useful concept that will help significantly simplify our discussion. Accordingly, in the following discussion, I employ the concept of a controlling nature solely within the parameters of these two assumptions.

COMMONSENSICALITY OF THE CONCEPT OF CONTROLLING NATURE

Our definition of a controlling nature assumes, of course, that such a thing exists. An obvious objection to this concept is that, in fact, no such thing does exist. But the objection is unfounded. The assumption that

---

69. In mixed versions of the Cosmic Inventor Model—where sometimes God directly causes events (as through divine remote-control command signals) and sometimes he lets the creation operate autonomously—the controlling natures of things are best conceived as having autonomous existence and as causing events through a sort of mechanical causation. In such cases, it is the controlling natures of things that determine cosmic events to the extent that the cosmos is functioning autonomously; and it is the creative will of God that determines cosmic events to the extent that God intervenes.

70. That is, the controlling natures *function* autonomously even though God created, designed, and willed into existence every controlling nature that exists.

everything has a controlling nature is completely commonsensical.[71] It may not take exactly that form to which—for the sake of our discussion—we have just restricted ourselves. That is, it may not be an entity with autonomous existence that mechanically causes the actions of that being of whom it is the controlling nature. But the existence of a controlling nature, *per se*, is beyond dispute.

To assert that everything has a controlling nature is not to assert something spooky. It is merely to assert that there exist objectively real principles that govern reality and cause it to be rationally ordered.[72] It is to assert that something exists that causes each creature to behave in a rationally ordered way.

Or, to put it still another way, it is to affirm the possibility of true knowledge. If there were no controlling natures determining the rational orderliness of things, there would be no objective, determinative patterns in human experience.[73] And if there were no determinative patterns in human experience there could be no knowledge; and no one can seriously believe in the impossibility of knowledge.[74]

Built into the very fabric of human intelligence itself—so foundational that no one can successfully ignore it—is the three-fold assumption that (1) orderly patterns are there to be discovered in human experience, (2) these orderly patterns correspond to a rational orderliness that is really objectively out there, and, most importantly, (3) *this objective orderliness must be caused by certain rational ordering principles.* (These are the controlling natures of things.) Innate human intelligence compels us to seek to identify those patterns and to understand the causes behind them. We cannot stop ourselves. So long as our intelligence is operative, we will seek the causes and explanations for the rational order of our experience.

Human beings are the most mysterious and complex participants in the

---

71. In the sense of 'commonsensical' defined above in chapter 3.

72. Whether they be the rational will and objectives of the Divine Mind, or the rationally-designed mechanisms of autonomously functioning existents.

73. The assumption I am making here is that some form of determinism is required to account for rational order in human experience. In the absence of rational minds or principles ordering our existence, we could expect only chaos and randomness. See chapter 8 for a fuller discussion of this point.

74. By 'a serious belief' I mean one in which a person's actions follow logically from the fact that one holds the belief. If a person says he believes X, but his actions are not logically compatible with X, then his belief in X is not a serious belief. No one consistently behaves as if they seriously believed that knowledge is not possible. And to the degree that anyone did, we would consider his condition pathological.

cosmic drama. Yet, even of them we expect behavior that manifests a discernible orderliness. Our concepts of "personality" and "character" reflect this expectation. They describe different aspects of the orderly, predictable behavior of individual human beings. They describe different aspects of the controlling nature of a human individual. A rationally ordered law of each and every individual makes him behave exactly as he does. Personality and character are the common terms we use to describe aspects of that law.

We rely on our knowledge of other people's personality and character on a daily basis. When we get married, sign contracts, vote for candidates, hire employees, or make any of a host of other decisions, we are making judgments based on our understanding of the controlling nature of individual human beings.

Human beings are incredibly complex. Consequently, we do not expect to gain a thorough and flawless understanding of a person's controlling nature. Notions of a person's character and personality are, at best, only rough approximations of the nature of that person. The controlling nature of a stone, on the other hand, is simple and easy to understand. A stone, unhindered, will always roll down hill in slavish obedience to the law of gravity. This is a straightforward aspect of its controlling nature. But however easy or difficult knowledge of a controlling nature may be to acquire, we always assume it is there and that it can, in principle, be known, even when such knowledge is, in practice, inaccessible.

Still, a skeptic might object that our having an indomitable expectation of finding a controlling nature in things does not make it so. If this expectation is built into human intelligence, so much the worse for human intelligence. Perhaps this expectation is nothing more than a quirk—a strange and meaningless psychological need.

Perhaps. But if so, then no true knowledge of anything is possible. If all of our beliefs are actually constructed to fulfill an invalid psychological need for rational orderliness, then none of our beliefs have any significance as knowledge; they cannot be assumed to be true—that is, to correspond to the way things actually are. But this is totally absurd. No sane, reasonable, intelligent human being can seriously maintain total skepticism.[75] Total skepticism is a game played by sophists, not a serious philosophical position.

It makes more sense (particularly in the light of Judaeo-Christian theism) to understand that our persistent expectation of finding a controlling nature in things is a God-given expectation, created by God to be the very foundation of human intelligence. It is an expectation that God created in

---

75. For that matter, neither can an insane and unreasonable human being *consistently* maintain total skepticism.

us to correspond to the fact that those natures really are there. In other words, if the Christian God is there, it makes sense to believe that the fundamental impulses that drive us as knowers correspond to the way objective reality actually is, so that true knowledge is possible. This is a basic assumption of the biblical worldview. God created the cosmos, and he created human beings to be capable of true knowledge of that cosmos. Consequently, he designed human intelligence to be adequate for the task.

So our fundamental assumption that everything has a controlling nature is not motivated by a misguided psychological need. It is foundational to human intelligence itself, the cornerstone of human knowing. If we reject this assumption, then we repudiate the very foundation of human intelligence and we reject the possibility of true knowledge of the cosmos at the same time.[76]

Consider what would happen if a human infant were born into this world without the assumption[77] that everything has a controlling nature. The baby would see a collage of colors. He might notice on one occasion that this collage of colors, shifting and dynamic as it was, included some consistent patterns that did not vary. But if he had no expectation that there was a reason for this pattern, if he had no expectation that there was some controlling nature that was giving rise to his experience, his only response could be, "Wow! How incredibly interesting! Those colors are staying together! What a remarkable random coincidence."

But this is not how the baby responds. Instead, the baby reasons, "Those colors are staying together. The only rational explanation is that they constitute a *thing*, an object. The fact that they are an object is what causes them to keep the same pattern. I'm not sure what the object is. I'll have to wait until I can talk and ask my mother, but I know it is something." My point is this: the very possibility of the human infant learning anything at all is based on the fact that the baby innately expects[78] his experience to be caused by controlling natures that he can come to know and understand.

---

76. A thorough defense of this statement would require a whole treatise on a biblical theory of knowledge. Obviously, it is not possible to have that discussion here. Chapters 3 and 8 indicate the direction that my construction of such a theory would take; but I cannot offer here a thorough exposition and defense of what I would hold to be a biblical epistemology.

77. Obviously this assumption is not something that the infant holds consciously and articulately. Indeed, it is not properly speaking a part of the baby's knowledge. Rather, it is what I would call a "pre-gnostic" assumption. It is not an assumption posited in theoretical thought; rather, it is a working assumption built into the very operation of human intelligence itself. To use a computer analogy, it is part of the ROM of human intelligence.

78. Again, not as a conscious expectation that he can articulate. See the note immediately above.

All things considered, it simply makes no sense to reject the notion that all things have a controlling nature.[79] It is just too commonsensical. We cannot help ourselves. We are forced to believe it by our own instincts. To reject it is to rebel against human intelligence itself.

BEING CLEAR ON CONTROLLING NATURES

It is crucial that I be perfectly clear what I mean by CONTROLLING NATURE. Consider the controlling nature of a stone. The controlling nature of a stone does not merely set boundaries on what a stone can be and how it can "act." Its controlling nature does more than determine that whatever the stone does must be stone-like. Rather, the controlling nature of a stone determines exactly what it will do on any given occasion. The controlling nature of a stone determines that it will fall from exactly this location at exactly this time at exactly this velocity having exactly these results. The physicist feels confident that, given enough information, he could predict the time, location, velocity, and results of the stone's falling. Why? Because he can have such a grasp of the stone's controlling nature that he can predict what its controlling nature will cause the stone to do.

BEING CLEAR ON THE CONTROLLING NATURE OF A HUMAN BEING

In the argument that follows we will concentrate especially on the controlling nature of human beings. Accordingly, an accurate understanding of what we mean by 'controlling nature' in their case is especially important. Three points are worth noting:

1. The controlling nature of a human being is not apart from the human being himself. My controlling nature is not separate and distinct from me, rather, it *is* me. My controlling nature is that in me—a part of my being, a part of the definition of who I am—that causes me to choose one thing rather than another.

---

79. A more concise but parallel assertion to the one that everything has a controlling nature might be this: Every action a creature takes is either uncaused (i.e., random), self-caused, or caused. The notion that every creature has a controlling nature is simply the suggestion that all of every creature's actions or choices are caused. None of them is uncaused (random); and none of them is self-caused.

2. The controlling nature of a human being is not just his human nature as we commonly understand that. My controlling nature does not merely put certain boundaries on the possible choices I can make. It does not merely dictate that my choices will be human-like. Rather, it is my own unique, personal, individual nature that specifically determines the specific, individual choices that I make as a distinct individual.

3. The controlling nature of a human being is not his individual will as that is sometimes understood. Many people conceive of the will as a decision-generating machine that makes it possible for a person to make decisions, but that does not determine the exact nature and content of those decisions. It's like a saw. A saw makes it possible for a man to cut wood. But the saw does not control the kind and location of the cut. Similarly, the human will is often conceived as a faculty that enables a man to choose, but it does not control what is going to be chosen and when. The human will, so conceived, is not one's controlling nature. The controlling nature of a distinct human individual is the causative force within him that determines specifically and exactly what that individual will choose when.

Creation *Ex Nihilo* as an Argument for Divine Determinism

The essence of the argument for divine determinism from divine creation is this: there are only two viable models whereby one can understand the Judaeo-Christian God as the *ex nihilo* creator; and, no matter which model one chooses (nor which version of that model one chooses) divine determinism is rationally required. To see this, I will proceed by considering the implications of the Cosmic Inventor Model and the Cosmic Author Model separately.

PRELIMINARY OBSERVATION ON MY PROCEDURE

I must first explain why I proceed as I do. In order to simplify matters, my discussion concentrates exclusively on the freewill choices of human beings. Obviously I am not maintaining that only freewill choices are divinely determined. My contention is that all cosmic events, of whatever nature, are divinely determined. But it is simpler to articulate my argument with respect to just the one type of event and not have to repeated-ly acknowledge all the other kinds of events that can occur. There are two reasons why I feel justified in limiting my discussion to human freewill choices:

1. This work is fundamentally a defense of divine determinism vis-à-vis limited determinism. As the label suggests, limited determinism is quite willing to allow that God determines many, if not most, cosmic events. Limited determinism is *limited* determinism precisely because it insists that some kinds of events are not divinely determined even though the majority are. Different limited determinists would specify different events as being outside the scope of God's causation. But virtually all limited determinists would include freewill choices among the class of events outside God's causation. Therefore, the freewill choices of human beings are particularly controversial. If my argument can show that creation *ex nihilo* entails divine determinism with respect to freewill choices, then I have successfully refuted limited determinism in the form in which it is usually found.

2. The arguments I offer for the divine determination of freewill choices could quite easily be adapted and applied to other types of cosmic events. Even though they would need to be modified somewhat, the substance of the arguments would be the same for every kind of cosmic event. Rather than tediously repeat the arguments with respect to each different kind of possible event, I have chosen to take the most difficult case—the divine determinism of freewill events—and let it stand for all cosmic events. I am confident that the same arguments could be made for the other kinds as well. Hence, though my arguments are framed as specific arguments for the divine determination of freewill choices, nevertheless the reader could easily satisfy himself that doing so has not invalidated these arguments as proof of the divine determination of all cosmic events.[80]

---

80. My premise is this: If God ultimately determines human freewill choice, then he must nec-essarily determine every other kind of cosmic event. Most limited determinists would readily accept this premise. Incidentally, the inverse of this premise (i.e., if God does not determine human freewill choice, then he does not determine every other kind of cosmic event.) is not true.

IMPLICATIONS OF THE COSMIC INVENTOR MODEL FOR DIVINE DETERMINISM

TWO WAYS CREATURES CAN FUNCTION WITHIN THE COSMIC INVENTOR MODEL

That there are, within the context of the Cosmic Inventor Model, two different ways to envision creatures functioning is apparent from my earlier descriptions of the different forms it can take:

1. God's creatures could respond—in accord with their created design— out of "mechanical obedience" to God's direct commands.[81] Just as the inventor of Robo-world could program his robots to respond to commands he sent them by remote-control signal, likewise, under the Cosmic Inventor Model, we could have been created by God to respond, mechanically, to command signals that God might send. If so, then, theoretically, our every move could be the direct result of God's direct command, and, hence, our every move would be directly caused by God.[82]

2. God's creatures—once created and initially set in motion—could function quite independently of God. God, having equipped them with a controlling nature, could have taken his hands off and left his creatures to chug along on their own, in strict mechanical obedience to their controlling natures. Just as the inventor of Robo-world could program his robots to function independently of any ongoing input from him, God could have equipped us with controlling natures that would allow us to function without any intervention from him. We would then operate out of mechanical obedience to the divinely-designed controlling nature that God placed in us initially.[83]

---

81. Throughout the ensuing discussion, when I refer to "mechanical" obedience, "mechanical" necessity, etc., I do not necessarily mean "physical" necessity. Physical necessity—i.e., strict necessity arising from the necessity of conforming to natural, physical laws—is the paradigm for what I mean; but it does not exhaust what I mean. I want to allow for the possibility (should it exist) that there are non-material, spiritual laws that direct cosmic events in a manner exactly analogous to the way physical laws direct natural events. Therefore, by "mechanical" necessity I mean to include not only the necessity that results from *physical*, mechanical causation, but also the necessity which results from *non-physical*, mechanical causation (if such exists).

82. The form of the Cosmic Inventor Model being described here is the Video Game Model or the Total Providentialist Model.

Or, we can function in some combination of these two ways. To whatever extent we function autonomously from God, we function as described in (2) above. To whatever extent we function in response to God's direct intervention, we function as described in (1) above—God's direct causation being able to override our controlling nature. Be that as it may, there remain just these two fundamentally different ways that freewill creatures might function (according to the Cosmic Inventor Model).

THE QUESTION OF INTEREST TO US

If, in fact, the first of the above models is the way we actually function, then the divine determination of our choices is clear and indisputable. If every choice is directly caused by God, then, by definition, we have the divine determination of freewill choices. But what if (in accord with the second model) we function autonomously from God—each of our freewill choices being determined not by God, but by the controlling natures that he gave us? What would then be implied as to the divine determination of our choices? If our controlling natures function independently from any direct, ongoing causative influence that God exerts on our choices, does it or does it not follow that our choices are divinely determined?

Most limited determinists base their judgment that God is not ultimately responsible for freewill choices on the assumption that our controlling natures can function autonomously from God. On the surface, the limited determinist's confidence seems unfounded. Even if we assume the functional autonomy of our controlling natures, is it not God—according to the biblical concept of creation—who created and designed our controlling natures? And if so, do our controlling natures not function in keeping with a design that originated from him? And if so, are not all of our choices ultimately determined by the design that God himself built into our controlling natures? Consequently, God is ultimately the determiner of all of our choices. Everything we choose has ultimately been determined by his creative will.

So while the divine determinist could argue that God, being the creator of my controlling nature, is thereby the ultimate determiner of my every choice even if my controlling nature operates autonomously, the limited determinist disagrees with this line of reasoning on the basis of one of the following two objections:

---

83. The form of the Cosmic Inventor Model being described here is the Park Fountain Model or Deistic Model.

THE FIRST OBJECTION TO THIS LINE OF REASONING

Granted, the biblical view of creation suggests that Adam[84] himself is created by God. But the Bible does not mean to suggest that Adam's controlling nature is created by God. God has created the fact of Adam's existence, but not the causes of his individual decisions (i.e., not his controlling nature). God causes Adam to exist; but Adam causes his own choices, not God.[85]

ANSWER TO THE FIRST OBJECTION

For the sake of argument, let us grant the limited determinist his assumption—namely, creation *ex nihilo* establishes that God created the fact of Adam's existence, but it does not establish that God created Adam's controlling nature. Given this assumption, where does Adam's controlling nature originate? What is the cause of its existence? I will examine all the logically possible answers to this question:

---

84. I shall use the name 'Adam'—in accordance with its original meaning—to mean "humankind" (as distinct from all the other types of living beings). For the sake of simplicity, I will use the term 'Adam' to represent any and every human being. I am not referring to the historical figure Adam, the first human being. I am using Adam, instead, as a variable place-holder to stand for any human being.

85. This is, in essence, the substance of Geisler's position. See Norman L. Geisler, *Philosophy of Religion* (Grand Rapids: Zondervan Publishing House, 1974), 401. Geisler argues that "No moral action is externally determined nor is it indeterminate. Moral actions are self-determined." There is a basic confusion in Geisler's position relative to mine. Certainly, Geisler does not mean that moral actions are self-determined in the sense that moral actions cause themselves. That, as we shall discuss later, would be absurd. Rather, Geisler means that Adam causes his own moral actions. No being external to Adam causes Adam's moral actions; and Adam's moral actions are not uncaused. But Adam's causing his own moral actions (Geisler's position) is equivalent to Adam's moral actions being caused by his own controlling nature (my position)—for, as I have already observed, Adam's controlling nature is his "self." The problem is this: Whereas Geisler and I both attribute moral actions to the same direct cause—Adam himself—Geisler stops his thinking there, assuming that the origin of moral actions is thereby solved. My argument is that attributing Adam's moral actions to Adam, though true, does not solve the problem of the ultimate origin of those moral actions. Where does the controlling nature or "self" which gives rise to Adam's moral actions come from? That, essentially, is the question to which we seek an answer—a question to which Geisler has provided no answer.

The Logically-Possible Answers

Nothing Causes Adam's Controlling Nature (It Does Not Exist)

The first possible answer is that nothing causes Adam's controlling nature because it does not exist. It is simply to assert that no controlling nature exists. Pure randomness controls the actions of Adam. His actions are not determined. They are not rationally ordered and patterned. Rather, indeterminism is the true explanation of his actions.

I have already dismissed this possibility in the arguments above. Such a perspective violates common sense. We could not bring ourselves to seriously believe this, try as we might. This is not a rationally satisfactory answer to our question.

Adam's Controlling Nature Is Self-Existent

The second possible answer is, again, that nothing is the cause of Adam's controlling nature, but in a different sense. According to this answer, Adam has a determinate controlling nature that causes his actions, but that controlling nature itself is caused by nothing outside itself. Rather, it is self-existent. It has always existed and must always exist as it does. It just is. No explanation of its existence is possible, nor needed.

Though this answer is logically possible, it is in direct conflict with the biblical doctrine of creation ex *nihilo* as we have defined it in this chapter. One of the primary assertions of the doctrine of creation *ex nihilo* is that no one and no thing, except God himself, is self-existent.[86] This answer requires that there be a whole host of self-existent beings. Not only God, but each and every controlling nature of each and every human being is self-existent!

This viewpoint would rewrite the biblical creation account to read:

> In the beginning was God and a whole host of little self-existent controlling natures. Now God created everything that is, and the self-existent controlling natures each picked one of these things to live in and control.

If the traditional doctrine of absolute divine creation *ex nihilo* understands the Bible rightly, then this position is biblically absurd. If we are going to take the biblical doctrine of creation seriously, this explanation for the origin of Adam's controlling nature is not satisfactory.

---

86. See the discussion of creation *ex nihilo* earlier in this chapter.

Adam's Controlling Nature Is Self-Creating

The third possible answer is that Adam's controlling nature is self-creating, self-originating, self-generating, and self-causing. It is not self-existent. That is, it is not eternal and uncaused. Its existence and nature are created, but it is self-created and self-determined and not determined by anyone or anything outside of itself.

Two major objections can be raised against this alternative:

1. It violates reason. The very concept of a self-creating being is irrational and nonsensical. The biblical concept of God, as traditionally understood, is not that he is self-creating and self-generating, but that he is eternal and self-existent. These are very different notions. The latter is ultimately meaningful and rationally possible, the former is rationally absurd. Therefore, the irrationality of the suggestion that Adam's controlling nature is self-creating is evident. It ascribes to a finite "thing," Adam's controlling nature, a power and ability that we do not even ascribe to the eternal, uncaused, self-existent, infinite God. Indeed, we would find it just as unthinkable and nonsensical to ascribe this ability to God as to ascribe it to Adam's controlling nature. Nothing can cause its own existence. The very notion is absurd.[87]

2. It violates the biblical account of creation. It violates the doctrine of creation *ex nihilo* as it has been explained in this chapter. One of the primary tenets of creation *ex nihilo* is that literally nothing comes into existence but that it is created by God. If the controlling nature of Adam is self-creating, then it comes into existence without being created by God. This is in direct contradiction to the traditional understanding of the biblical teaching.

---

87. In the same passage cited in note 85 above, Geisler argues that theism takes the view that "moral actions" are self-caused (as opposed to indeterminate or externally caused). As mentioned in note 85, Geisler does not mean by "self-caused" what I am criticizing here. He means to say that Adam, himself, causes his own moral actions. His actions are not uncaused, nor caused by something outside of Adam. In the terms in which I am arguing, however, this does not make his actions "self-caused." Even in Geisler's view, Adam's moral actions do not cause themselves! Rather, Adam's moral actions are, in terms of Geisler's categories, externally caused—that is, they are caused by Adam's controlling nature. We can legitimately call these actions self-caused (as Geisler does) in the sense that Adam, himself, is their cause—which is to say that Adam's controlling nature is their cause. But this is not the doctrine of self-generation that I am here rejecting as absurd.

But the limited determinist might object: I will grant that Adam's controlling nature is created by God, but there is "room to move" built into the very structure of Adam's controlling nature. It has the ability to fashion itself. So, the biblical doctrine is correct, nothing creates itself—so neither does Adam's controlling nature create itself. But whereas Adam's controlling nature does not create itself, it does—once created—develop, grow, change, and define itself as time goes on.

Confusing Adam's individual controlling nature with his generic human nature is what lends plausibility to this suggestion. The suggestion makes some sort of sense if we understand it to be simply that God did create Adam with a generic human nature, but that the generic human nature that God created in Adam did not, in and of itself, cause and determine Adam's individual controlling nature.[88]

But this suggestion would not solve anything. The question before us does not concern the origins of Adam's generic human nature. (I do acknowledge that such exists.) Rather, the question before us concerns the origins of Adam's controlling nature. Where does *that* come from? If the suggestion is that no such thing exists, because only a generic human nature exists, then we are back to the first alternative up above—a denial of the existence of a controlling nature. If we are suggesting, rather, that the individual controlling nature is able to create itself from out of the generic human nature, then we have not, in fact, advanced any beyond the nonsense of this present suggestion. To speak of an individual controlling nature creating or causing itself is absurd. Whether it is creating itself out of nothing or creating itself out of the already-existing stuff of a generic human nature makes no difference. It is still absurd. So to posit self-creation as an explanation of the origin of the specific, individual controlling nature of Adam is biblically and rationally unacceptable.

Adam's Controlling Nature Is Created By Some Other Self-Existent Being

The fourth possible answer is that, not the God of the Bible, but some other eternal, self-existent being (for example, God's cousin, George) created or determined Adam's controlling nature.

This is biblically unacceptable. One of the clear ramifications of the biblical doctrine of creation *ex nihilo* is that there exists one and only one

---

88. And this, of course is true. Adam's generic human nature does not determine his individual controlling nature. If it did, then every human being's individual controlling nature should be identical to the controlling nature of every other individual. If the individual controlling nature of Adam follows mechanically from the generic human nature alone, then there is no cause for any variation in individual controlling natures.

eternal, self-existent being. To propose otherwise is to run directly counter to the biblical teaching. No person who accepts biblical teaching would seriously propose this.

Adam's Controlling Nature Is Caused By Some Other Created Being(s)

The fifth, very popular, answer is that Adam's controlling nature is caused or determined by some other aspect of the created order. So, for example, God created Adam's genes. But it is his set of genes,[89] not God, that determines what his controlling nature will be.

It may very well be true that physical realities determine what Adam's controlling nature will be. Indeed, at least to some extent, it is certainly true. But to say that a set of genes (or some other combination of physical realities) determines Adam's controlling nature does not exclude God as being the one who ultimately determines his controlling nature. It only creates the illusion that divine causation is excluded. Indeed, if creation *ex nihilo* is true, then if genes (or whatever) do create Adam's controlling nature, ultimately it must be God who creates his controlling nature.

Adam's controlling nature is determined by his set of genes. His set of genes is, in turn, determined by physical laws of chemistry and biology— laws that were created and designed by God and that operate out of mechanical necessity in accordance with patterns that God established— in conjunction with certain choices his parents made. His parents' free choices, in turn, were determined by their controlling natures. Their controlling natures were determined by their sets of genes, that were determined by those same physical laws of chemistry and biology, in conjunction with certain choices their parents made. Their parents' free choices, in turn, were determined by their controlling natures…that were determined by those same physical laws of chemistry and biology in conjunction with certain choices the very first parents made. The first parents' free choices, in turn, were determined by their controlling natures, which were determined by their sets of genes, which were *determined by God*.[90]

---

89. No serious thinker would actually argue that genes and genes alone determine a person's every freewill choice. I just use genes as an example. It could be any physical or spiritual realities and any combination of physical or spiritual realities that one views as the cause of our choices. If these realities cause our choices out of some sort of mechanical necessity, then it is a species of the view that I am critiquing here. In particular, *it makes no difference whether these realities are genetic material or environmental factors.* Both sides of the nature/nurture or genes/environment debate are included within the scope of "some other aspect of the created order" as I envision that here. Whether that aspect of the created order is some part of the environment or the genetic inheritance, the argument holds the same either way.

Hence, if Adam's controlling nature is caused out of strict physical (or mechanical) necessity by any other aspect of created reality,[91] then—assuming creation *ex nihilo*—one is forced to recognize the ultimate determination of all things by the original inventor, God. For the same reason that the genius inventor of Robo-world is ultimately the one who determines all that transpires in that world, God, under our present assumptions, must similarly determine all things that transpire in our cosmos. In both instances, all subsequent events are the inevitable mechanical results of mechanical principles.

Adam's Controlling Nature Is Created By God

The final alternative is that God himself creates Adam's controlling nature. God, in creating Adam, does not merely create the fact of his existence, but he creates the unique, individual, distinctive nature that defines Adam as Adam and is—one way or another—causative of the choices Adam makes.

This alternative is quite compatible with both sound reason and the Bible.[92] No serious objection can be raised on either front—reason or the Bible—against understanding God's creative act in this way.

Conclusion

We have been seeking an answer to the question, "Where does Adam's controlling nature originate?" We have discovered that there are only two plausible answers: (1) it could be created by God directly, or (2) it could be caused out of mechanical necessity by the causative powers of other aspects of the created cosmos. Since the limited determinist wants to avoid

---

90. I would have to frame the argument of this paragraph differently if I were not assuming—for the sake of argument—that genes, alone, determined freewill choices. But the net result would be the same under any similar assumption. If our freewill choices are, ultimately, the mechanical result of certain mechanical laws (whether spiritual or physical), then ultimately our freewill choices are determined by those laws and the initial state of the cosmos—both of which were determined by God. This is the essence of my point in this paragraph.

91. This would be a form of natural determinism as defined in chapter 1. The conclusion here is that natural determinism in the context of a belief in divine creation *ex nihilo* is a belief in divine determinism mediated through natural determinism; but it is ultimately divine determinism nonetheless.

92. Actually, what I mean here specifically is that this answer is quite compatible with sound reason and the Bible with respect to the biblical view of creation—as that is traditionally understood. From the standpoint of the biblical and commonsensical view of human free will, this view in particular and the Cosmic Inventor Model, in general, is not compatible with sound reason and the Bible. This will become clearer as my argument progresses.

the former, the only plausible answer available to him is the latter: Adam's controlling nature originates from and is caused, mechanically, by other created realities.[93] But this answer does not accomplish what the limited determinist desires—an alternative to divine determinism. For, given the traditional biblical doctrine of absolute divine creation *ex nihilo*, Adam's controlling nature being caused out of mechanical necessity by other created realities is ultimately Adam's controlling nature being caused by the divine creator himself. In other words, this second answer logically entails divine determinism. Hence, it is no less an espousal of divine determinism than the first one.

The divine determinist reasons that since God creates the controlling natures of all things, he ultimately determines everything that transpires. The first limited determinist objection is, in effect, to deny that God creates the controlling natures of certain things. If he does not create the controlling natures of all things, then, perhaps, we can escape the conclusion that he determines all things.

But we have seen that rejecting the proposition that God creates the controlling natures of all things leads to a disappointing result for the limited determinist. When we assume that God is not the origin of our controlling natures, we find that there remains only one rationally and biblically acceptable alternative[94]—namely, our controlling natures originate as the mechanically necessary result of the interaction of other created realities. But this, as we have seen, ultimately implies divine determinism just as surely as if God were the direct creator of our controlling natures. Those other created realities that are the cause and origin of our controlling natures are ultimately created by God and function just as he has willed them to function. Our controlling natures, therefore, are ultimately determined by God. Even if they are not created directly by him, they are, as it were, created indirectly—being the necessary outworking of mechanical principles and laws that he did directly create.

This first objection, then—to deny that God creates the controlling

---

93. A real irony exists here. One of my contentions in this book is that limited determinists are right in their intuition to reject natural determinism and that their rejection of divine determinism results from their confusing divine determinism with natural determinism. In other words, limited determinism's "natural enemy" is natural determinism; and the limited determinist intuitively recognizes this. It is ironic, therefore—as I show in this argument—that the only strategy available to the limited determinist to avoid divine determinism, given the fact of divine creation *ex nihilo*, is to embrace natural determinism. And even that fails to avoid divine determinism.

94. But, as I noted in note 92, this is not truly an acceptable alternative in the light of all that the Bible teaches and in the light of all that common sense requires.

natures of certain things—offers no rationally and biblically acceptable line of reasoning by which to avoid divine determinism. If God is the creator of all things in any manner consistent with the Cosmic Inventor Model, then divine determinism is ultimately implied.

THE SECOND OBJECTION TO THIS LINE OF REASONING

The second objection that could be raised against the divine determinist's line of reasoning is this: Granted that God creates the controlling nature, nevertheless, he does not thereby determine the manner in which it will function in determining Adam's choices. Though God is the creator of Adam's controlling nature, he does not determine its functioning whereby it determines Adam's decisions. God created the fact that the controlling nature exists, but he did not create within it any laws by which its output (Adam's choices) is determined.

ANSWER TO THE SECOND OBJECTION

The most important response I can make to this objection is to note that a false distinction is being made here. The distinction between the existence of a controlling nature and the design according to which it functions to determine Adam's choices is fallacious. It makes no sense to say that God created Adam's controlling nature, but he did not determine the design according to which it functions. Once we grasp adequately what is meant by the controlling nature, we see that a controlling nature can no more exist apart from the design by which it determines Adam's choices than a mathematical expression can exist apart from the mathematical terms from which it is comprised. At its very essence, Adam's controlling nature is (or, at least, necessarily includes) that design or pattern according to which Adam's choices are determined.

A controlling nature without a design by which it determines Adam's choices would be like a computer with no programming. A computer without programming is not thereby left free to function as it freely chooses. Rather, it is paralyzed from functioning at all. Similarly, the controlling nature of Adam, if it had not been given any design by which to function, would be paralyzed. It would be unable to determine Adam's choices at all. It would not render Adam free to make uncaused and undetermined choices. It would render Adam a lifeless corpse, unable to do anything at all.

Whether God can create any particular X without creating the structure and design according to which it functions is questionable in its own right. I am not convinced that it would ever make sense to claim that God created the fact that X existed without creating the nature, design, and structure of X's existence. If such were possible, how would X be distinguishable from any Y that exists. Does not the fact that X is definable as X rather than Y necessarily entail that X has a given structure, design, and nature according to which it exists *and functions?* So I remain unconvinced that this suggestion can even make any sense. God creating X without creating the laws of its operation is perhaps outright nonsense.

But—for the sake of the argument—I will grant that it is possible, in general, for God to create X without creating the laws of its operation. But what might be possible in general cannot possible apply to Adam's controlling nature. The existence of Adam's controlling nature *is* its design. Adam's controlling nature is nothing else but the determinative cause of his choices. To say that Adam's controlling nature was created by God is, by definition, to say that the determinative cause of Adam's actions was created by God. If God created the *fact* of the existence of Adam's controlling nature, then he created the nature of its determinative control, for its existence *is*, in its essence, the nature of its determinative control.

Therefore, if God did create (either directly or indirectly) the controlling nature of Adam—and we have seen that this follows necessarily from the traditional doctrine of creation *ex nihilo*—then it follows that God ultimately determines all of Adam's choices. Adam's choices are necessitated by his controlling nature, and his own controlling nature is caused and determined by God. Ultimately, therefore, God determines Adam's choices.

CONCLUSION

Where has our argument brought us? If we assume the Cosmic Inventor Model, there are only four viable answers to the question of the origin of our actions—that is, answers that do justice to both reason and the traditional understanding of the Bible's teaching about creation:

I. The actions of God's creatures originate with God. God directly and immediately causes his creatures to act as they do. Just as the genius inventor of Robo-world could so construct his world that its every event was subject to his direct intervention by means of remote-control signals he would send, God could have so constructed the cosmos that every move his creatures make is in direct response to his expressed will, mechanically enforced upon them. *This is the view that God controls the actions of his creatures directly through remote control.*

II. The actions of God's creatures originate from the autonomous operation of the controlling natures of things; and these controlling natures are directly designed by God to operate exactly as he wished. The robots in Robo-world could have been made to function just as the inventor wished even though they functioned autonomously from him. The inventor could have designed them to act out of mechanically necessary obedience to the programming that he designed for each one. Likewise, God could have designed each of his creatures to respond out of some sort of "mechanical" necessity to its own particular controlling nature that he himself designed. *This is the view that God controls the actions of his creatures directly through pre-programming.*

III. The actions of God's creatures originate from the autonomous operation of the controlling natures of things; and these controlling natures are directly caused out of mechanical necessity by the interaction of various other aspects of the created order that ultimately also function out of mechanical necessity in accordance with a design that they were given by God. For example, if we could assume that the genes in a human's body are ultimately the cause of every particular decision he makes, then, in effect, his controlling nature is his particular set of genes. Furthermore, these genes operate by mechanical (chemical) necessity in accordance with physical laws that God himself designed. *This is the view that God controls the actions of his creatures indirectly, mediated through other created causes he designed.*

IV. They originate from any combination of any or all of the above.

As we have seen, no matter which of the above options one chooses, the divine determination of all cosmic events is the necessary result. If we want to remain faithful to the traditional doctrine of biblical creation and sound reason, we cannot conceive of God's relationship to the cosmos as that of cosmic inventor without finding that divine determinism is ultimately implied. *Hence, the Cosmic Inventor model of God as the creator* ex nihilo *of the cosmos rationally requires divine determinism.*

IMPLICATIONS OF THE COSMIC AUTHOR MODEL FOR DIVINE DETERMINISM

The very nature of the Cosmic Author Model is such that divine determinism is implicit in the very description of the model. If God is the one who moment-by-moment is creating every aspect of everything that exists and every event that occurs, then clearly he determines absolutely every-thing as divine determinism suggests. Therefore, *the Cosmic Author Model entails divine determinism by definition.* If the Cosmic Author model is the true model of God's relationship to reality,[95] then it necessarily follows that divine determinism is true.

THE ARGUMENT FOR DIVINE DETERMINISM FROM THE FACT OF DIVINE CREATION

At last, we are in a position to articulate the argument for divine deter-minism from the doctrine of creation *ex nihilo* succinctly from beginning to end.

OUTLINE OF THE ARGUMENT

There exist two, and only two, models whereby one can understand the relationship between God and created reality in such a way that the con-sequent view of God is consistent with (1) the traditional Judaeo-Christian (biblical) concept of the nature of God, and (2) the traditional under-standing of the biblical doctrine of creation *ex nihilo.* These two models are (1) the Cosmic Author Model and (2) the Cosmic Inventor Model.

No matter which of the two possible models one chooses, divine deter-minism is rationally required by that model. If one chooses the Cosmic Author Model, divine determinism directly follows by definition. If one chooses the Cosmic Inventor Model, divine determinism still follows. For under the Cosmic Inventor model, the four plausible explanations for the origin of controlling natures—explanations that do not violate the doctrine of creation *ex nihilo* nor common sense—all necessitate divine determinism.

Therefore—assuming (1) that common sense is a reliable guide to truth, (2) that the traditional Judaeo-Christian conception of the nature of God is true, and (3) that absolute divine creation *ex nihilo* is true—we can-not consistently conceive of God as the creator of the world without also conceiving him to be the determiner of all that occurs in the world. In other words, *if we want to assent to creation* ex nihilo *in the context of a tra-ditional concept of God, then we are forced to embrace divine determinism.*

---

95. I believe that the Cosmic Author Model is the true model of God's relationship to reality. However, for the purposes of this chapter, I have not assumed so. For the purposes of this chap-ter, I assume that either model—the Cosmic Author Model or the Cosmic Inventor Model—may indeed be the right one.

IMPORTANT OBJECTION TO THE ARGUMENT

An important objection remains. The above argument, it could be said, proves that God determines all things, but it does not prove that he *purposes* all things. Limited determinists do not object to divine determinism's contention that God determines all things so much as they object to its contention that God actually purposes all things. The above argument from creation *ex nihilo* establishes the former, but not the latter. It has shown that the Cosmic Inventor Model necessarily entails divine determinism, but it has not shown that it entails divine *providence.*[96]

Let me illustrate this objection by returning to our analogy between God and the genius inventor of Robo-world. We have seen that, given the nature of his relationship to Robo-world, the genius inventor actually determines everything that transpires there. Everything follows necessarily (mechanically) from the initial state in which it was set in motion and from the internal programming that directs its functioning. The inventor is the direct cause of both. But it does not follow—in fact, it clearly cannot be true—that the inventor of Robo-world actually purposes everything that occurs in Robo-world. Robo-world is so incredibly complex that it simply would not be possible for the human inventor to anticipate everything that will occur as a result of his programming choices and the original state in which he put Robo-world. Indeed, it may be fair to say that the inventor can predict virtually nothing beyond the first few minutes of Robo-world's operation.

By analogy, the same could be true of God. That is to say, while his status as creator *ex nihilo* logically requires that he be the ultimate cause of everything that occurs, it does not logically require that he ultimately purpose everything that occurs. Like the human inventor of Robo-world, God may perhaps be unable to predict what the implications of his original creative choices will be. In that case, while he ultimately causes everything that occurs, he does not purpose or plan everything that occurs, for, from the beginning, he did not and could not know what the results of his creative, causative choices would be.

ANSWERING THIS OBJECTION

The problem with this objection is that it relies on a false analogy. In one crucial respect, God is not analogous to the human inventor of Robo-world. The human inventor of Robo-world is just that, *human*—with all

---

96. By 'divine providence' here I mean to describe the *purposeful* control of all cosmic events.

the finitude and limitations that that implies. God is *not* human, and he does not suffer from the characteristic finitude and limitations implied by that. Only if we are prepared to jettison the traditional conception of God as omniscient, as unlimited in his ability to know, can we legitimately draw the necessary analogy between God and this human inventor.[97]

Under a traditional conception, God—unlike the human inventor—certainly could anticipate what the ramifications of his choices will be.[98] From a knowledge of its initial state and operative principles, God would know in exact detail the entirety of cosmic history. Hence, God (as traditionally conceived) could not create the cosmos without knowing—from its initial state and controlling principles—everything that would occur within it. Hence, in creating the initial state of the cosmos, God would necessarily be purposing all that would follow in cosmic history. If he did not want a particular course of cosmic history to occur, he had the option not to create it. He was not ignorant of what his creation would entail. The fact that he did create it, therefore, necessarily requires that he purposed it.[99] For an omniscient, unlimited God—who is unlike any finite, limited human being—to determine all things is to purpose all things.

One could still argue that, while God is capable of knowing the outcome of his choices in creation, he could—through an act of self-induced forgetfulness—prevent himself from knowing their outcome. While God was capable of purposing a particular cosmic history, through such self-induced forgetfulness, he could opt to create the cosmos blindly, allowing his initial creation to simply unfold however it would. In other words, God could have created the world and, at the same time, blocked himself from being cognizant of the ramifications of his initial creative choices.

What one gains by arguing this way is difficult to determine. Is it any less problematic to have God create death, evil, and destruction as the result of willful ignorance than to have him create it purposefully? I shouldn't think so. Indeed, if death, evil, and destruction were purposeful

---

97. Interestingly, Pinnock, in his defense of an extreme limited determinist position feels compelled to deny the omniscience of God in order to hold the position he wishes to hold with logical consistency. Pinnock is to be applauded for his logical consistency and intellectual integrity in this regard. See Clark Pinnock, "God Limits His Knowledge" in *Predestination & Free Will*, edited by David and Randall Basinger (Downers Grove: InterVarsity Press, 1986).

98. Indeed, given sufficient knowledge and the aid of a computer with adequate size and speed, I could imagine myself being able to anticipate exactly what should follow by mechanical necessity from the initial state of the cosmos given the nature of its controlling principles. If I can conceive of my doing this, surely the omniscient God can do this.

99. Leibniz has seen this as clearly as any other philosopher.

creations, there is at least a possibility that God's purpose was good and
noble rather than malevolent. In that event, God would be vindicated in
his creation of these evils. But if God made a willful choice to create blindly, in complete ignorance of the results—when he had it within his power
to have perfect knowledge of the results—it is difficult to know how he
could ever be morally vindicated in the light of what has transpired. The
result of his willful ignorance includes death, evil, and destruction. If this
result is not the product of noble purposefulness, then God's experiment
of closing his eyes and creating a cosmos to see what would happen was an
absurd and irresponsible (if not evil) choice.

Furthermore, it is not altogether true—as I stated earlier—that limited
determinism's objection to divine determinism is to the notion that God
purposes all things, not to the notion that God determines all things. Later
in this book I will discuss the various objections to divine determinism.[100]
Only one of the three major objections is specifically an objection to the
notion that God purposes all things. The other two are objections to the
notion that all events are said to be determined by God—quite apart from
whether they are purposed by him.

Conclusion

One cannot embrace the traditional conception of God, the traditional doctrine of creation *ex nihilo,* and the reliability of sound reason and
common sense and, at the same time, reject divine determinism without
being intellectually irresponsible. If all of my arguments have been sound,
this conclusion follows.

Is my reasoning sound? Consider the various points at which one might
take issue with the arguments in this chapter:

1. One may, of course, reject the reliability of reason as a guide to
truth altogether. But, as we have discussed earlier, this amounts to
intellectual suicide.

2. One may reject the traditional Judaeo-Christian conception of
God.[101] This would introduce possibilities that I have not discussed. It
would be easy enough to come up with a conception of reality that does
not imply divine determinism if we are permitted to either reject or
redefine divinity.

---

100. See chapters 9,10, and 11.

101. As, for example, Clark Pinnock is prepared to do. See note 97.

3. One may reject the doctrine of creation *ex nihilo*. But it is difficult to see how one can do this and remain faithful to the biblical revelation. However, if faithfulness to biblical revelation is not important, this is an effective way to avoid divine determinism.

4. Finally, one may reject my assumption that there are two, and only two, viable models for understanding the relationship of God to his creation. (To qualify as a viable model, it must—at a bare minimum—be compatible with a traditional conception of the nature of God and with the traditional doctrine of creation *ex nihilo*.) If there exists some third model that—while meeting these criteria—portrays a plausible relationship between God and his creation, then my conclusion may not be valid. For, if this yet-to-be-discovered model should happen not to necessarily entail divine determinism, then divine determinism is *not* the only logically possible conclusion to draw from our premises. Hence, the persuasive power of my argument in this chapter rests on an important assumption: *there exists no other model whereby God's relationship to his creation can plausibly be understood that is also compatible with creation* ex nihilo *and a traditional conception of the nature of God.*

I would expect most readers to readily grant me the first three points above. The fourth point may seem less certain. Given all the requisite assumptions, divine determinism necessarily follows, according to the arguments of this chapter. Accordingly, for the typical reader, divine determinism can be rejected only if he rejects the fourth point above—that is, only if he has a reasonable basis for believing that there exists a different, viable[102] model of God's relationship to his creation that does not imply divine determinism.

Ultimately, the reader will have to satisfy himself—one way or the other. If one is willing to be hasty, it would be easy enough to simply assume that this third, yet-to-be-discovered model is still out there. But, having given it considerable thought, I am convinced no third option exists, that there is no other conceivable model that fits all the criteria.[103]

---

102. The term 'viable' here includes the suggestion that such a model is consistent with a traditional conception of the nature of God and is consistent with the biblical doctrine of creation *ex nihilo*.

103. One important factor in my confidence at this point is my observation that the two models that I have proposed—the Cosmic Author Model and the Cosmic Inventor Model—cover all the logical possibilities for the nature of created existence. Logically, current created existence functions in one of three ways: (1) autonomously, (2) *not* autonomously, or (3) in part

If I am right, then one cannot reasonably conceive of a God who is truly the biblical creator *ex nihilo* who does not determine all things. The bottom line is this: *if nothing exists that has not been created by God, then it ultimately follows that nothing transpires that has not been determined by him.*

---

autonomously and in part *not* autonomously. My two models account for all of these logical possibilities. If current created existence does *not* function autonomously, divine determinism logically follows. If current created existence *does* function autonomously, divine determinism logically follows. And if it functions autonomously in part and, in part, not, then divine determinism still logically follows. It would appear that divine determinism is logically required by all of the logical possibilities for the current state of created existence.

CHAPTER SEVEN

DOES GOD'S FOREKNOWLEDGE IMPLY DIVINE DETERMINISM?

Does the Bible teach divine determinism? In effect, "yes." It is rationally required by two fundamental biblical truths: (1) the biblical concept of God's creatorship (as traditionally understood), and (2) the biblical concept of God's ability to foreknow future events. In chapter 6, I demonstrated that God's *ex nihilo* creatorship requires divine determinism. In this chapter I shall explore the implications of God's ability to foreknow the future—specifically, whether that capability necessitates divine determinism.

Some Essential Concepts

THE CONCEPT OF DIVINE FOREKNOWLEDGE

There are countless examples of God's knowing in advance what will transpire and letting his people know through his prophets. Such is the essence of prophetic prediction.

PETER'S DENIALS AS A PARADIGM CASE

But, of all the many specific examples of divine foreknowledge in the Bible, I will focus on just one: Jesus' prophetic prediction of Peter's denying him.[104]

> "Simon, Simon, behold, Satan has demanded permission to sift you like wheat; but I have prayed for you, that your faith may not fail;[105] and you, when once you have turned again, strengthen your brothers."

104. In addition to the account I cite from the gospel of Luke, Matthew and Mark also have accounts of Jesus' predicting Peter's denials (Matt. 26:31-35; Mark 14:27-31). Whether they record exactly the same occasion of prophetic prediction is not important for my purposes here. My arguments in this chapter will focus on just that occasion and those details recorded by Luke.

105. Relative to the issue of divine determinism, this is a significant statement in its own right. According to most versions of limited determinism, Jesus would be wasting his breath to pray

And he said to Him, "Lord, with You I am ready to go both to prison and death!"

And he said, "I tell you, Peter, the cock will not crow today until you have denied three times that you know Me."

Luke 22:31-38

Jesus makes this prediction during the hours of darkness.[106] The substance of his prediction is this: "before the daylight hours have finished dawning, you—Peter—will have denied that you know me and are one of my followers on three separate occasions." As the gospel accounts record, Peter did just what Jesus predicted. Before the next day had finished dawning, Peter had denied that he even knew Jesus on three separate occasions.[107]

Two aspects of Jesus' prediction are especially significant and dramatic:

1. In this prediction, Jesus is predicting a number of future freewill decisions by another human being.[108]

---

to God that Peter's faith not fail him. A human being's response of faith to God is a freewill decision that, according to limited determinism, is out of God's hands. Whatever God might cause and control, he does not cause and control our response of faith to him. If limited determinists were right in this respect, Jesus' prayer that God preserve Peter's freewill choice such that he continue in faith is inexplicable. It would be a prayer to God for something over which he has no control. Under a divine determinist understanding, on the other hand, Jesus' prayer makes perfectly good sense.

106. Specifically, it is late at night on the day before he was arrested or early in the morning (shortly after midnight) of the very day of his arrest. In reading the gospel accounts, one must remember that the Jews marked the beginning of their day at sundown. Hence, whether it was before or after midnight, by their reckoning this prediction would fall on the same day as Jesus' arrest.

107. I realize that it is a point of controversy whether the gospel accounts offer a coherent and consistent account of Peter's denials. I cannot take the time here to defend my belief that they do. Some Bible students have proposed harmonizations of the four gospel accounts of Peter's denials that are, in fact, rather artificial and contrived. For example, the proposal by Johnston M. Cheyney is rather contrived and forced. See Johnston M. Cheyney, *The Life of Christ In Stereo* (Portland: Western Baptist Seminary Press, 1969), 218-220. But these less than convincing proposals do not exhaust the possibilities for how the accounts could be harmonized. In a paper available through McKenzie Study Center, 1883 University St., Eugene, OR, 97403, I propose a harmonization which I believe to be both plausible and exegetically responsible.

108. Actually, it predicts several different freewill decisions by several different people. The complexity that that introduces makes Jesus' prediction all the more remarkable.

2. Jesus' prediction is sufficiently detailed that it specifies a time span within which these freewill choices are to occur. Specifically, it predicts that these freewill choices will occur before the second occasion of a cock crowing during the upcoming dawn.[109] Significantly, this rules out Jesus' prediction being a product of normal human intelligence. It is not explainable in terms of Jesus' astute insight into Peter's character. Undoubtedly he had such astute insight. But that alone cannot account for Jesus specifically predicting the number of occasions and timing of Peter's denials.

With these things in mind, I will use Jesus' prediction of Peter's denials as a paradigm or model case for all the prophetic predictions we find in the Bible. What the instances of prophetic prediction in the past show— to one degree or another—is that God had infallible, detailed knowledge of those predicted events while those events were yet to occur, while they were yet in the future. Even more importantly, they show that God had infallible, detailed knowledge of future freewill decisions yet to be made by human beings. This point is crucial. God's ability to foreknow freewill decisions is what creates an insoluble problem for limited determinism.

In my paradigm case, Jesus' prediction clearly reflects God's detailed, infallible knowledge: God knew that Peter would be in situations during the night where his association with Jesus would be suspected, he knew on exactly how many occasions Peter would be confronted with this suspicion, and he knew the chronology in sufficient detail to predict that it would occur prior to the second time the cock would crow the next morning.

From examples like this paradigm case, it should be clear that there can be no question with regard to *whether* God can infallibly know and predict the future. The question is *how*? What is it about God and his relationship to future events that makes divine foreknowledge possible?

EXAMINING SOME KEY CONCEPTS

Before I can answer this question, I need to define some terms and introduce some concepts. These will provide me with the conceptual language I need to construct my argument for divine determinism.

---

109. The specific detail that the denials would occur *before the second occasion of a cock crowing* was not a part of the prediction as Luke records it. It is a detail included in the prediction that Matthew and Mark record. (*Cf.*, Matt. 26:31-35; Mark 14:27-31)

Accordingly, the first portion of this chapter is a miscellany of observations, definitions, and concepts. Their relevance will only become evident when I employ these concepts in the argument that follows. I begin my investigation by introducing two models of divine foreknowledge—the Divine Clairvoyance Model and the Divine Disclosure Model. Next, I introduce the concepts of EVENT CLOSEDNESS and EVENT OPENNESS. Only then do I lay out my specific argument that divine determinism necessarily follows from divine foreknowledge.

TWO MODELS OF DIVINE FOREKNOWLEDGE

How is it that God is able to know the future in advance and predict what lies ahead? And of special importance, how can God know in advance what the freewill choices of human beings will be?[110] Since this last question is particularly problematic, our discussion will focus on it specifically. Our task, then, is to explain how God can possibly make a valid knowledge claim about a future event that is utterly dependent upon the freewill choices of human beings. There are really only two plausible explanations:[111]

1. God is the one who plans the future and will cause it to happen and bring it into being. He can predict in advance what will transpire precisely because he is the one who, when the time comes, will cause it to transpire in accordance with what he has planned. In other words, divine determinism is true. Accordingly, God can predict the future because he is the one who will totally determine it.[112] This option I call

---

110. One medieval answer to this question was that God can know the freewill choices of human beings because of his "middle knowledge." This answer has an appeal to certain modern Christians as well. For a discussion of whether middle knowledge is a helpful concept for explaining God's ability to foreknow the future, see appendix I.

111. This is a crucial assumption; my argument is vulnerable at this point—it depends on their being only two plausible options. If I have neglected a third serious option, then it is a distinct possibility that my argument is fallacious. However, I am confident that there is no viable third option.

112. Actually, an objection can be raised at this point: Even if we grant that God plans the future and is capable of bringing his plans to pass, that, in and of itself, does not necessarily entail divine determinism. For example, what if man makes autonomous choices that are not divinely determined, but God, who does determine man's physical environment, is able to so skillfully control that environment such that he can manipulate a man into making exactly that choice he wants him to make. In such a case, God can predict the future because he plans and controls it; but it would not be true that human choices are divinely determined. Hence, the Divine

the DIVINE DISCLOSURE MODEL. According to this model, prophetic prediction happens when the God who causes and determines all things discloses to his spokesman, the prophet, some specific aspect of what he, God, plans to cause to transpire in the course of cosmic history.

Note what is explicitly included as part of the definition of this model: *if a cosmic event is predicted by God, it must be the case that that event is caused (or determined) by God.* If God knows and can predict a future event precisely because he is the one planning and bringing to pass every specific detail constituting that event, then it directly follows that God does determine that event.

2. God has the ability to "see" every future event just as if it were a past event. This possibility I call the DIVINE CLAIRVOYANCE MODEL. According to this model, regardless of what cause, combination of causes, or absence of causes may give rise to a future historical event, God has the ability to "see" that future event just as surely as if it were a past event that he once witnessed and now vividly remembers. So even if a future event were uncaused and random, God could still know about its every detail, for he can "see" it or witness it in advance of its occurring in history.

The very point of this model is to find an explanation for divine foreknowledge that—unlike the Divine Disclosure Model—does not necessitate divine determinism. Hence, an implicit assumption within this model is that certain of the future events that God foreknows are, nevertheless, not caused or determined by him.

THE CONCEPT OF EVENT OPENNESS OR CLOSEDNESS

Consider Peter's denials of Jesus from Jesus' perspective at the time of his prediction—namely, as a future event. What were the prospects for Peter's denying Jesus in the future exactly as Jesus was predicting? If it was utterly impossible for Peter to do anything other than what Jesus was pre-

---

Disclosure Model could be true without divine determinism being true. My answer to this objection is simply that this suggested alternative to divine determinism—namely, that God controls human choices through infallible manipulation rather than through divine determination—should certainly be just as (if not more) problematic to the limited determinist as divine determinism is. If it can be argued that divine determinism precludes free will, then surely it can be argued that infallible divine manipulation precludes free will even more so. In any event, divine manipulation *is*, in fact, both unbiblical and uncommonsensical; for it contradicts the commonsensical and biblical teaching that man's choices are free and that man is accountable for them.

dicting, then the event was what I will call a CLOSED event. On the other hand, to whatever extent it was possible for Peter not to do what Jesus was predicting, to that extent it was what I will call an OPEN event. To put it another way: if an event is in some sense necessary, then it is closed; if it is in some sense not necessary, then it is open.

The Concept of Logical Openness or Closedness

Peter's denial of Jesus was a LOGICALLY OPEN event if it was logically possible[113] for Peter to do other than deny Jesus—that is, to do other than was being predicted. If Peter's denying Jesus was done out of logical necessity—i.e., if it was logically impossible for him not to do it—then it was a LOGICALLY CLOSED event.[114]

If I should predict that, tomorrow, two plus two will equal four, my prediction would be the prediction of a logically closed event. It is logically impossible for two plus two to fail to equal four tomorrow. Hence, it is logically closed. Similarly, if Peter's denial of Jesus (as viewed from the standpoint of Jesus' predicting it) was logically necessary (in the same vein as the logical necessity of two plus two equaling four), then it was logically closed. But if Peter's failure to deny Jesus would have done no violence to the laws of logic, as such, then it was a logically open event.

Common sense tells us that Peter's choice to deny Jesus was, of course, a logically open event. When we understand something to be a freewill choice (as was Peter's choice), we mean, in part, that it is not being necessitated by the laws of logic. For Peter *not* to deny Jesus was just as possible, logically, as was denying him. Neither was logically necessary.

---

113. By 'logically possible' I simply mean that it is possible without violating the laws of logic (those laws which any system of formal logic is attempting to systematically define). It is not possible for 2+2 to not equal 4 on logical grounds. The *definition* of two, the *definition* of addition, the *definition* of equality, and the *definition* of four all logically entail that 2+2 = 4. It is logically impossible for it to be otherwise. It is not that 2+2=4 just because "that's the way it is in this world"; rather, 2+2=4 *logically MUST BE that way* in this world. I am not denying that we could have a different name for '2', '+', '=', and '4'. Certainly we could call them something else. But the concept '2' (whatever we might name it), the concept '4' (whatever we might name it), the concept '+' (whatever we might name it), and the concept '=' (whatever we might name it) must always be related to one another such that 2+2=4.

114. For the sake of completeness we could include a separate discussion of the concept of ontological openness/closedness (or, metaphysical openness/closedness). However, for the purposes of this chapter, any definition I might give to ontological (metaphysical) openness/closedness would render it sufficiently akin to the concept of logical openness/closedness that it is not particularly helpful to distinguish them. Hence, I shall define logical necessity broadly enough in this chapter to include what one might rather call ontological or metaphysical necessity.

The Concept of Mechanical Openness or Closedness

Peter's denial of Jesus was a MECHANICALLY OPEN event if it was *mechanically* possible for Peter to do other than was predicted. But if it was *mechanically* necessary for him to deny Jesus—i.e., if it was mechanically impossible for him *not* to do it—then it was a *mechanically closed* event.

By 'mechanically possible,' I mean possible with respect to the physical and spiritual laws that govern our existence. The physical laws of nature are the most obvious example. To whatever extent it is impossible for physical laws to be violated, to that same extent physical laws make certain aspects of certain events physically (and mechanically) necessary. If there are analogous laws of a spiritual nature (and I am not assuming that there are), then, by 'mechanical necessity,' I mean necessity with respect to these natural and supernatural laws, combined.

The point, very simply, is this: Some things happen as the result of the mechanical outworking of basic laws or principles built into reality. If an event is the result of such a mechanical outworking, then it is mechanically necessary, or mechanically closed. If it is not, then it is mechanically open.

If I predict that, tomorrow, the earth will rotate on its axis, my prediction is the prediction of a mechanically closed event. It is mechanically impossible for the earth not to rotate on its axis tomorrow.[115] Hence, it is mechanically closed. Similarly, if it had been mechanically impossible (in similar vein to the impossibility of the earth's not rotating on its axis) for Peter *not* to deny Jesus, then it would have been a mechanically closed event. However, if Peter's not denying Jesus would have done no violence to any mechanical laws of the cosmos, as such, then it was a mechanically open event.

The natural determinist would say that Peter's denials *were* a mechanically closed event. His denials were the mechanical result of physical laws operating within his brain and body to produce a mechanically determined result. Hence, the denials were mechanically necessary. As we shall see, both limited determinism and divine determinism agree—against natural determinism—that Peter's denials were mechanically open. He did not act out of mechanical necessity. He made a freewill decision. And that,

---

115. I assume, in this example, the inviolability of certain physical laws. The question of the strict inviolability of physical laws is more complex than we need to get into here. For the sake of argument, I simply assume it, knowing that the truth of the matter is more complex than that. Leibniz's view of natural laws as "subsidiary general principles" is, I think, a helpful understanding of the status of natural laws. There is such a thing as mechanical inviolability, on the one hand, but it is too simplistic to see that inviolability as occurring at the level of the formulated laws of physics. Miracles are possible, in part, precisely because the formulated laws of physics are not the most basic, inviolable rational principles.

by definition, precludes the decision's being mechanically determined. For, to identify a decision as a freewill decision is—at least in part—to assert that it was physically and mechanically possible for the decision to have been other than what it was. This, I submit, is a commonsensical understanding of free will.[116]

The Concept of Theological Openness or Closedness

Finally, Peter's denial of Jesus was a *theologically open* event if it was *theologically* possible for Peter to do otherwise than predicted. But if it was done out of *theological* necessity—that is, if it was theologically impossible for him not to deny Jesus—then it was a *theologically closed* event.

When I speak of theological possibility, I am referring to its possibility with respect to the will and purpose of God. Some things result from the divine will unfailingly accomplishing its purposes. If an event results from such divine governance, and, hence, cannot fail to come to pass without violating the inviolable will of God, then it is theologically necessary, or theologically closed. If it does not result from the inviolable outworking of God's will, then it is theologically open.

If I predict that Jesus shall return, my prediction is the prediction of a theologically closed event. It is theologically impossible for our Lord not to return, for Jesus' return is an unchangeable aspect of the divine resolve. Hence, it is theologically closed. Similarly, if Peter's denials of Jesus were *theologically necessary* (in a vein similar to the necessity of the Lord's return), then those denials would have been theologically closed events. But, if Peter's *not* denying Jesus would have done no violence to the purposive divine governance of human events, then those denials were theologically open events. In other words, so far as the unfailing purposes of God were concerned, it would have been possible for Peter not to have denied our Lord.

The basic difference between the perspectives of limited determinism and divine determinism comes to this: divine determinism views Peter's denials (even from Jesus' vantage point as he is predicting them) as theologically closed events—for it holds all freewill decisions to be theologically-closed; but limited determinism would insist that his denials were theologically open events. Most forms of limited determinism, as we have seen, insist that human freewill choice is autonomous from divine causation.

Our two models for understanding divine foreknowledge and prophet-

---

116. As will become clear, my ultimate objection to natural determinism is that it violates common sense.

ic prediction directly reflect this same basic difference. The Divine Disclosure Model assumes that all events, including freewill decisions, are theologically closed. The Divine Clairvoyance Model insists that at least some of those events that God foreknows are theologically open—namely, events that are dependent on freewill choices.

THE INDEPENDENCE OF THE VARIOUS FORMS OF EVENT OPENNESS/CLOSEDNESS

Before I leave this subject, I must make something explicit: logical, mechanical, and theological openness (or closedness) are independent of one another. *It is entirely possible for an event to be closed in one of these senses while being open in the others.*

Events controlled by natural laws—for example, the law of gravity—are a case in point. It is *logically* possible for events not to be controlled by the law of gravity as we know it.[117] At the same time, given the cosmos as it is, this would not be *mechanically* possible. Natural events are, of mechanical necessity, subject to the law of gravity. Hence, the effect of gravity in a natural event is *logically open* while being *mechanically closed.*

This Independence as Crucial to the Distinction between Divine and Natural Determinism

Acknowledging this independence of the various forms of event openness and closedness is crucial. One of the greatest obstacles to the acceptance of divine determinism is the propensity to confuse it with natural determinism. Because the divine determinist wants to maintain the *theological* closedness of all cosmic events, it is assumed that he is espousing their *mechanical* closedness as well (i.e., natural determinism). But, to the contrary, the divine determinist wants to maintain the theological closedness of *all* cosmic events while maintaining—at the same time—the mechanical openness of *some* of those events (namely, freewill events). The limited determinist is willing to acknowledge that a natural event may be *mechanically* CLOSED while being *logically* OPEN. Analogously, the divine determinist asks us to acknowledge that a freewill event may be *theologically* CLOSED while being *mechanically* OPEN.

---

117. That is to say, we are not being illogical when we imagine a radically different sort of cosmos where the law of gravity (in the form we know it) does not apply. By way of contrast, we are being illogical when we imagine a cosmos where the law of contradiction does not apply. Where, for example, what does not exist exists.

As a case in point, consider divine determinism's perspective on Peter's denials. What if Peter had mustered up his courage to acknowledge his relationship to Jesus rather than deny it? Everyone can agree that there would have been no violence done to the laws of logic had he done so. Neither would there have been any violence done to the laws of physics. But, unlike the limited determinist, the divine determinist maintains that, had Peter done so, it would have been a violation of the inviolable will and purpose of God. Therefore, whereas Peter's denials were not logically or mechanically necessary, they were (according to divine determinism) theologically necessary. Whereas Peter's denials were logically and mechanically open, they were theologically closed. Hence, it was *logically* and *mechanically* possible that Jesus' prediction fail, but it was *not theologically* possible that it fail. Theologically, his denials *had to be*. The unfailing purpose of God had ordained it, and God was committed to causing it.

Both natural and divine determinism, therefore, maintain that Peter's denials of Jesus were inevitable. But there is a very important difference between divine and natural determinism: while natural determinism suggests that Peter's denials were inevitable because they were MECHANICALLY CLOSED, divine determinism suggests that Peter's denials were inevitable because they were THEOLOGICALLY CLOSED, while being MECHANICALLY OPEN.

As will become clear, this is at the heart of the most serious problem limited determinists have with divine determinism. The limited determinist rejects the notion that an event can be theologically closed while being logically and mechanically open. He insists that such is not possible. If an event is theologically closed, then, of necessity, it must be mechanically and/or logically closed as well. God closes an event (theologically) precisely by closing it mechanically or logically. Furthermore—claims the limited determinist—since divine determinism affirms that every event in human experience is theologically closed, it cannot make any sense out of the notions of logical and mechanical openness. If an event is closed by the determinative will of God, how can it make any sense to speak of it as being mechanically (or, logically) open?

On the other side of the issue, the divine determinist claims that an event can be theologically closed while being mechanically open. Further, he insists that he can make perfectly good sense out of the notions of logical and mechanical openness even though all events are theologically closed.

According to divine determinism, when God wills an event, he chooses among a set of alternatives, all of which are logically and mechanically possible. (In general, of course, he does not consider options that are logically and mechanically impossible.)[118] If God has only one logically-possible alternative available to him, then, of course, his choice is already decided for him by the dictates of logic.[119] In other words, his choice is logically determined, it is logically closed. Likewise, if God has only one mechanically-possible alternative available to him, then, of course, his choice is already decided by the mechanics of the situation.[120] The choice is mechanically determined, it is mechanically closed. In this way, says the divine determinist, a meaningful distinction can be made between events that are logically and/or mechanically closed, on the one hand, and those that are logically and/or mechanically open, on the other hand, even though they are both theologically closed. A mechanically (or, logically) closed event is an event that was mechanically (or, logically) closed to God as he contemplated his options for how to shape cosmic affairs. A mechanically (or, logically) open event was correspondingly open to God as he contemplated his options.

We can summarize our point this way: the divine determinist insists that any given freewill event is theologically closed (bound to be that way and no other because God has willed it), yet he is in no way suggesting that it is logically or mechanically closed (bound to be that way and no other because there exists no other logical or mechanical possibility open to God in directing human affairs). The contrast between this and natural determinism needs to be kept firmly in mind. Natural determinism explicitly espouses the *mechanical* closedness of freewill events.

EVENT OPENNESS OVER TIME

Time is one of the most mysterious aspects of reality. One of its mysteries is the transformation that occurs in the status of events by virtue of the passing of time. Consider our paradigm case:

---

118. I discuss in chapter 3 why God would not choose a logically impossible event. The question of whether God would ever choose a mechanically impossible event is a very complex question. See note 115 above.

119. For example, if God has already determined that X will exist, then the existence of X is a logically closed fact. God does not have the option of having X not exist. He could, in the future, have X cease to exist; but he cannot now have X exist and not exist simultaneously.

120. For example, if God has X fall from a tree, pulled by the law of gravity, then—without violating the physical structure of the cosmos which he has willed into being—God cannot choose to have X not fall toward the ground. That is, he cannot choose to have X hang suspended in mid-air. X's falling toward the ground, therefore, is the only alternative open to God—if he is to preserve the integrity of the created structure of the physical cosmos. In this regard, however, see note 115 above.

When we consider Peter's denials as being a future event (looking at them from the same standpoint Jesus did when he was predicting them), we notice that the event of his denials is a logically open event, a mechanically open event, and perhaps (if limited determinism is true) a theologically open event. That is to say, it is logically and mechanically possible that Peter will not deny Jesus; and perhaps it is possible that Peter's denial is not necessitated by the will of God.

Time passes. We arrive at the present—the actual occasion of Peter's denying Jesus—and move on into the future. Looking back on Peter's denials as a past event, we notice that its status has changed dramatically. The event of Peter's denials (which had been open before it occurred) is now an absolutely closed event.[121] That Peter did not *then* deny Jesus is not *now* LOGICALLY possible.[122] It is not *now* MECHANICALLY possible to change the fact that Peter *then* denied his Lord.[123] Neither is it THEOLOGICALLY possible to change the past event.[124] The event of Peter's denials of Jesus has been transformed through the passing of time. It has changed from a largely, if not absolutely, open event to an absolutely closed event.

This, indeed, is the nature of all cosmic experience. By the judgment of common sense, the future is largely, if not completely, open. But, in the present, the events of cosmic history become closed—fixed in metaphysical concrete. Out of all the possibilities for what could have been, some events become selected in the occurrences of the present and become established as components of actual, concrete reality. The past is the reality that results. The events of the past are absolutely closed and unchangeable, having become permanent, concrete reality by the magic of time.

---

121. I define 'absolutely closed' as simultaneously closed in all three of the senses I have defined above—logically, mechanically, and theologically.

122. It is now logically impossible for the past event of Peter's denying Jesus not to have occurred when it did. To say that past event X—which by virtue of the definition of a past event means that it occurred at some determinate time in the past—never occurred would be to formulate a contradiction—namely, past event X is NOT a past event.

123. It is now mechanically impossible for the past event of Peter's denying Jesus to be made to have never occurred when it did. No mechanical principles in the cosmos give one the means to transform a past event such that it can be made to have never occurred.

124. The will and purposes of God cannot *now* determine that the past event of Peter's denying Jesus never have occurred.

Argument For Divine Determinism

Having introduced the two models of divine foreknowledge and examined the notions of event openness and event closedness, I can now make my case for divine determinism in the light of divine foreknowledge. I proceed by defending a series of seven propositions, each one building on the previous ones and culminating in an affirmation of divine determinism.

FIRST PROPOSITION

PROPOSITION #1: *Knowledge of an event necessitates some sort of closedness to that event.*

When we speak of having knowledge of an event, we cannot validly do so unless that event is, in some sense, closed.[125] It may be theologically closed. It may be mechanically closed. It may be logically closed. But it must be closed in at least one of these senses before it is subject to a valid knowledge claim.

To see this, we need only observe that a valid knowledge claim involves, by definition, a proposition that is true. A claim that is false is not a valid knowledge claim. But, even more importantly, a claim that cannot be established either way (that is, as either true or false) cannot be a valid knowledge claim either. What I mean is this: if nothing determines, in principle, whether a claim is true or false, then it cannot constitute a valid knowledge claim.[126] It is not a matter of the human knower not being able to determine the truth-value of the claim—that is, whether it is true or false. Rather, it is a matter of its truth-value, *per se*, being indeterminate.

---

125. Strictly speaking, I should speak of *aspects* of events rather than *events per se*. Different events have different aspects to them and different aspects of the same event may differ in their status—that is, with respect to whether they are closed or open and in what sense they are closed or open. But to avoid being tedious, I am simply going to refer to events as if they were simple and not complex. The reader can keep in mind that what I really mean are particular, simple aspects of a given event. This short-hand does not affect the nature of my argument in any way. I use it merely for convenience.

126. Students of the history of logic may conclude that I am agreeing with Aristotelian logic against Stoic logic in this regard. In a sense this is true. However, as a divine determinist, I will ultimately maintain that there is no proposition about the future whose veracity cannot be determined in principle. In this regard, therefore, my position is more akin to that of the Stoics than it is to Aristotle. But whereas the Stoics believe in *logical* determinism, I am an advocate of *divine* determinism; these are significantly different positions.

The human knower cannot determine whether it is true or false precisely because nothing in reality has established it as either true or false. In such a case, to make a valid knowledge claim about the event is not possible. A valid knowledge claim must be one that is fixedly true, in principle.[127] When the claim itself is, in principle, neither true nor false, then such a claim cannot legitimately be called knowledge.

Consider our paradigm example. When I claim now to know that Peter denied Jesus, I make a valid knowledge claim precisely because Peter's denial of Jesus has, in truth, been established as a fact of history. In other words, Peter's denial is now a closed event. It, like all historical events, is ABSOLUTELY closed. But if I were to claim to know that you, the reader, will deny Jesus tomorrow, and if nothing in reality makes your denial a closed event[128] —i.e., neither God, physics, nor logic definitively necessitate your denying Jesus tomorrow—then I am being absurd. The event itself is not closed; it is not fixed in reality as fact; it is not made inevitable by some present aspect of reality. In truth, you may or you may not deny Jesus tomorrow. Accordingly, any claim that I might make about it could turn out to be true, but it could just as easily turn out to be false. Time and the unfolding of cosmic events will tell which. In the meantime, no valid knowledge of the event is possible. For how can I claim to have knowledge of the facts when the facts could turn out either way? By definition, a VALID knowledge claim is one that asserts something that reality dictates must be true.

SECOND PROPOSITION

PROPOSITION #2: *The Divine Disclosure Model is the only rationally acceptable model for explaining how divine foreknowledge is possible.*

As mentioned earlier, any viable explanation of divine foreknowledge must be able to account for the foreknowledge of events that are shaped by man's freewill choices. Most instances of prophetic prediction are pre-

---

127. Again, I do not mean that it must, as a practical matter, be one that the knower can justify—though that may be true also. Rather, I mean that—whether it can be practically justified or not— it must, as a matter of principle, either correspond to an established fact of reality or not correspond to that established fact of reality.

128. Note, I am NOT hypothesizing that I do not *know* of anything that would make your denial a closed event—although that may very well be required for a valid knowledge claim as well. Rather, I am hypothesizing that there *does not exist* anything in reality that would make your denial a closed event.

dictions of just this type of event. In the discussion that follows, only such instances are in view. How can God have foreknowledge of events that have been shaped by the freewill choices of men?

That future freewill events are absolutely open events is built-in to the very assumptions of the Divine Clairvoyance Model (and to the limited determinist perspective that supports it). Freewill events are not closed in any sense whatsoever. They are not closed logically or mechanically, for our commonsensical understanding of free will precludes that.[129] But—according to the assumptions of limited determinism—neither are they closed theologically. That freewill choices are not necessitated by the will of God is a foundational assumption of limited determinism. Furthermore, the very point of the Divine Clairvoyance Model is to offer an explanation of divine foreknowledge that does not require the divine determination of freewill choices. Hence, under the assumptions of this model, future freewill choices are not closed events in any sense at all.

The Divine Disclosure Model, on the other hand, holds that every divinely foreknown freewill event (as is true of all events) is in some sense closed. Whereas freewill events are acknowledged to be logically and mechanically open, no events—including freewill events—are acknowledged to be theologically open. By the assumptions of this model, all events are caused by God. Some events—for example, natural occurrences—may be mechanically (and perhaps logically) closed as well. But all events are, at the very least, THEOLOGICALLY closed.

Proposition #1 states that knowledge of an event necessitates some sort of closedness to that event. In view of that, predictive knowledge of future freewill choices is impossible under the Divine Clairvoyance Model. Under it, freewill choices are absolutely open events. According to proposition #1, no valid knowledge claim can be made of an absolutely open event. Therefore, under the Divine Clairvoyance Model, a valid prophetic knowledge claim with regard to future freewill events is not possible.[130]

Under the Divine Disclosure Model, on the other hand, such a knowledge claim is possible. Under that model, every event (including future freewill choices) is a closed event. Hence, according to it, all future events

---

129. Chapter 9 will discuss this and other ramifications of our commonsense conception of a freewill choice in more detail.

130. That is, it is not possible unless one—in order to preserve the theological openness of future freewill events—is willing to believe that future freewill events are either logically or mechanically closed—that is to say, unless one is willing to embrace either logical determinism or natural determinism. It is ironic that limited determinism can only avoid divine determinism by embracing natural determinism or logical determinism (its "natural enemies").

(including freewill events) meet the requirement of proposition #1 for a valid knowledge claim.

As we have seen, in order for an explanation of divine foreknowledge and prophetic prediction to be rationally and biblically adequate, it needs to be able to account for valid knowledge claims about future freewill choices. The Divine Clairvoyance Model cannot do this. The Divine Disclosure Model can. If these are the only two plausible explanations,[131] then—given that the Divine Clairvoyance Model is rationally unacceptable—it follows that *the Divine Disclosure Model is the only rationally acceptable explanation of divine foreknowledge and prophetic prediction.*

OBJECTION TO THIS ARGUMENT

At this point, one might object that I have dismissed the Divine Clairvoyance Model too hastily. I rejected it on the grounds that, by its own assumptions, it views future freewill events as absolutely open. But what if future freewill events are *not* open events under the Divine Clairvoyance Model? What if the situation is more complex than that?

Here is the problem: When one says that the Divine Clairvoyance Model views future freewill events as absolutely open, it does so from the standpoint of the human observer. Granted—from a human being's point of view in the present—future freewill events are absolutely open events. But what about from God's vantage point? From Jesus' perspective, Peter's denials were an open event. Was it so from God's vantage point as well? Or could it be that God was in a different time frame altogether and was not limited by the same standpoint in time that restricted Jesus' perspective?[132] If so, what would the status of this future (to Jesus) freewill event be from God's vantage point?

The present, like some sort of reality-creating machine, grinds forward into the future, turning future non-existent events into past actually-existing events. The present is a sort of metaphysical watershed. As Jesus stands in his present and looks past-ward, he sees freewill events that exist as actual and real closed events. As he looks future-ward, he sees no freewill events having any reality or actual existence; he sees event-openness. On Jesus'

---

131. See note 110.

132. That is, what if God is outside time altogether or is in an entirely different time frame from the one we are in? That is, what if God can arrive at knowledge from the standpoint of another, different time frame from ours at the same time that he has access to ours and can exist, act, and communicate within it?

time frame (the human time frame), his present time marks the transition between event openness and event closedness.[133] (See Diagram 7.1)

JESUS' TIME FRAME

Jesus' Past	Jesus' Future
Jesus' Present	Time of Peter's Denials

Diagram 7.1   Solid Line = Event Closedness
Broken Line = Event Openness

Now perhaps God, having access to an altogether different time frame, is able to adopt any point in the sequence of cosmic events as his present vantage point. That is, perhaps, God can "travel" through the sequence of cosmic history by means of another time frame and arrive at a point in that sequence of events that, though in the future to Jesus, becomes his (God's) present. Could it be that, as God passes through the sequence of cosmic events, events that Jesus will pass through in his future, these events become closed relative to God in exactly the same way that those same events will become closed relative to Jesus as his present moves on into the future? If so, then the same cosmic event (*e.g.*, Peter's denials) could be an open event to Jesus while being, at the same time, a closed event to God as he observes it from his distinctive standpoint relative to time. (See Diagram 7.2)

If this were so, then the argument against Divine Clairvoyance on the grounds that future freewill events are absolutely open would not hold. To God, the one who has foreknowledge of the event, these same future freewill events are absolutely closed events. They would be, as it were, past events to God. In this case, the requirement of proposition #1 is met. God—the one making the knowledge claim—is claiming to know something about what is, to him, an absolutely closed event. Therefore, in light of the possibility that God knows the sequence of cosmic events in Jesus' future from the standpoint of an altogether different time frame from the one Jesus is in, Divine Clairvoyance cannot be ruled out. It cannot be judged rationally unacceptable.

---

133. Speaking specifically of freewill events according to the basic assumptions of the Divine Clairvoyance Model.

ANSWERING THIS OBJECTION

Fundamentally, the answer to this objection rests in the fact that what marks the transition between event openness and event closedness is not the position of the observer in the sequence of cosmic events, it is the position of the participants in those events.

GOD'S TIME FRAME

Diagram 7.2   Solid Line = Event Closedness
                Broken Line = Event Openness

Why is it that our present time seems to be the point at which events pass out of the openness of the future into the closedness of the past? Is it because the present is the point on our time frame from which we observe cosmic events? Or is it because it is the point at which we create cosmic events—the point when cosmic events actually enter into existence? Surely, the transition from event openness to event closedness is found wherever the creators of cosmic events are acting and making choices. Our viewing cosmic events from the present is not the relevant factor in the open future becoming closed. Rather, it is the fact that we create cosmic events in the present that makes this so. The past is closed and the future is open because the present is that point in the march of time that our creation of cosmic events has reached.[134]

---

134. To begin with, I think it commonsensical that freewill events are caused and created by the freewill choices of human beings. Hence, if the determinative freewill choices have not been made, then it follows that the events which they create do not yet exist. As we shall see later, this is not in conflict with divine determinism. Divine determinism does not deny the decisive role of human free will as the cause of freewill events; it simply asserts a more ultimate cause behind the direct cause of freewill choice. But apart from common sense, given the foundational assumptions of limited determinism, the conclusion that freewill events gain their facticity—their closedness—from freewill choices and not from divine observation should be particularly appealing to the limited determinist. Limited determinism is consciously trying to avoid the suggestion that God causes freewill events in any sense whatsoever. The limited determinist favors

It is fallacious, therefore, to think that some observer on an altogether different time frame could experience, as closed events, events that are open (because they are future) to us. Even if God is on another time frame and even if God could, by virtue of that different time frame, adopt a present vantage point somewhere in our future, he would nevertheless not be able to observe events in our future as closed events. For his vantage point is not what marks the transition between the openness and closedness of cosmic events. God's presence at and observation of human events is not what gives actuality (or closedness) to the events of human history; the human actors do. God's presence as an observer cannot bring history into being. If the human actors have not been there to create it, then history is not yet there to be observed, it has not yet occurred. So even if God could travel into our future, he would find that there was nothing there to see.[135] The future has not occurred; the sequence of actual cosmic events does not include any events beyond our present. (Compare Diagrams 7.3 and 7.4)

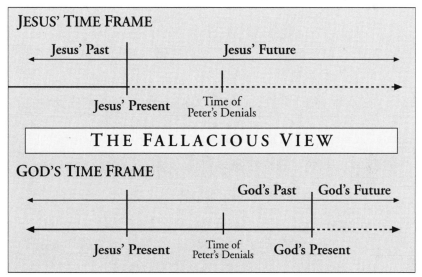

Diagram 7.3   Solid Line = Event Closedness
                 Broken Line = Event Openness

This fallacious view suggests that God's standpoint in the sequence of events marks the transition from event openness to event closedness. Note the solid line to the left of God's present.

---

the view that human beings autonomously cause freewill events. Hence, the view that the human actor (and not the divine observer) causes freewill events to come into being is very compatible with the limited determinist's fundamental agenda.

135. Clearly, then, divine foreknowledge must be qualitatively different from viewing future events as already there. This is the advantage of the Divine Disclosure Model over the Divine

Our rejection of the Divine Clairvoyance Model still stands. Since the true demarcation between event closedness and event openness lies in present time on the human time frame, proposing a different time frame for God does not change the fact that, under the Divine Clairvoyance Model, God would not be able to make any valid knowledge claims about freewill events that lie in our future. Future freewill events are absolutely open events (by the assumptions of the Divine Clairvoyance Model) precisely because they do lie in *our* future. Whether they lie in God's future is irrelevant. Regardless of where God situates himself in the sequence of cosmic events to observe them, the status of those events is nonetheless determined by the situation of the human actors, not by the situation of the divine observer. If the events have not yet been created, then God cannot make a valid claim to know about them on the basis of his having perceived them. *God cannot see what does not exist.* The Divine Clairvoyance Model, then, cannot account for divine foreknowledge of future freewill events. The Divine Disclosure Model, therefore, is the only rationally acceptable model for explaining how divine foreknowledge is possible.

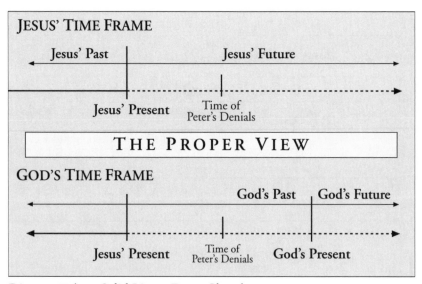

Diagram 7.4   Solid Line = Event Closedness
               Broken Line = Event Openness

This proper view suggests that our location in the sequence of events marks the transition from event openness to event closedness regardless of where God's standpoint might be located in the sequence of events. Note the broken line to the left of God's present.

FURTHER OBJECTION TO THIS ARGUMENT

The objector may still think that we have been too hasty. Granted, the true demarcation between event closedness and event openness lies in the present on the human time frame. Accordingly, when Jesus predicts Peter's denials, the future event of Peter denying Jesus cannot be closed—even to God. The future is, by its very nature, open. But what if all of reality exists in a multitude of different time frames. In that case, while the event of Peter denying Jesus is open in the time frame within which Jesus is making the prediction, it could be closed in an entirely different time frame. In this entirely different time frame, Peter could be actually present, denying Jesus. In this case, God's clairvoyance is plausible. Because he could transcend all the different time frames in which Peter exists, God could "view" the event within a time frame in which either (i) Peter is presently making his choice to deny Jesus, or (ii) Peter is looking back on his choice to deny Jesus as a past event. In either case, Peter's denial of Jesus would be a closed event that is determinate and available as an object of God's knowledge.

Under such a hypothesis, therefore, our rejection of divine clairvoyance would be unfounded. Our previous rejection of divine clairvoyance hinged on the fact that future events are not closed and, hence, not available as objects of divine knowledge. That is, since Peter did not exist in his future, he was not there to "close" the event of his denying Jesus through his freewill choices. But the notion being proposed here is that, as a matter of fact, Peter did exist in his future and he was there, making the freewill choice that closed the event of his denying Jesus. Granted, Peter was not there in the future of our ordinary historical time frame—the one in which he and Jesus lived. But in another time frame he was there, he did exist, and he was present—relative to that time frame—making the freewill choice that would put in historical concrete his denial of the Lord. Hence, Peter's denial of Jesus can be future (open) to him in one time frame while being past (closed) to him in another time frame. Under such an assumption, divine clairvoyance would, in fact, be plausible. If God transcended all possible time frames and had access to any and every one of them, then it would be possible for him to view the event of Peter's denying Jesus within whatever time frame was necessary in order to "see"

Clairvoyance Model. In the Divine Disclosure Model, the claim is never made that God can view future events as already there. Rather, the Divine Disclosure Model suggests foreknowledge of a completely different kind: foreknowledge due to a knowledge of what he, the determiner, intends or purposes to bring into being.

it as a closed event. But if God could view it as a closed event in this way, then it would be available to him as a valid object of knowledge. Hence, the objection raised against proposition #2 still stands. On these assumptions, divine clairvoyance would be possible.

ANSWERING THIS FURTHER OBJECTION

If a human being can and does exist within a multitude of different time frames, then I must retract my rejection of divine clairvoyance on the grounds that future events are not available to God as objects of knowledge. I must admit that, on this hypothesis, divine clairvoyance is a meaningful and plausible notion. But is the hypothesis that we exist on a multitude of different time frames plausible? Or, is it a flight of wild, nonsensical imagination?

I believe it is the latter. Individual existence on multiple time frames raises a whole host of unanswerable philosophical dilemmas. If I exist on a multitude of time frames, am I a multitude of different beings? Does any time frame have priority over the others? And if so, on what basis? If I exist on a multitude of other time frames, why is my conscious experience confined to this time frame? What does that mean? If we inquire far enough, existence in multiple time frames becomes a very problematic doctrine.

However, for the sake of argument, let us assume that it is a plausible suggestion. Even so, with respect to the concerns of the typical proponent of divine clairvoyance, it is self-defeating.

To see why, we must remember why divine clairvoyance is attractive to its typical proponent in the first place. It is attractive to its proponents because it would appear to be able to explain divine foreknowledge without resorting to divine determinism. That is, it explains how God can know the future without implying that God must determine the future. And why is that appealing? For if God determines the future, then future events are necessary and inevitable. That, specifically, is the conclusion that the typical proponent of divine clairvoyance is seeking to avoid.

But that is also why explaining divine clairvoyance in terms of the hypothesis of multiple time frames is self-defeating. For if God can know a future event precisely because on some time frame somewhere that event is a CLOSED event,[136] then that event is necessary and inevitable[137]—

---

136. Granted, on the multiple time frame hypothesis, a future event is not closed in the time frame within which ordinary experience is confined; but it is—by the very nature of the hypothesis—closed in some time frame. (This is precisely why it can work as an explanation for how God could know a future event.) But if—in some time frame—a future event is closed, then it

PART 2 | CHAPTER 7: DOES GOD'S FOREKNOWLEDGE IMPLY   165
DIVINE DETERMINISM?

the very conclusion that the proponent of divine clairvoyance was seeking to avoid in the first place. Hence, multiple time frames may indeed offer a basis from which we can achieve a plausible explanation of divine clairvoyance, but at a cost. It requires the admission that future events are, in fact, closed, necessary, and inevitable. That may be an acceptable price for some; but it is far too high a price for the typical proponent of divine clairvoyance.

Therefore, while one could, in truth, logically explain divine clairvoyance by means of the hypothesis of multiple time frames, this hypothesis is not available to the typical proponent of divine clairvoyance, for it explains divine clairvoyance only at the unacceptable cost of requiring that future events be closed, necessary, and inevitable. It would require that he concede that the future is already determined—the very thing he was trying to avoid by adopting divine clairvoyance.

On balance, therefore, divine determinism is a much less problematic doctrine than the doctrine of real existence on multiple time frames. Divine determinism may, and indeed does, strike us as "weird." But could anyone seriously deny the "weirdness" of real existence on a multiplicity of different time frames? It is at least equally weird. To resort to the doctrine of real existence in multiple time frames in order to avoid divine determinism is going to desperate lengths indeed.[138]

THIRD PROPOSITION

PROPOSITION #3: *The Bible's own explicit explanation for how God can have infallible foreknowledge is the Divine Disclosure Model.*

I am aware of only two passages that offer any explicit explanation for how God can know the future and make it known to us. These two explanations clearly reflect the Divine Disclosure Model rather than the Divine Clairvoyance Model:

---

is necessary and inevitable. An event which has already occurred in any time frame is a logically necessary event. An event which has been actualized within time (history) cannot, logically, be other than it is (was).

137. It cannot be closed in any sense without being necessary and inevitable.

138. See appendix C for a somewhat different approach to making this point.

For I am God, and there is no other; I am God, and there is no one like Me, declaring the end from the beginning and from ancient times things which have not been done, saying, *"My purpose will be established, and I will accomplish all My good pleasure"*; calling a bird of prey from the east, the man of My purpose from a far country. *Truly I have spoken; truly I will bring it to pass. I have planned it, surely I will do it.*

Isaiah 46: 9 - 11 (emphasis mine)

This passage clearly suggests that God's prediction of the future is nothing more than a declaration of his own purposes. God declares to his prophet what he intends to accomplish and is thereby confident that he is declaring the future itself. His prediction of the future, therefore, is based on his confidence that he can and will accomplish in the future what he now purposes to do when it arrives.

Surely the Lord God does nothing unless He reveals His secret counsel to His servants the prophets. A lion has roared! Who will not fear? The Lord God has spoken! Who can but prophesy?

Amos 3: 7-8

In this passage, too, the prophetic predictions that the Lord gives to the prophet are viewed as announcements of God's purposes. They are not announcements of what God has seen at his latest seance. Rather, they are simple statements of the will and "secret counsel" of God.

Amos is saying here that God will not act to bring about events in accordance with his will until he has first told his prophet what he plans to do so that the prophet can warn the people. But once God has spoken through his prophet, Amos warns, you better listen. If God says he'll do it, he'll do it!

In both of these cases, the explanation for divine foreknowledge is along the following lines: God knows what he purposes to do; therefore, he knows the future—for the future will turn out to be exactly what he purposes to make it. God plans and he brings his plans about. Therefore, when God tells you what he plans to do, you can be sure that that is what will happen.[139]

---

139. The objection could be raised at this point: "That is how you, Jack, interpret these passages. But, by your own admission in chapter 5, a person's pre-understanding directs the way he will interpret a biblical text. You see these verses as supporting the Divine Disclosure Model because that is the pre-understanding you bring to those texts. But I think you are wrong. I don't think these verses support the Divine Disclosure Model." I cannot deny that my pre-understanding

This is consistently the biblical explanation for God's knowledge of the future. It is, in essence, the Divine Disclosure Model. On the other hand, no biblical passage of which I am aware ever suggests that God is predicting the future on the basis of his direct perception (clairvoyance) of that future event. The biblical evidence, therefore, clearly favors the Divine Disclosure Model as the rational explanation for how God can know the future.

FOURTH PROPOSITION

PROPOSITION #4: *The Divine Disclosure model is the TRUTH with regard to how divine foreknowledge is possible.*

We can reasonably conclude that the Divine Disclosure Model is the true explanation of how God foreknows future events. This conclusion follows directly from propositions #2 and #3 on the basis of three important assumptions: (i) reason and the assumptions of common sense are a reliable guide to truth, (ii) the Bible is a reliable (indeed, infallible) guide to truth, and (iii) there exists no yet-to-be-discovered model for explaining divine foreknowledge that is just as rationally and biblically acceptable as the Divine Disclosure Model.

Logically, it would seem, only two possible models for understanding the possibility of divine foreknowledge exist. Given these two possible models, the dual authorities of reason and the Bible both commend the Divine Disclosure Model over the Divine Clairvoyance Model. If the only infallible avenues to truth that we have available to us—sound reason and revelation—both commend the Divine Disclosure Model, then to embrace it as TRUTH is reasonable.

FIFTH PROPOSITION

PROPOSITION #5: *If we know that an event was infallibly foreknown by God, then we know that that event was divinely determined.*

---

influences my interpretation. Therefore, I will concede that, in principle, there could be other interpretations of these two texts that do not imply the Divine Disclosure Model. But I am at a loss to know what those other interpretations would look like. If a plausible alternative exists to my interpretation of either of these passages, then my argument here is incomplete. I would need to show (if possible) that my interpretation of these texts is preferable to the proposed alternative. But I cannot make that case here, for I cannot even conceive of a plausible alternative.

As I have already shown, the Divine Disclosure Model, by its very nature, directly implies the divine determination of events that God foreknows. Therefore, when we know that an event has been foreknown by God, we know that it was determined by him as well. God cannot foreknow an event unless he is its cause. Therefore, events he predicts are events he will cause.

This conclusion is somewhat limited in scope. We have proved only that a certain sub-set of historical events—namely, those that God predicts through his prophets—can be known to be subject to divine determination. What about all the other events? My argument must continue.

SIXTH PROPOSITION

PROPOSITION #6: *Those events that we know were infallibly foreknown by God are not different in kind from any other cosmic event.*

We know—by the preceding argument—that the denial of Jesus by Peter is among those events that were divinely determined. What was the character of that event? Was it a fundamentally unique event, or was it like any other instance of a man denying Jesus?

I contend that Peter's denial is not fundamentally different in kind from any other freewill event. Peter willed to deny Jesus just as human beings throughout time have made their free choices. The same can be said of every event that God predicted through his prophets. The freewill choices that he predicted through his prophets were of like kind to all the other freewill choices throughout human history that God did not bother to predict. The Bible gives no hint of any fundamental difference in kind.

SEVENTH PROPOSITION

PROPOSITION #7: *Therefore, by induction, it follows that every cosmic event is infallibly foreknown by God, and, hence, divinely determined.*

Because the sub-set of events that God has foretold is not fundamentally different in kind from all other human events, we are justified in concluding, by induction, that all human events are subject to divine foreknowledge in exactly the same way that prophetically predicted events are. If God could know in advance that Peter would deny Jesus, then—for precisely the same reasons—he can know in advance whether you or I or anyone else will deny Jesus. And if the reason God can foreknow Peter's denial is because he will ultimately cause Peter's denial, then it follows that God can foreknow whether you or I will deny Jesus because it is he who would cause it to occur. In other words, all human events can reasonably be assumed to bear the same relationship to God as those that God has predicted. If the latter are divinely determined, then the former must be as well.[140] Hence, to conclude that all cosmic events are divinely determined because God has dramatically predicted some of them is eminently reasonable.

CONCLUSION

Proposition #7—our concluding proposition—is, in part, an affirmation of divine determinism. In seeking to understand how divine foreknowledge is possible, we have been led to acknowledge divine determinism. Nothing else—compatible with both the Bible and sound reason—can account for the nature and extent of divine foreknowledge. Therefore, to do justice to the biblical data with regard to God's ability to foreknow and predict the future, we are forced to embrace divine determinism as the most reasonable explanation.

Foreknowledge as Evidence Against a Common Objection

COMMON OBJECTION TO DIVINE DETERMINISM

I could stop here. The case for divine determinism from the fact of divine foreknowledge has been made. But a further point is worth highlighting—namely, the biblical data regarding prophetic prediction provides pointed counterexamples to the most important objection that lim-

---

140. This generalization would be invalid if there was any basis for believing that divinely fore-told—and hence, divinely determined—events were exceptional, extraordinary events. And if there was any basis for believing that it was only their extraordinary nature that made it possible for them to be divinely foreknown. But, as I have pointed out, there simply is no basis for believing that foretold events are extraordinary events in any other respect. Accordingly, divinely foretold events provide us with explicit data with regard to the relationship between God and human events—namely, they provide us with irrefutable evidence that God determines human events. And this conclusion can be assumed to hold for all human events—not just those events that God has foretold—for there is no basis for assuming that foretold events are qualitatively different from non-foretold events.

ited determinists have to divine determinism. The objection I have in mind is the alleged incompatibility of divine determinism with human free will and moral accountability. If God causes a person to make a choice, then that choice—it is alleged—is not and cannot be a freewill choice for which he is morally accountable.

Logically, then, we would expect the limited determinist to respond to the argument of this chapter with something like this: *As this line of reasoning suggests, it is true that events that were foretold by God must have been divinely determined. But since that is so, any human choices involved in the unfolding of those events cannot have been freewill choices, and they cannot have been choices for which the people who made them were morally responsible.*

INSTANCES OF DIVINE FOREKNOWLEDGE REFUTE THIS OBJECTION

But this is not consistent with the biblical data. If we look at the instances of prophetic prediction in the Bible, there can be no question that the biblical record views the actors in prophetically predicted events as making freewill choices and as being morally accountable for those choices. There is much evidence to this effect, and there is not the slightest hint to the contrary.

So, for example, the Bible does not exonerate Peter of his denials by virtue of the fact that God caused him to do it. Nor is he exonerated because, after all, he was just fulfilling Jesus' prediction and it simply had to be. Without any embarrassment at all, the Bible affirms two important things: (i) God can know of Peter's denials in advance precisely because he, God, is the one who determines the affairs of men, and (ii) Peter's denials are freewill decisions that speak unfavorably of his moral character—that is, they reflect cowardice, disloyalty, and lack of trust.[141]

In the biblical record, then, divine determinism and human moral responsibility are not viewed as incompatible. In instances of prophetic prediction, the Bible affirms both without any suggestion that they are in contradiction.[142] The assumption held by most limited determinists that

---

141. It is not necessary to defend this at length. It would require a rather superficial reading of the account to miss the intended contrast between Peter's claim of loyalty to the point of death based solely on empty bravado and the actual profound cowardice which he evidenced when tested. Clearly the text intends to expose Peter at his point of culpability, not to exonerate him through a "God made him do it" defense.

divine determinism and human responsibility are mutually incompatible is simply not an assumption that is shared by the biblical revelation.[143]

Conclusion of Part Two

Is divine determinism taught by the Bible? How we understand what the Bible teaches is, in fact, dictated by the pre-understanding that we bring with us to the study of the Bible. If we approach the Bible already believing in divine determinism, we will most certainly find texts that— interpreted accordingly—justify our belief. But if we come to the Bible believing in limited determinism, we will with equal readiness find texts that—interpreted accordingly—justify that belief. Accordingly, the crucial question becomes: which pre-understanding can I justifiably bring to the biblical texts?

When we consider two important biblical doctrines, we find that both these doctrines rationally imply divine determinism. These doctrines are (i) the traditional notion of creation *ex nihilo*, and (ii) the biblical concept of God being the one who is able to know the future in advance. We find that we have no rational explanation for either of these realities unless we assume divine determinism. Therefore, it would appear that the fundamental biblical teaching about the nature of God and his relationship to the created cosmos directly implies the divine causation or determination of all things. In other words, what the Bible teaches about God implies divine determinism.[144]

If we are to be faithful to the Bible's teaching with regard to the nature of God—we have no choice but to make divine determinism the pre-understanding that we take with us to the other relevant biblical texts. When we do so, we find a wealth of explicit references to God's role as the determiner of all things. Hence, the final answer to our question has to be "yes." The Bible *does* teach divine determinism.

---

142. And not ONLY in instances of prophetic prediction.

143. The assumption that most limited determinists make is not that divine sovereignty and human responsibility are incompatible; rather, it is that human responsibility is incompatible with divine determinism—as I have defined it. Many, if not most, limited determinists are willing to affirm that divine sovereignty and human accountability are mutually compatible by virtue of some sort of paradox. But to characterize divine sovereignty as I have characterized it in the doctrine of divine determinism is something they refuse to do; and they refuse to do so precisely because they believe it to be irreconcilable with free will and human accountability.

144. For another approach to the arguments presented in part two, see appendix L.

PART THREE
A BRIEF PHILOSOPHICAL CASE FOR DIVINE DETERMINISM

In the preceding chapters I sought to demonstrate that divine determinism is the philosophical position presupposed by the Bible. When we take all the biblical data into account, divine determinism emerges as the worldview most likely to underlie all that the Bible says and teaches. For one who accepts the biblical worldview as authoritative, the preceding chapters constitute an argument for divine determinism. Nothing more need be said.

But are there good reasons to embrace divine determinism apart from the authoritative teaching of the Bible? I believe there are. In this next part of my argument, I briefly explore a few of them.

Part 3 outlines a handful of important everyday assumptions that philosophically require determinism. If no version of determinism is true, we cannot plausibly account for how and why we hold these assumptions and why we live our lives in accordance with them. Accordingly, determinism of some sort is the only way to make sense out of our everyday life and experience. Much could be said in support of this contention. Part 3 is not a thorough defense. A complete defense of this claim would require a more extended discussion. My purpose here is merely to introduce a certain way of looking at the relevant issues and to suggest where I think the evidence ultimately leads.

My goal in part 3 is to demonstrate to the reader that, not only is divine determinism the assumption that most likely underlies biblical revelation, it is also the philosophical doctrine that most satisfactorily accounts for the nature of ordinary everyday experience. Accordingly, not only is it the biblical worldview, it is also the most philosophically compelling worldview.

CHAPTER EIGHT

DIVINE DETERMINISM AND THE DICTATES OF OUR EVERYDAY EXPERIENCE

The majority of philosophers who have considered the matter have concluded that determinism is the most reasonable understanding of reality.[145] They disagree with respect to the form of determinism; they differ with respect to what determines all of reality. But they all agree that reality is determined. A minority of philosophers reject determinism. And in my judgment, their rejection typically results from significant confusion or flawed reasoning. They do not really understand the issues. Sound philosophical reflection inevitably leads a person to embrace some form of determinism.

Why is determinism so widespread among philosophers who have given the subject due consideration? Very simply, because determinism is the only doctrine that can make sense out of the ordinary assumptions from which we interpret our everyday experience. In this chapter I shall attempt to show why determinism (and ultimately divine determinism) is the only view that can adequately account for how we experience and think about our lives.

Given a particular human choice, there are—if I am not mistaken— only three possibilities: either, (1) it is undetermined—the product of randomness, (2) it is spontaneously self-determined—the result of the actor spontaneously making the choice from within himself with no outside factors responsible for the nature of his choice, or, (3) it is determined. By a process of elimination, I will show that a choice (any choice whatsoever) must be determined. Neither of the other alternatives can adequately account for how we view our choices the way we do.

---

145. Here is a PARTIAL list of philosophers and/or philosophical schools who articulate one form of determinism or another: Homeric philosophy, Stoic philosophy, Epicurean philosophy, Augustine, Aquinas, Leibniz, Spinoza, Hobbes, Calvin, Luther, Edwards, Nietzsche. These are just the FEW that come immediately to mind. At the same time, recalling a notable philosopher who rejects determinism altogether is more difficult. Even Immanuel Kant, famous for his emphasis on human freedom, allows—arguably—for an ultimate determinism underlying human freedom. It is significant that so many philosophers who have seriously explored these questions embrace some form of determinism. They may not embrace DIVINE determinism; but they do embrace some version of determinism.

I begin my argument by clarifying what it would mean for a freewill human choice to be undetermined, self-determined, or determined, respectively. Then I do the same for impersonal physical events. Finally, I construct an argument to the effect that both impersonal physical events and freewill human choices must be understood as determined. Although my argument concerns impersonal physical events as well as human freewill choices, my main focus is whether "freewill" choices are determined. The reason for such a focus should be clear: "freewill" choices pose the greatest challenge to determinism in general and divine determinism in particular. Most people can accept that impersonal physical events are determined—determined by natural law and the inherent rational structure of the cosmos. But the status of freewill human choice is another matter. With regard to any form of determinism, the freewill choices of human beings are the phenomena most likely to be disputed. Accordingly, the argument of this chapter will focus on the status of "freewill" choices.

Defining Terms

Any particular choice must be either undetermined, self-determined, or determined. The precise meaning of each of these terms will not be obvious. I must define what I mean by them. I will first define each term with respect to human freewill choices, then I will define each of them with respect to impersonal physical events.

AN UNDETERMINED FREEWILL CHOICE

To maintain that a human freewill choice is undetermined is to maintain that it is radically random, that it is not explicable in terms of any cause or reason whatsoever. The choice is entirely happenstance. No cause and no reason determined that it should be THAT choice rather than some other.

Consider a person reaching down and picking up an agate off the beach. If the freewill choice to stoop down and pick up just THAT agate is an undetermined choice, then the choice to do so is not explicable in terms of any reason or cause. It just happened. It could have not happened at all, or the person could have chosen a different agate. Anything else the person might have done would have been equally consistent with any of the pre-existing causes or conditions. Nothing — absolutely nothing — explains why the person picked up THAT agate.

One could object that the person wanted to pick up the agate and that his desire to do so serves to explain his action. But even if we grant that, if his choice is undetermined, then his "desire" to pick up the agate is inexplicable. The desire may serve to explain the action, but nothing explains the desire. The desire was just there, out of the blue. There is no reason, no cause, and no explanation for the existence of his desire.

AN UNDETERMINED PHYSICAL EVENT

By analogy, to maintain that an impersonal physical event is undetermined suggests that it is radically random—not explicable in terms of any cause or reason whatsoever.

Consider a rock coming loose and rolling down the face of a cliff. If this event is undetermined, then there is no reason for the event; no cause can explain it. It just happened. It was possible for it not to have occurred at all. Or, something entirely different could have happened, and nothing that might have happened would have been inconsistent with any pre-existing causes or conditions. Nothing—absolutely nothing—explains why the rock fell down the cliff just then. The suggestion here is that we cannot even appeal to natural physical laws to explain the event. Nothing whatsoever explains the rock's behavior. The event is completely and truly random.

By random—or radically random—I mean more than the illusion of randomness. A random number generator on your computer is not a truly random process. If you were to type exactly the same key on your keyboard under exactly the same conditions one thousand times, your "random" number generator would give you exactly the same result one thousand times. We call it a random number generator only because the causal conditions that generate the number are so complex and so inaccessible to us that the result is utterly unpredictable. The program will generate a result that is beyond my ability to know and control. Therefore, while we can reasonably call it a "random number generator," observe that it is not "radically random" in the sense in which I am using that term. The "random" number produced by a random number generator is completely determined by the programming and hardware of the computer. The radical randomness I am referring to is far more radical. Randomness, as I am defining it, is where an event has absolutely no causes whatsoever. It is not merely that the causes cannot be known and the result predicted. There exist no causes determining the event at all. Even in principle, there is no accounting for why the event occurred as it did.

A SELF-DETERMINED FREEWILL CHOICE

To maintain that a human freewill choice is self-determined is to maintain that it is solely the product of the human chooser's individual will. It is to maintain that the particular choices made by a person are the spontaneous output of his particular will and that nothing outside his will can be said to cause or explain the choices that he makes. The will is sovereign over its own choices, generating them *ex nihilo* out of its own intrinsic nature. Nothing outside the will determines its function or output.

Consider the earlier example of a person reaching down and picking up an agate off the beach. If the choice to pick up just THAT agate is a self-determined choice, then the choice to do so is explicable solely and exhaustively in terms of the particular will of that person and in terms of the intrinsic nature of that will. No further reason can be given for why the person's particular will functioned just as it did and chose what it did. Nothing outside his human will is the cause or explanation for the operations of his particular will. Each particular human—with regard to his freewill choices—must serve as his own cause and his own explanation. So, with respect to our example, the particular human will of our beachcomber generated within itself the desire to pick up THAT particular agate, and absolutely nothing outside his will can explain why it generated that particular desire rather than another. Genetics cannot explain it, diet cannot explain it; not the environment, not childhood experience, not economic conditions—nothing whatsoever can explain the generation of such a desire by that particular human will at that time. Nothing other than the sovereign, spontaneous, *ex nihilo* free choice of that will itself.[146]

A SELF-DETERMINED PHYSICAL EVENT

To maintain that an impersonal physical event is self-determined is to maintain that each particular, impersonal object has its own intrinsic nature that is uncaused and undetermined by anything outside of itself. Any action of that impersonal physical object, therefore, will be caused and explained solely by its own individual nature, and nothing outside

---

146. This is the philosophical viewpoint typically advocated by the Bible-believing Christian who rejects divine determinism. As I shall demonstrate, it is a problematic position. He must reconcile his doctrine that God is the creator of the human will with his doctrine that the particular human will is radically sovereign over its own choices—such that nothing, not even God, causes or determines those choices. How can God create a will and not, thereby, determine how it will function? I discuss this problem later in this chapter.

that particular object can explain why it acted as it did or responded to its environment as it did.

Consider our example of a rock falling down the face of a cliff. If this event is a self-determined event, then it is explicable solely in terms of the particular nature of the particular rock that fell. No further reason can be given for why the rock fell as it did. Nothing outside the nature of that particular rock is a cause or explanation for its action. That particular rock's own nature generated within itself the action of falling down the cliff, and absolutely nothing outside the rock can explain why it spontaneously generated that particular action. If it was self-determined, then we cannot resort to natural laws of physics—not the law of gravity—to find an explanation. Nothing whatsoever outside the rock can explain the spontaneous generation of such an event.

This is a rather absurd position. No one today would even begin to seriously suggest it. But this is what this category of explanation would mean when applied to a physical, impersonal event.

A DETERMINED FREEWILL CHOICE

To maintain that a human freewill choice is determined is *not* to deny that the choice is the product of the particular, individual will of the chooser. Yet, at the same time, it is to maintain that something outside the person's particular will ultimately determines the operations and output of that will.

Consider once again the person picking up an agate. If the freewill choice to pick up just that agate is a determined choice, then the person's choice to do so is ultimately explicable in terms of something outside the particular will of the beachcomber. Granted, the particular human will generated within itself the desire to pick up that particular agate. But if the choice was determined, then something outside that will explains why it generated just that desire in particular. Some might suggest that human genes explain why the will chose as it did. Others might suggest that diet, body chemistry, environment, childhood experiences, economic conditions, or some combination of these things explain why the will chose as it did. The divine determinist, of course, is suggesting that God—the transcendent author of all things—determines why the will chooses as it does. Whatever the cause might be, if a human choice is determined, we are saying that something beyond the particular will itself ultimately explains the particular choice made by that will.

A DETERMINED PHYSICAL EVENT

To maintain—as almost everyone does—that an impersonal physical event is determined, is to suggest that each particular, impersonal object is subject to natural laws that dictate or determine how it will respond to its environment. Hence, any action of an impersonal physical object will finally be caused and explained by the laws of the cosmos to which it is subject.

Take our falling rock example—if that event is a determined event, then it is explicable in terms of physical laws that strictly dictate how the rock responds to its environment. The rock fell because gravity pulled it and—due to a variety of physical causes—there were no longer any countervailing forces to keep it from accelerating down the hill in accordance with Newton's laws of gravity. In other words, the wind, rain, and other physical factors made the rock "come loose" so that gravity pulled it down the cliff. This is, of course, the position held by any educated person today with respect to impersonal physical events.

SUMMARY

To better understand my definition of terms in this argument, I need to make a distinction. Consider once again the question of whether the freewill choice of a human being is self-determining. We must distinguish between a claim that the human will is *absolutely* self-determining and a claim that the human will is *derivatively* self-determining. If the human will directly determines its own choice X (*e.g.*, to pick up a particular agate on the beach) according to the structure of its own individual nature and operation, but the structure of its own nature and the character of its own operation is, in turn, explicable in terms of some other cause or causes (*e.g.*, its transcendent creator), then the human will could be said to be DERIVATIVELY self-determining. But if the human will directly determines its own choice X according to the structure of its own individual nature and the character of its own operation, and if the structure of its own nature and the character of its own operation is just a raw fact that is not, in turn, explainable in terms of any other cause or causes outside of itself (*e.g.*, a transcendent creator), then the human will could be said to be ABSOLUTELY self-determining. For the purposes of my argument in this chapter, we must take 'self-determining' to mean ABSOLUTELY self-determining. If one wants to claim merely that the human will is derivatively self-determining, then—as one can see from the above definitions—he is not denying the reality of determinism. A will that is derivatively self-determining is, in fact, being determined by some other cause outside of itself (*e.g.*, its creator). That being so, it is not really a philosophical alternative to determinism, it is just a particular version of deterministic theory.

Accordingly, the definitions discussed above can be summarized as they are in the following table:

	Impersonal Physical Event	Human Freewill Choice
Undetermined	Such an event is random; it is not explicable in terms of any causes or reasons whatsoever; it is completely and radically happenstance.	Such a choice is random; it is not explicable in terms of any causes or reasons whatsoever; it is completely and radically happenstance.
Self-Determined	Such an event is a product of the particular nature of a particular physical object; and each particular impersonal physical object is understood to have its own intrinsic nature, uncaused and undetermined by anything outside of itself. Its own particular nature functions as the sole cause and explanation for its response to its environment. (Under this view, the nature of a particular rock is not the nature of "a rock"; rather, it is the nature of "that rock in particular.")	Such a choice is a product of a particular human will; and each particular human will is understood to have its own particular nature, uncaused and undetermined by anything outside of itself. A person's own particular human will functions as the sole cause and explanation for the choices that he makes.
Determined	Such an event is caused by natural causes in conformity to natural laws inherent within the physical cosmos.	Such a choice is caused by something—either a natural, ordinary cause or a transcendent cause—that lies outside of the particular human will and ultimately determines what that particular human will shall choose.

The Argument

I will now examine both impersonal physical events and freewill choic-es. My task is to determine whether either could reasonably be understood to be undetermined, or alternatively, to be self-determined. I will argue that neither alternative makes any sense. Neither can reasonably be con-strued as undetermined, and neither can reasonably be construed as self-determined. I will argue that both alternatives—construing these events as undetermined and construing these events as self-determined—bring us into conflict with various everyday ordinary assumptions according to which we live our lives. By a process of elimination, therefore, we find that the only way we can make sense out of both impersonal physical events and freewill choices is by understanding them to be determined.

IMPERSONAL PHYSICAL EVENTS

ARE PHYSICAL EVENTS UNDETERMINED?

The first possibility to consider is whether impersonal physical events are undetermined—that is to say, radically random. After a little reflection, it should be clear that this makes no sense. We could never bring ourselves to assume that any event whatsoever is random and undetermined. We could never make any sense out of our experience if we were ever to allow for such a possibility. To see this, consider the following points:

1. *If the impersonal events in the physical universe are undetermined (random), then knowledge of the physical universe (i.e., science) is impossible.*

In our ordinary perception of things, science is a meaningful enterprise. But science is based on the assumption that occurrences in the physical universe are determined.[147] If physical occurrences are not determined, then no physical science is possible. Accordingly, our ordinary belief in the possibility of science presupposes that the physical events of the universe are determined.

One cannot discern laws of nature at work in physical events if those events do not, in fact, conform to such laws. If physical events are not

---

147. The increasingly popular appeal to Heisenberg's uncertainty principle as a defense of inde-terminacy is unsound. It merely betrays the prejudices of the modern trend toward irrational-ism. In truth, Heisenberg's uncertainty principle does not prove indeterminacy in natural events. For a brief discussion of this, see appendix B.

determined in accordance with some sort of rational ordering principle, then no knowledge of physical reality is possible, for knowledge of physical reality (science) is nothing else but a discovery of the rational ordering principles to which it conforms. Natural science, therefore, assumes the existence of rational principles that are the determinative causes and explanations of natural events. Science is impossible if events are not so determined.

If physical occurrences were uncaused and random, there would be no point in seeking to discover an order or pattern to those occurrences, for no pattern would be there. If perchance one did discern an order in random events, it could only be the result of his subjectively imposing that order on those events. He would be "seeing" something that was not actually there. Accordingly, it would not constitute true knowledge of objective reality.[148] Yet science understands its goal as exactly that—the attain-

---

148. By "true knowledge" of objective reality I mean a set of beliefs that accurately represent the way things actually are in reality as it is in and of itself. To have "true knowledge" of the physical order would involve an understanding of an order that does in fact exist as such in physical reality. It is not an order that exists in the mind of the scientist and dictates the way the scientist perceives reality; rather it is an order that exists in reality quite apart from how any scientist perceives it. I am not discounting Kant's insights here however. One can believe that one is acquiring true knowledge of objective reality as that reality is in itself without thereby denying that one's experience of that reality is a uniquely and peculiarly human experience of that reality. Just because one is confined or restricted to a human WAY of knowing (a la Kant) does not mean—as Kant tends to suggest—that one's knowledge is not a valid knowledge of THINGS IN THEMSELVES. If a computer only knows what it knows about the outside world—through sensors attached to it—in terms of digital information, does that mean that its knowledge is not of the outside world as it is in itself? Does that mean that it has not made meaningful contact with objective reality in itself? I don't think so. Neither does the fact that a human knows what he knows in terms of peculiarly human perceptions mean that what he knows is not a kind of meaningful contact with reality as it is in itself. To put it another way, I can agree with Kant that the way I perceive things is not necessarily identical to the way things exist in themselves without inferring that the way I perceive things does not necessarily correspond to the way things exist in themselves. These are two very different claims; claims which Kant, at times, seems to confuse.

Skeptics, encouraged but not supported by Kant, have never really altogether convinced the average person to abandon his commonsensical belief that things in and of themselves really do CORRESPOND to (even if they are not identical to) the way we perceive them. In other words, common sense says that the world of our phenomenal experience really does correspond to the way things are in and of themselves. A Kantian agnosticism with respect to things in themselves is ultimately rejected by common sense. But even if we were to concede a skeptical and agnostic interpretation of Kant which claimed that none of our knowledge is in any sense knowledge of reality in itself, the point being made in the text still stands: no true knowledge is possible if events are random. The scientist is seeking to understand phenomenal reality and the events we experience in the physical universe are phenomenal events. The point here is this: phenomenal events are necessarily determined events. If in no other way, they have been determined by the scientist who experiences them. Even if there could exist a truly random event in reality in and of itself, it would have to be a determined event in the phenomenal experience of a perceiver. Hence, even under a radical agnosticism inspired by (though not encouraged by) Kant, science

ment of true knowledge of the physical world as it actually is.[149] Therefore, to seek for order in the physical world—as science does—is to presume that such an order is actually there. But to presume that such an order is actually there, one must assume that there are, in fact, some ordering principles that determine what happens in the physical world. That is, one must assume that (1) some outside orderer (*e.g.*, a mind) determines and gives rational order to what happens in the physical world, or (2) the world itself is self-determining according to a rational orderliness inherent within its own intrinsic nature. But on either assumption the world is being ordered, shaped, caused, and determined in accordance with some sort of rational principles.

Therefore, if science is a valid means to true knowledge—and we all assume that it is—then physical events cannot be random and undetermined.

2. *If any impersonal event in any part of reality is undetermined, then no true knowledge of objective reality is possible.*

As I go about building my understanding of reality, experience-by-experience, I am forced to assume that every experience I encounter fits coherently into the order and structure of reality. If I did not make such an assumption, then no knowledge of any of reality would be possible.

The alternatives are to assume that either (1) no event fits into any order and structure (*i.e.,* everything is random and chaotic), or (2) some things are random and other things constitute the order and structure of reality. Clearly, no true knowledge of reality would be possible under the first alternative; everything, being chaos, would be inherently unknowable. But neither would true knowledge be possible under the second alter-

---

is seeking a *true* knowledge of the phenomena of the natural world; and those phenomena must necessarily be determined in order to be knowable. As a matter of fact, Kant's whole project was to establish the phenomena as rationally ordered and determined in order that he could explain how science is possible. That is exactly my point in the text.

149. Some philosophers of science have offered an alternative explanation for the purpose and goal of science consistent with the philosophical view that true knowledge of reality is not possible. This is not the prevailing view in the practicing scientific community however. The working assumption of the working scientific community (oriented, as it is, more toward common sense than toward contemporary philosophy) is that it is seeking to understand the physical universe as it really is. Even if some philosophically-minded scientist purports to subscribe to a redefinition of his task in accordance with a modern philosophy of science, the commonsensical belief that he carries into his laboratory—the one that he shares with all his colleagues—is that true knowledge of physical reality is possible.

native. For if some events were random and some not, knowledge could never begin. For how would I know which events to allow to inform my understanding of the rational structure of reality and which events to ignore? Without the implicit *a priori* assumption that everything can be assumed to fit coherently into the world order (and not to be random), knowledge could never get off the ground. We could never learn from our experience.

If truly random events could be assumed to exist, then—unless a child was equipped with a fairly comprehensive understanding of the structure of reality from birth—he would have no basis upon which to decide which events in his experience were a part of the structure of reality and which were random. Hence, he would be unable to learn about reality, for he could never know when an event was merely a part of the random noise of experience (and, as such, needed to be ignored) and when it was a piece of rationally-ordered objective reality that had to be incorporated into his picture of reality. Hence, if we cannot presume that every aspect of our experience fits coherently into the rational order of reality, then, logically, we can never learn anything from our experience. Or, at least, we could learn from experience only if we already possess an extensive understanding of the structure of reality. But this is not how it works. I do not possess an extensive understanding of the structure of reality before my learning begins. I begin from a minimal knowledge of reality and build a rather extensive knowledge of reality through life-experience. But as we have seen, this is possible only on the assumption that no event in all of reality can be viewed as random and undetermined.

The assumption that no event in reality is random (and, hence, that everything is determined) forms the foundation for all knowledge. This assumption is either true or false. If it is true, then true knowledge is possible. If it is false, then, while the illusion of knowledge is generated by this false assumption, in truth, there is no actual knowledge of reality. My "knowledge" is merely an order imposed on a reality that does not in fact possess any order. I am not coming to understand the world as it really, objectively, is. I am ordering it as I want. That is not true knowledge. Therefore, if reality is not in fact totally determined, then the only true knowledge is that no true knowledge of reality is possible for human beings.

Where do these two observations leave us? Just here: unless I am prepared to say that true knowledge of objective reality is impossible and that scientific knowledge of the cosmos is impossible, I am forced to conclude that all impersonal physical events are determined.

ARE PHYSICAL EVENTS SELF-DETERMINED?

If it makes no sense to construe impersonal physical events as undetermined, then they must either be self-determined or determined by something outside the physical event. No one would seriously suggest that the impersonal events in the physical universe are self-determined as I defined that above. To understand what such an assertion would mean is to reject it. To suggest that a physical event is self-determining is to suggest that each particular impersonal object involved in the event has its own intrinsic nature that is uncaused and undetermined by anything outside of itself. Hence, nothing outside the particular objects involved could serve to explain why they acted as they did or responded to their environment as they did. Their actions would be explained solely and completely by their own individual natures. To be specific, one could not resort to natural laws of the cosmos to explain the actions of particular physical objects. One would have to explain each particular object's action with respect to its own particular nature—not with respect to its generic nature (that is, its nature as a rock or a tree or a mountain), but with respect to its particular nature. This view is difficult to take seriously. It would imply, for example, that that volcano erupted yesterday because "that mountain is just like that." Surely this view makes no sense.

CONCLUSION: IMPERSONAL PHYSICAL EVENTS ARE DETERMINED

It makes no sense to believe that an impersonal physical event is undetermined and random. Furthermore, it makes no sense to believe that such an event is spontaneously self-determined by the physical objects involved. By process of elimination, then, only one option remains: an impersonal physical event is determined by something in the cosmos outside of the physical objects involved. This view accords well with popular assumptions today. The impersonal physical events within the physical universe are commonly assumed to be caused by and to conform to the rational structure of the universe, the natural laws. Granted, the natural determinist wants to say that the natural laws themselves are uncaused, that they were not created; that they are just there, inherent within the cosmos. But the actual physical events themselves are determined—with this the natural determinist concurs. Impersonal physical events are determined by the natural laws of the universe. They are not undetermined and random and they are not self-determining. They are determined.

HUMAN FREEWILL CHOICES

ARE HUMAN CHOICES UNDETERMINED?

Now we turn our attention to the freewill choices of human beings (or any other free moral agents that exist). Is a freewill choice undetermined and random? To answer "yes" is to suggest that a human choice is not explicable in terms of any cause or reason whatsoever. It is to suggest that any choice made by a human being is completely and entirely happenstance and absolutely uncaused. In other words, if a freewill choice is undetermined, it is radically random as defined earlier. If a freewill choice is truly undetermined, then, by its very nature, no necessitating principle—neither one outside nor inside the chooser—causes the choice. The choice does not reflect the operation of any rational principle of any kind.

Upon a little reflection, we see that the radical randomness of human choices makes no sense. We can cite two reasons:

1. *If human choices are undetermined, then we cannot adequately account for the phenomenon of human personality.*

That people have personalities is axiomatic. An individual person has an orderly and structured identity that, through experience, we can come to know and understand. This is what we call "personality." Human beings are very complex creatures. As such, their actions are not always predictable in practice. But in general terms, people behave in ways consistent with their own idiosyncratic network of choices. They are basically predictable—in the sense that the general character of their choices can be anticipated. And behind their more or less consistent network of choices is assumed to be a determinant "personality"—an individual nature that causes and accounts for the nature of the choices that that person makes.

The very concept of a personality is indicative of the fact that people's choices, responses, attitudes, tastes, etc. operate in accordance with discernible patterns. We come to know and understand a person's personality by observing the choices he makes. As we observe his choices, we begin to see discernible patterns. He always prefers X. He always avoids Y. He likes Z, but he doesn't like T. He tends always to be kind. He is never arrogant.

Now here is the crucial question: can personality or character be explained in terms of undetermined (random) choices? No! The very concept of "personality" points to a discernible pattern of behavior. Where does this discernible pattern come from? If an individual's choices are not determined by some determinant, rationally-discernible personality functioning as the ordering principle of those choices, then how do we account for the pattern to his choices that led us to ascribe personality to him?

Randomness cannot explain the phenomenon of "personality." Randomness can produce only chaos—the absence of any significant and meaningful patterns. And randomness involves the lack of predictability. But our ordinary concept of "personality" assumes both a significant pattern of behavior and a significant degree of predictability in human behavior. Human choices, the units of personality, if you will, cannot therefore be random. Random choices could not create those patterns within our experience that give rise to the concept of human personality. Human choices, therefore, must be either self-determined or determined, but they cannot be undetermined and random.

2. *If human choices are undetermined, then it would be impossible to understand human nature.*

By the same line of argument as in point (1) above, if human choices are neither determined nor self-determining, then knowledge of human nature is impossible. Granted, human nature is a very complex thing. There is much we do not understand about it. Perhaps there is much that we never will understand about human nature. But few of us are prepared to say that "human nature" is a fiction or an illusion. As complex as it is, our humanity seems to have order and structure to it. Human choices give evidence of that structure. They follow significant and meaningful patterns that show that the chooser is a human being like all other human beings.

If human choices were random or uncaused, would such a thing as human nature exist? Would a knowledge of that human nature be possible? No. It would not. Extending it further, would knowledge of the humanities and human sciences be possible? If human choices were random and uncaused, could we come to a meaningful understanding of history, psychology, sociology, economics, literature, art, or anything else involving human action? Again, the answer is no!

Where do these two observations leave us? Just here: unless I am prepared to suggest that there is no such thing as human nature, that a knowledge of human nature is impossible, that the phenomenon of "individual personality" is not objectively real, and that there can be no such thing as knowledge of an individual person (i.e., knowledge of his personality and character), then I am forced to conclude that freewill human choice is determined. It makes no sense to suggest that it is undetermined and random. Either human choice is determined by something outside the human chooser or by something within the human chooser—by the inner nature of that human chooser—but human choice is decidedly not random and undetermined.

ARE HUMAN CHOICES SELF-DETERMINED?

Human freewill choices must, therefore, be either determined or self-determined. We turn now to the possibility of self-causation. Can human choice be self-determined? Could human choice be the result of a human being's functioning as the cause of his own choices, independently of any outside causes?

As we saw above, no one would suggest that impersonal physical events are self-determining. Only in the arena of human choice is the possibility of self-determination seriously entertained. Human choices are what they are because each individual human will determines for and by itself what choices it will make. Nothing outside the human will shapes it or determines its operation—that is, no outside cause determines how and what it will choose. It is not determined by genetic activity, not by diet or environment, not by anything external to the actual will itself. In the final analysis, the human will, regardless of what factors may have an *influence* on it, determines its own choices. It is ultimately spontaneous and self-determining.

Why do so many people opt for such a view? Primarily because it seems to be the only theory that can account for our commonsensical belief in free will. As we have seen, it makes no sense to hold that our choices are undetermined—i.e., random. But to suggest that our choices are determined would seem to preclude human freedom. Hence, it would appear that only one option remains—self-determination. Only self-determination can account for human freedom while avoiding the absurd consequence that human choice is random.

Various forms of natural determinism have argued that human choices are determined by genetic realities, personal history, environment, or some combination of these things. No one would seriously argue that these are not important factors in human decisions. Clearly they are. But are they determinative? That is, do they control choices irresistibly? Do they *necessitate* the choices a person makes? That is the issue at question.

If one could isolate all the natural factors that serve to influence a person's choices, would that particular combination of natural influences—and it alone—be sufficient to explain the resultant choice? The natural determinist says "yes." He would say, "Give me such-and-such information about a person's natural condition and environment, and I will tell you what he will choose." At least, he would say that such a boast is valid in principle. But most people, on the basis of common sense, deny this. Although we can all agree that one's natural condition and environment play an important role in human decision—i.e., we can all agree they are important influences—nevertheless, our common sense tells us that they do not irresistibly determine human choice. We assume that another factor lying within the human will itself ultimately determines what choice one will make. From the point of view of common sense, if you had two people with absolutely identical biological conditions, with identical personal histories, with identical present environments, being confronted by identical choices, the two could quite conceivably make different choices. The natural determinist, on the other hand, would deny this. On his account, two such people must necessarily make exactly the same choice.[150]

But most people embrace the view that the human will is self-determining. They do so in order to reject natural determinism in favor of common sense. The decisive determiner of human choice cannot be a set of natural causes, for that would negate human freedom. What is it then? It must be something lying within the will itself. The human will must be self-determining.

Insofar as it represents a desire to avoid natural determinism and to preserve the commonsensical notion of free will, I cannot help but be sympathetic with this view. But in the end I have to reject it. One can reject natural determinism and make sense of the reality of free will without resorting to the overly grand and false claim that the human will is self-determining.[151]

What would be required for the human will to be absolutely self-determining as defined above? For the human will (or some aspect of it) to be self-determining, it would have to be UNCREATED. To create something (from nothing) necessarily involves determining the shape, structure, nature, and laws of its existence. Therefore, creation necessarily involves determinism, and being undetermined necessarily entails being uncreat-

---

150. See chapter 9 for a fuller discussion of free will and natural determinism.

151. To argue that the human will is self-determining in order to preserve the insight that natural factors alone are not adequate to explain the phenomenon of human choice is like arguing that computers are human in order to preserve the insight that computers are capable of logical operations. The concept of self-determination is too grand a claim. It is much more than is needed to preserve the modest insight that human choice is not determined by natural causes. We can preserve this insight without resorting to such a grandiose claim.

ed.[152] For if something is created by some creator X, it is X who has determined the nature and laws of its existence. But there are only two ways
that something can be uncreated: either (1) it is eternal and self-existent,
or (2) it is self-creating (capable of creating itself from out of nothing). An
absolutely self-determining will, therefore, would have to be either eternal
and self-existent or self-creating.

The latter is totally nonsensical. The human will cannot plausibly be
self-creating. How can something that does not exist (because it begins as
nothing) create itself from out of nothing and so begin to exist as a particular something? The former notion—the view that some aspect of the
human will exists eternally as self-existent—is not immediately implausible. Maybe our human wills are essentially eternal, self-existent entities. At
least, such a view is logically possible. God is eternal and self-existent, so
why not us?

But on closer examination this latter suggestion is not plausible either.
In the light of experience, it makes no sense to suggest that some aspect of
our being is eternal and self-existent. One of the most striking character-
istics of an eternal, self-existent being is the *necessity* of his existence. He is
not contingent, but necessary. His being is not contingent on the will of a
creator or on anything else. He exists because he must exist. He exists out
of metaphysical necessity. He exists because—quite simply—he cannot not
exist. Does that describe any aspect of human existence? Is my individual
human will or any other aspect of my being non-contingent and necessary?
It seems apparent from our experience that we are thoroughly contingent
beings. We do not exist because we have to exist. Our continued existence
is not necessary. It is entirely possible for us to cease to exist. And neither
was our existence up to now a matter of metaphysical necessity. It was
entirely possible for us never to have existed. Hence, we are not necessary
beings. We are radically contingent beings. But if we are not necessary
beings, it follows that we are not eternal, self-existent beings either.[153]

---

152. This specific claim is explicitly challenged by some. Some Christian philosophers have
attempted to maintain that God creates the existence of an individual's human will but DOES
NOT determine the output of that will. As Geisler seems to put it, God determines the "being"
or actual existence of a person and his will, but God does not determine the "becoming" or
ongoing choices and activities of a person and his will. See Norman L. Geisler, *Philosophy of
Religion* (Grand Rapids: Zondervan Publishing House, 1974), 401. I have already argued that
such a view is not tenable. It makes no sense to suggest that God can create the fact of an entity like the human will without determining the nature and structure of its operation—and,
hence, ultimately its output, its "becoming." To maintain that God can create the "being" of a
human will without thereby determining its "becoming" involves a philosophical confusion; for
it would be a philosophical impossibility. See my earlier discussion of this issue in different terms
in chapter 6, pp. 131-135.

To assert that our wills have necessary existence and that they are eternal and self-existent would fly in the face of all human experience. That does not stop people from believing it. People throughout human history have been willing to declare themselves gods, but the better part of reason is against it. Experience teaches us that we are totally contingent beings, dependent for every aspect of our existence upon someone or something else. But, if it makes no sense to believe that we are self-existent, then it makes no sense to believe that we are self-determining.

CONCLUSION: HUMAN CHOICES ARE DETERMINED

As we have seen, it makes no sense to believe that human choices are undetermined and random. Furthermore, it makes no sense to believe that human choices are spontaneously self-determined by the will of the chooser. With the exception of that aspect of ultimate reality that is truly eternal and self-existent (*e.g.*, God), nothing in reality can be self-determining, including the human will.[154] By process of elimination, then, only one option remains: all human choices are ultimately determined by someone or something outside the human chooser himself.

CONCLUSION

We have seen that—whether we focus on impersonal physical events or on freewill choices—we must assume that everything in all of reality is ultimately determined. Under no other theory can we account for these three everyday assumptions: (1) the fact of order in our experience, (2) the possibility of true objective knowledge, and (3) the fact of the radical contingency of human existence. Total determinism is the only view that is compatible with all three of these foundational aspects of human experience. Unless I am prepared to reject these fundamental, foundational beliefs, I am forced to conclude that everything in reality is determined—except, of course, for the ultimate determiner himself (or itself).

---

153. Mortimer Adler has a helpful discussion of necessary vs. contingent beings in his book *How To Think About God.*

154. One cannot deny the following claim: whatever serves as the ultimate ground of all existence is self-existent, eternal, and self-determining. But it makes no sense to attribute self-existence, eternality, and self-determination to anything whose existence is derived from this. If God is the ultimate reality, then it makes sense to claim that he is self-existent and self-determining. Likewise, if it makes sense to suggest that the cosmos is the ultimate reality, then it makes sense to claim that it is self-existent and self-determining. But nothing inferior in its being to that which is ultimate reality—because derivative from it—can reasonably be said to be self-existent and self-determining.

Who or What is the Ultimate Determiner?

The only question that remains is the identity of this determiner. The four that have been nominated throughout the history of human thought are these: (1) God—the eternal, self-existent creator of everything *ex nihilo*, (2) the cosmos—the eternal, self-existent complex of material and spiritual realities, including the gods, (3) the physical universe—the eternal, self-existent, intrinsically rational complex of matter and energy, and (4) me—the creator god of my own subjective reality, the only reality that exists for me.

As a Christian, I obviously vote for the first candidate. To spell out all the reasons for my vote would involve a total defense of why I believe in the God of Christianity and the Bible. I will forego that here. For now, what is important is to understand that any valid defense of God's existence will *ipso facto* be a defense of divine determinism—that is, that God is the determiner of all things. For to argue for the existence of God is to argue that a personal, self-existent being is the ultimate determiner of all reality.

As we have seen in this chapter, determinism is the only rationally sound conclusion that one can reach on the basis of human experience. If, similarly, it can be said that biblical theism is the only rationally sound conclusion that one can reach with regard to the nature of ultimate reality (and I think it is), then clearly divine determinism is the only rationally sound conclusion that one can reach on the basis of human experience.

Summary

Whether an event involves a human freewill choice or is an impersonal physical event, three options exhaust the possibilities for its origin: it is either undetermined, self-determined, or determined.

I argued that we cannot reasonably hold any such event to be undetermined. If we do, we are unable to account for: (1) the existence and knowledge of human personality, (2) the existence and knowledge of human nature, (3) the possibility of scientific knowledge, and (4) the possibility of knowledge in general. No theory of the origin of events that fails to account for these four foundational realities is a philosophically tenable theory. Accordingly, we must reject the view that any event can be undetermined.

Next, I argued that we cannot reasonably hold any such event to be self-determined. With respect to impersonal physical events, the suggestion is patently absurd. With respect to events involving human free will, the suggestion flies in the face of experience. The suggestion that human freewill choice is self-determining involves the suggestion that a human being (or at least his will) is eternal and self-existent. But this is in conflict with what seems apparent from our experience—namely, the radical contingency of human existence.

By process of elimination, then, every event that occurs in reality is best understood as determined, for to understand any event to be undetermined or self-determined—whether it involves free will or not— is problematic.

Philosophically, only some form of determinism can account for the important underlying assumptions that form the foundation of our experience. This is critical. If a philosophical theory cannot account for what I do and must implicitly believe, then that theory is suspect.[155] Determinism can and does account for the ordinary beliefs that I do and must embrace. The alternative theories cannot. This is of no small importance. Determinism of some sort is required in order to make sense out of the assumptions and beliefs that undergird ordinary experience. The only question that remains is what sort of determinism is required. My contention, of course, is that DIVINE determinism is required. To give a philosophical defense of that contention would require me to offer my philosophical defense for the existence of a transcendent creator God. That is outside the scope of this work. Suffice it to say, if the argument of this chapter is sound, then any philosophical defense of the existence of a transcendent creator God is *ipso facto* a philosophical defense of divine determinism.

---

155. As long as I am engaging in mere speculation (with my feet resting on my desk), I can, of course, embrace virtually any philosophical theory I want. Philosophical speculation can posit the randomness and indeterminacy of events, and it can posit the indeterminacy of human choice. But what merit is there to a philosophical theory that denies the very things which all of us at all times must implicitly believe when our feet are walking the sidewalk? It is ultimately disingenuous to subscribe to a theory of reality that is intrinsically alien to and incompatible with the beliefs that I must implicitly believe in order to conduct my life. A sensible theory of reality will reject the notion that any event in reality (including human choice) is random and undetermined; for to subscribe to such a notion is to presume that no true knowledge of reality is possible, but that is not what we in fact believe. All of us live as if we believe that a knowledge of reality is possible.

PART FOUR

MAJOR OBJECTIONS TO DIVINE DETERMINISM

In the preceding chapters I outlined compelling reasons for accepting divine determinism. For many people, these reasons are countered by what seem to be decisive arguments against it. In the next three chapters I will discuss the most influential arguments against divine determinism, demonstrating that they are invalid.

Three different, but related objections constitute the most important challenges to divine determinism. The first is philosophical in nature, the second is theological in nature, and the third is ethical in nature. They can be briefly stated as follows:

THE PHILOSOPHICAL OBJECTION

• To affirm both divine determinism and the existence of free will in a human being is a logical contradiction. Divine determinism is logically incompatible with human free will.

• We know beyond a doubt that human beings have free will.

• Therefore, since human beings have free will, it is logically impossible for divine determinism to be true.

THE THEOLOGICAL OBJECTION (VERSION 1)

• If God is perfectly good, then he could never be the ultimate cause of any evil; it would be contrary to his character.

• According to the Bible, God is not evil; he is perfectly good.

• Therefore, God could never be the ultimate cause of any particular event that was evil.

• If divine determinism is true, it follows that God must be the ultimate cause of every particular event that occurs in the world—evil as well as good. If God is not the ultimate cause of every particular event in the world—evil as well as good—then divine determinism is not true.

• Therefore, divine determinism cannot be true; for there are some events of which God cannot be the ultimate cause.

——————— or ———————

THE THEOLOGICAL OBJECTION (VERSION 2)

• The evil that exists in the world is of such a nature and of such an extent that no perfectly good being with the power to eliminate it would allow it.

• Therefore, God cannot be both perfectly good and have the power to eliminate it.

• According to the Bible, God is perfectly good.

• Therefore, it follows that God must not have the power to eliminate the evil in the world; it must have some other source that is outside God's control.

• If divine determinism were true, it would follow that God would have the power to eliminate the evil that is in the world.

• Therefore, divine determinism cannot be true.

THE ETHICAL OBJECTION (FORMAL VERSION)

• If divine determinism is true, then God will accomplish his will regardless of what a human being desires or wills to do. If divine determinism is true, the desires and volitions of human beings are irrelevant with respect to human choice and action.

• Accordingly, if divine determinism is true, then it is futile for any human being to strive to desire and to will what is good; for to do so would not affect one's choices or behavior.

• It is clearly false to say that it is futile for any human being to strive to desire and to will what is good. The Bible, as well as common sense, clearly presupposes that it is not futile for humans to strive to desire and to will what is good.

• Hence, divine determinism cannot be true.

————— or —————

THE ETHICAL OBJECTION (INFORMAL VERSION)

• Insofar as divine determinism does and can result in moral laxity, it is a dangerous doctrine.

• Accordingly, since divine determinism is a dangerous doctrine, it should be ignored and assumed not to be true.

In the following chapters I will discuss each of these objections. I will clarify the nature of each objection. I will analyze the underlying arguments in support of each objection. And I will show that, contrary to popular belief, none of them constitutes a compelling refutation of divine determinism.

CHAPTER NINE

THE PHILOSOPHICAL OBJECTION TO DIVINE DETERMINISM

THE PHILOSOPHICAL OBJECTION:

Divine determinism and the existence of free will in man are logically incompatible. We know beyond a doubt that man has free will. Therefore, since man has free will, divine determinism cannot be true.

If all we had to consider were natural, physical events, the arguments for divine determinism in parts 2 and 3 would be widely persuasive. Though not totally without problems, the absolute determination of every natural, physical event by God is a very plausible notion.[156] In fact, as we saw in the last chapter, sound reasoning from experience ultimately leads to a belief in some sort of absolute determinism. Philosophical reasoning is much more comfortable with determinism than with indeterminism or self-determinism with respect to physical events. The determinism of such events makes more sense.

Only when we consider choices made by free moral agents—particularly choices made by human beings—does philosophical reasoning begin to seriously balk at determinism. The divine determination of human choices appears, on the surface, to be logically incompatible with the notion that man has free will. And yet, absolute divine determinism (the viewpoint that I am espousing) entails that even an individual's "free" choices must be divinely determined.

The fact of human free will is a strong philosophical commitment that nearly all of us share. Reluctance to embrace a theory that seems incompatible with human free will is, therefore, quite understandable. The seemingly obvious incompatibility of free will and divine determinism is what constitutes the essence of the objection under consideration here. We know that people have free will. That the divine determination of human choices is not logically compatible with our exercising free will is *clear* and *obvious*. Divine determinism, therefore, does not and cannot extend to

---

156. The only problem which arises in connection with the divine determination of physical events is a *theological* problem: if God is the ultimate cause of "evil" physical events—destructive earthquakes, hurricanes, floods, famine, *etc.*—then his causing such "evils" would seem to indict his character.

human choice. Hence, divine determinism is not total and absolute. This is the argument to which the divine determinist must respond.

A PREVIEW OF THE CHAPTER

This chapter can be roughly divided into two halves. In the first, I clarify the exact nature of the argument from free will. In the latter half I offer the divine determinist's response to this argument.

I begin by clarifying the philosophical objection—the objection from free will—in three very important respects:

1. I analyze the objection from free will into a cluster of four sub-arguments that, taken together, capture the substance of the objection from free will. I do this in order to bypass the thorny questions that surround the prospect of defining "free will."

2. I demonstrate that the objection from free will is not a straightforward objection based on the clear dictates of common sense. Rather, it is in reality a deductive argument that extrapolates from the dictates of common sense with respect to ordinary experience to the transcendent reality of God. Such an extrapolation is not itself warranted by common sense. Rather, it relies on an implicit argument that involves a generalization from the nature of free will *vis à vis* ordinary reality to the nature of free will *vis à vis* transcendent reality. Such an argument may or may not be valid. Whether it is valid needs to be determined by careful reasoning, not by hasty assumption.

3. Finally, I articulate the logical structure of the four sub-arguments that—taken together—allegedly refute divine determinism by establishing the incompatibility of free will and divine determinism. In my articulation of their logical structure, I intend to make explicit the crucial and problematic step in each of the four arguments. Namely, each argument depends on the validity of identifying ordinary causation with transcendent causation. Each argument depends on extending the commonsense truths about ordinary causation, without qualification, to God as the transcendent cause.

In the second half of this chapter I offer a direct response to the four sub-arguments that constitute the philosophical objection. Having established that the philosophical argument is a deductive argument that involves a problematic extrapolation from the incompatibility of free will with ordinary causation to the incompatibility of free will with transcendent causation, I then evaluate the validity of this extrapolation. I argue that it involves a fallacious generalization. Then, having shown that the philosophical argument is based on a fallacious generalization, I conclude that no valid philosophical objection can be made to divine determinism on the grounds that it is incompatible with free will. No form of this objection has ever demonstrated that free will and divine determinism are logically incompatible. The objection has always simply assumed that they are incompatible, and it has done so merely on the basis of a false analogy to natural determinism.

PART I — Clarifying the Nature of the Philosophical Objection

Before discussing the merits of the philosophical objection, I need to develop its exact nature more fully.

THE PHILOSOPHICAL OBJECTION AS AN ARGUMENT FROM FREE WILL

What is it about the fact of "free will" that makes the determinism of human choice appear incompatible with it? It may seem that one should begin with a definitive definition of "free will." But trying to formulate an adequate formal definition of free will would prove rather difficult. What is the "will"? Is it actually a metaphysical entity? If so, does it have an independent existence from the mind or rationality, or is it simply a part of rationality? Is it perhaps not an actual entity at all? Is it maybe nothing more than a logical construct, a short-hand verbal device for describing the network of choices that an individual makes. What is it?

I want to bypass these thorny and perhaps unanswerable questions. Given our purposes in this study, I think we can safely do so. Rather than offer a rigorous definition of "free will," I shall analyze the argument from free will into four definable objections that I believe constitute its essence. If and when we object that divine determinism is incompatible with free will, essentially we are contending that divine determinism is incompatible with the four following convictions:

1. There exist many choices that men make that are "real" choices.[157]

2. There exist many choices that men make that are significant choices in that they have a significant impact on reality and that serve as part of the basis for a man's belief that he is significant.

3. There exist many choices that men make for which they are morally accountable.

4. There exist many choices that men make from which it is valid to infer the nature of their character and personality.

When people reject divine determinism because of the fact of free will, they are rejecting divine determinism on the basis of four distinct arguments: (i) divine determinism cannot be true because of its incompatibility with the fact that we experience "real" choices, (ii) it cannot be true because of its incompatibility with the fact that man is significant and makes significant choices, (iii) it cannot be true because it is incompatible with the fact of man's responsibility for his choices, and (iv) it cannot be true because of its incompatibility with the fact that we judge a man's character by his actions. I will elaborate on each of these in turn:

FIRST ARGUMENT CONSTITUTING
THE FREE WILL OBJECTION

The first line of argument involves the conviction that people really do have choices in human experience—a real possibility to choose one of many alternatives. Divine determinism implies the absence of any real choice. If divine determinism is true, then the only alternative available to a person is what God has willed to happen. What God has determined to be is what will in fact be—indeed, what must be. Consequently, the human being is not exercising any real choice. He may have the illusion that he is making a real choice, but the fact of the matter is that his choosing does not really involve choice at all. Hence, if divine determinism is true, real choice is not a reality. But if real choice is a reality, then divine determinism cannot be true. Only if I am prepared to deny the reality of real choice in my experience can I accept divine determinism.

---

157. I place 'real' in quotes to indicate that this is the most likely everyday term to be used by the objector in making this objection. I admit that it is a vague, ill-defined, and therefore problematic term; but I believe the discussions which follow will serve to adequately define what the objector means by it in this context.

SECOND ARGUMENT CONSTITUTING
THE FREE WILL OBJECTION

The second line of argument is closely related to the first. It involves the conviction that mankind is genuinely significant and that his significance is closely related to his ability to make significant choices. Divine determinism, it is argued, robs man of any significance because it denies the significance of his choices. How can divine determinism, which denies that man makes real choices, maintain the significance of his choices? Do human choices make any difference in the cosmos? How could they? According to divine determinism, what God wills reality to be is exactly what reality will be. Human choices are simply the mechanical outworking of the will of God. They do not significantly contribute anything to the course of the cosmos. The cosmos is on the course God has set for it and human choices do nothing to alter that. How, then, can human choices be anything other than insignificant reflexes that give flesh to the will of God? If divine determinism is true, then human choices have no significance. If we are prepared to deny the significance of human choices, then divine determinism is an option. But anyone who holds that human choices are significant can accept divine determinism only at the cost of contradicting himself.

THIRD ARGUMENT CONSTITUTING
THE FREE WILL OBJECTION

The third argument involves the well-established conviction that people are accountable for their choices. We praise people for the good and noble deeds that they do. We blame people and hold them morally culpable for their evil deeds. How—so the argument goes—could we hold people accountable for their choices if those choices were determined by someone else? If God determined that I would choose to kill someone, then how could I be held to blame? It was not *my* will that led me to kill, it was God's. How can I be held responsible when it was not *my will* that was the cause of my action? The proponents of this argument think the answer is clear: "I can't." So, if divine determinism is true, there exists no action or choice for which a man can be held morally accountable. But this is directly contrary to everything we have come to believe from experience. Man is morally accountable for his deeds. Unless we are prepared to reject the reality of human accountability, we cannot embrace divine determinism, for they are logically incompatible. If divine determinism is true, then human accountability is not; if human accountability is true, then divine determinism is not. Since experience teaches us that human accountability is real, divine determinism cannot be true.

FOURTH ARGUMENT CONSTITUTING THE FREE WILL OBJECTION

The fourth line of argument is closely related to the third. It involves another deeply imbedded conviction—that a person's actions and choices are indicative of what kind of person he is; that is, that we can draw conclusions about a person's character and personality on the basis of what he chooses to do, say, and think. Now, would that be possible if divine determinism were true? If my choices are not a result of my will, but of the will of God, then how could one legitimately draw any conclusions about *me* on the basis of my choices? My choices reflect the will of God, not the nature of my character. If divine determinism is true, then any inference from a person's choices to his character is not possible. But experience teaches us that such an inference is valid. Therefore, divine determinism cannot be true. Unless I am prepared to deny the validity of this universal daily practice, I cannot believe in divine determinism.

THE ARGUMENT AGAINST DIVINE DETERMINISM FROM FREE WILL

These arguments, taken together, are the essence of what people mean when they say that they cannot accept divine determinism because they believe in "free will." A belief in free will is the belief that (1) the choices men make are real rather than illusory, (2) man is a significant being who makes significant choices, (3) man is morally accountable for his choices, and (4) man's choices genuinely reflect his own character and personality. All four of these convictions are alleged to be incompatible with divine determinism. If this allegation is correct—indeed, if divine determinism is incompatible with any *one* of these convictions— then divine determinism is unacceptable, for it would be logically incompatible with undeniable fact.

If any one of these four free will arguments were valid, we would be forced to doubt the biblical and philosophical arguments that we earlier advanced in support of divine determinism. But I shall argue that none of these is correct. Divine determinism is not incompatible with any of these four free will convictions. I do not challenge the indubitability of any of these aspects of human free will. What I challenge is that any of these aspects of free will is in conflict with divine determinism. Divine determinism does not deny human accountability. It does not deny the validity of inferring a person's character from his choices. It does not deny the reality of human choice. And it does not rob man of his significance. These popularly accepted philosophical objections to divine determinism, I contend, are not valid objections at all. Divine determinism and free will are mutually compatible truths. Therefore, no indubitable truth from our experience makes it philosophically unacceptable to embrace divine determinism. Sound reasoning from experience offers no valid counter-arguments to the arguments we offered earlier in defense of divine determinism.

IS THE PHILOSOPHICAL OBJECTION
AN OBJECTION FROM COMMON SENSE?

The philosophical objection from free will rests on two very important assumptions. The first is that free will is an objective reality in human experience. The second is that divine determinism is logically incompatible with free will. Both of these assumptions need to be correct in order for this objection to work. That we humans have free will is commonsensical.[158] It seems equally commonsensical that divine determinism and free will are incompatible. Most of us immediately assume their logical incompatibility. It seems obvious to us. This nearly universal and automatic acceptance of its assumptions gives the philosophical objection its force:

> *Do we have free will?*
> *Of course, it's just plain common sense! Everybody knows that.*
> *Are divine determinism and free will logically compatible?*
> *No way! Everybody knows that. That's just plain common sense too.*
> *Then, clearly, divine determinism can't be true!*

Is this really so? Are divine determinism and free will truly incompatible? That is the crucial question that remains to be addressed in this chapter. But first, I would like to concentrate on a more specific ques-

---

158. I would part company with Gordon Clark due to his apparent willingness to fly in the face of common sense by denying the reality of free will. See, for example, Gordon Clark, *Religion, Reason, and Revelation* (Nutley, New Jersey: Craig Press, 1961),194-241. Although he has many helpful insights with regard to this discussion, he is too hasty in his willingness to jettison altogether the notion that free will is the basis for moral responsibility. See especially pp. 230-233.

tion— namely, is divine determinism's incompatibility with free will an *obvious* conclusion, reached simply and directly by common sense?

Recall that earlier I differentiated between common sense and kommon sense:

> **COMMON SENSE** *is that set of beliefs that any intelligent being could and should recognize as true, simply on the basis of his own personal mundane experience.*

> **KOMMON SENSE** *is that set of beliefs that is widely (if not universally) embraced by mankind everywhere.*

It may well be that *kommon sense* teaches the incompatibility of divine determinism and free will. In modern American culture, this assumption certainly appears to have wide acceptance. I do not presume to know whether all modern cultures universally accept the incompatibility of free will and divine determinism. Perhaps that is not the case. But modern secular post-Christian cultures overwhelmingly embrace the philosophical dogma that divine determinism is incompatible with free will. In our culture, then, we could understandably conclude that divine determinism's incompatibility with free will is kommonsensical. It is as taken-for-granted as any assumption can be in our culture.

Now if one were to confuse the concept of common sense with the concept of kommon sense, he might fallaciously conclude—on the basis of its kommonsensicality—that it is commonsensical to believe that free will and divine determinism are incompatible. But not all that is kommonsensical by virtue of its universal acceptance is truly commonsensical in the more meaningful sense defined earlier.[159]

This brings us then to the question that must be discussed here: While free will and divine determinism seem to be self-evidently incompatible, does it seem self-evident because it is a commonsensical belief or because it is a kommonsensical belief? In other words, is the fact that this incompatibility seems so self-evident an illusion created by its nearly universal acceptance by the culture around us (i.e., its kommonsensicality)? Or is it because this incompatibility is truly commonsensical in the sense that it is an inescapably rational belief?

To answer this question, I will do the following: First, I will identify the criteria used by common sense to judge whether or not a choice is a freewill choice.[160] Second—for the sake of making an instructive

---

159. See my discussion of this point in chapter 4.

comparison—I will apply those criteria to human choice on the assumption that natural determinism gives an accurate description of human choice. Finally, I will apply those same criteria to human choice on the assumption that divine determinism gives an accurate description of human choice. By this process, we will be able to determine whether or not the criteria of common sense judge divinely determined choices to be freewill choices.[161]

FREEWILL CHOICES AND THE DICTATES OF COMMON SENSE

Most people intuitively recognize that natural determinism and free will are mutually incompatible. They do not typically couch their objections in exact or philosophically rigorous language; but the vague, everyday language they use provides important clues to the fundamental criteria that their ordinary common sense uses in discerning freewill acts from those that are not. When confronted by the determinist's claims, most people would respond, "Then you don't think people can be blamed for their crimes." When the determinist tries to insist that his determinism does not contradict the fact that people are morally accountable for their acts, most people would then respond, "But how could they be to blame? It's not their choice to commit the crime!" Or, alternatively, "But how could they be to blame? They didn't have any choice in the matter!"

These intuitive responses suggest the two most important criteria that people apply routinely to distinguish acts that involve free will from those that do not. These are commonsensical criteria learned through rational reflection on our experience. They are, I submit, the practical criteria that

---

160. This chapter is written in response to the commonly held belief that divine determinism is not commonsensical. My thesis is that it *is* commonsensical or, at least, that it is not incompatible with common sense. I contend that divine determinism only appears uncommonsensical due to the popularity of the DOGMA that divine determinism and free will are logically incompatible. It is not my purpose here to defend the criteria used by ordinary common sense in judging whether a choice is a free will choice. My assumption is that these commonsense criteria are readily recognized and immediately acceptable to the reader. To give a thorough defense of the validity of common sense and its dictates lies outside the scope of this work. It would require a thorough presentation of my entire theory of knowledge in order to defend it. My purpose in this chapter is merely to identify the criteria used by ordinary common sense and to show that such criteria do NOT judge divinely determined choices to be incompatible with free will.

161. The discussion in the following section relies on the important distinction between natural determinism and divine determinism. For an explanation of this distinction, see chapter 1.

ordinary common sense acknowledges are determinative of free will. Here they are more formally:

1. *An act did not involve a freewill choice unless that choice "belonged to" the person who did the act. If it was not his choice, then it was not his freewill decision and he is not morally culpable.*

2. *An act did not involve a freewill choice unless it was physically possible for that person to have acted differently from what he did. If he did not really have a choice, then it was not a freewill decision.*

Both of these criteria remain vague and need further explication. Specifically, what does our ordinary common sense understand by the concept of a choice "belonging to" a person? And what exactly does our ordinary common sense understand by it being "physically possible for an action to have been different"? To clarify these two concepts, it will be helpful to analyze our commonsensical evaluation of a number of hypothetical situations:

SITUATION #1—*Some dirty, low-down, no-good varmint comes and overpowers me. He takes hold of my hand and forces a loaded gun into my palm. Then he squeezes my finger and makes me pull the trigger while he aims the gun at someone to shoot and kill him.*

Now, under these circumstances, did I kill of my own "free will"? Am I morally accountable for the murder? My finger pulled the trigger. Can I be judged guilty of the crime? Did I have a real choice in the matter?

Ordinary common sense says "No!" Of course I'm not to blame. Of course I'm not a murderer. Why not? Very simply because the choice to kill was not "my choice." It didn't "belong to" me, and common sense dictates that I cannot be held accountable for a choice that did not "belong to" me.

As we can see, one of the first questions ordinary common sense asks is whether the choice was "mine." Clearly, in this instance, the choice to shoot and kill someone belonged to the dirty, low-down varmint who overpowered me. I did not fire the gun as an act of free will. I, therefore, am not morally culpable. I am not the murderer, he is.

Nor did I have any real choice in the matter. I played no significant role in the murder. Why not? Because it was physically impossible for me to have acted any differently.162 It was physically impossible, under the circumstances, for me not to pull the trigger. My attacker had overpowered me. Ordinary common sense says that, if it was physically impossible for me to act differently, then I did not have a "real" choice in the situation, and my role was not a significant one. I contributed no more and no less to the murder than the gun did. I was simply a tool in the real murderer's hand.

As ordinary common sense evaluates this situation, both practical criteria identified above are employed: (1) Was the choice or action one that "belonged to" me? (2) Was it physically possible for my course of action to have been different?

From this example, we are able to identify what immediate criteria ordinary common sense employs to judge whether an act "belonged to" me and whether an action "could have been different":

A choice or action "belongs to" someone if that choice or action is a function of his individual choice rather than a function of someone else's individual choice being imposed upon him by means of overpowering coercion.

A choice or action "could have been different" if it were not the result of coercion by means of an overpowering physical force external to the person.

Note, in this particular case, the exact nature of the coercion that occurred. It is *physical* compulsion. Therefore, the specific criterion that ordinary common sense is applying in this situation is this: a choice or action involves a freewill choice only if it is *physically* possible for the act to have been different from what it was in exactly the same circumstances.

SITUATION #2—*A robot, operated by remote control by some human being (probably the same low-down varmint), shoots and kills a person.*

Did the robot kill of his own free will? No! Our common sense evaluates this situation in just the same way as the last one—with one very instructive exception. In this example the immediate criterion employed by our ordinary common sense to determine whether the act "belonged to" the robot is somewhat different from the one used in the last example. The human who is manipulating the robot by remote-control is not manipulating the robot by overpowering him, rather he is simply using his

---

162. Indeed, if more physical resistance on my part would have made a difference, then to the extent that I chose not to resist, to that extent I did make a real choice, did play a significant role, and am morally culpable.

knowledge of the robot's electronics to make the robot respond as he wishes. The will of the human is what is reflected in the robot's actions, not the will of the robot. But yet the human's imposition of his will does not, in this case, take place through overpowering coercion. It takes place through the exploitation of general laws and principles of created reality. The robot's actions are not a function of its own individual contribution to the choice, rather they are a function of mechanical and electrical engineering—engineering that utilizes general laws and principles that operate according to physical necessity. We can see the import of this more clearly in the following examples.

SITUATION #3—*A robot has been pre-programmed to respond in any and every situation. This robot has been programmed to seek out and to shoot and kill a particular person. Having been programmed accordingly, the robot has been set loose to operate "on its own." The robot finds and shoots the designated person.*

Unlike the last situation, there is no human controlling the robot's moment-by-moment action. The robot was pre-programmed to evaluate each situation and respond in accordance with its own programming. Is such a robot acting of its own free will? Is this robot morally accountable for the killing? Would we judge the robot a murderer? Is the robot making "real" choices and making a significant contribution to the flow of events? Common sense would say "No!"

Surely we would not judge such a robot culpable for this killing. We would not punish it for the evil it did, we would disable it. We would wish to stop the robot from destroying a human life, but we would not punish it or seek vengeance on it if it did. We might as well seek vengeance on a mountain for killing a friend in a landslide, or on a heat-seeking missile for downing a friend during battle. The robot, like the mountain or heat-seeking missile, simply does what it does out of physical necessity. We see this same thing in our next example.

SITUATION #4—*A Grizzly bear mauls and kills a camper.*

What does ordinary common sense say about animals like this grizzly? Does ordinary common sense suggest that this grizzly is acting out of free will? Does ordinary common sense dictate that we should hold animals morally culpable for their actions? That they are volitional creatures making "real" choices? No, it does not.

We do not punish bad or dangerous animals, we destroy them. We may not want them around, but we do not blame them for acting as they do. Why not? Very simply because we identify them to be sophisticated, organic robots designed by God. In principle, they would be no different from the man-made mechanical robot in situation #3 above. No less than mechanical robots are, their lives and actions are dictated by necessary physical laws of the created order—by instinct. They do what they do as a reflection of those laws, not as a reflection of some independent, individual contribution that they make.[163] They are simply a unique convergence and manifestation of physical laws. We do not see the actions that animals take as "belonging to them." An animal's choice does not reflect the contribution of his individual will; rather, it reflects the unique convergence of physical circumstances and physical laws that make him a unique creature. But the animal is not making choices to become what it will become. There are no existentialists among the monkeys.

Therefore, the grizzly is not to blame, physical law and circumstances are to blame. The animal is not culpable, for the choice did not belong to him. Nor could the animal "help it." He could not act any differently from the way he acted. He acted out of physical, biological necessity.

SITUATION #5—*A man finds himself in the position of being the only man alive who can prevent a terrorist's bomb from exploding and killing thousands of people. To prevent the explosion, he must hold a plastic strip between two contact points until the bomb can otherwise be disarmed. Due to a complex set of implausible circumstances, no one is in a position to help him for several days. The man becomes so weary that he falls asleep in spite of his noblest efforts to stay awake. His hand drops the plastic strip, electrical contact is made, and thousands of people die in the explosion.*

What does ordinary common sense say about this situation? Is the man, despite his noblest efforts, guilty of a selfish and cruel act—choosing his own sleep over the lives of thousands of other people? Can we pass moral judgment upon this act? No, of course not. It is perhaps unthink-

---

163. It does not affect the force of my argument if the reader does not grant that an animal acts out of physical (specifically, biological) necessity. My point here is NOT to defend a particular view of animals. It is to defend a particular conception of free will. If one believes that animals act out of physical necessity, then he believes that they do NOT act out of free will. If, on the other hand, one believes that animals act freely and NOT out of physical necessity, then to that extent he also believes that animals do have free will. My point is the opposition of physical necessity to free will. Whatever one's view of animal choice, I contend that we all can agree on this incompatibility of instinct and free will.

able for several reasons. But one of them is our awareness that falling asleep can be a semi-automatic response and that, once asleep, hand movement is an unconscious act. Once the man goes unconscious, his hand's movement becomes involuntary, and it makes no sense to hold someone morally culpable for an involuntary act.

Some aspects of human existence parallel our analysis of animal behavior. Some human actions are involuntary, the result of biological necessity rather than purposive choice. Why might a man be morally culpable for falling asleep while on guard duty, but not for falling asleep after several days of keeping a bomb from exploding? Because the latter case is arguably an automatic, involuntary response of the man's body. But the former case is not (assuming the first man is relatively well rested before his guard duty). Though the latter man has tried desperately not to fall asleep, he must eventually pass out from exhaustion. We would judge it unconscionable, in such a case, to hold the man morally blameworthy for something that was an involuntary response of his body. Why? Because the action is not a reflection of the individual contribution of his will. It is a reflection of general biological laws. He is not to blame; the laws of nature are to blame. So even within my own being, common sense recognizes a distinction between actions I take that "belong to me," and actions I take that do not "belong to me." If an action was involuntary, then it didn't really belong to me. It merely reflected biological laws. But if it was voluntary, it reflected an individual contribution I made and therefore it was a choice that "belonged to me." There is another reason this man is not to blame for his involuntary responses. His involuntary responses could not have been other than they were. Due to physical necessity, he had to fall asleep. He did not really even have a choice in the matter.

In these last four hypothetical situations, we have seen an additional immediate criterion being employed by our ordinary common sense to determine whether an action "belonged to" someone and whether it was "physically possible for an action to have been different"—namely,

A choice "belongs to someone" if and only if that choice is a function of some aspect of his being that is independent of the general laws of nature and, hence, only if that choice itself is not a function of general laws of nature and principles of physics.

It is physically possible for a choice or action to have been different only if that choice or action was not exclusively the result of the normal operation of general laws of nature.

Notice that our ordinary common sense understands these two things to be mutually exclusive: if a choice is the function of general physical laws and principles, then it cannot be a function of one's free will; if it is a function of one's free will, then it is not a function of general physical laws.

We can summarize our conclusions thus far: In order for an action to satisfy our concept of a "freewill" choice, that action must (i) involve a choice that "belongs to me," and (ii) involve an action that could have been other than what it was. Furthermore, in order for a choice to qualify as one that "belongs to me," the choice must not be the result of necessary physical laws nor the result of overpowering coercive action on the part of another. Otherwise, any other choices that I make are my choices, they "belong to me," and they qualify as "freewill" choices for which I am morally accountable. And similarly, when we say that a freewill choice must involve a choice that could have been other than it was, we mean that it must have been physically possible for my actions in exactly that same situation to have been different. The key thing to notice is that *physical* possibility is the criterion we are applying.

SITUATION #6—*There is an alien from outer space who is an immaterial, non-physical, spiritual being who has mastery of natural laws that are not even in principle knowable to physicists, who study only the laws of the physical universe. By using such unknowable laws, the space alien is capable of completely enslaving the will of a particular human being such that that human being will and must do whatever the alien wills him to do. He thereby wills that a particular man murder another; and the man does so.*

What does common sense tell us about this situation? It tells us that the human is not morally culpable for murder. The one who is culpable is the space alien who willed the murder, not the human whose will was merely the reflection of the will of the space alien. Why do we judge the situation so? Although there is neither physical coercion nor a physical necessity born of physical laws, there is nonetheless a *natural* necessity born of *natural* laws. The natural laws in question may be neither knowable nor accessible to us, but that is not relevant to our judgment. The fact that some natural laws of the natural order necessitated a particular choice or action is sufficient for us to conclude that such a choice does not "belong to" that man. Likewise, it is sufficient for us to conclude that the choice could not have been other than it was. On both counts, we do not consider it a "freewill" choice by the criteria of common sense.

In the light of this final situation, we can revise the two immediate criteria that our ordinary common sense employs to judge both whether an action "belonged to" someone and whether it was "physically possible for an action to have been different"—namely,

> *A choice "belongs to someone" if and only if that choice is a function of some aspect of his being that is independent of the general laws of nature in the broadest possible sense and hence only if that choice is itself not a function of those general laws of nature.*

> *It is physically possible for a choice or action to have been different only if that choice or action was not exclusively the result of the normal operation of general laws of nature in the broadest possible sense.*

I summarize the preceding discussion in the diagram that follows. As we can readily see from the diagram just below, the criteria for determining whether or not an act involves free will can be reduced to two specific criteria: an act can be judged to involve free will if and only if—

Commonsense Criterion #1: *the act was not the result of coercion by means of an overpowering external force; and*

Commonsense Criterion #2: *the act was not the result of inviolable laws of nature (construed in the broadest possible sense) operative within the actor himself.*

SUMMARY OF THE COMMONSENSICAL CRITERIA
FOR DETERMINING A FREEWILL ACT

What common sense would determine to be the necessary implications of an act's being a freewill act:	The immediate, corresponding, expanded criteria applied by common sense in order to determine whether an act involves a freewill choice:		
(1) The act involves a "real" choice.	An act involves (1) a real choice that (2) has significance as a choice if and only if that act is of such a nature that	It is physically possible for an act to have been other than it was if and only if—	(a) the act was not the result of coercion by means of an overpowering external force; and
(2) The act involves a truly significant choice.	(A) it was physically possible for it to have been other than what it was.		(b) the act was not the result of inviolable laws of nature operative within the agent himself.
(3) The agent of the act in question is morally accountable for the act.	An act involves (3) moral culpability and (4) the possibility for character inference from that act if and only if that act is such that	An act can justly be said to "belong to" the actor if and only if -	(a) the act was not the result of coercion by means of an overpowering external force; and
(4) It is valid to draw conclusions from an act about the character of the person who is the agent of the act.	(B) it can justly be said to "belong to" the actor.		(b) the act was not the result of inviolable laws of nature operative within the agent himself.

So, having established what common sense dictates must be the criteria for determining whether something involves free will or not, what can we say about freewill choices *vis à vis* natural determinism?

FREEWILL CHOICES, NATURAL DETERMINISM, AND THE DICTATES OF COMMON SENSE

I defined natural determinism as any variety of determinism that believes that the determination of human choice lies in some sort of natural force within his physical environment—whether biological, psychological, chemical, economic, sociological, mechanical, or whatever.[164] If one holds that one or another of these forces physically necessitates human choice, then he ascribes to a form of natural determinism. It is important to emphasize that natural determinism involves the notion of physical or natural necessity. Natural determinism holds that man's choices are necessarily what they are because of the inviolable control of some natural force or forces.

Applying the criteria of common sense, then, we can see that common sense immediately finds natural determinism to be a theory that excludes free will. Natural determinism, by definition, explicitly posits that all human choice is explainable in terms of inviolable natural laws operative within the human actor himself. But, as we have seen, this directly fails one of the criteria that common sense uses to determine whether an act is a "free" choice or not. Therefore, if natural determinism is true, no human choice is a "free" choice according to the dictates of common sense.

Many natural determinists insist nonetheless that natural determinism and free will are not incompatible. They cannot bring themselves to deny the reality of free will, so, rather than deny it, they incorporate it into their belief system—assuming uncritically that there exists no incompatibility between the natural determinism they espouse and the free will they are forced by common sense to acknowledge. They smuggle free will into their belief system without realizing—perhaps without taking the time to realize—that the notion of free will is logically incompatible with the implications of natural determinist theory.

Natural determinists who seek, inconsistently, to embrace free will typically try to cloak that inconsistency by proposing an inadequate analysis of common sense. Consider, for example, the philosopher David Hume. Hume rejects the notion that a free will must be an undetermined will. He proposes that we understand a freewill choice to be a choice that results

---

164. For a description and definition of natural determinism, see chapter 1.

from within my own volition rather than from the coercive influence of someone or something external to me. Hume has rightly identified and employed *one* of the two criteria of common sense. But the second criterion has completely escaped his notice—namely, that to be a freewill act, an act can never be the result of inviolable laws of nature operative within the actor himself. Because he ignores this second criterion, Hume can accept the compatibility of free will and natural determinism. Had he applied both of the criteria of common sense, it would be clear to him that such an assertion is patently false.

By Hume's analysis of free will, he would have to judge the grizzly bear and the two robots mentioned above as having "free will." In each case the bear and the robots acted in a manner consistent with the operations of their own inner "decision-making" processes. No external coercive pressure was operative. Each acted according to its own volition (such as it was). But surely this runs afoul of common sense, proving that Mr. Hume has not adequately analyzed our commonsensical notion of free will.

All natural determinists who insist that there is room in their theory for free will have similarly failed to give an accurate or complete analysis of the dictates of common sense. In the end, one thing should be clear: According to the dictates of common sense, natural determinism—the theory that all human choice is physically necessitated by some natural force or forces—excludes free will from human experience. If free will is a real phenomenon, as common sense suggests it is, then natural determinism falsely describes human choice.

FREEWILL CHOICES, DIVINE DETERMINISM, AND THE DICTATES OF COMMON SENSE

The situation is very different with divine determinism. If we apply these same criteria of common sense, we find nothing in the doctrine of divine determinism that excludes free will. Granted, neither does common sense demonstrate that they *are* compatible—i.e., divine determinism may very well be logically incompatible with a belief in free will, but common sense is not adequately equipped to pass judgment on the question.

We must remember exactly what divine determinism is positing. Divine determinism says there exists a creator God who creates absolutely everything—including each particular human choice. Therefore, what a man does is done out of the necessity of creaturely dependence. Every choice is absolutely controlled and determined by the creator of that choice. Every choice is what it is, not out of physical, logical, nor even natural necessity, but rather out of a sort of ontological necessity. If that particular choice is to have existence at all, it must be exactly what he who gives it existence created it to be.

What do the criteria of common sense say about this doctrine? Divine determinism is not positing a God who controls our every choice by external coercion, overpowering us and forcing us to do what we do not want to do. Hence, divine determinism is clearly not incompatible with free will by the first criterion.

But neither is divine determinism positing the existence of natural laws that create human choices out of physical or natural necessity. Divine determinism readily acknowledges that a choice that I might make could have been different, so far as physical and natural necessity is concerned. My genes, my social environment, my training, nothing in my physical or natural environment required that my choice be what it was. Rather, it was the creator God who made my choice to be what is was. In any given physical situation (i.e., genes, culture, personal upbringing, body chemistry, etc.), God could have caused my choice to be different from what it was—he could have created a different choice. He was free. His hands were not tied by my physical situation and natural circumstances. Therefore, there was no physical or natural necessity to my choice. There was only a divine, theological necessity—a necessity that transcends the physical and natural reality in which I find myself. Therefore, neither does the second criterion of common sense rule out the divine determination of freewill choices.

Divine determinism is not positing a kind of determinism that is immediately and obviously incompatible with our commonsensical notion of human freedom. Divine determinism sees me as a being who is ultimately, in very significant respects, free of the physical cosmos and of nature in the broadest sense. I am free of my genes; I am free of my environment. True, I am not free of my creator. But I am free of physical (natural) necessity. And this is all that is required in order for common sense to decide that, in a meaningful sense, "I have free will." "Free of what?" we ask. "Free" of the physical cosmos; "free" of nature in the broadest possible sense. Therefore, divine determinism and the dictates of common sense are not in conflict. The kind of freedom that common sense insists we have, divine determinism allows.

Can we conclude therefore that divine determinism and free will are not logically incompatible—that they do not involve a contradiction? No, that concludes too much too soon. The criteria of common sense are adequate tools to use in everyday mundane life to establish blame and to make judgments with respect to character. But they are not adequate to the task of making a judgment about the larger philosophical question of transcendent causation. If a God who transcends all of reality absolutely determines everything in that reality, what does that mean with regard to moral blame and the assessment of character? The criteria specifically honed to determine, within reality, which of our acts are free are simply not adequate nor appropriate tools to use in making judgments about a God who exists *outside of* all reality. You can't hammer a nail with a fingernail file. You can't determine the compatibility of divine determinism and free will using the everyday criteria of common sense regarding ordinary causation. We will need to educate ourselves and develop a new set of criteria that are useful and adequate to the task at hand—namely, to the task of judging whether a created reality that has been caused by a transcendent reality can be said, without logical contradiction, to involve free will.

Most people—if they entertain the question at all—assume that divine determinism and free will are logically incompatible by the dictates of common sense. Why do they assume so? Has their analysis of common sense resulted in a different set of criteria for assessing the status of human choice? Do they, in accordance with those different criteria, find that divine determinism is clearly and unmistakably incompatible with free will? I think not. Rather, the notion that common sense judges divine determinism and free will to be incompatible is not really an assessment of the dictates of common sense at all. Instead, such a conclusion is based on an implicit argument wherein one extrapolates from the dictates of common sense to a conclusion about divine determinism and transcendent causation. I will attempt to convey the exact nature of this implicit argument:

The Argument that Divine Determinism Is Incompatible with Free Will

PREMISE ONE: *Any human choice that is caused by the physical necessity of overpowering coercion or by the physical necessity of natural processes is not a freewill choice.*
  • Premise 1 is justified by the dictates of ordinary common sense.

PREMISE TWO: *Any human choice that is caused by anything whatsoever (as opposed to being self-caused or uncaused) is not a freewill choice.*
  • Premise 2 is justified by a logical extrapolation from premise 1 by means of generalization. If a human choice that is caused by a physical (natural) cause is not a freewill choice, then we can generalize and say that a human choice that is caused by *any cause whatsoever* is not a freewill choice.

PREMISE THREE: *According to divine determinism, every human choice is caused by God.*
- Premise 3 is justified by the definition of divine determinism.

CONCLUSION ONE: *According to divine determinism, no human choice is a truly freewill choice—i.e., free will does not exist.*
- Conclusion 1 follows by deduction from premise 2 and premise 3.

CONCLUSION TWO: *If free will does exist, then it is logically impossible for divine determinism to be true.*
- Conclusion 2 follows by logical deduction from conclusion 1.

In the next part of the chapter I will argue that this is a fallacious argument. My purpose here is to establish a prior point: If I maintain that divine determinism and free will are logically incompatible, whether I am right or wrong, I do not do so on the basis of plain common sense. Rather, I believe it on the basis of a much more complex logical deduction that is utterly dependent upon the validity of a generalization—namely, it is dependent on premise 2 above. As the following section will show, this problematical deduction or generalization plays exactly the same role in each of the four sub-arguments that, in effect, define the philosophical objection from free will.

THE PHILOSOPHICAL OBJECTION —
ANALYZING THE ARGUMENTS

We are now in a position to understand more thoroughly and accurately the philosophical objection to divine determinism. In our discussion thus far we have made three crucial discoveries:

1. The philosophical objection involves the conviction that divine determinism is incompatible with four indubitable beliefs:

   a) belief in the reality of free choice,

   b) belief in the significance of men's choices,

   c) belief in the moral accountability men have for their choices and acts, and

*d) belief in the logical relation between men's choices and their charac-
ter and personality.*

2. It is a valid and true belief, handed to us by common sense, that a choice
or act that is done out of physical necessity cannot be held to be truly free,
nor significant, nor morally blameworthy, nor reflective of character or
personality.

3. The philosophical objection, though based on the commonsensical
belief in (2) above, is in fact a logical deduction from that commonsense
proposition and may or may not be a valid deduction. It is not itself—as
is usually supposed—a straightforward commonsensical belief.

Let us consider a formal presentation of the four sub-arguments that
comprise the philosophical argument against divine determinism. We will
deal at more length with the first sub-argument since it is the most commonly recognized of the four.

THE FIRST SUB-ARGUMENT
AGAINST DIVINE DETERMINISM

STEP ONE: *Men do not make real choices if every choice they make is made
out of physical necessity.*

If a choice is physically coerced or "programmed in" by the laws of
nature such that it couldn't have been otherwise, then it would be invalid
to call it a real choice—that it involves a choice is mere illusion. This
premise is deemed valid on the grounds that it is commonsensical (in the
right sense of the word). It is a transparently sound induction from ordinary, mundane experience according to the laws of induction and the fundamental assumptions upon which all human knowledge relies. If this
premise can be called into question, there is no aspect of human knowledge that cannot be called into question.

STEP TWO: *Men do not make real choices if every choice they make is made
out of necessity.*

This conclusion is justified on the grounds that it is a valid generalization from the premise in step 1 above. If the physical necessity of a choice
is incompatible with that choice being a *real* choice, it follows that the

necessity of a choice—in any sense of necessity whatsoever—is incompatible with that choice being a *real* choice. This simply follows by generalizing from the first premise. The assumption, of course, is that what disqualifies choices that are physically necessary from being real choices is the necessity of those choices. The fact that it is *physical* necessity is incidental. Though we have little or no experience with any kind of necessity other than physical necessity, to generalize beyond physical necessity to other kinds of necessity (even though we have no direct experience of them) is nevertheless presumed to be valid.

STEP THREE: *Divine determinism asserts that all human choices are caused by God and hence every human choice is made out of necessity.*

This follows immediately from the definition of divine determinism as we have defined it.

STEP FOUR: *Therefore, if divine determinism is true, then the belief that men make real choices is not true.*

This follows by straightforward deduction from the conclusion in step 2 and the premise in step 3.

STEP FIVE: *If the belief that men make real choices is true, then divine determinism is not true.*

This follows by straightforward deduction from the conclusion in step 4. Formal logic teaches us that the contrapositive of a true statement is necessarily true. Step 5 is the contrapositive of step 4. Since step 4 has been established to be true, then step 5 is necessarily true.

STEP SIX: *The belief that men make real choices is true.*

This premise is justified on the same grounds as the premise in step 1—common sense. This is a basic induction from human experience. It relies upon fundamental assumptions of common sense and the principles of induction. If this premise can be questioned, there is no aspect of human knowledge and human intelligence that cannot be questioned. The alternative to accepting this premise is total skepticism.

STEP SEVEN: *Therefore, divine determinism is not true.*

This follows by straightforward deduction from the conclusion in step 5 and the premise in step 6.

THE OTHER THREE SUB-ARGUMENTS

The other three sub-arguments parallel this first one exactly. Rather than go through each one separately, I refer you to the charts on the following pages. The charts lay out the corresponding steps of each sub-argument. The defense for each step of each argument would be identical or analogous to the defense of the corresponding steps of the first argument discussed above.

THE FIRST TWO SUB-ARGUMENTS THAT COMPRISE THE PHILOSOPHICAL ARGUMENT

Sub-argument #1	Sub-argument #2
Step one: A person does not make REAL choices if every choice he makes is made out of physical necessity.	**Step one:** A person's choices are not significant if every choice he makes is made out of physical necessity.
Step two: A person does not make REAL choices if every choice he makes is made out of necessity.	**Step two:** A person's choices are not significant if every choice he makes is made out of necessity.
Step three: Divine determinism asserts that all human choices are caused by God and hence that every human choice is made out of necessity.	**Step three:** Divine determinism asserts that all human choices are caused by God and hence that every human choice is made out of necessity.
Step four: Therefore, if divine determinism is true, then the belief that human beings make REAL choices is not true.	**Step four:** Therefore, if divine determinism is true, then the belief that a human being's choices are significant is not true.
Step five: If the belief that human beings make REAL choices is true, then divine determinism is not true.	**Step five:** If the belief that a human being's choices are significant is true, then divine determinism is not true.
Step six: The belief that human beings make REAL choices is true.	**Step six:** The belief that a human being's choices are significant is true.
Step seven: Therefore, divine determinism is not true.	**Step seven:** Therefore, divine determinism is not true.

THE OTHER TWO SUB-ARGUMENTS THAT COMPRISE THE PHILOSOPHICAL ARGUMENT

Sub-argument #3	Sub-argument #4
Step one: A human being is not morally accountable for his choices if every choice he makes is made out of physical necessity.	**Step one:** A person's character and personality cannot be judged on the basis of his choices if every choice he makes is made out of physical necessity.
Step two: A human being is not morally accountable for his choices if every choice he makes is made out of necessity.	**Step two:** A person's character and personality cannot be judged on the basis of his choices if every choice he makes is made out of necessity.
Step three: Divine determinism asserts that all human choices are caused by God and hence that every human choice is made out of necessity.	**Step three:** Divine determinism asserts that all human choices are caused by God and hence that every human choice is made out of necessity.
Step four: Therefore, if divine determinism is true, then the belief that human beings are morally accountable for their choices is not true.	**Step four:** Therefore, if divine determinism is true, then the belief that a human being's character and personality can be validly judged on the basis of his choices is not true.
Step five: If the belief that human beings are morally accountable for their choices is true, then divine determinism is not true.	**Step five:** If the belief that a human being's character and personality can be validly judged on the basis of his choices is true, then divine determinism is not true.
Step six: The belief that human beings are morally accountable for their choices is true.	**Step six:** The belief that a human being's character and personality can be validly judged on the basis of his choices is true.
Step seven: Therefore, divine determinism is not true.	**Step seven:** Therefore, divine determinism is not true.

SUMMARY

Although we commonly believe that divine determinism and free will are clearly incompatible by the dictates of common sense, I contend that such is not the case. Rather, it is the dictates of kommon sense that make this belief seem so clear and obvious.[165] A close examination of what com-

---

165. I strongly suspect that the kommonsensicality (i.e., the nearly universal acceptance) of the incompatibility of divine determinism and free will is, at least in part, a product of either the Enlightenment or of Romanticism. (But I must leave it to the intellectual historian to either vin-

mon sense dictates relative to what divine determinism asserts reveals that, in fact, the seeming incompatibility of free will and divine determinism (i.e., the kommonsensicality of their incompatibility) is actually based on a debatable logical deduction that may or may not be valid. It is not, in fact, based on a simple, direct application of the dictates of ordinary common sense.

This is an important point for those of us whose theory of knowledge credits highly the dictates of common sense. For us, if common sense ruled that divine determinism and free will were incompatible, then divine determinism would be decisively refuted. But if, in fact, common sense does not directly judge divine determinism and free will to be incompatible—if, instead, their incompatibility is the conclusion of a deductive argument that contains a controversial premise, a problematic generalization—then it behooves us to postpone our rejection of divine determinism until we can determine whether that logical argument is, in fact, sound. In the next section I will argue that the argument is, in fact, fallacious and that, therefore, the philosophical objection to our belief in divine determinism is not a valid objection. Common sense, as it turns out, will not oppose divine determinism. It will support it.

PART II — Answering the Philosophical Objection

To answer the philosophical objection to divine determinism, I must demonstrate that its four sub-arguments are not sound arguments. As I did in the analysis and exposition of those sub-arguments, I will concentrate on the first sub-argument in my response. My response to the other three sub-arguments would be essentially identical to my response to the first. Therefore, it will not be necessary to spell out my response to each of

---

dicate or refute this suspicion.) It seems likely that it is a philosophical dogma that has, as a legacy from history, become a part of the taken-for-granted assumptions of western civilization, and which no longer comes under any scrutiny—philosophical or otherwise—in our culture. It seems self-evident to us that divine determinism and free will are incompatible, because it is part of the cultural baggage we are handed as we enter the world. Since it is immune from examination, we never discover that its apparent self-evidence is an illusion, and that the actual logical basis for the belief is a rather problematic logical deduction based on a fallacious generalization.

It is part of my suspicion that other cultures in world history would not have been nearly so ready to assume the incompatibility of divine determinism and free will as modern western civilization. [Again, I must leave it to the historian to say for sure.] If so, Christians in other civilizations would not have had nearly the same degree of difficulty affirming divine determinism as does the modern Bible-believing church.

them explicitly. Looking at the first sub-argument, then, how should we respond?

The crucial step in the argument is step 2—*men do not make REAL choices if every choice they make is made out of necessity.* Step 2 involves a crucial deduction from the commonsensical premise in step 1—*men do not make REAL choices if every choice they make is made out of* physical *necessity.* Is this a valid deduction? That is the crux of this argument. I have no quarrel with step 1, and I have no quarrel with steps 3 through 7 of the sub-argument. If step 2 is valid, then 3 through 7 follow out of logical necessity. The whole argument hinges on this conclusion in step 2. Is it a valid deduction from step 1?

In step 2, the objector to divine determinism concludes that just as common sense dictates that a choice that is necessary due to physical causation is not a REAL choice, so also a choice that is necessary due to *any sort of causation* is not a REAL choice. A cause is a cause is a cause—so the argument goes. The fact that the necessity of a choice is due to a physical cause in particular is not relevant. If a choice is caused, it is caused. If it is necessary, it is necessary. Consequently, since common sense tells us that a physically necessitated choice is not a REAL freewill choice, it follows that a choice necessitated by any cause whatsoever will not be a REAL freewill choice.

But this is exactly the point where this argument is unsound. One cannot, without independent supporting evidence or argumentation, generalize from physical causation to any and every sort of causation. One cannot validly conclude that because every house in Mill City is made of wood, every house everywhere is made of wood. Neither can one validly conclude that because a choice made out of physical necessity is not a real choice, a choice made out of any sort of necessity is not a real choice. This invalid generalization fails to account for the distinction between different kinds of causes. Its assumption that a cause is a cause is a cause is hasty and fallacious.

At least one crucial distinction needs to be made when we talk about causes. There are, on the one hand, those that I shall call "ordinary causes," and, on the other hand, there are those that I shall call "transcendent causes."[166] An ORDINARY CAUSE is any cause (whether an object, a force,

---

166. There are undoubtedly several important distinctions in the ordinary usage of the word "cause" and the corresponding network of concepts. A thorough and definitive analysis of causation would be helpful here, but it is outside the scope of this work. Furthermore, I do not think a thorough analysis of causation is necessary to the argument of this work. This one distinction between "ordinary" and "transcendent" causation is, I think, sufficient to advance my arguments.

or a state) that is a part of created reality. A TRANSCENDENT CAUSE is
any cause that exists outside of some specific created reality such that it is
not itself a part of that created reality.[167] In the biblical worldview, the
only possible candidate for serving as a transcendent cause of the cosmos
is the transcendent creator God. This distinction is a very simple and obvious one, but—as will become evident—it is a very important one.

Obviously, physical causes fall within the category of ordinary causes.
But God, who—by divine determinist theory—is the ultimate cause of
everything in the cosmos, must be classified a transcendent cause.

In step 2 of the first sub-argument against divine determinism, the
deduction is made that since physical causes (a species of ordinary cause)
preclude choices from being REAL freewill choices, then all causes—
including God as the cause of everything (the unique transcendent
cause)—preclude choices from being REAL freewill choices. This generalization involves an inductive leap across the ordinary and transcendent
cause distinction. Is this leap valid or invalid? The argument against divine
determinism hinges on this question.

This inductive leap presents itself as eminently commonsensical. Why?
Primarily because it is barely even noticed. Indeed the distinction itself is
seldom, if ever, recognized. Without acknowledging the distinction, all
causes are treated the same. All are viewed as ordinary causes and our commonsense intuitions about ordinary causation are applied uncritically.

Furthermore, even if the distinction is recognized, one's first inclination
is to understand a transcendent cause as being exactly analogous to an
ordinary cause. At first glance, it appears that I have nowhere else to go in
order to get any training in the nature of transcendent causation. If the
only training my intuitions have received is in the rules and implications
of ordinary causation, then understandably I could not be expected to
understand a transcendent cause in any way other than by direct analogy
with ordinary causation.

But both of these notions are mistaken. A transcendent cause is not
exactly analogous to an ordinary cause. As I will show, there are some very
crucial differences between them. Furthermore, that our intuitions are
untrained in the nature of transcendent causation is simply not true.
Certainly, our intuitions with respect to ordinary causes are much better

---

167. What does it mean to exist outside of created reality? I mean more than simply existing outside of the material cosmos. I mean more than existing outside of the present age. I mean to literally be beyond created reality itself. Beyond heaven, beyond hell, beyond the angels, beyond
the revelation of God himself as Yahweh, beyond Satan, beyond the whole spiritual realm of created reality. See diagram #4.1 and the accompanying discussion in chapter 4.

trained and stronger. Ordinary causes abound whereas transcendent causes do not. But the fact remains that we do have experience with transcendent causes, and we can, in fact, understand exactly what is involved in the
nature of transcendent causation. Our intuitions work with the concept of
transcendent causation all the time—most notably, when we consider the
relationship of a man to the creation of his imagination. For example, if
we consider the relationship between the author of a novel and the imaginary reality that he creates in that novel, we are considering the nature of
transcendent causation, for that relationship is exactly the relationship of
a transcendent cause to its effect.

The creator God is not the only existing transcendent cause. Any
human being who creates within his own imagination a reality that he
himself is "outside of," and not a part of, is functioning as the transcendent cause of that imaginary reality. Therefore, there is a useful and
instructive analogy between a human author's relationship to the works of
his imagination and God's relationship to the works of his creative will.
This, in turn, means that the divine AUTHORSHIP of all reality is the all-
important metaphor for understanding the relationship between God and
the reality he creates and controls.[168] We must understand God to exist as
the AUTHOR of reality and to have a sort of authorial control over that
reality; only then are we understanding God's providential control over
reality appropriately—as its TRANSCENDENT cause. Any other conception of God's providence and sovereign control—any other metaphor—
will conceive of his providence as a kind of ORDINARY cause—a very misleading error. But the Bible—and divine determinism-contend that God
is more than just the most powerful ordinary cause in the universe. He is
the transcendent cause of everything.

With a little reflection, it becomes quickly apparent how apt the
analogy is between God's providence—as the divine determinist under-

---

168. The Westminster Confession betrays the fact that it has failed to make a distinction
between ordinary causes and transcendent causes—and even more importantly, that it has failed
to recognize that an author is a transcendent rather than an ordinary cause—when it denies that
God is the "author" of sin. (Westminster Confession, chap. 5, sec. 4) Indeed, my point in this
book will be that a recognition that God is the *author* of evil rather than the *agent* of evil is the
crucial distinction that allows both divine determinism and free will to be true simultaneously.
The Westminster Confession, failing to make a distinction between these two very different relationships, is trying to deny that God is in any way the AGENT of evil by purporting that he is
not the AUTHOR of evil. This same failure is evident among others in the Reformed tradition.
The Reformed tradition's failure to make this vital distinction—between ordinary and transcendent causation—has prevented it from reaching final clarity with regard to the nature of free will
and human accountability in the light of their doctrines regarding divine sovereignty, divine
election, and divine predestination.

stands it—and the author's relationship to an imaginary world he creates. What is a character (in an author's novel) that he should resist the author's will?[169] The author of a novel is the one in whom each character in his novel "lives, moves, and has his being."[170] The character in a novel could not think a thought, make a move, nor even exist, but for the will of the author. Each character's existence, and every minute detail of his life is completely, utterly, and unvaryingly a function of the author's will. But this is exactly the relationship that the divine determinist (and, indeed—as we saw in earlier chapters—the Bible) purports to exist between God and the whole of created reality, including ourselves. To understand the nature of God's relationship to reality, we can analyze a familiar situation that is indeed analogous—that of the author of a book in relation to the fictional reality he is creating within his book.

Let me summarize. The author of a novel is the transcendent cause of everything that happens in his book just as God is the transcendent cause of everything that happens in reality. To understand the implications of God's being the cause of everything, I can turn to the only apt analogy to God's providence that I have ever experienced: the author's absolute determination of every detail of the imaginary reality of his novel. I must not turn to physical causation. A physical cause is not a transcendent cause. It is an ordinary cause. The analogy to physical or mechanical causation will only mislead me with respect to God's control over his creation. It will lead to the sort of fallacious reasoning found in the philosophical objection to divine determinism outlined earlier in this chapter.

AN ANALYSIS OF TRANSCENDENT CAUSATION

What then is involved in transcendent causation? Or, more important-ly, what is not involved? Let us consider some of those propositions that our common sense considers axiomatic for ordinary causation and consider whether common sense deems them equally valid for transcen-dent causation.[171]

---

169. Compare with the claim regarding God in Romans 9:19.

170. Compare with the claim regarding God in Acts 17:28.

171. The axioms to which I am referring are those commonsensical axioms that I argued earli-er were the criteria used by common sense in determining whether a choice was a freewill choice or not: (a) a freewill choice is a real choice; (b) a freewill choice is a significant choice; (c) a freewill choice is one for which the person is morally culpable; and (d) a freewill choice is one from which the person's character and nature can be validly inferred. There is a fuller discussion of these in the early part of this chapter.

IS THERE AN ANALOGY TO THE FIRST AXIOM
OF ORDINARY CAUSATION?

The first axiom of ordinary causation is this: (i) *if a choice is caused by a physical cause (i.e., an ordinary cause) and is physically necessary, then it is not a REAL freewill choice because it is not a real CHOICE at all.* Does this same axiom hold true of a choice caused by transcendent causation? Is it axiomatic that if a choice is "transcendentally" necessary, then it is not a REAL freewill choice because it is not a real CHOICE at all? Does common sense dictate that if a human action is ultimately caused by a transcendent will then it does not involve a real freewill choice? No! It does not.

Consider the choices made by the characters in a novel. Such choices certainly qualify as choices that are ultimately caused by a transcendent cause; they are utterly under the control of the transcendent author who has willed them into existence. No character in a novel would act as he did, think as he did, nor be what he was apart from the will of the author. Furthermore, the author's will is irresistible. Whatever the author wants a character to do, think, or be, that's what he does, thinks, and is. Now, what does our common sense tell us about the choices made by these characters? Are their choices not REAL choices? Do we relate to these characters as beings who "had no choice"? No! We relate to them as beings with decidedly real choices, as beings who certainly could have done and thought differently.

That is why, in reading a novel, we alternately feel regret and joy at the choices these characters make. We do not typically respond in casual indifference because, after all, "they aren't really making a choice." We relate to them as characters who have freely chosen as they have. Therein lies the nobility, the tragedy, the poignancy, and the drama of what we are reading.

What are we thinking? We know the characters are nothing more and nothing less than the outworking of the will of the author. Why, then, do we allow ourselves to react to what they do as if they were free moral agents? Because—though they may not be free of the ever-present authorial will that has granted them existence in the first place—they are free in every other respect. Their choices are not physically or logically necessary in the context of the imaginary reality they inhabit. It is not as if—given the imaginary reality created in the novel—the choices these characters make are the only choices that were logically or rationally possible. That is not how we perceive their choices. The fact of the matter is, they could have chosen evil rather than good. They could have chosen selfishness over generosity. They could have entertained perverse thoughts rather than pure thoughts, and still the rational coherence of the author's imaginary world would have remained intact. There truly were other alternatives for these characters. They were REAL choices before them, and they chose what they chose in complete freedom and autonomy from all the other realities within the world of the novel. The real universe created in the novel had not rendered their choices a necessity. Hence, they were completely and utterly free within the world of that novel. Recognizing that, we readers do not hesitate to relate to their choices as REAL choices that could have been different.

Our common sense understands and is quite comfortable with a certain paradox here: the character in a novel is faced with very REAL choices and yet he must do exactly what the author wills him to do. The character chooses what he does, not out of some necessity inherent in the imaginary world of which he is a part, but rather, out of the necessity of doing what the author has decided he will do. The characters' choices are "authorially necessary" or "transcendentally necessary" (if you will), but they are not physically or logically necessary. Our common sense understands and is quite comfortable with this paradox. The character in a novel is faced with very real choices that he must freely make, and yet he must and will do what the author wills. The choices that he freely makes are utterly and completely determined by the author of his existence, and yet they are *free* choices that he freely makes.

IS THERE AN ANALOGY TO THE SECOND AXIOM OF ORDINARY CAUSATION?

Consider next the second axiom of ordinary causation: (ii) *if a choice is caused by a physical cause (i.e., an ordinary cause) and is physically necessary, then it is not a freewill choice because it is not a* significant *choice.* Does this same axiom hold true for transcendent causation? Is it equally axiomatic that if a choice is caused by a transcendent cause and is "transcendentally" necessary then it is not a freewill choice because it is not a significant choice? In other words, if a human action is caused by a transcendent will, does it fail to involve significant choice on the part of the human actor? No! That is not the determination of common sense.

Roughly the same thing can be said about this as about the first axiom. Whereas a choice done out of physical necessity is not deemed a significant choice by common sense, yet a choice done out of "transcendent" or "authorial" necessity *is* deemed a significant choice. Once again we can see this clearly in the transcendent causation exemplified in a novel. The choices made by the characters in a novel are genuinely significant. They are utterly determinative of the course of the fictional history being created in the novel. The plot could not and would not proceed as it does without the characters choosing as they do. The choices of each character are absolutely determinative in shaping the story of which they are a part.

Again, common sense is quite comfortable with a paradox: The character in a novel is faced with significant, reality-shaping choices, and yet he will (and must) do exactly what the author wills him to do. According to common sense, it is not an either/or proposition. It is not a matter of choosing whether the author shapes the plot of his book or the characters, through their choices, shape the plot of the book. Clearly, it is both. The author shapes the story of the novel and the characters shape the story of the novel. To be exact, the author shapes the story of the novel in and through the freewill choices that the author determines his characters will make. The story cannot proceed as it does without the characters choosing as they do. Yet the characters cannot and will not choose as they do apart from the author's creatively determining their freewill choices. Our common sense has no trouble negotiating this paradox. The character in a novel is faced with significant, life-changing choices that he must freely make, and yet he must inevitably do what the author of his existence transcendently determines.

ARE THERE ANY ANALOGIES TO THE THIRD AND FOURTH AXIOMS OF ORDINARY CAUSATION?

When we turn to the final two axioms of ordinary causation, the distinction between an "ordinary" cause and a "transcendent" cause becomes even clearer: (iii) *if a choice is caused by a physical cause (i.e., an ordinary cause) and is physically necessary, then it is not a freewill choice and the person making the choice is* not morally accountable *for that choice,* and (iv) *if a choice is caused by a physical cause (i.e., an ordinary cause) and is physically necessary, then it is not a freewill choice and* nothing *about the character or personality of the person making the choice can be inferred from that choice.*

Do analogous axioms hold true for transcendent causation? Is it equally axiomatic that a person cannot be held morally accountable for a choice that results from some transcendent cause? And is it equally valid to say that one cannot infer anything about the character or personality of a person whose choices have been determined by transcendent causation? Once again, the answer is "No!" These are not valid axioms when we have TRANSCENDENT causation in view.

If a character in a novel commits a murder, do we blame the character for his deed? Of course we do. We may find ourselves even hating him for his cruelty. And we most certainly pass judgment on his character; we may very well conclude that he is utterly evil.

How is it that we can do that? According to the logic of ordinary causation we shouldn't be able to respond to the character as we do. The character couldn't help it. He had to do whatever the author made him do. We can't blame the poor guy for a murder that the author made him do. And why should we judge the poor guy's character so harshly? He might be truly a nice guy. He acted cruelly because the author willed him to do so. And no character can resist the will of his author.

Such is the logic of ordinary causation. But that is not the logic that controls our commonsensical reaction to the characters in a novel. We blame and commend these imaginary characters for their deeds and choices. We find it right and natural to use their choices as the basis upon which to form a judgment about their characters and personalities. Why? How? How can we do so in such defiance of the logic of ordinary causation? There can be only one explanation: we are applying an entirely different logic to the phenomenon of transcendent causation from that which we apply to the phenomenon of ordinary causation. The logic of transcendent causation—the logic we intuitively recognize to be applicable in the case of an author's transcendent control over his characters—is radically different from the logic of ordinary causation. It has an entirely different set of axioms.

SUMMARY OF OUR ANALYSIS
OF TRANSCENDENT CAUSATION

The implications of ordinary causation and the implications of transcendent causation are very different. Common sense tells us that ordinary causation (including primarily physical causation) is logically incompatible with the attributes of what we call freewill choices. A choice that has been determined by an ordinary cause is not real, not significant, not morally assessable, and not a valid datum for the determination of a person's character. But that same common sense tells us that a choice that has been determined by a transcendent cause is all of those things—i.e., real, significant, morally assessable, and a valid datum for the determination of a person's character. If so, then a choice's being determined by a transcendent cause is not incompatible with its being a freewill choice. A choice's being determined by an ordinary cause clearly is incompatible with its being a freewill choice, but no such incompatibility exists when its determinative cause is transcendent. Before we can proceed any further, we must pause to respond to a very natural and common objection.

AN OBJECTION: THE LOGIC
OF ORDINARY CAUSATION IS *NOT* DIFFERENT
FROM THE LOGIC OF TRANSCENDENT CAUSATION

We have just contended that the logic of ordinary causation is different from the logic of transcendent causation. We noted that we do not naturally apply the logic of ordinary causation to cases that clearly involve transcendent causation— for example, to the case of characters in a novel whose actions are transcendently caused by the author of that novel. Instead, transcendent causation has an entirely different logic of its own.[172]

But someone may raise the following objection: True, the logic does seem to be different; but the difference in logic is not due to a fundamental difference between ordinary and transcendent causation. Rather, it is due to the fact that the characters in a novel are not real. They are imaginary.

Consider a specific example: an author, Arthur, writes a novel in which a character, Killroy, murders another character, Deadmore. Now, according to the argument I sketched above, our commonsense intuitions do not find it reasonable to convict Arthur or find him culpable for the murder. I offered an explanation for this: namely, the fact that Arthur's relationship to the fictional characters in his novel—to Killroy, to Deadmore, and to the whole imaginary world of his novel—is a TRANSCENDENT relationship. Arthur is the transcendent creator of these characters and of all their actions, including this murder. As the transcendent creator and cause of Deadmore's murder, he is not the one who is morally responsible for it. He did not *commit* the crime, he *created* it. Creating a murder is a significantly different action from committing one. They do not amount to the same thing.

But why? Why is he not morally culpable for what he transcendently causes or creates? My contention is that it is due to the nature of transcendent causation. Transcendent causation, unlike ordinary causation, is not the kind of overpowering physical coercion that requires us to shift

---

172. By "a logic of its own," of course, I do not mean that there exists literally another kind of logic. From my discussion in chapter 3 it should be clear that I am convinced there is, strictly speaking, only one kind of logic. Here I refer to "logic" in the looser sense often used in everyday language. The point is that what logically follows from the fact that some choice has been "transcendently" caused is not the same as what logically follows from the fact that some choice has been "ordinarily" caused. A common, short-hand way to say this is simply to say that the "logic of transcendental causation" is different from the "logic of ordinary causation."

moral culpability. If the direct agent of a murder has been overpowered and coerced (ordinary causation), then we shift blame from the agent committing the murder to the one whose coercion made him commit the murder. But transcendent causation leaves moral culpability intact. The character who commits a murder is morally accountable for that murder because he is the one who committed it. That, after all, is how the morality game is played: whoever commits a deed is morally accountable for it. The author, Arthur, who created the character and the murder, is not morally accountable for *committing* the murder. This is so precisely because he did not commit it, he only created it, and creation of this sort is an act of transcendent causation.

But one might object: Granted, our intuitions do find it unreasonable to blame the author of a novel for a murder committed by one of his characters. But it has nothing to do with the fact that the author is a transcendent cause. Rather, it is because the crimes committed in a novel are not real, but imaginary. The author cannot be blamed for a murder that has not really occurred—that is, for a strictly imaginary murder. Isn't this the real reason we do not blame an author for the crimes he creates?

According to this objection, I have based my argument upon sleight-of-hand illusion when I use the analogy of an author to describe God's relationship to his cosmos. It may appear to demonstrate that a transcendent cause is not morally culpable; it may appear to show that transcendent causation does not nullify the reality of free will. But, in fact, authorship does not demonstrate any such thing. In reality, there is no real crime in a novel for which the author could be culpable, and the free will that exists in his characters is as "imaginary" as anything else in his novel. Hence, an author's relationship to the fictional reality he creates in a novel has nothing at all to teach us about God. Certainly it cannot prove that transcendent causation does not preclude free will, for there is no analogy between God and an author. The author of a novel creates no REAL thing, only imaginary things, while the works of God's hands are REAL. Therein lies the significant, decisive difference between God's relationship to the world and an author's relationship to his novel. God is related to REAL things as their creator; the author's relationship is to merely imaginary things.

ANSWERING THIS OBJECTION

There are three things that need to be said in response to this objection.

PART ONE OF MY RESPONSE TO THIS OBJECTION

It is certainly true that the murder that occurs in a novel is an imaginary one. Why did I choose an imaginary—rather than a real—evil for my analysis of transcendent causation? Am I trying to deceive the reader? Am I claiming to prove a difference based on transcendent causation when the difference hinges on something else entirely—the difference between reality and fiction? It will help my case to explain why I chose an example that involves only imaginary realities.

As a matter of fact, I chose an imaginary murder precisely because there exists no other instance where we humans can experience and hence relate to the concept of transcendence. None of us does—nor ever possibly could—transcend the reality in which we exist. We are ourselves creatures, inextricably a part of this created reality. None of us has ever experienced—nor will we ever experience—being above or outside the creation of which we are inescapably a part.

Consider, then, the case of a murder. How could we ever know, first-hand, what are the moral implications of being the creator of a murder? Who of us has ever created (rather than committed) an actual, real murder? We most certainly understand the moral implications of committing a murder. That is a part of our direct experience. But who of us has the power to create the freewill choice to commit murder in another person? Such is an experience that none of us will ever have. Accordingly, in trying to determine whether the transcendent cause of a crime bears any morally accountability for it, we have no experience to draw upon. We have no experience upon which we could base any conclusion. We have never been a transcendent cause of anything in our reality.

We have, however, been the transcendent cause of things within imaginary realities of our creation. Indeed, that is the one and only way in which we ever could be a transcendent cause. We can create an imaginary murder. We could never create a real one.

This is why my argument must appeal to the case of an imaginary murder. I must analyze a *bona fide* instance of transcendent causation. But the only way I can be a transcendent cause is in relation to the products of my imagination. Hence, when my argument seeks to understand moral culpability relative to an imaginary murder, I do not introduce the element of its imaginary nature in order to create a specious, illusory argument. Rather, it is because no other scenario exists that could afford us the opportunity to understand the implications of transcendence. If we do not analyze a situation in which transcendent causation does, in fact, occur—namely, over the creations of my imagination—then what situation are we going to find that will permit us to analyze transcendent causation?

PART TWO OF MY RESPONSE TO THIS OBJECTION

In the example above, I argued that we do not blame Arthur (the author of the novel) for Killroy's murder of Deadmore because holding the transcendent cause of an evil deed morally accountable for it is contrary to common sense. According to the objection under consideration, this is not right. The correct explanation (so the objection claims) lies in the fact that the murder of Deadmore is imaginary, not real. At first glance this sounds like a plausible explanation. But on closer examination, the imaginary status of the murder does not adequately explain why we hold Arthur blameless.

Look at it from "inside" the story. Suppose that the imaginary Killroy were to be apprehended by an imaginary police force and brought to trial before an imaginary jury. Would it make sense for this imaginary jury to acquit Killroy on the grounds that Killroy did not commit a real murder? Even if—from our perspective as readers—this sounds plausible, from the perspective of this imaginary jury, this would be ridiculous. From their perspective, they are trying Killroy for a real murder.

The "reality" of the murder is relative.[173] Relative to our author (Arthur) and the objective existence of which he is a part (including us readers), the murder is not real. But relative to the imaginary jury, the murder is very real. It is just as real as they are! Arthur did not write a fictional story about an imaginary murder. He wrote a fictional story about a real murder—a real murder within the fictional world he created. Relative to this imaginary jury that is a part of that imaginary world, the murder is a real one. Accordingly, it would be unthinkable—even bizarre—for the jury to acquit Killroy on the grounds that the murder he had committed was not a real one.

Now what if Arthur (the author) were to be brought to trial before this same imaginary jury. We have suggested that, commonsensically, Arthur should not be held culpable for the murder that he created. He is not the murderer. He is the author of the murder. But here is the crucial question: why not? Why should he not be found guilty? Because—as the objection suggests—the murder was not a REAL one? No! Relative to the imaginary jury that, hypothetically, is trying Arthur, the murder he is being tried for is quite real. The not-real argument could never even arise in this imaginary jury's deliberations. Yet a guilty verdict would be bizarre and unthinkable just the same.

---

173. My point here hinges on the idea that reality can exist on different "levels," that things can exist in "degrees." For a further discussion of this concept of reality, see appendix D.

Why the not-guilty verdict then? It can only be because Arthur's state of transcendence relative to the novel renders him unimpeachable for the crimes he created in that novel. To create whatever he chooses is the author's prerogative. He cannot be judged accountable for his characters' actions for, as I said before, he creates those actions; he does not commit them. An author cannot create the world he chooses to create (the author's prerogative) without creating the characters and actions that that world requires. But the rules that make up the moral structure of objective reality implicate the agent or committer of a crime, not the transcendent creator of a crime.

We have made two important observations in this thought experiment wherein we imagine Arthur being put on trial by a jury within his novel: (i) the question of whether Deadmore's murder was real or imaginary would not even arise, it would be a non-issue to such a jury (they would take the "reality" of the murder for granted), and (ii) it is inconceivable that such a jury would convict Arthur of this crime. So, according to my own commonsensical intuitions, while I expect this jury to be reluctant to blame Arthur for Killroy's deed, yet I expect them not to hesitate with respect to the REALITY of Killroy's deed. Therefore, my reluctance to judge Arthur morally culpable for Deadmore's murder results not from the murder's lack of reality relative to me, rather it must result from an acknowledgement of Arthur's prerogative as the transcendent author. Common sense recognizes that a transcendent author (the transcendent cause) is not morally accountable for any particular deed which a creature might commit in the reality of which he is the transcendent creator.

This raises a further question. Am I suggesting that an author is above good and evil in the writing of a book? Is there no moral accountability for what an author writes? And by analogy, then, am I suggesting that God is above good and evil? Am I saying that God could do literally anything he wants to do in creating the history of the world and never in any sense whatsoever be morally accountable for what he creates?

My answer to both questions is "No." In the case of an author, I am not suggesting that Arthur is above good and evil. Like any human being, Arthur must and will be judged by the standards of goodness, and the act of writing his novel is one of the acts for which he will be judged. But, with regard to the novel, for what exactly will Arthur be judged? Will he be judged for the crimes and evils that are committed by the characters in his novel? No. As we have seen, Arthur cannot be held morally accountable for the actions of his characters. Rather, moral judgment of his creation of the novel will be based on two things: (i) the purpose of and motive from which he wrote the novel in the first place, and—to some extent, at least—(ii) the overall impact of the novel on its readers. If Arthur's purpose for writing the novel is consistent with what is good and right, then his act of writing the novel was, to that extent, a good thing. Similarly, if the overall impact of the novel on its readers was morally good, then, to that extent, the writing of the novel was a good act. But if Arthur's purpose was evil and the overall impact on its readers was harmful, then writing it was evil; it ought never to have been written. So, while Arthur is not morally culpable for the deeds committed by the characters in his novel, he is nonetheless morally culpable for the novel's creation, taken as a whole.[174] He is not above good and evil. He too is subject to moral judgment. But he must be judged only for that which he did, in fact, do. He must be judged only for that of which he was, in fact, the agent. Arthur was not the agent or the doer of any of the crimes he authored in his story. So he cannot be judged for those. But he was the agent of an act of creation. He created a reality—a reality that included a murderer, Killroy, within it. He must ultimately be judged for the creation of that world he authored. Taking that world as a whole, it was either morally good that he brought it into being, or it was morally evil that he brought it into being. For that Arthur must be judged.

The same is true of God. God is not above good and evil. He too is subject to moral judgment. Either God is good or he is evil. The standard by which we can legitimately judge God's moral character is essentially the same standard we apply to one another.[175] Indeed, it is ultimately the same standard he applies to us. But, as with Arthur, God must not be judged on the basis of deeds he did not commit. He must not be judged on the basis of the deeds committed by his creatures. Rather, he must be judged on the basis of the deed he did commit—namely, the deed of cre-

---

174. Is my argument here that the "end justifies the means"? In one sense, "yes." However, to argue that the end justifies the means is only fallacious if one is arguing that inherently unjust or evil means can be considered justified by virtue of some good end that they achieve. That is, of course, fallacious moral reasoning. But I am not arguing that an author who creates an act of murder is employing an inherently evil act as the means to a good end. Rather, I am contending that there is nothing inherently evil about the act of creating the deed of murder in the first place. It is morally reprehensible to BE a murderer; but it is not morally reprehensible to create murder as a part of some larger reality that one is creating—assuming that the reality you are creating is, overall, not morally objectionable. My contention, therefore, is that the creation of a murder in one's novel can be a morally permissible means to a good end. This is not "the end justifying the means" in any morally problematic or fallacious sense.

175. This needs to be qualified. As the text goes on to make apparent, God, the creator, has prerogatives we do not have. Any moral assessment of God must take that fact into account. But it is outside the scope of my purpose here to enter into a thorough discussion of all the differences that exist between passing moral judgment on God *vis à vis* passing moral judgment on man.

ating this reality in which we find ourselves. Would a morally good creator have created *this* reality, taken in its entirety? Is God's motive and purpose in creating this reality consistent with goodness—even perfect goodness? Will the overall result of God's having created this reality be consistent with what a perfectly good God would want? If so, then God is a good God. If not, then God is evil and we must not hesitate to judge him so. The moral structures of reality require it. Even God himself must be subjected to the scrutiny of moral judgment that he created us to engage in. God, then, is not above good and evil. But, in passing moral judgment on God, we must not ignore his role as the transcendent cause of everything. We must take into account his truly unique status. We must not apply moral judgment to him as if he were just one of us—as if he were merely another "ordinary cause" within the web of reality. As the transcendent creator he has a unique prerogative—the prerogative to make reality be whatever he wants it to be. While many of the people and deeds he creates are evil, God is not guilty of evil for creating them. It is God's prerogative to create both good creatures and evil creatures. There is nothing evil in that.[176] If he is to be judged evil, it can only be because his creation, taken as a whole, is an evil story that should never have been conceived.[177]

---

176. Some want to argue that even as the transcendent creator whose prerogative it is to create both good and evil, a good God would never create evil. To do so implicates him in that evil. Not because he is morally accountable for the deed; but because, as its creator, it reflects poorly on his own moral character. For, in order for God to create an evil event, he had to have the ability to conceive of evil. Is the act of conceiving evil not an evil act itself; and is the ability to do so not already an indictment against God's character? The reasoning seems to involve something like the following assumption: in order to create something, that which is created must already, in some sense, exist within the nature and being of the one who creates it. There may be some truth to this in the context of human creation. But clearly this cannot be so in the case of divine creation from out of nothing. God created yellow without being yellow; God created physicality and materiality without being either; God created the taste of sweetness without tasting sweet. Likewise, cannot God create moral evil without himself being morally evil? Furthermore, to conceive of evil is not the same thing as to have an "impure thought." When a human being has an impure thought, he is actually *desiring* what ought not be desired, or *valuing* what ought not be valued. To create evil as a part of his creation, God need neither desire it nor value it. He can hate it and abhor it at the same time that he creates it and employs it to accomplish the overall good purposes that he intends.

177. Will it ever be possible, in principle, to form any judgment as to the propriety of the story God has created? I believe so. I believe that at the end of time—when all that can be known about this present age is known—anyone whose moral judgment is not stunted by the effects of sin will look at all that God has accomplished in the world and will praise him for his wisdom, for his creativity, and especially for the purity of his goodness.

PART THREE OF MY RESPONSE TO THIS OBJECTION

Let us keep in mind the issue at hand: Why exactly do we not feel compelled to hold the author of a novel morally accountable for a murder that occurs within his novel? Is it because the murders contained in his story are not real, but imaginary? Or is it because it is his prerogative, as the author and transcendent cause, to create whatever realities he wants to create within his story?

I have offered one reason why the imaginary nature of the murder cannot adequately account for why we do not blame the author. There exists yet a second reason: moral culpability is not limited to objective realities. To put it another way, being merely imaginary is no defense against moral blame.

Take Jesus' teaching, for example—"every one who looks on a woman to lust for her has committed adultery with her already in his heart."[178] Is Jesus suggesting that a man who lusts for a woman has committed an objectively real act of adultery? Of course not. His point is that to lust after a woman—to have an inappropriate desire to be sexually intimate with a woman other than one's wife—is the moral equivalent of adultery. But he is not suggesting that it is objectively real adultery. Clearly, it is adultery in the imagination—imaginary adultery.

Jesus' teaching is very significant for the issue at hand. Even though the lust of which Jesus speaks does not involve an objectively real act of adultery, a man is morally culpable for it nonetheless. A man can and will be held morally accountable for an act of adultery that exists only in his imagination. By this standard, then, Jesus could never let Arthur off the hook for a murder he created in his imagination on the grounds that it existed only in his imagination and not in objective reality. If he were to exempt Arthur from condemnation, it would have to be on some other basis.

Suppose that Arthur actually did have a perverse desire to kill—either someone in particular or someone in general. Let's suppose that his motive for including Killroy's murder of Deadmore in his novel was to give expression to this perverse murderous desire in his own heart. In such a case, the murder in his novel would be a true reflection of his own heart's desire. Would Jesus hold Arthur morally culpable for the creation of the murder in this event? Yes! I think so. The fact that it was not an objectively real murder would not make him any less culpable for it. Still, his culpability would not be for committing the murder. He did not do that. Neither would his culpability be for his creating the murder *per se*. Rather,

---

178. See Matthew 5:28.

it would be for the perverse murderous desires that gave rise to his creation of the murder. In our previous analysis—where we decided that Arthur was not culpable for Deadmore's murder—we were assuming that Arthur's story did not involve giving expression to some perverse desire in his own heart.

Pornography is another example of this same point. Am I morally culpable for reading about and perversely enjoying intrinsically immoral sexual experiences in my imagination? Or am I held blameless because those experiences are imaginary and not objectively real? Jesus, I think, would say "No!" I am not blameless. Never mind that they are not real acts. To enjoy perverse sexual encounters in my imagination reflects an evil and corrupt heart just as surely as would acting out those same desires in objective reality. The fact that, in such an instance, I do not engage in REAL acts does not exempt me from moral culpability.

Therefore, in light of Jesus' and the Bible's overall perspective on evil and moral culpability, the objection under examination is without force. Our reluctance to attribute moral accountability to an author is not due to the imaginary, not-real status of the novel. Biblically, such a fact by itself could never exempt Arthur from moral culpability. Our reluctance, therefore, arises from something else. What is that something else? It can only be what we have already suggested—Arthur's status as a transcendent cause. According to our commonsensical and rational understanding of the rules of morality, the author—the transcendent cause of an evil deed— is not the one who is morally culpable for any deed he creates. Rather, it is the creature who commits the crime, the character who perpetrates the murder. The author who conceives of it and creates it cannot reasonably be held accountable.

Our original contention remains valid. An author's relationship to the characters in his novel gives us important information about the nature and "logic" of transcendent causation. An author is the transcendent cause of the freewill choices that his characters make. His transcendent causation of these freewill choices does not preclude them from being genuinely free choices. It does not preclude our holding the characters accountable for their choices and judging their characters on the basis of those choices. Neither does it preclude our deeming their choices significant, nor deeming them REAL. Accordingly, since God is the transcendent cause of human choices in a manner analogous to the way an author is the transcendent cause of his characters' choices, we can see that God's divine determination of all of our choices does not preclude our choices from being truly and genuinely free. In other words, once we have come to a correct understanding of the nature and logic of transcendent causation, we can see clearly that divine determinism and human free will are not at all incompatible.

SUMMARY OF OUR REFUTATION
OF THE PHILOSOPHICAL OBJECTION

We are now in a position to summarize what is fallacious in the four sub-arguments that comprise the philosophical objection to divine determinism. The second step in each of these arguments involves a fallacious generalization.[179] Failing to take into account the distinction between ordinary causation and transcendent causation, these arguments mistakenly generalize from the character of ordinary (physical and mechanical) causes to the character of all causes whatsoever (including transcendent causes). If a person's choice is caused by some ordinary cause, that ordinary cause would physically necessitate that choice and it would not therefore be a freewill choice. Generalizing from that commonsensical fact, they conclude that if a person's choice is caused by and necessitated by any cause whatsoever, then it would not be a freewill choice. But, as we have seen, this conclusion is simply false. Transcendent causes are of such a nature that they can necessitate a creature's choices without precluding the reality of them being truly freewill choices. At first glance, this seems implausibly paradoxical. But it is an inescapable truth. Examining the author's relationship to the characters in his novel is a helpful way to arrive at an intuitive grasp of this truth.

We saw earlier that the validity of the philosophical argument against divine determinism ultimately hinges on this crucial second step in all four of the sub-arguments. If this second step in each argument were valid, then divine determinism would be philosophically indefensible. But step two is fallacious; none of the sub-arguments is sound. As a consequence, there exists no problem with the doctrine of divine determinism from a philosophical point of view. Divine determinism is not refuted by the philosophical objection, for—contrary to the objector's claim—it does not preclude free will. Divine determinism and free will are completely compatible concepts, so our earlier arguments in support of divine determinism still stand. In spite of the initial plausibility of the philosophical objection, divine determinism remains the most reasonable theory that can account for all the data and make the best sense out of reality, knowledge, and the Bible.

---

179. Each of the four sub-arguments was discussed earlier in this chapter.

Conclusion

Much confusion results from a failure to separate our consideration of divine determinism from that of natural determinism. Many people rightly reject natural determinism on the grounds that it precludes free will. But mistakenly, they think that they are equally right to reject any and every form of determinism on the same grounds. As the arguments of this chapter have shown, the case against natural determinism cannot legitimately be generalized to refute all forms of determinism whatsoever. Most notably, it cannot be generalized to refute divine determinism. Divine determinism, unlike natural determinism, is compatible with free will. Therefore, the truth of human freedom does not stand as a refutation of divine determinism in the same way that it stands as a refutation of natural determinism. Ordinary causation—the causation assumed by natural determinism—is a fundamentally different sort of thing from transcendent causation—the causation assumed by divine determinism.

CHAPTER TEN

THE THEOLOGICAL OBJECTION
TO DIVINE DETERMINISM

THE THEOLOGICAL OBJECTION:
In light of what the Bible teaches us—namely, that God is a perfectly good being—divine determinism and the existence of evil in the world are logically incompatible. God, being a perfectly good being, cannot be the cause of any evil. Or—even if we concede that God could, in certain cases, cause some particular evils in order to accomplish a greater good—he certainly cannot be the cause of the whole extent of the evil that actually exists in the world. The nature and extent of the actual evil in the world is inexcusable. It follows, therefore, that there must exist sources of evil in the world that are beyond God's control. It further follows that divine determinism cannot be true, for there exist some aspects of reality-namely, these sources of the actual evil—that are not determined and controlled by God.

The philosophical objection to divine determinism—discussed in the last chapter—is an objection to determinism in general. It is an objection to natural determinism just as surely as it is an objection to divine determinism. In this respect, the theological objection is quite different. Due to its very nature, the theological objection is leveled against divine determinism in particular. It has no force against natural determinism.

Furthermore, while the philosophical objection must begin with the virtually universal belief that humans have free will, the theological objection must begin with the not-at-all-universal belief that a morally perfect God exists. If the existence of a morally perfect God is not granted, the theological objection cannot get off the ground. As such, the theological objection is an objection that is entirely without force outside the context of theistic belief. Only a theist who believes that God exists, that God is omnipotent, that God is morally perfect, and that evil truly does exist in the world can possibly feel the force of the theological objection. The person who has rejected any one of the above assumptions would not be phased by this objection. In other words, the theological objection is unmistakably part of an in-house debate among fellow Judaeo-Christian theists.[180]

---

180. For a fuller discussion of this point, see appendix F, *A Detailed Analysis of the Theological Objection to Divine Determinism.*

One further point of comparison: both objections are raised against the extension of God's determinative power to everything. Generally speaking, God may be said to be the first cause of all of reality, but he does not cause every particular thing within it. Some things within reality are outside his control. In this regard the two objections agree. But they differ with respect to exactly which set of things they would identify as outside the scope of God's determination. The philosophical objection contends that divine determinism would preclude free will. Hence, it insists that freewill decisions are outside of God's control. The theological objection, on the other hand, contends that divine determinism would preclude the perfect goodness of God. Hence, it insists that the occurrence of evil is outside God's control.

Accordingly, the philosophical objection, standing alone, would readily concede that God is the determinative cause of natural evil—devastating earthquakes, tornadoes, hurricanes, famine, etc. But the theological objector is unwilling to concede this. The suggestion that God causes any evil whatsoever is precisely what this objection opposes. The theological objector assumes that God cannot be the cause of any evil whatsoever. If a devastating earthquake is truly evil, then God did not cause it. If God did cause it, then, while devastating, it is not truly evil. It may be difficult to understand how an earthquake with such apparently evil consequences is not evil, but—if God is its cause—it cannot be an evil occurrence. This is the underlying perspective that forms the foundation of the theological objection to divine determinism.

In a similar vein, the theological objection, taken alone, would have no problem with the suggestion that God is the determinative cause of some (or even all) of our freewill choices—so long as those choices were morally good. So, for example, God could be the cause of our choice to act in compassion toward someone. But this is the very thing the philosophical objector is unwilling to concede. From the standpoint of the philosophical objection, a choice is only truly a freewill choice if God did not cause it. It makes no difference whether that choice is morally good or morally evil. It cannot qualify as a moral choice at all if God—not an autonomous human will—caused it.

Both the theological and philosophical objections are seeking to establish boundaries to the determinative control of God. While the philosophical objection opposes the extension of God's causation to freewill choices, the theological objection opposes the extension of God's causation to anything evil, whether it is the result of freewill choices by men or the result of the impersonal forces of nature.

Clarifying the Theological Objection

The theological objection is founded on the contention that the following three beliefs are mutually incompatible: (1) a belief in divine determinism, (2) a belief in the perfect goodness of God, and (3) a belief in the reality of evil. Belief in the perfect goodness of God and belief in the reality of evil are incontestable aspects of Christian belief. Hence, it logically follows that if Christian belief is valid, then divine determinism is not.[181] The crux of the objection, therefore, is the alleged logical incompatibility of the above three beliefs. There are two different forms that this objection can take. I will examine each.

THE WEAKER FORM
OF THE THEOLOGICAL OBJECTION

An assumption that undergirds the theological objection is the assumption that if God is the cause of my acting in a particular way, then it is God, not I, who is morally accountable for my deed. The assumption undergirding the philosophical objection reverses the emphasis—namely, if God is the cause of my acting in a particular way, then I am not morally accountable for my deed, God is. While the philosophical objection focuses on the absence of moral accountability in me, the theological objection focuses on the fact that God must be morally accountable.

Beginning from this initial assumption, consider a specific action I might take. If God is the ultimate cause of an evil deed that I commit—as divine determinism would assert—then God is the one who is ultimately to blame for it. But divine determinism extends God's determinative control—and, with it, his moral accountability—to everything. Hence, God is morally accountable for every deed done by every human being everywhere throughout time. With that in mind, how then can we consistently maintain that God is a perfectly good being while affirming divine determinism? For if God is ultimately accountable for every individual evil deed that human beings perform, he can hardly be credited with moral perfection. We must either concede that God is evil, or we must concede that divine determinism is false. But we cannot simultaneously embrace divine determinism and the moral perfection of God.

---

181. See appendix F, *A Detailed Analysis of the Theological Objection to Divine Determinism*.

THE STRONGER FORM
OF THE THEOLOGICAL OBJECTION

A second form of the theological objection is stronger in force in the sense that it is more difficult to refute. It presents a decidedly more difficult challenge, for a completely adequate response cannot be formulated that does not rely upon ultimately subjective perceptions. This form of the objection focuses on the nature and extent of evil in the world, not simply on the fact of evil in the world. It does not insist that God is culpable for each individual act of evil—as the weaker form of the objection does. It merely asks whether a world with the nature and extent of evil that ours has could be totally determined by a perfectly good God.

I have already agreed that God is not above moral judgment altogether. He can and must be held accountable for what he has created. The moral structure of reality demands it. As we have seen, we must take care in passing such judgment that we don't hold him accountable for things for which he is not legitimately responsbile. We must keep in mind that God is the author and creator of all and that he has all the prerogatives of such.

But whether God can legitimately be blamed for a man's particular evil choices becomes irrelevant to this stronger form of the argument. God can certainly be blamed (or praised) for reality as a whole. He can and must answer for the whole of existence. He can be held accountable for bringing this created order into being at all. The stronger form of the theological objection attacks divine determinism at exactly this point: how can it be maintained that a perfectly good God who is completely in control of every facet of reality would purposely will into existence a reality that contained within it the nature and extent of evil that this one does? Would a perfectly good God who was perfectly in control of everything create a world that included murder, rape, unthinkable inhumanity, wanton cruelty, devastating natural disasters, disease, war, child molestation, and starvation—to mention just a few? This, so the objection maintains, is unthinkable. But this is precisely the sort of reality we live in. So either God is not the determiner of all things (as divine determinism asserts), or God is not as good as he is purported to be. But we cannot maintain God's complete determinative control over every facet of reality at the same time that we maintain God's perfect goodness. God cannot be both perfectly good and the creator of this evil world in which we live. But surely God is morally perfect! (Or so our theology asserts.) Therefore, he must not be the determiner of absolutely everything. Evil enters into reality from some other source—uncaused and undetermined by God.

We must take note of the subtle but important shift in strategy from the weaker argument to the stronger one. The stronger form of the objection does not attempt to suggest that, given divine determinism, God would be to blame for every particular act of evil that is committed; rather, it suggests that God can legitimately be blamed for the overall moral quality of the reality he has created. If the God who has everything totally under control has chosen to bring an evil and cruel world into being, then how can he legitimately claim to be a good God?

This objection itself is employed by many different people with many different agendas. Something like this objection is employed by the atheist against theism. The atheist argues that given the nature and extent of evil in the world, it is not reasonable to believe in the existence of a God who is both all-powerfully in control and perfectly good. The atheist's goal, of course, is to persuade the theist to give up his belief in the existence of God altogether. This classic argument against the rationality of belief in the existence of God is known as THE ARGUMENT FROM EVIL. But the argument from evil *per se* is not under scrutiny in this chapter.

Something like this objection is also employed by certain non-traditional Christian theists (for example, those who believe in Process Theology) to defend their belief in a finite, not-all-powerful God. The finite-God theist argues that given the nature and extent of evil in the world, it is not reasonable to believe in the omnipotence of God. We know that God is perfectly good, they argue. If he were all-powerful as well, then he would eliminate the evil, pain, and suffering in the world. Since he obviously is not eliminating them, it follows that he must not have the power or ability to do so. In other words, he is not all-powerful. But again, this is not the objection that is under scrutiny in this chapter either.

To defend the traditional view of God as simultaneously good and all-powerful is not my purpose. For a Christian believer who takes the biblical text seriously, this is not even in question. Only by disregarding (or misinterpreting) significant portions of biblical teaching can one accept a non-traditional view of God as finite and limited in power. My purpose is to defend divine determinism as a biblical doctrine to people who desire to take biblical teaching seriously. I direct my arguments to traditional theists who care what the Bible teaches. If such as these object to divine determinism, I am seeking to answer their objections.

So, what is this stronger form of the theological objection posed by those who uphold a traditional view of the nature of God and yet reject divine determinism? It goes something like this:

As the Bible maintains, God is ultimately sovereign over and in complete control of the outcome of human history. But how are we to reconcile God's sovereign control over reality with the nature and extent of the evil that exists within it? There can be only one way to effect such a reconciliation. We must assume that there are certain realities, certain phenomena, certain events, and certain forces that are outside the scope of God's direct causation and determination. Evil must arise from these other realities. God is not the source and cause of evil. It is these other realities (for example, human free will) that cause evil.

But if certain facets of reality are outside God's control, how do we still maintain that he is sovereign? While God does not directly control non-divinely-determined forces like free will, he can nevertheless indirectly control their outcome. God's power, creativity, and intelligence is such that he can sovereignly control the ultimate outcome even of free choices that were not directly caused by him. Accordingly, he can guarantee that his good pre-ordained purposes will be achieved, because—by manipulating that portion of reality that is directly under his determinative control—he can control the final outcome of choices and forces that were not directly under his control. In other words, God is so exceedingly wise, clever, and powerful that he can manage to bring his good purposes to pass out of any and every event that occurs even when he was not the first and direct cause of that event. So, for example, I may introduce sin and evil into the world through a freewill choice that I make, but that does not prevent God from cleverly combining the results of my sinful choice with the results of other things that he directly determines such that he ultimately accomplishes the good and perfect result that he had ordained from the beginning.

Under such a viewpoint, God's sovereignty and moral perfection are successfully reconciled with the nature and extent of evil in the world. On the other hand, if we accept the notion that every facet of reality is directly caused and determined by God—as divine determinism does—then it becomes impossible to reconcile God's sovereignty and moral perfection with the nature and extent of evil in the world. Accordingly, in light of the evil that exists in our world, the only way we can rationally affirm the biblical concept of God as both sovereign and good is by positing that certain aspects of reality (such as human free will) are beyond the determinative control of God. In other words, only by rejecting the doctrine of divine determinism.

This then is the strong form of the theological objection to divine determinism—an objection by traditional theists who uphold a traditional conception of God's sovereignty and goodness but who reject divine determinism as I have defined it in this book. They do so on the grounds that, if we add the doctrine of divine determinism to the biblical conception of God, then our concept of God becomes incompatible with the nature and extent of evil in the world. Only by rejecting divine determinism can a biblical notion of God be plausibly reconciled with the nature and extent of the evil that exists.

Answering the Theological Objection

IN ITS WEAKER FORM

To answer the weaker form of the theological objection, we need only recognize that it mirrors one of the sub-arguments of the philosophical objection. By disposing of the philosophical objection in the last chapter, we have already disposed of this form of the theological objection.[182]

The crux of this objection, as in the philosophical objection, lies in the assumption that God is morally culpable for the evil he creates. As we saw in the last chapter, the problem with this assumption is its failure to distinguish between a transcendent cause and an ordinary cause and its failure to recognize that these two different kinds of causes have radically different natures.

In divine determinism, God is a transcendent cause, analogous to the author of a novel. The logic of transcendent causation does not permit a shift of moral accountability from us, the agents of evil deeds, to God, their transcendent cause.[183] Yes, we do make evil choices. Yes, God is ultimately responsible for them as their transcendent cause. But we—not God—are morally culpable for the choices we make. Just as the characters in a story and not the author of the story are morally culpable for the choices authored in them in the unfolding of their story, so we are responsible for the choices God authors in us. Therefore, though evil choices do exist in the world, God is not the one who is morally culpable for those choices. My evil choices, therefore, provide no ground upon which to challenge God's goodness. My evils do not appear on his record; they appear only on mine.

Similarly, God is not morally culpable for the evils that occur by the agency of impersonal forces. As the transcendent cause of the created order itself, God—though totally in control of what transpires—is not morally

---

182. For a full discussion of my response to the corresponding portion of the philosophical objection and, hence, to the weaker form of the theological objection, see chapter 9.

183. See chapter 9 for a full discussion of this point.

accountable for what transpires. We do not consider the author of a book morally blameworthy for the accidental death of one his characters in a flood. Why? Because that is the nature of transcendent causation. Transcendent causation does not entail moral culpability at the level of an individual impersonal event. Similarly, God is not morally culpable for the "acts of God" that lead to negative or adverse consequences.[184]

IN ITS STRONGER FORM

The crux of the matter with respect to the stronger form of the theological objection is whether there exists any possibility, in the light of the evil world we live in, of reconciling the goodness of God with the sovereignty of God on the assumption that divine determinism is true. The objection states that there is not. It argues that we must reject divine determinism because, if we do not reject it, we will be unable to reconcile the existence of the biblical God (sovereign and good) with the nature and extent of the evil that is in the world. If the objection is wrong about this—that is, if in fact there is a way to reconcile the existence of God as sovereign and morally perfect with the existence of this evil world while maintaining a belief in divine determinism—then the objection fails completely. Its entire force as an objection rests on the merits of this claim: divine determinism and the nature of the evil that exists cannot be reconciled. To answer the objection, therefore, I must show how divine determinism is, in principle, compatible with the existence of the evil in the world.

To do so, I turn once again to the author/novel analogy. Consider the author of a particular novel. A particular novel includes many different moral realities. It includes everything from impatience to murder, disease, and war. Upon reading such a novel, could we justifiably conclude that it

---

184. Nowhere in this book do I argue specifically that a transcendent cause of impersonal events is not morally culpable for those events. But I believe it is self-evident. If the transcendent cause of the acts of free moral agents is not morally responsible for those acts, then likewise the transcendent cause of impersonal events is not morally responsible for those events. There is only one notable difference between the two types of events. There does exist moral accountability in the case of free moral agency— namely, the free moral agent who does the deed is morally culpable. But in the case of an impersonal event, there exists no moral culpability at all. Granted, we might be tempted to make God—the transcendent cause—morally culpable for an impersonal event. For who else could we blame? Yet we must resist the temptation. There is no logical reason why there has to be any moral accountability at all in the case of an event where no free moral agency is involved. Indeed, I would argue that denying the existence of moral culpability in the case of impersonal natural events is eminently commonsensical.

was written by an evil man? The question is not whether we know that the author is evil. (If we believe the Bible's teaching, we know that he is evil. He was born a sinner.) The question is whether we could validly conclude that he was evil merely on the basis of his novel.

We can approach this same question another way. Could Jesus (one who, according to orthodox Christian theology, was morally perfect) have written that novel? Would it have been morally possible for him to have done so?

Common sense says, "yes." Without jeopardizing or compromising his morally perfect character in any way, Jesus could have written such a novel. So presumably we would not be justified in concluding that an author is evil on the basis of the content of such a novel.

Granted, some novels that contain evil are indeed evil creations. Pornography is an example. It not only contains evil within it, its very existence is motivated by, panders to, and serves the purposes of evil. But other novels that contain evil are not similarly evil. At least, in theory we can conceive of one that is not.

The evil of a story must not be judged on the basis of whether it contains evil within it. Rather, it must be judged on the bases of (a) the motive behind the story, (b) the purpose it accomplishes, and (c) the final effect that it has. If the motive behind it is pure, its purpose is righteous, and its final effect is good, then the story is a good creation, not an evil one. It is one that a morally perfect person would be morally justified in creating, regardless of what particular evils may exist within its pages.

By analogy, the same can be said of God, who (according to the doctrine of divine determinism) is the divine author of all reality. The fact that this reality contains evil, suffering, and cruelty is not sufficient in and of itself to justify the conclusion that a good God could not be its author. The mere existence of evil within this reality does not justify the judgment that it is evil rather than good. Before we can judge the moral quality of our reality, we would need to know the ultimate motive behind its creation, the purpose for which it was created, and the nature of the final outcome. If we find that the motive, purpose, and result (or any one of them alone) are evil, then we can legitimately say that this reality is evil and a perfectly good God could not possibly have determined its every feature. But if the motive, purpose, and overall result are, in fact, good and right, then this reality—regardless of all the evil that is contained in it—is nevertheless a good creation—one of which a morally perfect God could be the author.

IS REALITY EVIL?

The critical question, then, is the moral nature of this reality in which we dwell. Is this reality that God has created evil or good? More specifically, what are the motive behind, the purpose for, and the overall result of the creation of this reality? Are these good or evil?

If they are incontrovertibly evil, then the stronger form of the theological objection stands. A morally perfect God could not be totally and absolutely in control of the reality that exists and divine determinism cannot be true. But if the motive behind, purpose for, and ultimate outcome of reality are good, then the theological objection fails. The mere fact that particular evils exist within reality is no indicator of any moral flaw in its creator. Hence, under such an assumption, a morally perfect God could reasonably and morally be the creator of this reality. Regardless of the particular evils it contains, there is no incompatibility between the moral perfection of God and God's total control of this reality.

So what is the fact of the matter? Is reality, in fact, good? Or is it evil? Everyone can agree that the evidence is mixed. Some of what we experience would seem to point to the goodness of God. Other aspects of our experience would seem to suggest that God may be evil.

To make a decision about the moral quality of this reality is particularly problematic in light of the fact that none of the three important considerations—namely, the motive behind, the purpose for, and the final outcome of this reality—can yet be fully known to us. We have no direct experience of the whole of reality from beginning to end. But without such experience, we are in no position to make a judgment with respect to the moral character of created reality. Surely no one can presume to finally know whether reality is good or evil when he has not yet seen the last chapter. Whether God is good or evil will finally be decided on the basis of the whole story. How will it all turn out? What will have been the final result? What will have been God's point in all of this? What will have been his ultimate motive? No one can possibly yet know. At least, not on the basis of experience. But until we can know such things, we are in no position to judge.

For this strong form of the theological objection to have any force, one must presume to know that the nature and extent of the evil that exists in this world is such that a perfectly good author of all reality, who controlled every detail of reality, would never have authored this one. But such a conclusion is just presumption. How could one know that? On what basis? Having only such a limited and narrow perspective as human experience gives, how can I confidently know that the nature and extent of evil in the world does not ultimately serve some perfect purpose that is being achieved by a perfectly good divine author who, with utterly pure motives, is directing the entirety of cosmic history toward a perfect outcome? The opponent of divine determinism presumes to know that this is not the case. I cannot be so presumptuous. I do not have the kind of clarity that permits me to know what evil would and could fit a morally perfect author's purposes and what could not. Maybe the evil that exists in the world is ultimately irreconcilable with what a morally perfect being would author. Then again, maybe not. I cannot know from my present standpoint. One day we will all know firsthand. In the end, when all has been said and done, we will—with our own eyes—see whether the final result was utterly and entirely good from beginning to end, or whether the outcome—to the extent that it is a good one—was only good because it was cleverly snatched out of the jaws of evil by a clever, sovereign God. But as we sit here now, we must sift through puzzling and ambiguous evidence. We do not have a clear vision one way or the other. To presume to be able to judge from our own experience is arrogant. To presume to be able to see is to presume to have the perspective of God himself.

The theological objection to divine determinism, therefore, fails. In order to succeed, it must show that divine determinism cannot possibly be compatible with the nature and extent of the evil that exists in the world. But the theological objector has never demonstrated that point. He has only dogmatically asserted it, having no firm foundation for his assertion. The objection has emotional appeal, certainly; for to separate the God we serve as far as possible from the horrendous evils we see in our experience is emotionally appealing. But as emotionally appealing as it is, the theological objection is groundless. It has offered no argument for believing that the evil that exists in the world makes divine determinism untenable.

That God is good is foundational to the divine determinist's (as indeed to any traditional Christian's) view of the world. It is not wishful thinking. The divine determinist has reasons for such a confidence. While he acknowledges the ambiguity of the data of life experience, he has other reasons—other evidences—that give him a basis for confidence in the goodness of God. He has what he believes to be a reasonable and intellectually responsible confidence that God is perfectly good.[185]

---

185. It is outside the scope of this work to spell out the nature of the evidence that results in the Christian's conviction that God is good. To do so would be tantamount to a defense of the Christian faith itself. My purpose in this book is not to defend Christianity in the face of its critics. Rather, my purpose is to defend the doctrine of divine determinism as rationally and biblically required by the nature and content of Christian faith. If the reader is a non-Christian, unconvinced of the goodness of God, then divine determinism is neither relevant nor problem-

As a consequence, the divine determinist trusts God. He assumes that the things that God does are ultimately good, even though they cannot be clearly and unambiguously seen to be good. Ambiguous and problematic evidence does not dissuade him from his confidence. His basis for believing that God is good is so secure that evidence that seems ambiguous and problematic is not sufficiently unsettling to compel him to alter his view. The only thing that would cause a divine determinist to change his mind about the goodness of God would be some clear and incontrovertible evidence that God is ultimately evil or capable of evil. Heretofore—so far as the Christian is concerned—no such evidence has been forthcoming. Accordingly, the theological objection fails to have any effect on him. Granted, if reality were evil, then a morally perfect God could not be in absolute control of it. But the divine determinist does not assume that reality is evil. Rather, he assumes that reality (for all the evil that it contains) is ultimately good. Hence, there is no logical tension in his beliefs. A morally perfect God in absolute determinative control of an ultimately good reality is logically unassailable. The divine determinist firmly believes that experience itself will vindicate his assumption of God's goodness in the end. Reality will be shown to be truly good. That being the case, divine determinism is not vulnerable to the theological objection. Reality will be shown to be truly good—according to the divine determinist's expectations—precisely because a perfectly good God is totally in control of authoring every facet of it.

Summary and Conclusion

There are two forms that the theological objection to divine determinism can take:

1. The first assumes that were God the ultimate cause of every particular evil, he would thereby be culpable for every particular evil and could not then be seen as morally perfect. Since the moral perfection of God is so foundational to Christian belief, Christian belief and divine determinism are therefore—it is argued—logically incompatible.

---

atic. It is a non-issue. It is only in the face of the Christian assumption that God is perfectly good that divine determinism has to even answer the theological objection. That is what I am attempting in this chapter. I leave it to another time and place to defend the Christian assumption of God's goodness that gives rise to the theological objection in the first place.

This argument is fallacious. It fails to see that God, as the ultimate cause of every evil, is not the ordinary cause of those evils, but is rather their transcendent cause. As such, no moral culpability for those evils is attributable to him.

2. The second form of the objection assumes that, if God were the ultimate cause of everything in reality, his moral character would ultimately be reflected in the moral quality of that reality. It further assumes that—due to the extent and nature of the evil that exists—the moral quality of this reality is evil. The powerful, sovereign God may very well be capable of salvaging reality by bringing good out of the evil that exists. But the reality that exists is inherently evil. And it is evil in such a way that no morally perfect creator with any sovereign control over his creation would have ever willingly brought it about that such a reality exists. Since we can be confident of the moral perfection of the creator, there is only one explanation for the evil state of the created order: its morally perfect creator does not totally and absolutely cause nor determine everything that transpires within reality. Only by rejecting divine determinism can we account for the nature and extent of evil in the world without casting aspersions on the moral character of God.

This argument is also fallacious. A reality that contains evil is not necessarily an evil reality. It is logically possible for an ultimately good reality to contain horrendous evil within it. What this form of the theological objection must prove, in order to make its case successfully, is that reality taken as a whole is in fact evil. That is, it must prove that the nature and extent of the evil in the world is incompatible with the whole of reality having an ultimately good purpose with a perfectly good outcome. That has not and indeed cannot be shown. Hence, this form of the theological objection is without force. It has done nothing to demonstrate the incompatibility of the goodness of God, absolute divine determinism, and the nature and extent of the evil that exists in the world. It dogmatically asserts such incompatibility, but it has done nothing to demonstrate it. It assumes the very thing that it needs to prove if this objection is to serve as a refutation of divine determinism.

CHAPTER ELEVEN

THE ETHICAL OBJECTION TO DIVINE DETERMINISM

THE ETHICAL OBJECTION

If divine determinism is true, then it is futile for men to strive to be good. God will accomplish his will regardless. But this is contrary to fact. We know that it is not futile for men to strive to be good. (It is a fundamentally common-sensical assumption that striving to be good is a prerequisite to good choices and actions.) Hence, divine determinism cannot be true.

In the final analysis, the ethical objection is an objection to what is per-ceived to be the inevitable practical result of believing in divine determin-ism. To believe in divine determinism, it is argued, must inevitably result in moral laxity or passivity.

If everything I do is ultimately decided by God, then what is the point of diligently striving after moral goodness? If God wants me to be good, then I will. If he doesn't, I won't. And nothing I do can change it. So, why try? Such is the practical attitude that must necessarily result from a belief in divine determinism.

But the truth is that we are all under obligation to diligently pursue moral goodness. We will attain to moral goodness only by striving after it. Therefore, the practical implication of divine determinism—namely, that moral diligence is pointless—is directly contrary to the truth. Now if a theory or worldview has implications that are not true, one is forced to assume that the theory itself is not true. Therefore, divine determinism is untenable as a worldview. In truth, we are morally obligated to strive for goodness. Yet divine determinism entails moral indifference and passivity. Divine determinism, therefore, is wrong.

This third objection to divine determinism combines elements of the previous two. It is somewhat philosophical in nature, but it is also some-what theological in nature. Specifically, it is ethical in nature. Like the philosophical objection, it is really only an objection to extending divine determinism so far as to include the freewill choices of men. And like the theological objection, it is only a forceful objection to those who hold a particular worldview—specifically, the Judaeo-Christian worldview. It is only forceful against those who recognize moral laxity to be in contradic-tion to what is true.

The ethical objection is more of an intuitive gut reaction than it is an argument. It is rarely spelled out rigorously by the objectors. Therefore, to answer it, I must try to translate the intuition behind it into a more systematic form that can then be analyzed.

It seems to me that this objection actually takes two different forms. First, it can exist as a reasoned argument against divine determinism. This objection attempts to argue that moral laxity is the logically necessary implication of divine determinism. (I will refer to this form of the argument as the FORMAL ETHICAL OBJECTION.) Secondly, it can exist as a utilitarian argument against divine determinism. This objection, while acknowledging that moral laxity may not be logically required by divine determinism, insists that moral laxity is psychologically inevitable nonetheless. And, assuming this, it argues for rejecting divine determinism on the basis of its inevitable negative effects. (I will refer to this form of the argument as the INFORMAL ETHICAL OBJECTION.)

The Formal Ethical Objection

Let us examine the formal objection in the form of a relatively rigorous argument. The argument would go something like this:

STEP 1: *If divine determinism is true, then God is the cause of my choosing to do whatever good thing I do and God is the cause of my choosing to do whatever evil thing I do.*

This follows directly from the definition of divine determinism as we have defined it in this work.

STEP 2: *If divine determinism is true, then God's will is irresistible; whatever he wills comes to be.*

This too follows directly from the definition of divine determinism as we have defined it in this work.

STEP 3: *If God is the cause of my choosing to do whatever I choose to do, then I will necessarily do whatever good thing God wills me to do and I will necessarily do whatever evil thing God wills me to do.*

This follows directly from step 2 and from the concept of causation as it is defined in this work with respect to divine determinism.

STEP 4: *If divine determinism is true, there exist absolutely no realities that could prevent me from doing whatever good thing God wills me to do nor whatever evil thing God wills me to do.*

According to step 1, if divine determinism is true then God is the cause of my choosing to do whatever I do—whether good or evil. According to step 3, if God is the cause of my choosing to do a good (or an evil) thing, then I will necessarily do whatever good (or evil) thing God wills me to do. It follows from steps 1 and 3 that if divine determinism is true, then I will necessarily do whatever good (or evil) thing God wills me to do. It follows directly from this—by the very nature of necessity—that if divine determinism is true, then there can exist absolutely no realities that could prevent me from doing whatever good (or evil) God wills me to do.

STEP 5: *If divine determinism is true, my own lack of desire and volition to do some particular good that God wills me to do could not prevent me from doing it, and neither could my own lack of desire and volition to do some particular evil that God wills me to do prevent me from doing that.*

This follows directly as a specific instance of the conclusion reached in step 4 above.

STEP 6: *If divine determinism is true, to strive to attain to a desire and volition to do good things is futile with respect to the ability to actually do them.*

This follows directly from step 5. If God, apart from desire and volition in me, is the cause of the good things that I actually do, then striving to have a desire and volition to do good is an irrelevant and unproductive enterprise. It cannot result in my doing any good deeds except and unless God wills them. And if God *does* will that I do them, then I necessarily will do them whether I have striven to have a desire and volition to do them or not.

STEP 7: *If divine determinism is true, then to strive to have a desire and volition to do good things is pointless and futile.*

This follows directly from step 6.

STEP 8: *If to strive to have a desire and volition to do good things is not pointless and futile, then divine determinism is not true.*

This follows directly from step 7. The contrapositive[186] of a true statement is necessarily true. Step 8 is the contrapositive of step 7. Since our argument has concluded that step 7 is true, it follows directly that step 8, its contrapositive, is true.

STEP 9: *If what the Bible teaches about morality is true, then to strive to have a desire and volition to do good things is not pointless and futile.*

This follows from an inductive study of the Bible's teaching. Explicitly and implicitly, in a number of ways, the biblical perspective is that to strive after goodness—that is, to seek to desire it—is one of the defining features of what it means to be a truly authentic human being in the light of who God created us to be. It is assumed throughout that those who do good are those who have desired goodness and willed it for themselves. Furthermore, the biblical perspective is that to do so—to strive after goodness—will be rewarded with success. ("Blessed are those who hunger and thirst after righteousness, for they shall be satisfied."-Matthew 5:6)

STEP 10: *If what the Bible teaches about morality is true, then divine determinism is not true.*

This follows directly from step 8 and step 9 above.

STEP 11: *What the Bible teaches about morality is true.*

This is a premise that is foundational to the Christian believer's faith. The Christian believes that it is rationally defensible and grounded in sound reason.

STEP 12: *Therefore, divine determinism is not true.*

This follows immediately from step 10 and step 11 above.

---

186. The contrapositive of a statement of the form "If A, then B" is "If not B, then not A." It is axiomatic in formal logic that the contrapositive of a true statement is necessarily true.

Answering the Formal Ethical Objection

YAHWEH-THE-JUDGE
OR YAHWEH-THE-TRANSCENDENT

To analyze the Formal Ethical Argument, we must draw a crucial distinction between two very different relationships that God sustains with respect to created reality. At particular moments in human history the transcendent creator God has taken up specific roles within the drama of history and has revealed himself to certain people—most notably the Jewish people—and has promised to sustain a particular relationship with them.

God told Moses to call him Yahweh.[187] Yahweh wanted to be the God of Israel, and he wanted Israel to be his people. As such, he promised to sustain a relationship with Israel where he would serve as law-giver and judge, on the one hand, and as the one who would bless them, protect them, prosper them, and sustain them on the other. In exchange, he asked of Israel that they obey and honor him by keeping his law. Yahweh, the maker of this covenant with Israel, presents himself as a being in a covenant-relationship to Israel. He will make a law that he wants Israel to keep. Then he will wait to see what Israel will do—pleading with them to obey him and warning them that he will judge them with destruction if they do not. Now, why would a God who, according to the thesis of this book, is in absolute control over every aspect of his creation have to plead with and warn Israel? Could he not simply "author" their obedience? How do we reconcile Yahweh the covenant-maker with the transcendent creator God we are seeking to understand in this work?

In sorting out the biblical evidence, we must make a distinction between who Yahweh ultimately is—the transcendent author of all reality—and who Yahweh presents himself to be in relationship to human beings—the one who desires a covenant relationship with his people. When Yahweh makes a covenant with Israel, pleads with Israel, exhorts her, woos her, and ultimately judges her, God is presenting himself to Israel only in a limited role: as a law-giver and covenant-maker. He clearly is not revealing himself in the fullness of who he is. On the other hand, when he predicts Israel's future restoration and obedience and when he declares that God's promises are going to come to pass regardless of the stubbornness of the nation's heart, Yahweh's transcendent authorship of

---

187. In my judgment, *Yahweh* is best understood to mean "HE WHO *IS*".

the whole of history is clearly being manifest. So, while Yahweh is the transcendent author of all of history and of all reality, he sometimes presents himself to mankind in a more limited role: as their covenant-maker, lawgiver, and judge. In the remainder of this work, when I refer to God as he ultimately is in his fullness, I will call him Yahweh-the-Transcendent. When I refer to the more limited role in which God often discloses himself to men within the unfolding drama of history, I will call him Yahweh-the-Judge.

Yahweh-the-Judge is the king and judge of all the earth. Yahweh-the-Judge sits exalted in the heavens. All power and all might is in his hands. Yahweh-the-Judge is sovereign.[188] Yahweh-the-Judge is magnificent. Yahweh-the-Judge is all-powerful. But he is not being conceived as transcendent. Rather, Yahweh-the-Judge is God revealing himself within a particular role within this reality. He is the sovereign God who must be worshipped. He is the judge before whom every creature must stand and give account. He is the mighty savior who can either save or destroy. He is a force to be reckoned with within our reality. But he is not being conceived as a transcendent reality. He is being conceived as an actor within the drama of cosmic history and not as the author of cosmic history itself.

And yet Yahweh-the-Judge is one and the same with the transcendent creator God who exists above and beyond all of reality. Yahweh-the-Judge is ultimately Yahweh-the-Transcendent. Yahweh-the-Judge is a particular manner in which Yahweh-the-Transcendent has manifested himself within reality. Yahweh-the-Judge is Yahweh-the-Transcendent having presented himself as a character within the drama of history. Yahweh-the-Transcendent, the author of all reality, revealed himself by writing himself into the script as Yahweh-the-Judge, the Lord and God of Israel and of all mankind. Yahweh-the-Judge, and he alone, is Yahweh-the-Transcendent.[189] Now it is important to note: in presenting himself to us as Yahweh-the-Judge, he never ceased to function as Yahweh-the-Transcendent. (The very idea is absurd.) Yahweh-the-Transcendent simply "embodied" himself in the role of a character in the drama that he was

---

188. See my discussion of the meaning of 'sovereign' in chapter 4.

189. This, of course, was the point God (Yahweh-the-Judge) kept stressing to Israel. He, Yahweh-the-Judge—not the Baalim of the Caananites, nor Molech, nor any other so-called god—was the true God. In other words, no other so-called god was the unique God who was identical to Yahweh-the-Transcendent. Alongside Yahweh-the-Judge's claim to be the one true God, Yahweh-the-Transcendent, no heathen god of the surrounding nations could make any legitimate claim to be a god at all.

190. I am not suggesting Yahweh-the-Judge had a body. Clearly he did not. He "embodied" himself only in a manner of speaking.

(and is) transcendently creating.[190] Yahweh-the-Judge is a revelation of Yahweh-the-Transcendent. He is only a *partial* revelation of Yahweh-the-Transcendent, but he is a revelation nonetheless.

The above distinction is very important. The failure to make it misleads us into thinking that the ethical objection to divine determinism is plausible. As Yahweh-the-Transcendent, God does not (by definition) function as an ordinary cause within reality. He is the transcendent cause.[191] But as Yahweh-the-Judge, he presents himself as an agent acting in history as an ordinary cause. Throughout human history he has so presented himself. Most notably, when Yahweh-the-Judge commands mankind to "be holy as I am holy," he is doing so as an ordinary cause. As Yahweh-the-Judge he presents himself as seeking to motivate, move, and influence through the ordinary process of pleading, warning, exhorting, and persuading. He cannot change our behavior. We must choose to change our own behavior. He cannot make us righteous. He can only plead with us to be righteous. He cannot make us be his people. He can only promise us certain blessings if we choose to be so. In this way, Yahweh-the-Judge presents himself in a specific role where he serves as an ordinary cause of human behavior, not as its transcendent cause.

GOD AND RIGHTEOUSNESS

For the sake of our discussion of the Formal Ethical Objection to divine determinism, the relationship between God and righteousness[192] is crucial. Is God the cause of my good deeds on the one hand and of my evil deeds on the other? This is the claim made in step 1 of the Formal Ethical Objection.

Whether the claim is true depends upon whether we are referring to God as Yahweh-the-Judge or as Yahweh-the-Transcendent. It makes all the difference whether we mean God, the transcendent cause of human choice, or God insofar as he presents himself as the ordinary cause of human choice.

Yahweh-the-Judge made a covenant with Israel. His desire becomes quite clear in the context of that covenant. Yahweh-the-Judge desired that his people be holy as he is holy. Righteous living is the will of Yahweh-the-Judge. Indeed, not only did he desire it, but he made it clear that his peo-

---

191. See chapter 9 for a discussion of the distinction between an ordinary cause and a transcendent cause.

192. By 'righteousness' I mean a quality of life and behavior that manifests itself in deeds of goodness. I use 'righteousness' as a synonym for godliness, god-likeness, and goodness.

ple (and by implication, all people) were under obligation to be righteous. He would judge them accordingly. Everything God did in relation to Israel is, to some degree, calculated to persuade them to pursue righteousness.

But for as much as Yahweh-the-Judge wanted his people to be righteous, and for all the warning, pleading, exhorting, persuading, and motivating that he did to try to bring it about, he did not get what he wanted. The history of Yahweh-the-Judge's dealings with the Jews is a story of his frustration. Israel remained contrary. Their "hardness of heart" controlled the result. Yahweh-the-Judge's exhortations, threats, and promises were without positive result. They were ineffectual in the face of the willful sinfulness of man.

Why? Why could Yahweh-the-Judge not succeed in making Israel obey him? Did he lack power? Is Yahweh-the-Judge simply outgunned by the power of evil? Is God too weak to bring his will to pass? Is he simply no match for the sinfulness of mankind? That is most certainly not the perspective of the Bible. Yahweh-the-Judge's lack of power is not a problem. He had more than ample power. The problem lay in the will of Yahweh-the-Judge. Yahweh-the-Judge did not desire coerced holiness, but genuine holiness. He wanted holiness that would result from the free choice of his people, not from his own coercive power.

Yahweh-the-Judge, unlike Yahweh-the-Transcendent, did not have the option of causing Israel to be holy without coercing them. Yahweh-the-Judge, by virtue of the nature of his role, could function only as an ordinary cause with respect to the choices and actions of human beings. He does not function as the transcendent cause behind reality. Even as Yahweh-the-Judge, he could have caused Israel's obedience. He could have caused it irresistibly. But he would have done so only at the cost of nullifying the free will of each Israelite. The Israelite would have obeyed out of free will only if the final, determinative, ordinary cause of his obedience lay within his own heart and mind. If, instead, the final, determinative, ordinary cause of an Israelite's obedience lay within the power of God, then his choice would not have been a freewill choice. What allowed human sinfulness the upper-hand is Yahweh-the-Judge's unwillingness to nullify free will by using his great power coercively.

The implications of this are important. Yahweh-the-Judge has no intention of being the ordinary cause of human choice. Yahweh-the-Judge is not the ordinary cause of either good or evil deeds. He declines to be; he desires not to negate free will. Therefore, in response to the question we raised earlier, the answer is "no." God (insofar as we are talking about Yahweh-the-Judge) is not the cause of my good deeds on the one hand and my evil ones on the other.

But if we are talking about God as Yahweh-the-Transcendent, things are different. As the author and transcendent cause of literally everything that transpires in reality, Yahweh-the-Transcendent is the transcendent cause of every choice of man. Every good deed performed by man is caused (transcendently) by Yahweh-the-Transcendent, and every evil deed is likewise (transcendently) caused by him. He is, in a meaningful sense, the cause of both the good deeds and the evil deeds of all of mankind. Therefore, responding once again to the question we raised earlier, the answer is now "yes." God (insofar as we are talking about Yahweh-the-Transcendent) is most certainly the cause of my good deeds on the one hand and my evil ones on the other. But we must remain clear as to exactly in what sense this is true. *Yahweh-the-Transcendent is legitimately viewed as the* transcendent *cause of every human deed. But he is in no sense the* ordinary *cause of any of them.*

STEP-BY-STEP ANALYSIS

Keeping in mind the distinction between Yahweh-the-Transcendent and Yahweh-the-Judge and all the ramifications of such a distinction, it becomes apparent that the Formal Ethical Objection suffers from ambiguity from the outset:

ANALYSIS OF STEP 1

STEP 1: *If divine determinism is true, then God is the cause of my choosing to do whatever good thing I do and God is the cause of my choosing to do whatever evil thing I do.*

Who is God in this premise? Is it Yahweh-the-Transcendent or Yahweh-the-Judge? And further, in what sense is this step asserting that God is the cause of my choices? Is it asserting that God is their *ordinary* cause, or their *transcendent* cause? The truth or falsity of this premise hinges on exactly which is being claimed.

Divine determinism clearly does maintain that Yahweh-the-Transcendent is the transcendent cause of every choice I make, both good and evil. But in no way does it suggest that he is the ordinary cause of these choices. Furthermore, so far as what divine determinism maintains, Yahweh-the-Judge is the cause of human choice in no sense whatsoever. He is neither its transcendent cause nor its ordinary cause. Yahweh-the-

Judge seeks to influence and persuade, but he does not cause, determine, or necessitate any human choice. Man is free to obey him or disobey.

Step 1 is true, therefore, only under this one specific interpretation:

STEP 1A: *If divine determinism is true, then Yahweh-the-Transcendent is the transcendent cause of my choosing to do whatever good thing I do and Yahweh-the-Transcendent is the transcendent cause of my choosing to do whatever evil thing I do.*

ANALYSIS OF STEP 2

In step 2 of the Formal Ethical Objection we are faced with exactly the same situation. The will of Yahweh-the-Transcendent is irresistible. But Yahweh-the-Judge's will is clearly *not* irresistible. We have already seen that Yahweh-the-Judge refused to coerce obedience from his people, Israel, and they did, in fact, resist him. Step 2 is true if and only if it reads:

STEP 2A: *If divine determinism is true, then Yahweh-the-Transcendent's will is irresistible; whatever he wills comes to be.*

God's will is irresistible because a transcendent cause does, by the very nature of transcendent causation, have irresistible control over his creations. But we will be tragically misled by this premise if we conceive of God's will as an invincible ordinary cause. God's will is not irresistible because he is stronger and more powerful than any other ordinary cause within reality. Rather, his will is irresistible because he is the creator of reality. What further inferences we draw from this premise will differ greatly depending upon which understanding we have of it. Conceiving of God as the most powerful and, therefore, the determinative ordinary cause is a false premise and will lead us to false conclusions. Only under the conception of God as the transcendent cause and creator of all of reality is this premise true.

ANALYSIS OF STEP 3

Step 3 does, indeed, follow directly from step 2. But only if both are understood in the same vein—namely, it is Yahweh-the-Transcendent, not Yahweh-the-Judge, who must be in view in order for each of these steps to be valid. So we have:

STEP 3A: *If Yahweh-the-Transcendent is the cause of my choosing to do whatever I choose to do, then I will necessarily do whatever good thing Yahweh-the-Transcendent wills me to do and I will necessarily do whatever evil thing Yahweh-the-Transcendent wills me to do.*

To understand step 3 with reference to Yahweh-the-Judge would be totally invalid. From step 2, which had Yahweh-the-Transcendent in view, it would be utterly fallacious to infer something about Yahweh-the-Judge. Furthermore, as we have already seen, the condition "If Yahweh-the-Judge is the cause of my choosing to do a good or evil act" will never be fulfilled (in contradistinction to the condition "If Yahweh-the-Transcendent is the cause of my choosing to do a good or evil act"). Yahweh-the-Judge is never in any sense the cause of any of our choices.

ANALYSIS OF STEP 4

This inference does follow directly from steps 1 and 3, if indeed we have Yahweh-the-Transcendent and not Yahweh-the-Judge in view. Hence, we have:

STEP 4A: *If divine determinism is true, there exist absolutely no realities that could prevent me from doing whatever good thing Yahweh-the-Transcendent wills me to do nor whatever evil thing Yahweh-the-Transcendent wills me to do.*

But, to avoid being misled, this inference needs to be more precisely stated. There is a significant logical jump from step 3a to step 4a—a jump from "…then I will necessarily do whatever good or evil thing Yahweh-the-Transcendent wills me to do" to "…there exist absolutely no realities that could prevent me from doing whatever good or evil thing Yahweh-the-Transcendent wills me to do." This is a complex deduction that is not, and should not be, directly apparent. It is basically sound, I think. But while the deduction is basically sound, it is so only when the conclusion is rightly understood. We must take great care to understand what is and is not being asserted by this conclusion.

The intuition behind this inference is very simple: As the transcendent creator God, no created thing is capable of thwarting Yahweh-the-Transcendent in his effort to make creation what he wills it to be. That is exactly at the heart of what divine determinism affirms. Hence, no divine determinist will quarrel with this. But does it follow from this that "*no* realities could prevent …(what) Yahweh-the-Transcendent wills…."? No! It does not follow. Let me explain.

One very important thing *could* prevent what God wills—namely, a contradictory or rationally inconsistent reality. Granted, no such reality can, in actuality, thwart God's will, for God, the creator, would simply not allow such a reality to exist. But were God—contrary to his own will—to bring such a reality into existence, it would indeed prevent God from accomplishing his will.

We have been arguing in this book that, to have a biblically consistent worldview, one must embrace what I have called divine determinism. It can likewise be said that, to have a biblically consistent worldview, one must uphold both the rationality of God and the rationality of the created order.[193] According to the Bible, God is a rational being (indeed, he is the very source of reason and intelligence) who has created and continues to create everything in accordance with a unifying rational structure or pattern. This rational order to reality is what makes reality knowable to intelligent beings. Were there no patterns within reality that were discernible to human rationality, then no real knowledge would be possible.

From the biblical perspective, it is not arbitrary that God creates in accordance with a rational order. It is required by the very nature and character of his being. God is a "rationality freak" who requires that reality be rationally orderly. For God to tolerate rational incoherence is no more possible than for him to tolerate evil. Just as God's holiness precludes the possibility of his doing evil, his rationality precludes the possibility of his doing anything illogical, rationally inconsistent, or intellectually chaotic.[194]

As discussed in chapter 3, the rational patterns that dictate God's creative activity are, at least in part, discernible to us. The recognition of these patterns is a major part of what we call knowledge. Science is the discovery of those patterns that exist in physical reality. One of the fundamental rational patterns—apparent to both common sense and scientific investigation—is the pattern of cause and effect. Every event within reality has an ordinary cause that brought it about.[195] It is part of the created order—part of the rational pattern that God follows in creating history—that

---

193. See my earlier discussion of this in chapter 3.

194. I hope that what I am saying here is clear enough in light of my discussion in chapter 3. God can certainly do things that seem irrational and that appear to be rationally inconsistent from the standpoint of our limited perspective. My point has to do with the ultimate nature of things. God will not and cannot do anything that is ultimately irrational and ultimately inconsistent in the larger scheme of things.

whenever he creates an event, he also creates other antecedent realities from which that event follows out of rational necessity. We recognize these antecedent realities as the ordinary cause or causes of that event. God—in creating the flow of history—is bound by the pattern of cause and effect just as surely as he is bound by goodness. It is part of the rational order of created reality that he, by his very nature, is committed to.[196] Therefore, God cannot cause (transcendently) something to happen in reality without also causing (transcendently) its rationally appropriate ordinary causes as well.[197]

This brings us back to the point under discussion. Are there any realities that could prevent God (Yahweh-the-Transcendent) from accomplishing his will? "Yes," and then again, "No." "Yes" in the sense that, if God were to create a set of circumstances that rationally required a particular effect, then God—by his own rationality—is under obligation to create

---

195. Actually, whether every event has an ordinary cause is problematic. For example, I am inclined to think that human volition has *no* ordinary cause. It is this fact that explains why we typically tend to view human volition as "uncaused" or "self-caused," notions that, strictly speaking, are absurd. What our common sense is seeking to come to terms with in the typical view is that human volition has a transcendent cause but no ordinary cause. Or, at least, that its ordinary cause (namely, "the will") is simply an epiphenomenon of its transcendent cause. The free volition of free moral agents stands alone, I believe, as a reality independent of but contributing to the chain of cause and effect. It is unique in having no ordinary cause. But causation is a very complicated concept that is worthy of much more rigorous analysis than I can give it here in this book. For the purposes of this book, I will ignore these more complex issues. The outcome of any further investigation of these matters would not, I am confident, affect the points I am making here in this argument in any way. Throughout the rest of this chapter I will speak of the human will as the "ordinary cause" of one's volitional choices. While this may not be strictly accurate, it is true enough for our purposes. It is particularly important to distinguish the ordinary cause of my volition from its transcendent cause. To do so, we must locate the ordinary cause of my volition within the workings of my own will. But in speaking in such a way, I do not discount the very likely possibility that, in fact, my volition has no ordinary cause at all.

196. There is an important difference between God's commitment to goodness and God's commitment to cause and effect. God is committed to cause and effect in this reality we live in, but it is logically possible for God to have created a reality without cause and effect. In another reality—an entirely different created order—God may not have been committed to cause and effect. But in ANY reality he created, God would be committed to goodness. The parallel to goodness, then, is not cause and effect (that is, the specific rational order we find in our world); rather it is rationality itself. Like goodness, any reality God created would find God committed to the rational coherence and consistency of that reality. God is as incurably rational as he is incurably good.

197. The reader who is familiar with medieval philosophy and theology will recognize that I am describing the distinction that the medievals made between God as the primary cause of some aspect of reality and the secondary causes of that same aspect of reality. While the medievals knew that God was the creator of all reality and everything in it, they recognized that he often (if not always) worked through secondary causes to make occur what he willed to occur. Their concept of a secondary cause parallels in important ways my concept of an ordinary cause.

that effect as well. God is thereby "thwarted," in a sense, from creating the absence of that rationally required effect. But "No" in the sense that, if God has created a set of circumstances that rationally require a particular effect, nothing whatsoever (other than God's own will) could stop God from simply changing the circumstances (through his power as transcendent author) until what is rationally required is the absence of the effect rather than its presence.

Let's look at an example. Suppose God (Yahweh-the-Transcendent) caused (transcendently) an apple to become detached from its stem. The event that is rationally required (in the light of the rational structure of the divinely created order and a host of unstated assumptions[198]) is for the apple to bonk Sir Isaac Newton on the head. Now, if God—out of deference to Sir Isaac's head—willed to prevent him from being hit, could that be accomplished? "Yes," and "No."

"Yes," insofar as God is quite capable of creating other realities that would render it no longer rationally required that the apple bonk Newton on the head. For example, God could create in Newton the desire to do a handstand at just the right moment—thereby altering what is rationally required. Now, the apple must either miss him entirely or hit him on the feet. Or, God could cause a tremendous gust of wind to blow the apple to the side. Then—by rational requirement—it must miss Newton's head.

In another sense, however, we must answer "No." If God's will were to prevent Sir Isaac from being hit by the apple, there is a set of realities that could prevent God (Yahweh-the-Transcendent) from accomplishing his will. Specifically, for God to cause the apple to become detached from the tree, to have all other aspects of reality stay unchanged, and to still have Newton go unbonked is not possible. Under this set of circumstances, it would be irrational for God to create the event such that Newton—in defiance of the laws of physics—was not hit by the apple.[199]

---

198. The host of unstated assumptions would include things like: there is a man Sir Isaac Newton; he is sitting under an apple tree; he is located directly beneath the apple that is about to become detached from its stem; etc.

199. But this raises an interesting question. Could God have the apple fall to within 6 inches of Sir Isaac's head and then stop there, suspended in mid-air? Would it be irrational of God to do that? It clearly would not be irrational if he used secondary causes to accomplish it. Some unknown force field that effectively canceled out the force of gravity and brought the apple to rest, for example. But could God create this effect *ex nihilo*, without employing secondary causes, and still have it be a rational event? While this is a difficult question, I am inclined to think that he could. If he were to attribute the effect to himself insofar as he has revealed himself as Yahweh-the-Judge who has a role in the course of cosmic events, then the effect would have an ordinary cause. The ordinary cause would be the power of Yahweh-the-Judge, the God most high. This would render the event entirely rational. The effect would be utterly explicable. We

Now let us consider the claims in step 4a directly. Could God cause me to do a good thing (in accordance with his will) and create the simultaneous realities that (i) I do not want, in any sense, to do that good thing, (ii) I do not choose to do that good thing, and (iii) I am not being physically coerced to do that good thing? No! To do so would be to violate the rational structure of the created order—specifically, it would be to violate the rational structure of the psychology of human choosing. Accordingly, this is something God would be unable, by his very nature, to do. Realities (i), (ii), and (iii) rationally require that I not do the good thing that God wants me to do. For God to transcendentally cause me to do that good thing anyway—without replacing realities (i), (ii), and (iii) with a new set of realities—would be something God is incapable of doing. In the language of step 4, realities (i), (ii), and (iii) would "prevent me from doing the good thing that God willed me to do." Only by transforming the present realities can God cause me (transcendentally) to do the good thing he wills me to do.

As is perhaps clear already, two things contribute to the logical confusion that results in the deduction in step 4 of the original version of the Ethical Objection:

First Source of Confusion

The reasoning in step 4 fails to reckon with the fact that God has boundaries.[200] There are limits on what Yahweh-the-Transcendent, the transcendent cause, will and will not—and indeed, can and cannot—do. God's own nature, character, and purposes establish boundaries that he cannot cross. Failing to notice this creates the illusion that nothing in created reality would or could be incompatible with anything else in created reality. In the light of this illusion, step 4 can be misconstrued to suggest that there is nothing incoherent about a person doing a good deed while neither desiring nor choosing nor being physically coerced to do it. As we have seen, this simply is not so. Doing a good thing is utterly incompati-

---

once again see the import of distinguishing between Yahweh-the-Transcendent and Yahweh-the-Judge. Some people are reluctant to attribute the miraculous signs that God performed to any secondary causes at all. They feel that to attribute them to anything other than the raw power of Yahweh-the-Judge as their ordinary cause is to diminish their significance as a sign and wonder. This makes no sense to me. Whether Yahweh-the-Judge uses other secondary means to demonstrate his power or whether he uses his raw, unmediated power makes no difference to the significance of the sign—namely, they reveal that Yahweh-the-Judge has absolute control over the whole of reality and, therefore, deserves to be heeded and acknowledged.

200. I first discussed this in chapter 3.

ble with a lack of desire, volition, and coercion. God will not and cannot create such a rationally chaotic state of affairs. It would offend his rational sensibilities.

Second Source of Confusion

Secondly, step 4 results from a confusion of Yahweh-the-Transcendent with Yahweh-the-Judge. We saw above that step 4 is a valid inference if it has Yahweh-the-Transcendent in view. It is not a valid inference if it has Yahweh-the-Judge in view.

To mistakenly understand step 4 with reference to Yahweh-the-Judge rather than Yahweh-the-Transcendent presents a faulty and misleading picture of God. God, rather than being the divine author, is perceived to be the divine bully. Rather than seeing him as the transcendent cause, it views him as an overpowering and invincible ordinary cause.

This false picture of God logically leads to a false dilemma upon which the whole Formal Ethical Objection turns. If divine determinism is proposing that Yahweh-the-Judge is the cause of human choice, then logically I am faced with a choice: either God (Yahweh-the-Judge) is the determinative cause of my choices, or my own volition (my own desires and willings) is the determinative cause of my choices. Since both are ordinary causes, they cannot both be the determinative cause of my choices. Either God's causation is determinative, or my own will's causation is determinative, but they can't both be determinative.[201]

Clearly, this becomes the crux of the argument against divine determinism. Divine determinism is seen to have chosen God (Yahweh-the-Judge) as the cause of human choice, thereby precluding one's own will and volition as the cause of human choice. Given this false dilemma, either God (Yahweh-the-Judge) causes my choices or I do. Divine determinism, then, renders volitional striving futile and pointless. Why exert myself in trying to choose what is right? My will does not govern my actions anyway. God does.

But the picture changes completely when I recognize that step 4 is valid only if Yahweh-the-Transcendent is in view. It ceases to be valid when Yahweh-the-Judge is in view. Yahweh-the-Transcendent is not an irresistible ordinary cause. He is a transcendent cause. Accordingly, that the

---

201. Granted, God's will and power could exert influence on me simultaneously to the influence of my own desires and volition. But only one of them can be the *decisive* influence such that it is the determinative cause of my choice. To whatever extent God's (Yahweh-the-Judge's) influence could be determinative, to that extent it would be coercive. If it were irresistibly coercive, then what would happen to moral accountability for that volition? See the discussion in chapter 9.

determinative cause of human choice could be both God (Yahweh-the-Transcendent) and one's own volition simultaneously is no longer unthinkable. They are not identical kinds of causes. *Volition is the ordinary cause of human choice. God is the transcendent cause of human choice.* For a human will to be the determinative ordinary cause of human choice while the divine will is the transcendent cause of that very same choice is not at all problematic. Both can be equally determinative of an event without any logical conflict.

Take Newton's falling apple. What caused it to fall? Gravity? Or God? Divine determinism quite readily acknowledges both as the determinative cause of the event. One can affirm both without contradiction. Similarly, divine determinism sees no conflict in affirming both human volition and God as the determinative causes of human choice and action. Human volition is the determinative ordinary cause. God is the determinative transcendent cause. Accordingly, to affirm the latter does not require me to reject the former—viewing it as futile, pointless, and irrelevant. Indeed, the rational order of things requires both causes to be present for any event to transpire.[202] In order for an effect to follow, not only must there be a transcendent cause, there must also be the requisite ordinary cause.

This is where the confusion contained in step 4 can lead to the fallacious reasoning of the Formal Ethical Objection. The Formal Ethical Objection is unsound because it fails to recognize that, as divine determinism sees it, human volition and divine causation are not on a par and, hence, are not mutually exclusive. Divine determinism does not force me to choose one explanation over the other. Both are valid explanations of human choosing, and both must be operative. The transcendent will of Yahweh-the-Transcendent must determine my choices, but my own desires and volition must determine my choices as well. Accordingly, contrary to the objection, the absence of any desire and will to do the specific good thing that God wants me to do could and would (so long as this lack of willingness persists) prevent me from doing it. By misconstruing divine causation as just another ordinary cause powerful enough to be determinative, this argument assumes that divine causation precludes the possibility that human volition is the determinative cause of human choice. This simply is not true. Divine determinism fully recognizes that human volition is the determinative cause of all human choice and action.

---

202. Human volition is a likely exception. It may very well have no ordinary cause. See note 195 above. I will proceed to speak as if human volition is the ordinary cause of my choices and free actions even though, strictly speaking, this may not be the truth about the free actions of free moral agents. They may—so far as ordinary causation is concerned—be uncaused, having only a transcendent cause.

ANALYSIS OF STEP 5

STEP 5: *If divine determinism is true, my own lack of desire and volition to do some particular good that God wills me to do could not prevent me from doing it and neither could my own lack of desire and volition to do some particular evil that God wills me to do prevent me from doing that.*

As a direct inference from step 4, step 5 suffers from exactly the same confusion as step 4. In one sense step 5 is true, however. Specifically, if a desire to do evil rather than good exists in me, such a desire is no obstacle to God's causing me to do good. The existence of a preference for evil over good at the present moment does not prevent God from replacing my desire to do evil. Whereas in the present moment my desire may be for evil, in the next future moment my desire may be for good. In this sense, of course, the conclusion in step 5 is a true and necessary implication of divine determinism.[203]

But in another sense step 5 is not true. So long as God causes the desire to do evil rather than good to continue in me, God cannot rationally cause me to do the good deed he commands me to do. Therefore, whereas my own present lack of desire and volition to do some good deed that God wills me to do, strictly speaking, could never ultimately prevent me from doing it, yet the continuing lack of desire and volition to do that same good deed must necessarily prevent me from doing it. Whether step 5 is true or not is dependent upon which of these is meant. The following reformulation of step 5 would be true:

STEP 5A: *If divine determinism is true, my present lack of desire and volition to do some particular good that Yahweh-the-Transcendent wills me to do could not prevent me from doing it and neither could my present lack of desire and volition to do some particular evil that Yahweh-the-Transcendent wills me to do prevent me from doing that.*

But this reformulation of step 5 would be false:

---

203. It is this fact, of course, which is the solid foundation of the Christian's hope. This fact is a source of tremendous joy, comfort, and encouragement for the believer. No amount of stubborn rebellion on my part can ultimately thwart God's purpose to grant me my full inheritance as a child of God and the fullness of the blessing that goes with it. See chapter 2 for a fuller discussion of this point.

STEP 5B: *If divine determinism is true, my continuing lack of desire and volition to do some particular good that Yahweh-the-Transcendent wills me to do could not prevent me from doing it and neither could my continuing lack of desire and volition to do some particular evil that Yahweh-the-Transcendent wills me to do prevent me from doing that.*

ANALYSIS OF STEP 6

STEP 6: *If divine determinism is true, to strive to attain a desire and volition to do good things is futile with respect to the ability to actually do them.*

We can see now that the conclusion reached in step 6 is false and that the Formal Ethical Objection is logically flawed. It has led us astray. By the logic of divine determinism, to strive to attain a desire and volition to do good deeds is not at all futile and pointless.[204] Indeed, it is very necessary! The volition to do good deeds is an absolutely essential prerequisite to a person's doing them. It is the necessary ordinary cause of a person's good deeds. If that cause is not present, it is rationally impossible for the effect to be present. In other words, you cannot do good deeds without wanting to do them.[205] So, far from being futile, striving after the desire and volition to do good deeds is an essential prerequisite to good deeds being done. Step 6 is utterly false.

So where does the argument go wrong? Step 6 is a valid inference from step 5 only if we construe step 5 as step 5b. But as we argued above, step 5b is false. I can embrace step 5b only if I fail to see that a lack of desire and volition to do some particular good thing is logically incompatible with choosing to do it; and, further, only if I fail to recognize that divine determinism's claim is that God (Yahweh-the-Transcendent) is the transcendent cause of human choice, not the determinative ordinary cause of human choice. Divine determinism does not reject the commonsensical notion that human desire and volition constitute the determinative ordinary cause of human choice.

---

204. To strive to attain a desire and volition to do good without reckoning with the only way human beings can attain it—namely, as a gift of God's grace—is indeed futile in an entirely different sense from the one being proposed by this argument. This argument proposes that divine determinism renders striving after goodness futile *in theory*. Christian theology asserts that striving after goodness (as opposed to trusting God for it as a gift) is futile *in practice*. These are two entirely different and distinct issues. We must not confuse the two here.

205. Throughout this present discussion, I am discounting physical coercion. Furthermore, one can, of course, do something with good effect without doing so intentionally. But that would not qualify as a good action in the sense in which I mean it in this context.

ANALYSIS OF STEP 7 THROUGH STEP 12

The argument is straightforward from step 7 through step 12. If step 6 were sound, then steps 7 through 12 would likewise be sound. But since step 6 can be seen to be unsound, then the argument of steps 7 through 12 lead to an unsound conclusion as well, being based upon a faulty premise in step 6.

CONCLUSION

It simply is not the case that divine determinism logically requires that one understand striving to be good as a futile and pointless exercise. On the contrary, divine determinism perceives striving to be good as an essential prerequisite to doing good. If one does not strive after good, he will never do good. To conclude that moral laxity is logically implied by divine determinism is a faulty and simplistic understanding of the theory.

The Informal Ethical Objection

The demonstration that divine determinism, rightly understood, does not logically require moral laxity does not stop the ethical objection. The objection continues:

Divine determinism may not logically justify moral laxity, strictly speaking, but it leads to moral laxity just the same. It takes a pretty sophisticated understanding of divine determinism to know that moral laxity is not justified by it. People aren't that sophisticated. Even though it may be strictly fallacious for them to do so, most people will, in fact, think that divine determinism permits moral laxity. Accordingly, divine determinism gives them the excuse they need to be morally lax.

It is difficult to know exactly what this argument is supposed to be. It seems that there are three possibilities. I will explain and respond to each of the three possibilities:

FIRST POSSIBLE FORM OF THE
INFORMAL ETHICAL OBJECTION

Perhaps the argument is this: Divine determinism is not worthy of our affirmation because it is a doctrine that can be and is used to rationalize evil behavior.

RESPONSE TO THE FIRST POSSIBLE FORM OF THE INFORMAL ETHICAL OBJECTION

This is an utterly unworthy objection. What theory is not vulnerable to the creative distortions of the evil human mind? Theoretically, anything could be used as a basis for rationalizing my evil. Anything! So long as my inferences need not be logically sound, there is no premise that could not be turned into the "logical" foundation for evil by some specious rationalization.

If to embrace any theory that could be used to rationalize evil is a mistake, then none of us should be Christians. Christianity has been used as the logical basis for the crusades, the inquisition, imperialism, and innumerable other blatant evils throughout human history. Shall we encourage people to avoid Christianity because they might fallaciously use it to rationalize evil? That is a stretch. By the same token, it would be absurd to discourage acceptance of divine determinism simply because someone might employ it to rationalize their moral laxity. If divine determinism is true, as this work has argued, then it needs to be accepted regardless of what people may do with it.

Obviously, the use of a doctrine or a theory is of no relevance to the question of whether it is true. If validly derived ramifications of a theory are contradictory, incoherent, or evil, then one has a legitimate basis for rejecting that theory. But the fact that faulty inferences from a theory could be employed to rationalize or justify evil behavior is not a legitimate basis for rejecting it. Such is of no relevance to the truth or worthiness of the theory. False inferences can neither condemn nor recommend a doctrine, regardless of what practical results might follow.

SECOND POSSIBLE FORM OF THE INFORMAL ETHICAL OBJECTION

But perhaps the argument intended involves a more sophisticated statistical argument: Whereas 90% of those people who believe in divine determinism live morally lax lives, only 30% of those people who do not believe in divine determinism live morally lax lives. Therefore, not believing in divine determinism is morally preferable to believing in it.

The "advance" over the last interpretation of this argument is that, though anything can be exploited for purposes of rationalizing evil, not everything is exploited to the same degree in practice. Perhaps what this objection is suggesting is that divine determinism is, in fact, exploited as a rationalization for moral laxity to such a significant degree that the actual, demonstrable effect of the doctrine is to promote immorality. Thus, it is argued, we ought to discourage people from embracing the doctrine.

RESPONSE TO THE SECOND POSSIBLE FORM OF THE INFORMAL ETHICAL OBJECTION

The first thing to note is that such an argument involves a blatant disregard for truth. What relevance does the social effect of a belief have with respect to its truthfulness? None! If something is true, it is true. It makes no difference what unfortunate impact a belief might have. Our goal as knowers is to understand reality the way it actually is. To try to enforce or promote beliefs according to any other standard (such as their social benefit) is to fly in the face of everything intellectual integrity demands of us. It can never be good and right to believe what is not true—regardless of how socially beneficial we may deem it. To believe what is not true is evil.

Is divine determinism true? Then we must embrace it without regard to its negative social effect. If it is not true, then we must reject it with equal disregard for its positive social effect.

Furthermore, I suspect this argument is based on a myth. I doubt very seriously that a careful and accurate study would discover the kind of statistical patterns that this objection assumes. It is more likely that the majority of people who truly believe in divine determinism are diligently seeking after righteousness, not living lives of moral laxity.[206] I do not have hard scientific data at hand any more than the objector does, but I seriously doubt that divine determinism has the negative moral impact that is often alleged.

But even if the alleged statistical pattern did exist, to argue that such a statistical pattern establishes the existence of a cause and effect relationship is fallacious. It would be silly to argue, for example, that because everybody who breathes air dies, breathing air must be the cause of death. Likewise, it would be silly to argue that because 96% of professional basketball players are over six feet tall, playing professional basketball makes people grow tall. A statistical relationship does not, in and of itself, establish cause and effect. So even if the alleged statistical pattern does exist, it would not follow, necessarily, that belief in divine determinism produces or promotes moral laxity. There could be a completely different network of cause and effect relationships that bring about the statistical pattern.

Here, for example, is an obvious possibility: Anyone who wants a theological justification for moral laxity will tend to see in divine determin-

---

206. Especially if we are careful to distinguish between fatalism and divine determinism, two very different doctrines. See appendix E.

ism a theology that they can readily misconstrue in order to rationalize their moral laxity. Hence, people wanting a theological rationalization for moral laxity will tend to gravitate toward divine determinism. I, frankly, do not think that this is true. But if it were, it would explain a statistical correlation between moral laxity and belief in divine determinism that does not entail that moral laxity is caused or promoted by one's belief in divine determinism.

THIRD POSSIBLE FORM OF THE INFORMAL ETHICAL OBJECTION

This brings us to the final suggestion as to what this informal objection might be arguing: Divine determinism is a complex and confusing doctrine. It is very easy to misconstrue it to imply that striving after moral goodness does not matter. Hence, from a moral standpoint, it is a doctrine best left ignored and assumed not to be true. In other words, since it is a dangerous doctrine—a doctrine that can easily lead to moral laxity—it should not be entertained.

RESPONSE TO THE THIRD POSSIBLE FORM OF THE INFORMAL ETHICAL OBJECTION

This understanding of the objection involves the same blatant disregard for truth as the other interpretations of the objection. In the final analysis, what difference does it make how confusing, complex, and dangerous a belief is to its truthfulness? General relativity theory is complex, confusing, and easily misunderstood. Does that mean it is not true? Theories of the atomic structure are dangerous (people use them to build atomic bombs). Does that mean we should reject the theories? Belief in justification by virtue of God's grace can be easily misunderstood and is, in that sense, a dangerous doctrine. Should we pretend, therefore, that justification is not the result of God's grace? This is not clear thinking.

Beyond that, the doctrine of divine determinism need not be as confusing and as easily misunderstood as it is assumed to be. Understanding God as our author, who is creating us like characters in a story, brings the nature of transcendent causation and *ex nihilo* creation into a realm that is readily accessible to our commonsense intuitions. We do not have to find divine determinism and its implications for human responsibility to be as mysterious and incomprehensible as we typically do. It's not easy, of course. We are dealing with one of the most intellectually challenging concepts in all of human thought. But it is not hopeless. We can understand who God is in relation to us and learn to think skillfully, intuitively, and accurately within the worldview of divine determinism.

As we do so, it will become increasingly obvious how unthinkable and unjustified moral laxity is in the light of divine determinism. If divine determinism is true, there is one and only one logically sound choice a person can make: to strive to imitate the holiness of God. Granted, if God does not will it to be, then, left to myself, I will not and cannot make it happen. I am at God's mercy in that sense. But, if I do not strive after holiness, it is guaranteed that I will not attain it. To choose to strive after his holiness (something that will only happen as God, in his mercy, determines me to do) is the only wise and logical choice. God may decree that I will not be wise and logical. But the fact that to strive after righteousness is what I ought to do will always remain the truth. Divine determinism does not imply anything different.

Conclusion

The ethical objection to divine determinism, regardless of what form it takes, fails. It fails because it is based on a false understanding of what divine determinism is and how it is to be conceived. Rightly understood, divine determinism promotes moral goodness, not moral laxity. There can be no valid objection to divine determinism on the basis of its ethical implications.

PART FIVE
CONCLUSION

CHAPTER TWELVE

TOO WEIRD TO BE TRUE?

In this final chapter, I offer a brief description and summation of the argument of this book followed by some comments on how we ought to think about the apparent weirdness of its conclusions.

Brief Summation of the Argument

I have argued that the Bible teaches divine determinism—the perspective that literally nothing whatsoever occurs in reality that has not ultimately been determined by God himself. My argument for divine determinism has been based on the fact that both the biblical concept of God as the creator *ex nihilo* and the biblical understanding of the nature of God's foreknowledge logically require divine determinism. Hence, divine determinism must be assumed to be the underlying worldview of the Scriptures. I further argued that, from a philosophical point of view, divine determinism is required if we are to have a sound logical foundation for the most basic indubitable assumptions of common sense. I then argued that the superficially compelling objections to divine determinism are not rationally compelling at all. The problem with these objections is that they do not fully grasp what divine determinism actually is, and they have a faulty understanding of its implications. Each of them fails to consider the radically different character of a transcendent cause *vis à vis* an ordinary cause. To grasp clearly what divine determinism is and what it implies, one must consider carefully the implications of God's being truly transcendent. God is not the divine bully who controls all of reality through coercive force. It is not merely that God is tough enough to force reality to do what he wants. Rather, God is the divine author of all reality. He creates every minute detail of reality exactly as he wants it to be. When he is seen as the divine bully, God's sovereign control over all things spells the death of free will and human responsibility. Clearly, that would be rationally unacceptable. But when he is viewed correctly as the transcendent author of all reality, no logical conflict exists between God's sovereign control over all things, on the one hand, and important, indubitable notions such as free will and human responsibility on the other. The net conclusion is this: Divine determinism is a philosophically sound, a philosophically necessary, and a philosophically unobjectionable doctrine that is advanced by the Bible as its underlying worldview. We have no other responsible choice but to embrace divine determinism as the truth.

But, a very important point needs to be made. Belief in divine determinism does not replace my ordinary perception of, experience of, and thinking about reality. Rather, it explains the underlying relationship of reality to God, its author. It explains the metaphysical realities that underlie my ordinary, everyday experience. The conclusion of this book is not that we are forced by sound biblical reasoning to reject our everyday commonsensical perceptions and embrace divine determinism instead. Rather, it is that divine determinism describes the underlying reality that accounts for the everyday perceptions of reality that we have. We need not reject our commonsensical perceptions of our experience in order to embrace divine determinism. We can embrace both. They are not mutually exclusive.[207]

The debate over the relationship between God's sovereignty and human responsibility has been long and enduring. If there is anything new and fresh in what I have advanced in this book, it would be these three inter-related things: (i) an understanding of God as radically and absolutely transcendent, (ii) a recognition that an important and fundamental difference exists between the logic of ordinary causation and the logic of transcendent causation and an insistence that we not confuse the two as we reflect on the issues involved in this debate, and (iii) a recognition that we can arrive at an intuitive grasp of the logic of transcendent causation by analyzing the relationship of a human author to the choices made by the characters in his story, since an author radically transcends the product of his imagination in a way analogous to God's transcendence of his creation. I submit that these three elements of my argument bring about a substantial advance in our understanding of the sovereignty of God beyond the traditional understanding of divine sovereignty and the traditional terms of this debate.

Can We Believe Something So Weird and Unnatural?

One very common reaction to the conclusion reached in the argument of this book goes something like this: "Your arguments are very interesting and very persuasive, but I cannot accept divine determinism nonethe-

---

207. See appendix H for a full discussion of this point.

less. My beliefs must be based strictly on the Bible. Your view is dependent upon a set of philosophical beliefs that are not explicitly taught by the Bible. As clever and imaginative as your strategy for reconciling divine sovereignty and human responsibility is, it is not the teaching of the Bible, so I cannot entertain it. I'll just stick to what the Bible teaches."

As pious as this response may seem, it is fundamentally ignorant of the important issues involved. Limited determinism (or any of the other alternatives) is no less dependent upon a set of philosophical beliefs than is divine determinism. This is an unavoidable truth: how we interpret the Bible is dependent upon what set of assumptions we bring to the Bible, including our philosophical assumptions regarding the nature of God, transcendence, reality, and moral accountability. Whenever an interpretation of the biblical text arises out of our pre-understanding[208] (and the philosophical assumptions contained in that pre-understanding), it will seem eminently "natural." It will seem that we are just "reading what is there" and not importing any foreign ideas into the text. Correspondingly, another interpretation—arising out of some other person's prior philosophical commitments—will seem "unnatural" to us. It will seem that they are "reading their philosophy into the text." But we fail to appreciate that their reading and interpretation of the biblical text does not seem "unnatural" to them. Their reading of the text seems just as "natural" to them as mine does to me.

Why is this so? Because reading—by its very nature—is a process of understanding or construing the meaning of the words on a page in correspondence with what I already believe ("know") to be true. Only one who is ignorant of the actual dynamic of verbal communication could ever articulate the goal of biblical interpretation as "making sure that I don't read anything into the Bible," or as "just reading the Bible for what it says without interpreting it." By its very nature, all verbal communication requires the hearer or reader to "read something in." All verbal communication involves words that are inherently ambiguous and mean nothing at all until the audience "interprets" them. And some of what we will read into the Bible (or any other communication) will be our philosophical assumptions. The point we must appreciate is this: *every interpretation of the Bible by every interpreter of the Bible involves importing one set of philosophical assumptions or another into one's understanding of the text.* To believe that one is reading his Bible without importing any prior philosophical assumptions into his understanding of the text is simply to be naive about the nature of verbal communication.

---

208. See chapter 5.

The goal of the interpreter is to make sure that the philosophical assumptions that are shaping his interpretation of the text correspond with the philosophical assumptions that shaped the author's intended meaning of the text. When they match, valid interpretation results and communication has occurred. If my interpretation of a text seems more "natural" to me than yours does, that does not make my interpretation right and yours wrong. If my interpretation is based on a view of God and reality that is radically different from that of the biblical authors, then, regardless of how "natural" it feels to me, it is not a valid interpretation.

We cannot escape the fact that, if we want to come to an understanding of the relationship between divine sovereignty and human responsibility, we must engage in philosophical reflection as a part of the process. We cannot escape the need for that. If we do not engage in philosophical reflection, if we do not subject our prior philosophical commitments to scrutiny, then we will unwittingly impose a philosophical framework on the biblical text without any basis for knowing (i) whether it is a sound set of philosophical assumptions, and (ii) whether it is a philosophical framework that corresponds to the one embraced by the biblical authors.

This is exactly my assessment of why modern Christianity finds divine determinism so implausible. Modern Christians have inherited a philosophical framework that includes various assumptions that necessarily preclude the possibility of divine determinism—various assumptions about free will, moral accountability, the nature of what is real, and other important philosophical issues. But they have never subjected their philosophical framework to any serious scrutiny. They have not adopted this framework after careful consideration. They drank it in with their mother's milk. Accordingly, two important things have escaped their notice: (i) their philosophical framework is incoherent and unsound, and (ii) the biblical authors wrote out of a radically different understanding of reality, an entirely different philosophical framework. As a result, modern Christians are doomed to misinterpret the Bible with respect to the issue of divine sovereignty. Until they are willing and ready to engage in the requisite philosophical reflection, they will continue interpreting their Bibles in the light of a fundamentally unsound philosophical framework that is not the framework of the Bible itself. And all the time they will think how "natural" their understanding of the biblical text is.

Admittedly, therefore, philosophical reflection is a necessary precondition for becoming persuaded of divine determinism. But this should not be viewed with suspicion, as if it were an indictment against divine determinism, for philosophical reflection is a necessary precondition for becoming persuaded of anything that is true. Whether we like it or not, we were created to be philosophers and we all *are* philosophers. We will either be good philosophers or bad philosophers, but we can never avoid being philosophers, for no route to truth can avoid resolving the various philosophical issues that pertain.

Nevertheless, many will still not be prepared to embrace divine determinism as it has been portrayed in this book. It is simply far too radical, far too unfamiliar, and far too weird to accept. Our previous understanding (our "pre-understanding") has seemed to serve us well over all these years. It would seem reckless, foolhardy, and disloyal to throw it away now.

To leave the security afforded by intuitions that are familiar and launch out into a way of perceiving reality that is wildly unfamiliar is a frightening prospect. And yet, this has to be our experience whenever we undergo a revolution in our thinking.[209] All revolutionary changes in one's worldview are unsettling. Our initial conversion to the Christian faith was unsettling. But being unsettling didn't make it wrong. Certainly it was worth the temporary feeling of insecurity to have taken the step to believe. So if reason requires us to embrace divine determinism, we must not let our emotional longing for security prevent us from following reason's lead. It always takes a while to get used to a new paradigm. It takes time to become acclimated to any radically new model for understanding reality. (And, admittedly, divine determinism is a radically new model.) But, in time, one can feel just as comfortable and secure with the new paradigm as with the old. The issue must not be whether it feels comfortable and secure right now. The issue must be whether it is true.

Should we be bothered by the fact the divine determinism appears to be a small, minority viewpoint? The vast majority of Christians, it would seem, reject it. Though that's true, one must remember that the vast majority of people reject Christianity also. But that doesn't make the Christian faith untrue and invalid.

One of the most important forces that gives rise to the beliefs we embrace is the power of culture and tradition. Some things seem true and believable to us simply by virtue of the fact that everyone around us believes them. By the same token, other things seem implausible and false simply by virtue of the fact that no one around us believes them. The cultural environment that gives credence to beliefs in this way is what sociol-

---

209. However, divine determinism rightly understood is not a revolution in our way of thinking in the sense that it overturns or transplants our ordinary way of thinking about and perceiving reality. For a full discussion of this and a related issue see appendix G and appendix H. It is very important to be clear as to exactly how and in exactly what sense the paradigm of divine determinism is "new."

ogists call a PLAUSIBILITY STRUCTURE. Modern Christian culture is a plausibility structure that rejects the doctrine of absolute divine determinism. To hold a belief contrary to the plausibility structure within which one is immersed is never easy. Secular culture is a plausibility structure that supports the doctrine of atheistic, naturalistic evolution. Accordingly, it is extremely difficult to function within secular culture and not see atheistic, naturalistic evolution as utterly plausible. The actual absurdity of the doctrine becomes invisible to us through the force of the plausibility structure. Similarly, to function within modern Christian culture and not accept the doctrines of limited determinism as obvious is difficult. Through the force of the plausibility structure, the incoherence and absurdity of those doctrines has become invisible to the modern Christian. A plausibility structure covers a multitude of logical sins when it comes to our willingness to accept certain beliefs.

Should we be bothered, then, by the degree to which those around us reject divine determinism? Not if we are persuaded that it is the only sound, reasonable worldview. If divine determinism is soundly rational and decidedly biblical, then its lack of acceptance is not an indictment against the doctrine. It is an indictment against the culture that rejects it.

While modern Christian culture would tend to see divine determinism as a truly weird point of view, divine determinism would not have seemed at all weird to most Christians throughout most of history. The prevailing view of God from the earliest origins of the Church, throughout the Middle Ages, and down to recent times was of God as the primary (ultimate) cause of everything in his creation. All other causes were only secondary causes. God was the primary cause of everything that was and everything that occurred. And X being caused by some secondary cause did not preclude X from also being caused by God, the primary cause. This view was commonplace throughout most of Christian history. Furthermore, God was considered the primary cause of all things because he was thought to exist at a level of reality above and beyond the level we inhabit. He existed outside our reality and served as its reason or cause. To employ one of the favorite descriptions of God by the medieval philosophers and theologians, God is the *ens realissimus*, THE MOST REAL BEING. God, the super-real being, is he who has imparted reality to us lesser beings, who exist on a lower level of reality. To people who acknowledged God as the *ens realissimus*, the doctrine of divine determinism would not have seemed weird or implausible. Divine determinism would have been a logical extrapolation from their basic understanding of God.

I am not suggesting that the typical medieval would have readily embraced divine determinism. I don't know that. But it would not have seemed outlandish and weird to him, for it is consonant with his philosophical framework in a way that it is not with the modern philosophical framework. From the narrow perspective of the twentieth and twenty-first centuries it will appear that divine determinism is acceptable to only a very small minority and deemed weird by the vast majority. But from the broader standpoint of the entire history of Christian thought, the vast majority of Christians would have found divine determinism eminently plausible. I am not suggesting that divine determinism *per se* was accepted by the vast majority of Christians throughout history. I am suggesting that they embraced an understanding of God that naturally and logically entails divine determinism, for God as the *ens realissimus* (the most real being) has been the prevailing concept of God throughout Christian history. In the end, that is what this study concludes: God is the most real being, *ens realissimus*, the one in whom "we live and move and have our being."

APPENDICES

APPENDIX A

DIVINE DETERMINISM AND ITS ALTERNATIVES

The chart below compares divine determinism with other possible positions with respect to the issue of ultimate causes:

	Physical events that happen mechanically in accord with natural laws and that do not cause harm to anyone	Physical events that happen mechanically in accord with natural laws and that do cause harm to someone	Morally good actions by humans (or superhuman beings) for which they are typically morally responsible	Morally evil actions by humans (or superhuman beings) for which they are typically morally responsible
Natural Determinism	NATURE	NATURE	NATURE	NATURE
Non-Determinism	NATURE	NATURE	FREE WILL	FREE WILL
Limited Determinism*	NATURE GOD	NATURE SATAN GOD	FREE WILL GOD	FREE WILL SATAN GOD
Divine Determinism	GOD	GOD	GOD	GOD

* When more than one ultimate cause is indicated, it means primarily that an individual limited determinist will assign a different ultimate cause to the same category of cosmic events on a case-by-case basis. So, for example, he may designate the ultimate cause of natural physical event A to be *nature*. At the same time, he may designate the ultimate cause of natural physical event B to be *God*. Events A and B belong to the same class of cosmic events, but they are assigned different ultimate causes. This reflects the primary difference between limited determinism and non-determinism. The limited determinist's God is "sovereign" over his creation and can, as he wills, intervene. Secondarily, the list of multiple causes is intended to reflect the fact that there are differences among different limited determinists. One limited determinist may be inclined to assign a particular ultimate cause to a class of cosmic events more readily than would another limited determinist.

*When more than one ultimate cause is indicated, the causes are listed in the order of likelihood that a limited determinist would assign this cause to this category of cosmic event. (Likelihood is based on my own subjective judgment.)

*The limited determinist is willing to entertain the notion that different events have different ultimate causes. For example, the limited determinist includes *God* as a possible cause of harmful natural events, because he can allow that on some occasions—for example, the divine judgment of a person or nation—God may use nature to do harm. But the limited determinist, unlike the divine determinist, is unwilling to maintain that God is the ultimate cause of any and every harmful event in nature.

APPENDIX B

THE DETERMINACY OF PHYSICAL EVENTS AND HEISENBERG'S UNCERTAINTY PRINCIPLE

The popular appeal to Heisenberg's uncertainty principle as a defense of indeterminacy is unsound and uncompelling. It merely betrays the prejudices of the modern trend toward irrationalism. Heisenberg's uncertainty principle does not prove *indeterminacy* in natural events. It only proves uncertainty with respect to either location or momentum of a sub-atomic particle. To extrapolate from that and conclude that physical events are undetermined is not at all justified. To say that I, an observer in space and time, cannot know both the location and the momentum of a sub-atomic particle is not at all the same as saying that there exists nothing that determines both the velocity and location of that sub-atomic particle. The confusion comes from the popular fallacy of equating determinacy and predictability. The person who infers indeterminacy from unpredictability is assuming the validity of the following proposition: if an event is not, in principle, predictable from physical data that are, in principle, available to a human observer, then it follows that that event is not determined by any physical realities. Now the inverse of this proposition is true. Namely, if an event is predictable from physical data by a human observer, then it follows that that event is determined by physical realities. But the initial proposition is not true. To be unable to predict an event does not logically require the indeterminacy of that event. To more readily see that this is fallacious, consider an equivalent proposition, the contrapositive of the proposition under consideration: if an event is determined by physical realities that are, in principle, knowable, then it follows that that event is, in principle, predictable from physical data that are, in principle, available to a human observer. Clearly this is not necessarily true. Consider weather prediction, for example. One can quite readily see that an event could be physically determined without being predictable, even in principle. Accordingly, the absence of predictability does not entail the lack of determinism. And if we consider the hypothesis that an event is determined by a non-physical, transcendent cause, then it is even more certain that the inability to predict an event from physical data does not entail its whole-sale indeterminacy. What misleads the philosophically naive scientist to conclude that Heisenberg's uncertainty principle is evidence of indeterminacy is his acceptance of this latter, fallacious proposition—namely, that the inability to predict an event from physical data implies that the event is indeterminate.

APPENDIX C

DIVINE CLAIRVOYANCE AND DIVINE DETERMINISM: ANOTHER APPROACH

Is it possible for God to know the future by seeing the future (divine clairvoyance) when the future does not yet exist in our present time? Here is another way to frame this question:

Suppose that we map every spatial location in the cosmos at any given time t_m (a time defined relative to my own existence such that t_0 was at the point of my conception) onto the points contained within a circle, and suppose that we assign a unique descriptor $D_m S_n$ to each point n in the circle such that the descriptor accurately and exhaustively describes the state of affairs at spatial location S_n at time t_m. Now we will have an infinite set of circles where any given time t_m has a circle C_m and the set of descriptors $\{D_m S_n$ for $n = 1$ to infinity$\}$ corresponding to it. Now consider each circle C_m placed one after the other consecutively, forming a cylinder. If we extend this cylinder into eternity in both directions, it would represent a complete description of everything that ever occurred in reality over the whole extent of all time. Now the question is this: does the cylinder that we have just defined exist statically or dynamically?

If it exists statically, then the entirety of the cylinder is just there, existing unchanged at all times relative to my time. In this case, my experience is just a matter of entering sequentially into the experience of what is, always has been, and always will be real.

If this cylinder exists dynamically, then the actuality of the cylinder progresses sequentially as I pass through time sequentially. In other words, C_m comes into real existence only as I come to exist at t_m. In this case, reality is progressively growing and increasing as I progress through time. If I exist at t_m then C_{m+1} does not yet have real existence.

In order for divine clairvoyance to make any sense, then the cylinder of reality described above must be static, not dynamic. For only on the assumption that C_{m+1} actually exists can God "see" and report to me what will happen at t_{m+1} when I am at time t_m. But C_{m+1} only exists on the static view. On the dynamic view it does not exist. Hence, the critical question is whether the cylinder of reality is static or dynamic.

One can salvage divine clairvoyance by proposing that the cylinder of reality is static. But one makes such a proposal at a price. The price is this:

(i) The hypothesis that the cylinder of reality is static is a bizarre doctrine. If one is seeking to avoid believing divine determinism because it strikes one as a weird belief, he has not gained much. For belief in a static cylinder of reality is at least as weird, if not more so.

(ii) Belief that the cylinder of reality is static makes everything that occurs in the future logically determined and, hence, necessary and unavoidable. If the future just is what it is, then it cannot be other than what it is. Hence, if one is inclined to reject divine determinism on the grounds that divine determinism makes the future necessary, then he has not gained anything. The future is just as necessary under the cylinder-of-reality-as-static doctrine as it is under divine determinism.

Therefore, divine clairvoyance can be salvaged as a rational belief if one is willing to embrace the cylinder-of-reality-as-static doctrine. But if one embraces the cylinder-of-reality-as-static doctrine, he gains nothing over divine determinism; for any objectionable result that one was trying to avoid by rejecting divine determinism is implied by the cylinder-of-reality-as-static doctrine as well.

APPENDIX D

WHAT IT MEANS TO BE REAL: THE ANCIENTS, THE BIBLE, AND US

We moderns have a very different concept of 'real' from the one that has prevailed throughout most of history. In fact, we moderns do not have a particularly clear notion of what we mean by 'real'. Our conception is quite vague and nondescript. We tend to understand 'real' to mean something like "having tangible existence." Rocks, trees, animals, desks, chairs, and walls are indubitably real, for they are clearly tangible. Abstract things are harder for us to assess. On the one hand it would strike us as odd to say that love, justice, truth, and beauty are *not* real, yet it strikes us as equally odd to say that they are real. Certain concrete, tangible things incorporate beauty or truth or justice into their relationships to other tangible things. Those tangible things are real. But to say that the abstraction truth itself is real or that justice itself is real, that is a bit of a stretch for the typically modern person.

A very different conception of 'real' existed among the ancients. Their conception of real meant something more like "not being vulnerable to having its existence disappear." If something was real, its existence was lasting and durable. If something was not real or less real, its existence was fleeting, ephemeral, and highly vulnerable.

Plato represents the ancients well in this regard. Plato believed that the desk chair I am sitting on is only barely real. Someone could take a hatchet and blow torch to my desk chair and transform it in a few minutes. It could be made into a pile of kindling and a bunch of scrap metal in no time. No longer would the desk chair exist. But the *idea* of the desk chair—that is, some person's conception of what it had been—is not vulnerable to the hatchet and the blow torch. A craftsman could build me another desk chair just like the one that had been destroyed, for the idea or conception of what it had been continues to exist. (Even when every particular desk chair of like kind has been destroyed.) The only way to keep another desk chair completely out of existence would be to destroy every person who could grasp the conception of that desk chair and construct another one just like it. But even if we destroyed every human being, that would not destroy the idea or conception of a desk chair. For the idea would still exist as something to be grasped and understood by some human being somewhere, if ever one were to exist again. There seems to be no possibility whatsoever of destroying the idea of a desk chair. Somehow, somewhere, eternally, it exists. It can never *not* exist. Accordingly, for Plato, the IDEA of a desk chair is exceedingly and especially REAL. The IDEA exists at the most supreme level of being REAL. But particular desk chairs that people sit on are considerably less real. Their vulnerability to being removed from actual existence is so great that they barely partake of REALITY at all, for what is truly real is what exists and cannot not exist. The truly REAL is what continues to exist eternally.

To be clear, these two conceptions of reality—the modern and the ancient—are very different notions. They share very little in common. Indeed, the only common element is that both of them view reality as defining a certain mode of existence. However, they define very different modes of existence as REAL. The modern notion defines the real as that which has tangibility and materiality. The ancient notion defines the real as that which has permanence and is not vulnerable to cessation of existence.

Four things are very striking about these contrasting conceptions of the real:

(i) The modern view tends to see reality as a digital concept. That is, something is either real or unreal. There are no degrees of reality. By way of contrast, the ancient view tends to see reality as an analog concept. That is, reality can exist in degrees. Neither view logically requires its respective notion. The modern view would not have to view reality as a digital concept; and the ancient view would not have to view reality as an analog concept. But this is how each conception of reality sees it. Consequently, ancients felt very comfortable speaking of one thing being more real than another. Moderns don't speak that way at all. Such speech confuses us. (What are you talking about? *More* real? How can something be *more* real? Either it has tangible existence or it doesn't. How can something have more tangible existence than something else?) But to the ancients, it made perfectly good sense to assess the degree to which something was real by the degree to which it was vulnerable to its existence ceasing.

(ii) To the ancients, it made perfectly good sense to recognize that some levels of reality were dependent upon higher levels of reality in a non-reciprocal kind of way. The desk chair I am sitting on could not exist at all if the universal idea of desk-chair-ness did not exist. But desk-chair-ness can exist whether there are any desk chairs in the world or not. Accordingly, my desk chair's existence is clearly dependent upon the existence of a higher order of reality—the realm of reality in which desk-chair-ness exists. But that higher order of reality is not at all dependent upon the existence of this realm in which tangible desk chairs are sat upon. So, the ancients claimed, this realm we inhabit is *less* real than the higher order realm of reality upon which this inhabited realm depends for its very existence. The ancients were very comfortable with the notion that there are *levels of reality* existing in interdependent relationships to one another. We moderns do not think in these terms at all. Reality is reality. There are no levels of existence.

(iii) While the modern notion clearly tends to ascribe ultimate reality to the tangible and material, the ancient notion tends to ascribe ultimate reality to the intangible and the immaterial. To the modern, the visible, concrete, physical world has the primary claim to being real. To the ancient, the invisible, unseen, spiritual world of abstract ideas and intangible minds has the primary claim to being real.

(iv) Both of these respective conceptions of the real reflect a deeper philosophical worldview. These conceptions of the real are not universal notions rooted in common sense. They are notions that emerge out of a larger conception of what the cosmos is and where it comes from. The prevailing modern conception of the real is the direct result of the naturalistic materialist philosophy that prevails in the modern world. The ancient conception of the real is the direct result of their firm belief in a multi-storied cosmos where a spiritual reality (of one kind or another) is a higher realm upon which this realm we live in is dependent. With the modern rejection of any and all spiritual interpretations of the cosmos, a new conception of what is real had to take the place of the old. But universal human experience has not changed. What has changed is the prevailing philosophical worldview through which we interpret the world. Neither the modern nor the ancient conception of what is real has a greater claim on common sense than the other. Both follow from their respective philosophical theories of the cosmos.

How does the biblical perspective compare to these two conceptions of reality? All things considered, the biblical worldview is much closer to the ancient notion of reality than to the modern notion. That is not to say that the Bible reflects the ancient view in its entirety. The biblical worldview is not the Platonic worldview. Indeed, the early intrusion of Platonic thought into Christian thought steered Christianity away from a biblical worldview to a significant degree. There are serious differences between the Platonic worldview and the biblical worldview. And this is particularly true of their respective views of the REAL. Most notably, what is ultimately real for the Platonist is THE REAL —an eternal realm of ideas upon which all other existence depends. What is ultimately real for the biblical authors is *The Creator God*—a personal, rational being. This is neither a trivial nor an inconsequential substitution. But it is outside the scope of our concerns here to explore these differences. Suffice it to say that the biblical worldview clearly is not the Platonic worldview, nor is it any of the other ancient worldviews. The biblical worldview is clearly and significantly distinctive among ancient philosophies, but it is much more akin to them than it is to the modern worldview. Certainly that is true with respect to the notion of what is real. Consider these three comparisons:

(i) The biblical notion of real, like all other ancient notions, is amenable to recognizing degrees of reality in a way that the modern notion is not. To speak of God as "more real" than we are is not, within a biblical framework, nonsensical. And the Bible freely speaks of the eternal plans and purposes of God as "more real" than the passing, ephemeral circumstances of our ordinary, everyday lives. Although John does not use the notion 'real' to make his point, John clearly wants to emphasize the superior reality of the person who chooses to do the will of God when he writes—"Do not love the world, nor the things in the world. If any one loves the world, the love of the Father is not in him. For all that is in the world, the lust of the flesh and the lust of the eyes and the boastful pride of life, is not from the Father, but is from the world. And the world is passing away, and also its lusts; but the one who does the will of God abides forever." (I John 3:15-17, NASV) Notice that John's fundamental argument hinges upon the ephemerality of the world and the eternality of the things of God. "In what should we invest our lives and existences?" John is asking. "In things that are passing away? Or in things that will endure forever?" The true child of God is the one who has discerned what is lasting and eternal—that is, what is truly and ultimately real—and has invested his life in those things, thereby securing the eternality of his own existence. He who invests his life in the things of this world will pass away along with the world itself, for the tangible, physical, material world that seems so real to us now is, in fact, truly temporary and fleeting. Only a fool would invest his existence in finding fulfillment in the fleeting.

(ii) The biblical worldview clearly understands different levels of reality. Clearly God exists on a whole different level of reality than do we and the world in which we live. We could look many different places in the Bible, but consider Psalm 102, "He has weakened my strength in the way; he has shortened my days. I say, 'Of old You did establish the earth; and the heavens are the work of Your hands. Even they will perish, but You still endure; and all of them will wear out like a garment; like clothing You will change them, and they will be changed. But YOU are the same, and Your years will not come to an end. The children of Your servants will contin-

ue, and their descendents will be established before You." (Psalm 102:23-
28, modified from the NASV) This Psalm gives explicit expression to the
pervasive biblical notion that God is eternal, unchanging, and ultimate
while all that he has created is utterly dependent upon him for its existence. When he chooses to, God will change the created order like a man
changes his clothes. The created order is inferior in the nature of its being.
It will "wear out." The created order is the "work of God's hands." Had
God not created, the creation would not exist. God, on the other hand,
has always existed and always will. His existence is dependent on no one
and no thing. God, the creator, clearly possesses a superior sort of reality
to that possessed by the created order. God exists above and beyond this
creation, on a higher level of reality. God is more real than we are. God is
more real than anything else that exists. He is, as the medievals were
inclined to put it, "THE MOST REAL BEING."

The New Testament speaks of yet another sense in which there are levels of reality. Since God is more real than the created order, the purposes,
promises, and plans of God are—by extension—more real than the circumstances of our lives here and now. Accordingly, the apostle Paul can
write, "Blessed be the God and Father of our Lord Jesus Christ, who has
blessed us with every spiritual blessing in the heavenlies (in the heavenly
places) in Christ...." (Ephesians 1:3, modified from the NASV) The spiritual blessings that God has purposed to grant us exist in a realm that is
more real than this realm. Whatever may seem to be real and appear to be
true in our realm is nothing compared to what exists as real and true in the
mind and purpose of The Most Real Being. Because of our discipleship to
Jesus, the Messiah, there exist blessings *really* in store for us that are more
real than any of the sorrows, difficulties, or obstacles of our lives here and
now. In another letter, Paul writes, "If then you have been raised up with
Christ, keep seeking the things above, where Christ is, seated at the right
hand of God. Set your mind on the things above, not on the things that
are on earth. For you have died and your life is hidden with Christ in God.
When Christ, who is our life, is revealed, then you also will be revealed
with Him in glory." (Colossians 3:1-4, NASV) When Paul exhorts them
to set their minds on "the things above," he is encouraging the Colossians
to focus and concentrate on values that are more real and more ultimately true than those of ordinary earthly existence. Clearly the New
Testament authors recognized that there were levels of reality in this sense.
Some things were simply more permanent, more ultimate, and more substantial than others. The purposes, will, promises, and values of God are
clearly more real and more true than the changing circumstances of our

lives and the values shaped by lives lived in the midst of ordinary circumstances. In this sense, therefore, there are levels of reality.

(iii) Clearly, in parallel to other ancient views, those things that the Bible holds to be ultimately real and ultimately true are invisible, intangible, immaterial, and spiritual realities, not the material, tangible realities of life here and now. On this point the biblical view is closer to the ancient than to the modern worldview.

Understanding the biblical conception of the real *vis à vis* the modern and ancient views is important. Contemporary Christians far too often adopt a modern notion of the REAL when they seek to understand the relationship between divine sovereignty and human responsibility. This is a critical mistake. The modern notion of the REAL is a concept completely foreign to, and in conflict with, the biblical notion of the REAL. It is a concept rooted in atheistic, naturalistic, materialist philosophy. It is not a commonsense notion that can be usefully employed to unpack the valid implications of the biblical worldview.

The existence of levels of reality is an assumption that is central to the claims advanced in this book. My whole argument hinges on the meaningfulness of thinking in terms of different levels of reality. The modern Christian, completely enculturated in a modern notion of what is REAL, will tend to dismiss as radical and bizarre the central tenet of my defense of divine determinism—namely, that God is more real than we are. But what may seem weird to the modern Christian would have seemed quite obvious and transparent to most Christians throughout history—indeed, to most peoples throughout history. What creates the sense of unfamiliarity that we experience as "weirdness" is our peculiarly parochial conception of the REAL rooted, as it is, in a decidedly recent philosophical worldview. God's existence above us as more real than we are is not an offense to our common sense. It is an offense to the rather inadequate and distorted sense of the REAL that we have inherited from the modern godless culture in which we live.

APPENDIX E

DIVINE DETERMINISM AND FATALISM

A common response to the doctrine of divine determinism among modern Christians is that divine determinism leads to fatalism. By that, they could mean one of two things: (i) divine determinism logically entails fatalism, or (ii) divine determinism results in a fatalistic frame of mind in the one who embraces it as a doctrine. I will consider each of these claims.

(i) 'Fatalism,' in the sense in which I mean it here (and that is the sense that the average person gives to the term), describes the view that whatever is going to happen is going to happen, *no matter what.* Whatever is fated to happen is indeed going to happen and nothing whatsoever can prevent it. The suggestion under consideration is that fatalism (so defined) is the logical consequence of the doctrine of divine determinism.

Clearly this is not true. Nothing in the doctrine of divine determinism suggests that if God has willed for X to occur, X will occur *no matter what.* On the contrary, in willing X to occur, God is also willing all of the ordinary causes of X as well. So, for example, if God wills that I murder person P out of a murderous rage induced by intense jealousy, then God must not only determine my act of murdering P, he must also determine my intense jealousy and murderous rage. Fatalism, as vaguely understood by the average person, would suggest that if God wills that I murder person P out of a murderous rage induced by intense jealousy, then it makes no difference whether I take steps to successfully avoid the intense jealousy and the murderous rage. I will murder P anyway. This is clearly not what divine determinism implies. If, in fact, steps could be taken whereby I could successfully avoid the intense jealousy and the murderous rage, then my act of murdering person P out of a murderous rage induced by intense jealousy could indeed be prevented. (In fact, even if I did end up murdering P, it would not have been out of a murderous rage induced by intense jealously. Hence, it would not have been what God had willed.) Divine determinism does not entail that what God wills to happen will happen *no matter what.* Rather, it entails that all that God wills to happen will happen, including the entire nexus of preconditions and causes that give rise to what he wills to happen. So, if God wills for me to murder person P out of a murderous rage induced by intense jealousy, then it is necessarily the case that I will develop an intense jealousy, that it will develop into a murderous rage, that I will have no desire to take steps to prevent the jealousy and rage, that I will freely and willfully choose to be jealous and murderous, and that nothing anyone does or says to me will be effective in inducing me to repent of my jealousy or rage. But it does not follow from this that *no matter what might happen* I will do what God has determined that I will do. It makes all the difference in the world what might happen!! If someone did say something to me that induced me to repent of my jealousy and rage, then, of necessity, I would not and could not go on to murder person P out of a murderous rage induced by intense jealousy. So it very much matters whether or not someone successfully induces me to repent. I will only do what God has willed that I do on the condition that I end up not repenting of my jealousy and rage. But there is a real and consequential choice before me. If I repent of my jealousy and rage, I will not murder P. If I do not repent of my jealousy and rage, I will murder P. The stakes are high. The consequences of my choice are great. Divine determinism does nothing to undermine the consequential nature of the choice before me. But while it does not alter the consequential nature of the choice I face, it does predict what my choice will be. If God has so determined, I will choose not to repent. Or, at least, I will not choose to repent.

Fatalism is a very different viewpoint. If fatalism—as popularly understood—were true, then my choices would be completely inconsequential. If I am going to murder P *no matter what*, then it makes no difference whether I repent of my jealousy and rage or not. What is going to happen is going to happen no matter what I do and choose. Clearly, this is not what divine determinism maintains. Hence, divine determinism is not fatalism. According to divine determinism, it makes all the difference in the world what I choose and what I do. It is just that what I do and what I choose, down to the minutest detail, is ultimately determined by the divine author of my being.

(ii) A 'fatalistic frame of mind,' in the sense in which I employ the phrase here, is the frame of mind a person can adopt wherein he is unmotivated to take any steps to affect the outcome of his life in any way. The source of the lack of motivation is his belief that it makes no difference what steps he might take. The outcome will be the same no matter what.

We have already seen that divine determinism does not logically entail the belief that it makes no difference what steps I take, that the outcome will be the same no matter what. But while it may not logically entail such a belief, does it, as a matter of course, lead to a fatalistic frame of mind nonetheless?

There is no evidence that it does. Granted, one can find individuals who, at some stage of their lives, have been inclined toward a fatalistic frame of mind. Such individuals may, in fact, consider divine determinism a convenient way to justify their fatalistic frame of mind. But three things need to be noted about such individuals: (a) Typically, this is a fleeting and temporary condition. One would be hard pressed to find an individual who persists in a fatalistic frame of mind out of a settled conviction and a permanent frame of mind. (b) Typically, such individuals have a superficial, inadequate, and distorted understanding of the doctrine of divine determinism. They are typically confused and mistaken about the valid implications of their belief. (This should not be surprising. Divine determinism and the issues that surround it are among the more intellectually challenging issues a human being can ever face.) (c) When the real source of the fatalistic frame of mind becomes clear, it is typically not the person's belief in the doctrine of divine determinism. It is typically something else. Usually it involves a strategy for dealing with moral failings. If I can believe that nothing I do affects the outcome of my life, then I need not take real responsibility for the moral failings in my life, for there is nothing I can do about it. This can be an attractive strategy for dealing with the guilt of moral failure. In such a case, divine determinism—or, more accurately, a superficial and distorted understanding of divine determinism—becomes a convenient basis for rationalizing one's fatalistic frame of mind by casting it in a form that seems intellectually respectable. But, in such a scenario, it is not my belief in divine determinism that has led to my fatalistic frame of mind. It is my strategy for coping with guilt due to moral failings. A bastardized form of the doctrine of divine determinism has served only as a convenient means to rationalize my fatalism.

Divine determinism, correctly understood, does not logically entail fatalism, nor does it lead, psychologically, to a fatalistic frame of mind. These cannot, therefore, be legitimately offered up as reasons to reject divine determinism.

In light of the above discussion, it is highly unfortunate that much of the philosophical literature discussing the issues would denominate my position as THEOLOGICAL FATALISM. To give them the benefit of the doubt, these philosophers would probably define theological fatalism in such a way that it means just what I mean by 'divine determinism'. But to label this position as they do is highly misleading and ultimately tendentious. Divine determinism is significantly different from fatalism as the latter term is popularly and typically understood. Accordingly, it does not serve the interests of clear communication to invite a confusion of these two radically different points of view. This is one of the reasons that I have chosen the label 'divine determinism' over 'theological fatalism' even though the latter is the more conventional term among those religious philosophers who discuss this topic.

APPENDIX F

A DETAILED ANALYSIS OF THE THEOLOGICAL OBJECTION TO DIVINE DETERMINISM

The theological objection to divine determinism is an objection raised in the context of Judaeo-Christian conceptions of God and reality. The relevant question could be framed as follows: given that the Judaeo-Christian God exists and given that reality contains evil, does this God determine and control absolutely everything in reality (as divine determinism would maintain) or not?

It is assumed by the theological objection to divine determinism that everyone who is party to this discussion would agree on four basic assumptions:

1. GOD EXISTS.

2. THE GOD WHO EXISTS IS PERFECTLY GOOD.

3. THE GOD WHO EXISTS IS SO POWERFUL AS TO BE ABLE TO TOTALLY CONTROL AND DETERMINE EVERYTHING IN REALITY.

4. EVIL EXISTS IN THE WORLD.

It is further assumed that the single difference between those who would subscribe to divine determinism and those who would not is as follows: the proponent of divine determinism would add the following assumption to the list of basic assumptions above; the opponents of divine determinism would not—

5. THE GOD WHO EXISTS DOES, IN FACT, TOTALLY CONTROL AND DETERMINE EVERYTHING IN REALITY.

There are now a total of five different propositions that are relevant to the discussion. The crux of the theological objection to divine determinism is its contention that the five propositions above are logically incompatible. Logically, the incompatibility of these five propositions could be attributable to any one (or more) of these five assertions being false. Temporarily abandoning the context of Judaeo-Christian belief, people have challenged each of these different propositions at various times. Here are the five different logical possibilities for identifying the source of the alleged logical incompatibility of these five propositions:

A. THE ILLUSION ARGUMENT
—a rejection of the validity of proposition (4), a rejection of the existence of evil.

This position maintains that propositions (1), (2), (3), and (5) are all true and, hence, that the false assumption is proposition (4). Evil does not, in fact, exist. The apparent existence of evil is explained as some sort of illusion. (Christian Science doctrine takes this or a similar position.)

B. THE ARGUMENT FROM EVIL
AGAINST THE EXISTENCE OF GOD
—a rejection of the validity of proposition (1), a rejection of the existence of God.

This position is a popular atheistic argument against the existence of God. It maintains that proposition (4) is true, but that proposition (1) and, hence, (2), (3), and (5) are all false. God does not, in fact, exist. (Many atheists subscribe to this argument.)

C. THE EVIL GOD ARGUMENT
—a rejection of the validity of proposition (2), a rejection of the goodness of God.

This position maintains that propositions (1), (3), (4), and (5) are all true and, hence, that the false assumption is proposition (2). God is not perfectly good. (Many atheists fallaciously point to this alternative as the only valid alternative to (B) above.)

D. THE FINITE GOD ARGUMENT
—a rejection of the validity of proposition (3), a rejection of the omnipotence of God.

This position maintains that propositions (1), (2), and (4) are all true and, hence, that the false assumptions are propositions (3) and, therefore,

(5). God is not capable of totally controlling and determining all that occurs in reality. God is small, limited, weak, and finite rather than omnipotent and infinite. (Various versions of Process Theology take this position.)

E. THE SELF-LIMITING GOD ARGUMENT
—a rejection of the validity of proposition (5), a rejection of divine determinism.

This position maintains that (1), (2), (3), and (4) are all true and, hence, that the false assumption is proposition (5). God does not control everything that happens. One is forced to this conclusion if he affirms the validity of propositions (1)–(4) and yet believes that (1)–(5) are logically incompatible. God is omnipotent and infinite and capable of controlling reality absolutely [proposition (3)]. Therefore, we must assume that God has, for whatever reasons, purposely limited his own control and determination of reality. The net result is that God does not determine the whole of reality and that proposition (5) is not true. (This is the typical position of most Christians who reject divine determinism.)

Now, as we said above, the theological objection to divine determinism is raised in the context of Judaeo-Christian belief. The proponents of this objection, holding a Judaeo-Christian worldview, view propositions (1)–(4) above as a logically coherent whole (and a coherent whole to which (5) is not admitted). Therefore, in the context of universally-accepted Judaeo-Christian belief, we can frame the options as such:

I. DIVINE DETERMINISM [proposition (5)] IS FALSE

II. THE FOUNDATIONAL ASSUMPTIONS OF THE JUDAEO-CHRISTIAN WORLDVIEW [propositions (1)– (4)] ARE FALSE

III. THE FIVE PROPOSITIONS [propositions (1)–(5)] ARE NOT LOGICALLY INCOMPATIBLE.

In terms of these three options, position (E), the self-limiting God argument, is an instance of option (I) above. All the other four logical possibilities, (A)–(D), are instances of option (II).

The force of the theological objection as an argument against divine determinism, therefore, hinges on the fact that both the proponents of divine determinism and its detractors share a common set of assumptions. Namely, they share the set of assumptions that forms the foundation of the Judaeo-Christian worldview, propositions (1)–(4). If, as the theological objection assumes, there can be no doubt but that the five propositions are logically incompatible, then the divine determinist is placed on the horns of a dilemma: either divine determinism is not true after all [I], or the foundations of the Judaeo-Christian worldview are false [II]. The theological objection rests on the fact that no one will easily reject his foundational beliefs, nor should he do so. This argument assumes that the Judaeo-Christian worldview forms the divine determinist's most foundational beliefs. So, when faced with the option of choosing between his Judaeo-Christian worldview in general and his doctrine of divine determinism in particular, there can be little doubt but that he will choose his Judaeo-Christian worldview over his commitment to divine determinism. Thus, by suggesting to the divine determinist that he is faced with exactly this dilemma—either his Judaeo-Christian worldview or his divine determinism—the theological objection is urging the rejection of divine determinism in favor of the foundational beliefs of Christianity. Obviously, therefore, the theological objection has no real force in discussion with one who would readily jettison the Judaeo-Christian worldview, or who has never subscribed to it in the first place.

There remains one important question: if, as the above anaysis suggests, the dilemma that the theological objection tries to create is between one's Judaeo-Christian worldview and divine determinism, then why does my presentation of the theological objection in chapter 9 present the dilemma as between divine determinism and the goodness of God?

I explain the theological objection as I do in chapter 9 precisely because that is the way the theological objection is most popularly presented. But why is it popularly framed in this way?

We can understand why, I think, if we consider carefully what the force of the objection is intended to be. The force of the theological objection results from creating a dilemma between the Judaeo-Christian worldview and divine determinism. It creates a dilemma of the following form:

If divine determinism is true, then it is not logically possible for X to be true.

The emotional and subjective power of this argument rests on X being equal to the Judaeo-Christian worldview. So, the dilemma reads:

If divine determinism is true, then it is not logically possible for the Judaeo-Christian worldview to be true.

But when the dilemma is stated in this form, it is not immediately apparent that it is true and, therefore, it is not rhetorically forceful enough. Why should it be the case that if divine determinism is true, the Judaeo-Christian worldview cannot be true? To increase rhetorical force, it is strategic to state the dilemma as between divine determinism and a specific belief foundational to the Judaeo-Christian worldview wherein the incompatibility with divine determinism seems apparent. The four fundamental assumptions that comprise the Judaeo-Christian worldview, (1)–(4), leave us four possibilities:

a) If divine determinism is true, then it is not logically possible for the existence of God to be true.

b) If divine determinism is true, then it is not logically possible for the omnipotence of God to be true.

c) If divine determinism is true, then it is not logically possible for the existence of evil to be true.

d) If divine determinism is true, then it is not logically possible for the perfect goodness of God to be true.

The first two will not create the desired dilemma. Divine determinism is certainly not logically incompatible with God's existence. It logically requires it. Hence, (a) would be absurd, not persuasive. Furthermore, divine determinism is clearly not logically incompatible with God's omnipotence. Rather, it requires it. So the second option, (b), is just as absurd as the first.

We are left then with options (c) and (d). The popular presentation of the theological objection to divine determinism amounts to creating a dilemma between these two options:

e) If divine determinism is true, then one or the other of the following must be the case: (i) it is not logically possible for the existence of evil to be true, or (ii) it is not logically possible for the perfect good ness of God to be true.

If we were to insist that evil does truly exist, then dilemma (e) gets reduced to the fatal dilemma (d) above—

d) If divine determinism is true, then it is not logically possible for the perfect goodness of God to be true.

On the other hand, if we insist that God is perfectly good, then dilemma (e) gets reduced to the fatal dilemma (c) above—

c) If divine determinism is true, then it is not logically possible for the existence of evil to be true.

Either way, we are forced to make a choice between divine determinism and one of the beliefs that is foundational to the Judaeo-Christian worldview. So, either way I must choose between divine determinism and the coherence of the Judaeo-Christian worldview. As we saw above, this essential dilemma—between divine determinism and the Judaeo-Christian worldview—is the ultimate strategy being employed by the theological objection to divine determinism.

Popularly, the strategy typically takes for granted the Judaeo-Christian assumption that evil does in fact exist and then maintains that one must therefore (in the light of that assumption) reject the perfect goodness of God. However, the same goal could be achieved by accepting the Judaeo-Christian assumption that God is perfectly good and then maintaining that one must therefore (in the light of God's perfect goodness) reject the reality of evil. From a logical point of view, the fact that the former is the more usual strategy is strictly arbitrary. Both would accomplish exactly the same thing. Both would force a dilemma between divine determinism and the Judaeo-Christian worldview and thereby make divine determinism objectionable and implausible.

APPENDIX G

DECISION-MAKING
AND DIVINE DETERMINISM

The person who has an inadequate understanding of the doctrine of divine determinism may misunderstand its implications for decision-making. He may assume that discerning the answer to the question—What is the sovereign decree of God?—is a legitimate component of the decision-making process. It is not.

Divine determinism does not alter the fact, obvious to common sense, that decision-making involves fundamentally two things: (i) discerning what is wise to do, and/or (ii) discerning what is desirable to do. The questions that an ordinary human being faces, therefore, are (i) what would be the wise thing to do in this situation, and (ii) what do I want to do in this situation? The question of what God has sovereignly decreed that I shall do in this situation does not and, logically, should not enter into one's deliberations at all. There is no profit in my even asking myself that question. The sovereign decree of the author of all existence will inevitably manifest itself through those choices that I ultimately make after considering only what I want to do and what I believe is wise to do. God determines my choices by determining (i) what I will want to do, (ii) what I decide is wise to do, (iii) whether I will be inclined to do what I want to do or whether, in this particular situation, I will be inclined to forego doing what I want to do, and (iv) whether I will be inclined in this particular situation to do the wise or the unwise thing. These are the components of normal decision-making in ordinary experience. While God sovereignly and transcendently authors my ultimate beliefs and desires with respect to a given situation, they are *my* beliefs and *my* desires, and I experience them in that ordinary way familiar to all of us. Hence, the psychology of decision-making is not the least bit affected by the fact that it is the ultimate author of all reality who creates the components of my decision-making and determines their content.

It makes no sense and it is of no profit whatsoever, therefore, to confront the question in advance: what has God sovereignly decreed that I do in this situation? The only question I need confront is this: what shall I choose to do in this situation? The sovereign decree of God will make itself known through the choice I make.

In general, acceptance of divine determinism does not require us to alter the way we understand and experience everyday, ordinary reality. Divine determinism is a doctrine that explains what lies beneath the surface of ordinary, mundane experience. It is not a doctrine that demands that we transform the way we understand and experience everyday, mundane reality. (See appendix H.) This is as true of decision-making as it is of every other aspect of ordinary experience.

APPENDIX H

DIVINE DETERMINISM: REFORMING OR NON-REFORMING DOCTRINE

There are two kinds of philosophies: those that ask us to reform the way we see and experience things, and those that merely seek to explain what lies behind the way we see and experience things. The former we might call a 'reforming doctrine,' the latter we might call a 'non-reforming doctrine'.

The theory of atoms is the latter, *non-reforming* kind of philosophical (scientific) doctrine. When the physicist suggests that the table in front of me is, in reality, a collection of atoms bound to one another in particular patterns by atomic forces while existing in empty space, he is not asking me to exchange my commonsensical understanding of the table for a scientific one. He is not proposing that I transform the way I experience reality; nor is he asking me to transform the way I perceive the table. Rather, he is attempting to explain more fully the metaphysics of what lies beneath and behind my ordinary, mundane experience. The scientist's atomic theory does not displace my old way of looking at the table for a new one. I can, without contradiction, view the table both ways. The old way is valid and true. The new way simply answers further questions and seeks deeper understanding of what lies below the surface of my experience.

The New Testament teaches that this world, this present age, is passing away and that one must not seek his or her fulfillment in the things it has to offer. One is wise to place one's hope in the age that is to come. This New Testament teaching, in contrast to atomic theory, is clearly a *reforming* doctrine. The New Testament authors are asking me to transform the way I look at my life and experience right now. I must stop viewing it as the end all and be all of my existence and view it, instead, as a temporary, short-lived stepping stone to another existence, one that is above and beyond this one. This is asking for a significant and radical transformation of my ordinary outlook on life. I am to exchange one way of looking at life for another, to displace my old way of looking at life for a new one.

If we have come to rightly understand divine determinism, we will recognize that divine determinism *per se* is a *non-reforming* doctrine. Divine determinism is not proposing that I transform the way I experience reality. Rather, it is attempting to explain more fully the metaphysics of what lies beneath and behind my mundane experience. It does not ask me to exchange one way of looking at ordinary experience for another. I can, without contradiction, view my mundane experience in two distinct ways. It is not asking me to displace my old way of looking at reality for a new one. The old way remains valid and true. In proposing a new way to look at reality, divine determinism intends only to promote a deeper understanding of what underlies the surface of our experience. Accordingly, to embrace divine determinism does not require that I set my commonsensical understanding of ordinary experience aside. Leaving my commonsense understanding intact, it simply proposes that there is more to be known than ordinary perception alone can reveal. If we look deep enough, we will discover that there exists a transcendent author of the surrounding reality. Divine determinism is not suggesting that the divine authorship of reality is visible on the surface of our experience, nor that what is visible is an illusion. Rather, it is suggesting that there is more to reality than meets the eye. Accordingly, divine determinism is not saying:

> "I know it looks to you like you make your own freewill decisions. But that is not true. That is an illusion. In reality, God makes your decisions. You don't. Stop believing the illusion. Stop believing that you are free. Come to see and understand that you are not free. Your every step is determined by the will of God."

On the contrary, divine determinism is saying something like this:

> "Obviously, the uncoerced decisions we all make are decisions that arise out of our freedom as free moral agents. While that is true, we can look deeper and ask ourselves wherein the power and reality of our being as free moral agents lies. And what do we find? We find that it does not lie in ourselves, as if we were self-existent beings. It lies in the will of the one who is the author of our very being and all that our being includes. So our freewill choices are authored by the same one who authors all of reality in the first place. My reality, my history, my substance, my choices, my desires——everything about me ultimately derives from the creative will of God. Am I a creature who exercises a free will? Yes, absolutely! Do I exist as a free creature from and of myself? No, of course not! If God did not will my existence, I would not exist. If God did not will my choice, my choice would not be made. If God did not will that my choice be a free choice, it would not be free. Nevertheless, while it is true that I am not autonomous, for God is the author of my being, yet my

being *is* just what it appears to be. I am a free-will creature who makes freewill choices. That is what God has authored me to be. That is what I appear to be. That is what I experience. And that is what I am."

So divine determinism *per se* is a non-reforming doctrine. After I come to believe it and embrace it, it leaves everything just like it was before I believed it.

However, while I must insist on the non-reforming nature of divine determinism *per se*, there are doctrines that are logically founded on divine determinism that are *reforming* in nature. The doctrine of unfailing hope that the gospel teaches, with divine determinism as its basis, is a reforming doctrine. If we live without hope in this world, we are invited, by the implications of divine determinism, to transform the way we look at and experience human existence. We are to live in hope in this world, not in despair. We are to exchange our desperate view of reality for a hopeful one, based on the sovereign, determinative grace of he who authors my being.

As we saw in chapter 2, there are many important practical and life-changing ethical, spiritual, and existential implications of divine determinism, implications that should reform our outlook on life. But while divine determinism has many significant reforming implications, as a theory of the metaphysics of being, it remains thoroughly non-reforming in nature. It does not transplant my ordinary, familiar way of looking at reality. It supplements it, answering questions about what lies ultimately at the root of ordinary experience without requiring any change in the way I perceive the nature of ordinary experience.

APPENDIX I

WHAT ABOUT MIDDLE KNOWLEDGE?

The following essay was originally published in 1995 under the title "Does Middle Knowledge Solve the Problem of Divine Sovereignty?" It was included in Volume Two of *The Grace of God, the Bondage of the Will*, edited by Thomas R. Schreiner and Bruce A. Ware, published by Baker Books, a division of Baker Publishing Group, 1995. Substantially the same essay is reprinted here with permission from Baker Book House Company.

In his paper, "Middle Knowledge: A Calvinist-Arminian Rapprochement?" William L. Craig suggests that the views of the medieval Spanish Jesuit, Luis Molina (1535 - 1600), amount to a reconciliation of the views of Calvinists and Arminians.[210] Accordingly, he recommends that we give fresh consideration to Molina's views, especially to his notion of divine middle knowledge. Craig is confident that if modern participants in the Calvinist-Arminian debate were to adopt Molina's notion of divine middle knowledge, we would see a closing of the gap that now divides them.

My purpose in this essay is to offer a personal reaction to this particular call for reconciliation. Craig maintains that Molina has shown us how divine sovereignty and the absolute autonomy of the human will are compatible concepts. Accordingly, if I, a Calvinist with respect to my views on divine sovereignty, would adopt Molina's views on the matter, I could concede to my Arminian brother the reality of absolute human autonomy without compromising my commitment to divine sovereignty. And by doing so, I would greatly reduce the gap that divides us. Here then is the question I wish to address in this essay: Can I, a Calvinistic divine determinist,[211] embrace Molina's conception of middle knowledge and thereby see my way clear to affirm the absolute autonomy of the human will?

My discussion, in four major sections, will explain Molina's theory of divine foreknowledge and middle knowledge in the context of the problem he was attempting to solve; assess whether Molina's theory of divine foreknowledge and his conception of middle knowledge are philosophi-

---

210. Published in *The Grace of God, the Will of Man: A Case for Arminianism*, ed. Clark H. Pinnock (Grand Rapids: Zondervan, 1989), 141-164.

211. By "divine determinist" I mean to denote one who believes that absolutely every aspect of everything that occurs in the whole of reality is ultimately caused and determined by God.

cally and biblically viable concepts and whether they reconcile divine sovereignty and human autonomy in the way that Craig and Molina claim that they do; address an underlying assumption in Craig's and Molina's appeal—namely, that Calvinism cannot give an adequate account of human freedom; and summarize the reasons why I am unmoved by Craig's appeal to embrace Molina's distinctive solution to the divine sovereignty/human freedom question.

Molina's Theory of Divine Middle Knowledge

To understand Molina's concept of divine foreknowledge and the concept of middle knowledge that accompanies it, we need to understand it as the solution to a problem he thought it solved.

MOLINA'S PROBLEM

In Molina's day, as today, the prevailing philosophical assumptions forced one to choose between two opposing theological positions, Calvinism and Arminianism. But, as Molina saw it, both positions are deficient when judged strictly from the standpoint of biblical teaching. Each holds some things that are right and some things that are wrong. The truth revealed in biblical teaching upholds some aspects of each of these opposing systems. It repudiates aspects of each as well.

To be specific, Molina believed that these four doctrinal positions capture the Scripture's teaching with respect to the points at issue:

1. The freewill choices of a human being are such that they always could have been other than they were. If person P freely does X at time T under the set of circumstances C, it is always true that P could have done not-X at exactly the same time and under exactly the same set of circumstances. Nothing necessitated that P do X at time T. Other than the resolution of P's own will at the time of his choice, nothing made it necessary that P do X at that time. Hence, there was no predetermination of P's choice of X by any cause. The human will is autonomous and functions independently of every other reality, including the will of God. I will refer to this first doctrine as a belief in the *absolute autonomy of the human will,* or as a belief in *absolute human autonomy.*

2. At the same time, God knows infallibly every detail of every event that will occur in the history of the cosmos. He knows all this before anything has transpired in time. I will refer to this second doctrine as a belief in the *de fide*[212] *doctrine of divine foreknowledge* (where *de fide* means, literally, "of the faith").

3. God is the ultimate and final cause of every detail of every event which will occur in the history of the cosmos. I will refer to this third doctrine as a belief in the *de fide doctrine of divine providence.*

4. God's choice ultimately determines who will be saved and who will not be saved. I will refer to this fourth doctrine as a belief in the *de fide doctrine of divine election.*

We can summarize his views by saying that Molina believes in *the absolute autonomy of the human will* at the same time that he believes in the *de fide* doctrines of *divine sovereignty*. (By the *de fide doctrines of divine sovereignty* I mean to denote the *de fide* doctrines of divine foreknowledge, divine providence, and divine election. Throughout this essay, when I refer to the *de fide* doctrines of divine sovereignty I mean to denote strictly the preceding definitions.)

Calvinism, by way of contrast to Molina, willingly embraces the *de fide* doctrines of divine sovereignty but rejects the absolute autonomy of the human will. Conversely, Arminianism embraces the absolute autonomy of the human will but rejects the *de fide* doctrines of divine sovereignty.

The problem, as Molina saw it, was that both Arminians and Calvinists were stuck in their respective systems. Their philosophical and theological commitments forced them to embrace the doctrines that are entailed by their respective systems rather than the doctrines advanced by biblical teaching. Molina attempted to find a way for both Arminians and Calvinists to break out of their respective systems.

---

212. In Molina, *Concordia* 4.52.10 we read, "And this last point is surely demanded by the freedom of the created will, a freedom that is no less *de fide* than are that same foreknowledge and predestination, as was shown at length in Disputation 23." Translation is from Luis Molina, *On Divine Foreknowledge* (Part 4 of the *Concordia*), trans. with an introduction and notes by Alfredo J. Freddoso (Ithaca: Cornell University Press, 1988). All subsequent citations from Molina are taken from this translation by Freddoso. In a footnote Freddoso writes, "A doctrine that is *de fide* (literally, of the faith) is one explicitly affirmed by the Church in a solemn manner (for example, in a creed or conciliar decree)." Molina, *On Divine Foreknowledge*, 169 n. 14. Molina's commitment to the doctrines of foreknowledge, providence, and election was based on his conviction that these doctrines were the established doctrines of the Church. My use of the title *de fide* to describe these doctrines is intended to reflect Molina's conviction that these were officially established church doctrines. See also Molina, *Concordia* 4.53.21.

THE KEY TO SOLVING THE PROBLEM

Why do Calvinists feel compelled to reject the absolute autonomy of the human will? Because they understand the absolute autonomy of the human will to be incompatible with the *de fide* doctrines of divine sovereignty. If the human will is autonomous, then it would be impossible even for an all-knowing God to have the foreknowledge that *de fide* theology says he has, to exercise the providential control it says he has, and to choose the saved in the way it says he does. In view of their commitment to the *de fide* doctrines of divine sovereignty, Calvinists are forced to reject the absolute autonomy of the human will.

And why do Arminians feel compelled to reject the *de fide* doctrines of divine sovereignty? Like Calvinists, Arminians believe that the absolute autonomy of the human will and the *de fide* views of divine sovereignty are incompatible. If the human will is autonomous, then God cannot have the foreknowledge, providential control, and power to elect that the *de fide* doctrines say he has. So, in view of their commitment to the absolute autonomy of the human will, Arminians are forced to reject the *de fide* doctrines of divine sovereignty.

Calvinists and Arminians agree fundamentally on an important point: the autonomy of the human will can in no way be reconciled to the *de fide* views on divine sovereignty. Where they disagree is at which pole of the contradiction the truth lies. So the two positions are at an impasse; there is no third way so long as the terms of the discussion remain here. If divine sovereignty and human freedom are incompatible, then there are only two choices: either Calvinism (which accepts divine sovereignty at the expense of human autonomy) or Arminianism (which accepts human autonomy at the expense of divine sovereignty).

Clearly, the assumed incompatibility of divine sovereignty and human autonomy channels Calvinists and Arminians into their respective systems. If Molina is to accomplish his agenda—if he is successfully to clear the way for both divine sovereignty and human autonomy to be embraced simultaneously—he must refute the prevailing dogma that divine sovereignty and human autonomy are incompatible. In other words, he must achieve their philosophical reconciliation.

MOLINA'S CONCEPT OF MIDDLE KNOWLEDGE

Middle knowledge is the key to Molina's reconciliation of divine sovereignty and human autonomy. To understand the concept of middle knowledge, let us engage in a bit of science fiction.

Imagine a genius human inventor named Egbert who created a whole world. (Call it Robo-world.) First, he created a huge building with thick, totally-impenetrable walls, floor, and ceiling. Then he invented a computer and other equipment capable of counteracting every effect of the outside world within this building. Gravity, magnetism—all were canceled. As a consequence, the inside of the building was completely devoid of any physical laws; all had been nullified. More computers and machines were then invented to create an entirely new physical environment exactly to the specifications of Egbert. Inside the building, everything, down to the very least physical law, was totally controlled by Egbert's computers.

Next Egbert invented scores of robots and programmed them all to move, act, communicate, and learn. He programmed each so that it had extremely detailed instructions as to how to respond and act in any specific set of circumstances. Furthermore, he equipped each robot so that he could control its movements and actions by remote control. Therefore, each robot would be controlled either by its own internal programming or directly by the inventor when he might override the robot's programming.

Finally, Egbert set all the robots and a variety of inert props in exactly that initial state he wanted. And with the push of a button, he started Robo-world in motion.

Before programming his various computers, Egbert had carefully mapped out all of the various possibilities for what Robo-world could look like. He mapped out in exact detail every world that he could possibly achieve. Once he had defined the physical laws that would obtain, the programming that he would give to each of his robots and ruling computers, and the initial state of Robo-world, he was able to predict, moment by moment, exactly what would occur throughout the entire history of each of the possible Robo-worlds.

After he had predicted the exact history of every possible Robo-world, Egbert then selected the possible Robo-world that he decided he wanted to bring into being. He programmed all the computers and set up the initial state necessary to bring exactly that possible world about; then he pushed the button and set it in motion. The result was precisely the Robo-world that he had wanted to bring into being.

Our genius, Egbert, already knows, before he pushes the button, exactly what will transpire at every moment of this Robo-world that he is about to bring into being. He had already mapped out its entire history before he ever decided to create it. So, with respect to the actual Robo-world, Egbert has *absolute foreknowledge*. Furthermore, he has providential-like control over this actual Robo-world, for everything that transpires in it has ultimately been brought about by his design, his act, and his choice.

As Molina understands it, God's creation of the actual world we live in is very much like Egbert's creation of Robo-world. Before he created anything, God had mapped out every detail of every event of every possible world. He considered each possible world (given his utterly detailed and exhaustive knowledge of each one) and chose the one he wanted to bring into existence. He then created the world that he had decided he wanted to bring into existence.

But there is a significant difference between Robo-world and our world. Robo-world is peopled by nothing but robots. Every creature in Robo-world has its every move totally determined by the programming and the engineering of Egbert. But our world is different. Alongside the biological and physical "machines" in our world are free moral agents, human beings. Human choices and actions are not determined by programmed instructions that God wrote for each human will. On the contrary, human choices are "free." They are autonomous, independent of any determining reality.

It is easy to see how Egbert could have mapped out every moment of every possible Robo-world; every move that is made in that world is determined by him and his choices. Given his exhaustive knowledge of the laws and principles that would obtain in any possible Robo-world, he could understandably predict exactly what would happen. Similarly, it is easy to see how God could predict the entire history of any possible world that he might create—if we ignore free-will creatures. Apart from them, everything else would be governed by physical laws and principles of which God had a complete and infallible understanding.

But what happens when you bring free-will creatures into the picture? According to Molina, nothing changes. God, unlike Egbert, is capable of knowing what choices a particular free-will creature will make in a specific set of circumstances. God is as capable of predicting the choice of one of his free-will creatures as Egbert is of predicting the choice of one of his robots. That God could have such knowledge is a mysterious and marvelous feat, of course. But God is more than a genius; he is God. And God can do such a thing. *This special and marvelous knowledge of what a particular free-will creature will do in a specific set of circumstances is what Molina calls middle knowledge.*[213]

Because of God's middle knowledge, God is capable of doing with respect to the actual cosmos what Egbert could do with respect to Robo-

---

213. For the purposes of this essay, I will not discuss why it is called middle knowledge. For a helpful discussion of that question, see William Lane Craig, "Middle Knowledge: A Calvinist-Arminian Rapprochement?" in *The Grace of God, the Will of Man*, 141-164, esp. 144-151. See also Molina, *On Divine Foreknowledge*, 23 and 47.

world. Before creating anything, he could map out the entire history of each and every possible world ahead of time and then, on the basis of an exhaustive knowledge of every detail of the history of each possible world, choose which possible world he wanted to bring into being.[214] Because of his ability to have middle knowledge, the free choices of the free-will creatures he would create in any possible world presented no obstacles to his mapping out the history of that world. He knew what each particular creature would choose in each and every situation. Hence, he could predict exactly the outcome of every event in every possible world.

As Molina understands it, this is how our world is situated with respect to God. The world that now exists is a world that God created, having freely chosen to do so. Of all the possible worlds he could have created, this is the one he wanted to bring into existence. And when he made his choice, he did so with an exhaustive knowledge of every detail of every event that would transpire within it throughout the full extent of its history.

THE RECONCILIATION OF DIVINE SOVEREIGNTY AND HUMAN AUTONOMY

It should be clear that Molina's understanding of God's foreknowledge is compatible with the *de fide* doctrine of divine foreknowledge. Under Molina's view, God foreknows every aspect of every event that will occur in our world.

Furthermore, under Molina's views, everything that occurs in our world is ultimately the result of God's free choice to create just this world in particular. Hence, he is the ultimate cause of every aspect of every event in our world. This includes his being the ultimate cause of everything that occurs due to the choices of free-will creatures. In creating the possible world that he did, he was causing to come into existence every freewill decision that every free-will creature in that world would ever make. So Molina's God exercises a divine providence that is just as extensive as that which he exercises in the *de fide* view of divine providence.

Finally, no less than in the *de fide* doctrine of election, Molina's God

---

214. Strictly speaking, Molina believes that the priority of God's foreknowledge of every possible world, his choice of a possible world to create, and his decision to do so constitute not a temporal priority, but a logical one. He sees all three of these events as temporally simultaneous. I have, for the sake of simplifying my discussion, chosen not to introduce this subtle complication into my exposition of Molina's views; it does not in any way affect my understanding or critique of them. See Craig, "Middle Knowledge: A Calvinist-Arminian Rapprochement," 145, for a discussion of this issue.

elects those particular individuals who will be saved. That set of particular individuals who will come to salvation in this world is ultimately determined by the free choice of God. God created this particular world in which exactly this set of people, and not some other set, will (as a result of their own autonomous choice) choose to believe and to be saved. By his choice to create this particular world, God is the one who determines who will be saved and who will not.

But what is especially interesting to Molina is this: although his conception of divine foreknowledge (which is based on divine middle knowledge of the choices of free-will creatures) upholds the *de fide* doctrines of divine sovereignty, it also upholds a belief in the absolute autonomy of the human will. The free-will creatures who people this world are truly free. God does not cause them to choose what they choose. Nothing makes them choose what they choose. Their choice is nothing more than the resolution of their own will. Under Molina's view, therefore, we can acknowledge divine foreknowledge, divine providence, and divine election without in any way redefining or compromising our concept of human freedom.

So Molina thinks that, by means of middle knowledge, he has discovered a way to preserve a full-bodied commitment to the reality of human autonomy while accepting the *de fide* doctrines of divine sovereignty. In other words, he has found a way to embrace the truth lying at the core of Calvinism without rejecting the truth lying at the core of Arminianism, and vice versa.

The Viability of Middle Knowledge

Molina's views, as we have seen, depend upon his concept of middle knowledge. They therefore assume that middle knowledge is a viable and coherent concept. But is it?

THE SURFACE PROBLEM WITH MIDDLE KNOWLEDGE

On the face of it, middle knowledge presents a problem: is it possible for God to know that X is true when nothing determines or necessitates that X be true? It is difficult to see how.

Take Peter as an example. Jesus predicted that Peter would deny him three times during the night of his arrest, before the dawning of the next day. How did Jesus—or, more importantly, God—know this about Peter? If Molina is right, God had middle knowledge of Peter's denials. He knew

Peter so thoroughly that, knowing all the circumstances Peter would find himself in, he knew exactly how Peter would respond in each of those circumstances.

But how could he know that? If Peter's will is what Molina says it is—utterly autonomous—then nothing at the time of Jesus' prediction necessitates that Peter deny Jesus. In fact, Molina's view requires that Peter could have done otherwise. If Peter had chosen to do so, he could have been courageously loyal to Jesus instead of denying him. He acted the coward because he chose to, not because he had to. But if nothing whatsoever necessitated the choices that he made, up to the time that he made them, how could God have known what those choices would be? Peter's choices were not determined ahead of time. So, if they had not yet been decided, how could God know the outcome of those decisions? No one, not even God, can know the outcome of an autonomous decision that has not yet been made, can he? To assert the possibility of such knowledge is problematic.

MOLINA'S RESPONSE TO THIS PROBLEM

In spite of this surface problem, Molina nonetheless thinks that middle knowledge is possible. Craig explains Molina's defense:

Now it might be asked how it is that by knowing his own essence alone God is able to have middle knowledge concerning what free creatures would do in any situation. Molina and his compatriot and fellow Jesuit, Francisco Suarez, differed in their responses to this question. Molina's answer is alluded to in the words of the initial citation above: "because of the depth of his knowledge." According to Molina, God not only knows in his own essence all possible creatures, but his intellect infinitely surpasses the capabilities of finite wills so that he understands them so thoroughly that he knows not only what they could choose under any set of circumstances, but what they would choose. In another place Molina speaks of "his immense and altogether unlimited knowledge, by which he comprehends in the deepest and most eminent way whatever falls under his omnipotence, to penetrate created free choice in such a way as to discern and intuit with certainty which part it is going to turn itself to by its own innate freedom." Because his intellect is infinite, whereas a free creature is finite, God's insight into the will of a free creature is of such a surpassing quality that God knows exactly what the free creature would do were God to place him in a certain set of circumstances.[215]

MOLINA'S DUAL ACCOUNT OF MIDDLE KNOWLEDGE

Molina's explanation of the possibility of middle knowledge seems to incorporate two significantly different accounts of middle knowledge. On the one hand, his official account of middle knowledge is to describe it as a direct, noninferential, intuitive knowledge that God has. God knows immediately (and noninferentially) that person P will do X at time T. On the other hand, there are intimations of a very different account.[216] He subtly implies that middle knowledge is God's ability to infer infallibly that person P will do X at time T on the basis of his infinitely thorough knowledge of the will of P.[217] This implicit, covert account of middle knowledge plays an important role in Molina's presentation of his doctrine. It helps to make an otherwise problematic account of divine middle knowledge seem less problematic.

THE OFFICIAL ACCOUNT:
NONINFERENTIAL KNOWLEDGE

In his official account of middle knowledge, Molina appeals to the magnificence of God and his abilities.[218] The possibility of middle knowl-

---

215. Ibid., 150. See also Molina, *Concordia* 4.52.11.

216. This is a central claim of this essay; it is crucial to my argument. It is potentially controversial. Some defenders of Molina would, most likely, want to dispute the existence of this different, second account of middle knowledge. Ideally, of course, my essay should go on to present a thorough defense of the existence of this second account. I do cite, in the following pages of text and footnotes, what I think is the most important evidence that a second account influences Molina's thought and the formation of his doctrine. But to finally demonstrate this claim would require a much more detailed and technical discussion than I can present here. I am confident that such a defense could be made.

217. To my knowledge, Molina never makes clear exactly what he understands the will of a person to be. Neither is it made clear, therefore, of what the knowledge of a person's will would consist. Molina's vagueness on the nature of the will leads to considerable confusion as to exactly what God's knowledge of an individual's will is. Precisely because of this confusion, Molina can operate according to two very different accounts of middle knowledge at the same time without being adequately aware of the logical tension that results.

218. Molina appeals to the magnificence of God's knowledge in a variety of ways. Among them, he appeals to God's "most profound and inscrutable comprehension" (Molina, *Concordia* 4.52.9), to his "absolutely profound and absolutely preeminent comprehension" (ibid., 4.52.11), to his being able to comprehend free-will creatures with "infinite excess" (ibid., 4.52.12), to "the infinite and wholly unlimited perfection and acumen of His intellect" (ibid., 4.52.29), to "the acumen and absolute perfection of His intellect" (ibid., 4.52.33), and to the "perspicacity and depth of the knower over and beyond the things known" (ibid., 4.52.35).

edge finds its explanation in the fact that God's knowledge is deep, immense, and unlimited. If God's knowledge of a particular finite will is infinitely thorough, how could it help but include a complete knowledge of everything that that particular person will choose in any and every situation? This account assumes that God's knowledge of what a particular person will do is a kind of immediate, intuitive knowledge. God does not infer or deduce what P will do from other things that he knows about P. Rather, he knows what P will do directly, immediately, and noninferentially.

This account of middle knowledge does not answer the question as to how middle knowledge is possible. It tells us instead why an answer will not be forthcoming. In effect, Molina's response is this: "How is God able to have middle knowledge of what person P will do, when P has not yet decided himself what he will do? Because he's God; that's how!" This is an appeal to divine "mystery." It is as if Molina were to say: "I shouldn't dismiss the concept of middle knowledge just because I can't make any sense of it. God 'works in mysterious ways,' 'his ways are not our ways,' ...."

An appeal to divine "mystery" is a common but suspicious move. At times the mysteries we embrace are incomprehensible to us not because they are mysteries, but rather because they are nonsense. Nonsense masquerading in the respectable dress of mystery is still nonsense. So, before we settle for an appeal to divine mystery, we can reasonably ask for assurance that Molina's concept of middle knowledge is a coherent concept. Perhaps it is incomprehensible because it is an incoherent notion, not because, for lack of being God, we are incapable of imagining such a lofty feat. Consequently, if Molina wants us to embrace his views, he must offer a more compelling answer than "he's God; he can do it." The problematic question remains: If the human will is absolutely autonomous, how can we reasonably assert that God is able to foreknow what persons with autonomous freedom will choose?

In my judgment Molina, throughout all his discussions of this subject, implicitly suggests an answer to this latter question by means of an unofficial account of middle knowledge. At the same time that he officially disallows it, he subtly and covertly relies on a fundamentally different account of middle knowledge to render his doctrine plausible.

THE COVERT ACCOUNT: INFERENTIAL KNOWLEDGE

Molina's official account of divine middle knowledge is marked by some curious features. To focus on the most important one: it is interesting that Molina predominantly presents divine middle knowledge as a deep and profound knowledge of the faculty of choice and only rarely as a knowledge of the choice itself, that is, the outcome of a particular event of choosing.

> Finally, the third type is *middle* knowledge, by which, in virtue of the most profound and inscrutable comprehension of each *faculty* [emphasis added] of free choice, He saw in His own essence what each such *faculty* [emphasis added] would do with its innate freedom were it to be placed in this or in that or, indeed, in infinitely many orders of things—even though it would really be able, if it so willed, to do the opposite, as is clear from what was said in Disputations 49 and 50.[219]

> But God knows the determination of a created faculty of choice before it exists because of the infinite and unlimited perfection of His intellect and because of the preeminent comprehension by which He comprehends *that faculty* [emphasis added] in His essence in a way far deeper than that in which it exists in itself; and thus …He knows which part it will in its freedom turn itself toward.[220]

Molina's characteristic description of middle knowledge is curious; and it is significantly problematic in the light of what he officially claims middle knowledge to be. If middle knowledge is what Molina's official account says it is, the most apt description of it would be an intuitive, noninferential knowledge of the actual choice itself, that is, of the outcome of a particular event of choosing. Why, then, does Molina explain it in terms of a profound knowledge of the faculty that will make the choice? By Molina's own official account, it would seem that the nature of a person's faculty of choice does not determine, cause, or otherwise necessitate the choice he will make. How, then, is a knowledge of Peter's faculty of choice even relevant to the issue of what Peter will choose? If his faculty of choice does not determine or necessitate what choices Peter will make, a thorough and deep knowledge of his faculty of choice will not provide God with any knowledge of what choices he will actually make. (Nothing is gained by stressing that God's knowledge of Peter's faculty of choice is infinitely deep.) Yet this is Molina's official account: God knows what choices Peter will make in a particular situation precisely because, due to the "infinite and wholly unlimited perfection and acumen of His intellect," God has

---

219. Ibid., 4.52.9.

220. Ibid., 4.53.1.14. See also ibid., 4.52.10, 4.52.11, 4.52.33, and 4.53.2.31. These citations reflect how Molina most frequently portrays divine middle knowledge.

"the most profound and inscrutable comprehension" of Peter's "faculty of free choice."[221]

Molina's characteristic explanation of middle knowledge is at odds with his own official account of it because Molina has unwittingly imported a different account of middle knowledge into his own conception of it. According to this second, covert account, middle knowledge is possible because it is based on an inference from God's infinitely thorough knowledge of the particular will itself. God could know that Peter would deny Jesus because he thoroughly understood Peter's will. Peter has not yet made any decision. He has not yet even confronted the choice in question. But that is no obstacle to God's being able to know what Peter will do. God's in-depth knowledge of Peter himself, the one who will be making the decision, allows him to infer what Peter will decide from the thorough knowledge he has of who Peter is.[222]

This inferential account of middle knowledge has a distinct advantage over Molina's official account: it is comprehensible and rationally plausible. It does not simply appeal to the mystery of God and dogmatically assert that middle knowledge is possible because of the unfathomable immensity of God.

Even we mere human beings are capable of certain forms of middle knowledge of the inferential sort. My wife knows that, were she to offer me a piece of pie tonight, I will accept it. My wife knows that I will drink a cup of coffee when I arise in the morning. She knows that, out of a sense of duty, I will go teach my class tonight whether I feel like it or not. These are all forms of middle knowledge. My wife knows what I will choose, of my own free will, in specific situations in the future. And she is not guessing. She knows what I will do. This is exactly the sort of middle knowledge that Molina wants to ascribe to God.

But the middle knowledge we possess is significantly limited. My wife does not and cannot foreknow what future circumstances I will confront. Consequently, no matter how well she knows me, she cannot predict with unfailing accuracy all that I will eventually do. Even more importantly, even if she has a thorough grasp of the situation and knows me as well as

---

221. Ibid., 4.52.9 and 4.52.29.

222. See ibid., 4.52.10, 4.52.11, 4.52.12, 4.52.13, and 4.52.30. These passages all strongly suggest an account of middle knowledge that relies heavily on the notion that a person's choice results from the operations of his own will and that, as a consequence, to have a profound knowledge of the person himself and of his will shall necessarily give one a knowledge of what choices he will make. The citations in note 220 reflect this same conception of middle knowledge.

any human being can know another, she still could be wrong. I could surprise her. I could, for some inexplicable reason, refuse the pie or the coffee. I could decide to be utterly irresponsible and not show up for class. However unlikely, I may act out of character in a way that my wife could never predict.

Here is where Molina's insistence that God's knowledge is deep and infinitely thorough is important. Whereas my wife could be surprised and find me choosing what she never would have predicted, God cannot and will not be similarly surprised. My wife's knowledge of me is finite; God's is infinite. My wife is surprised because there will always be subtle aspects of who I am and how I think that she does not understand. But not God; his understanding is infinitely thorough. No aspect of my will and being is beyond his understanding. God, therefore, can have utterly certain and totally infallible middle knowledge; his grasp of who I am is perfect.

It seems undeniable that this is Molina's real, working conception of middle knowledge, and it is utterly incompatible with his official account.

THE LOGICAL TENSION IN MOLINA'S ACCOUNT OF MIDDLE KNOWLEDGE

As we have seen, there are two important aspects to Molina's project. He wants to affirm the absolute autonomy of human choice. (For Molina, true autonomy would mean that human choice is not caused, not determined, and not necessitated by anything whatsoever.) Molina also wants to affirm that divine middle knowledge is a rationally coherent doctrine.

In order to achieve the former goal, Molina must affirm that nothing whatsoever determines in advance of a person's choice what that choice will be. He must affirm that no external causes necessitate the choices a person will make. But if he is committed to espousing this sort of human autonomy, then he cannot explain middle knowledge as a sort of divine inference. For, on the assumption that nothing whatsoever determines or necessitates Peter's choices, how could God infer what Peter will do? There is nothing to serve as the basis for such an inference. Peter's choice is not caused by anything; it is not determined or necessitated by anything. Hence, there is absolutely no basis from which God could infer the choice that Peter will make. Consequently, the only account of divine middle knowledge which is logically available to Molina is one wherein God has direct, immediate, intuitive knowledge of a yet unformed and undetermined choice that Peter shall make. Logically, therefore, if Molina is to successfully espouse true human autonomy, he has no choice but to conceive of middle knowledge as an intuitive, noninferential knowledge of voluntary choices. Officially, this is the account he wants to give,[223] for it succeeds at reconciling human autonomy with divine middle knowledge. But, as I have been suggesting, it is not that simple; the other aspect of Molina's project is not satisfied by this official account of middle knowledge.

Molina's official account of middle knowledge does nothing to demonstrate the rational coherence of the doctrine (unless one is satisfied with a dogmatic declaration of the possibility of divine middle knowledge backed by an appeal to mystery). To understand middle knowledge as rationally compelling, therefore, Molina is constantly drawn to a radically different conception of middle knowledge—to a conception of middle knowledge as a sort of inferential knowledge.

The concept of middle knowledge is rendered plausible when it is viewed as an inference based on God's thorough knowledge of the forces at work within each person—the forces that determine and necessitate his choices. We have a kind of middle knowledge of one another's future choices. If divine middle knowledge is to be comprehensible to us, it will be by analogy to the sort of middle knowledge we possess. So, if divine middle knowledge is understood to be inferential in nature, it becomes analogous to our own and is thereby made comprehensible to us. Accordingly, over and over Molina is seduced into describing middle knowledge in a way that suggests just such an account. Middle knowledge as a form of divine inference is the implicit, covert account of middle knowledge which underlies everything that Molina argues.

But, as we have just seen, an account of middle knowledge as a form of inference is utterly incompatible with Molina's official account. It presupposes that God could have prior knowledge of some reality that will somehow cause, determine, or necessitate the voluntary choice that an individual will make in the future. If God is going to infer what Peter will choose, he must infer Peter's future choice on the basis of something he knows about Peter now. In other words, if something about Peter now necessitates that Peter will deny Jesus at a particular time in the future, then if God knows that relevant thing about Peter, he can know (infer) that Peter will deny Jesus. But if, as Molina maintains in his official account, nothing whatsoever necessitates or determines any of Peter's free choices,[224]

---

223. See ibid., 4.53.1.10-14. Molina appears to consider and explicitly reject something much like what I am calling his covert account of middle knowledge. Although he officially rejects it, he covertly relies upon it.

224. An important question can be raised about this. Is Molina's position that nothing whatsoever causes, determines, or necessitates the voluntary choices of a human being? Or, is Molina's position that nothing other than the person's will itself causes, determines, or necessitates the

then there exists nothing from which God could infer Peter's choices. So, if human choice is absolutely undetermined and uncaused in the way that Molina officially maintains, then Molina's covert account of middle knowledge is logically incompatible with that official account. There can be no divine inference from God's knowledge of a person's faculty of choice to the choices he will make if, officially, the choices a person makes are in no way necessitated by that person's faculty of choice. Nonetheless, Molina's writings are fraught with this tension. He officially espouses middle knowledge according to one conception of it (as direct, intuitive knowledge), but he attempts to render it plausible with language informed by a very different conception of it (as inferential knowledge). The two conceptions are incompatible. Middle knowledge must be viewed either as a sort of mysterious noninferential knowledge, or as a sort of inferential knowledge; but logically we cannot have it both ways. Yet this is exactly what Molina attempts to do.

We can summarize the tension in Molina's account this way: what is required for Molina to succeed at making middle knowledge comprehensible (and therefore plausible and beyond suspicion) is in fatal tension with what is required for Molina to succeed at coherently maintaining the absolute autonomy of the human will. To reconcile divine sovereignty and human autonomy, Molina offers an official account of middle knowledge wherein human autonomy is assumed at the outset. But to convince us that this official account of middle knowledge involves a viable and plausible concept, he resorts to descriptions of middle knowledge wherein the predetermination of human choice is logically assumed—thereby nullifying and denying human autonomy. Hence, he takes back with one hand what he has given us with the other.

---

voluntary choices of a human being? It seems that Molina is not clear on this point. When he is intent on pressing his official account in order to maintain human autonomy, he seems to emphasize explicitly the notion that nothing causes or necessitates human choice. But when he slips into reasoning in accordance with his covert account (in order to render the notion of divine middle knowledge as plausible as possible), he clearly seems to think that a person's actions arise from and are determined by the will of that individual. His double-mindedness on this issue seems to be an exact reflection of his double-mindedness on the nature of middle knowledge; for the two issues are intimately related to one another. Furthermore, as I suggested (n. 217), all of Molina's confusion is exacerbated by the vagueness of his concept of the human will.

CAN MOLINA'S COVERT ACCOUNT RECONCILE MIDDLE KNOWLEDGE WITH HUMAN AUTONOMY ?

But perhaps the equivocation we have discussed is sloppiness on the part of Molina. His equivocation on the nature of middle knowledge aside, is Molina not right? Do we not have in middle knowledge the key to reconciling divine sovereignty and human autonomy? If we were to hold Molina to an inferential account of middle knowledge (the account that is more rationally compelling), would he not be able to thereby reconcile human autonomy and divine foreknowledge?

Under my view as a divine determinist, it is clear how God's infinitely thorough knowledge of Peter's will could explain how God can foreknow what Peter will choose. God, the creator of Peter's will, determines the character and workings of that will. The character of Peter's will shall in turn determine what choices he will make. Therefore, if God understands the character and workings of Peter's will with infinite thoroughness— which is to understand his own design and purpose in the creation of Peter's will—then he will certainly be able to predict what Peter will choose. But all this assumes that there is a chain of causes leading up to the choices that Peter makes and that God, the creator, is the ultimate author and determiner of that chain of causes and the choices which ultimately result. But what if we assume human autonomy instead? Can inferential middle knowledge still adequately account for divine foreknowledge?

According to his (covert) inferential account of middle knowledge, Molina attempts to offer the same explanation of divine foreknowledge as does the divine determinist: namely, Peter's choices are determined by the nature and workings of Peter's will. Consequently, if God has an infinite knowledge of that will (its nature and its mode of working) he will be able to predict its output—Peter's choices. One's choices are the necessary reflection of who one is. So, if God knows Peter perfectly, then from whom he is he should be able to infer what he will choose.

But how can this account be available to Molina? Molina's whole project is to affirm divine sovereignty without compromising human autonomy. If he acknowledges that Peter's choices are necessitated by the nature of Peter's will, that is tantamount to acknowledging that Peter's choices are necessitated by God; for God is the creator and designer of Peter's will.[225]

---

225. Some scholars would object that Peter's choices being necessitated by the nature of Peter's will is not tantamount to their being necessitated by God. They would agree that Peter's will is designed and created by God. They would argue, however, that God is responsible for and determines the existence of Peter's will but is not responsible for and does not cause the dynamic

Molina cannot consistently offer such an answer. In order to be consistent, Molina must insist that whom God has created Peter to be does not dictate what Peter will choose in any given situation. Otherwise, Peter's choices are not truly autonomous; they have been determined by the character of his will which was, in turn, designed and determined by God. For Molina, then, Peter's choices cannot be necessitated by the God-given nature of Peter's will.

Consequently, Molina must affirm one of two things: either who Peter is does not ultimately dictate what he will choose, or who God created and determined Peter to be is not the whole of who Peter is, that is, who Peter is at any given time is in part determined by the free, autonomous choices Peter has already made over the course of his life (choices that were not determined by whom God created him to be). In other words, who Peter is, is in significant measure, self-determined.

If Molina affirms the latter—that is, who Peter is, is ultimately determined by Peter, not by God—then how can he appeal to God's infinitely thorough knowledge of Peter's will to explain how middle knowledge is possible? He replaces one question with another—namely, how it is possible for God to have an infinitely thorough knowledge of Peter's will? If at any given time, who Peter is has not yet been fully decided, then how is it reasonable to think that at any given time God can know Peter with infinite thoroughness? Who Peter is depends on the outcome of his next autonomous choice.

If Molina affirms the former proposition—that is, who Peter is does not determine what he will choose—then knowing who Peter is, is of no help toward knowing what he will choose. In that case, an infinite knowledge of Peter's will cannot explain God's middle knowledge. From God's infinitely thorough knowledge of Peter's will, no conclusion can be drawn as to what Peter will choose, for the nature of Peter's will does not determine his choices.

---

workings of Peter's will. In other words, God creates Peter's will without in any way determining how it will function and what it will choose. He creates it to be free from everything, even from his own determinative control. It is outside the scope of this essay to explore this issue at length. But such a claim is fraught with philosophical confusion. How can God bring X into existence without thereby defining the nature of X, which will be determinative of how it will function and behave? If God has not defined its controlling nature, in what sense is it X that God has brought into existence (rather than not-X)? Suffice it to say that my argument assumes that there is an inextricable link between God's creating something and God's determining the nature of its being and functioning in reality. Hence, to create Peter's will is to create the nature, essence, and mode of working of Peter's will. If not—if God does not determine its nature, essence, and mode of working—then in what sense is it distinctively Peter's will that God has created, and how do we explain the origin of its nature, essence, and mode of working?

Hence, to be consistent with the position that humans are autonomous beings, inference from God's infinite knowledge of Peter's will cannot satisfactorily explain the possibility of divine middle knowledge. His infinite knowledge of Peter's will is either irrelevant with respect to middle knowledge or it is as mysterious and problematic as middle knowledge itself (and hence has no explanatory value). In his covert, inferential account, therefore, Molina has produced no explanation of divine middle knowledge that is consistent with his assumption of human autonomy. (His explanation works only to the extent that human choices are assumed to be ultimately predetermined by God.) We are left with our original problem unanswered and unresolved: if the human will is absolutely autonomous, then how can we reasonably assert that God can know (infer) what it will choose in a given set of circumstances?

Middle knowledge based on inference (Molina's covert account of middle knowledge) gains its plausibility only under the assumption that human choice is not autonomous but is ultimately predetermined by the will of God. If our choices are not the result of a causal chain of which God could have knowledge, then God cannot infer what choices we will make from the nature of their causes. The sort of human autonomy upon which Molina insists precludes the sort of antecedent causation of our choices from which our choices could be inferred. Since human autonomy, as Molina conceives it, does not allow for human choice to have any antecedent causes, it would be impossible for God to infer a human choice from its antecedent causes. Hence, on the assumption of human autonomy, Molina is unable to make the possibility of inferential middle knowledge plausible.

SUMMARY: AN ASSESSMENT OF MOLINA'S DOCTRINE

Molina's exposition of middle knowledge involves a subtle confusion of two incompatible accounts of middle knowledge. He shifts which account of middle knowledge he wants us to consider, depending upon the question at issue.

When the question at issue is whether human autonomy and divine sovereignty are compatible, Molina would have us focus on his official account of middle knowledge: middle knowledge as God's mysterious ability to know directly and immediately what a particular person, acting in absolute autonomy, will do in a particular situation in the future. This official account of middle knowledge, if it can be shown to be a coherent and intelligible concept, successfully reconciles divine sovereignty and human freedom. It assumes the reality of human autonomy and by means of middle knowledge accounts for the attributes of divine sovereignty without compromising that autonomy. Insofar as we are satisfied to leave it at that, Molina has given us a believable account of how divine sovereignty and absolute human autonomy are compatible.

But if we are not satisfied to leave it in the realm of mystery, if we ask how divine middle knowledge is possible—given that it is supposedly a knowledge of choices which are as yet undecided by those who will make them—then Molina would have us shift our focus to his covert account of middle knowledge: God's ability to infallibly infer from the character of a person's own will what that person shall choose in a particular situation in the future. By means of this account, Molina does succeed in making middle knowledge comprehensible and plausible. Even we who are finite creatures have this sort of middle knowledge of one another. We infer what another person will do from the knowledge we have gained of his character. If we can have middle knowledge of this sort, certainly God can have it even more so, for he knows us with an infinite thoroughness.

So middle knowledge makes sense if it is a sort of inferential knowledge. But, in conceding this to Molina, we fail to keep his original project in view: to reconcile divine sovereignty and absolute human autonomy. Hence we fail to notice that, under Molina's plausible, covert account, human autonomy is not reconciled with divine sovereignty; rather, human autonomy is denied. As we saw, middle knowledge based on inference gains its plausibility only under the assumption that human choice is not autonomous but is ultimately predetermined by the will of God.

The force of Molina's defense of middle knowledge depends upon our failure to notice how very different his covert account of middle knowledge is from his official account and, more importantly, upon our failure to notice the contradictory ramifications of these two different accounts. If we do notice, then we realize that he has failed in his attempt to give us a compelling account of middle knowledge that does not compromise human autonomy. It is easy not to notice, for Molina's discussions involve a sort of philosophical sleight-of-hand wherein he gives us different, conflicting accounts of middle knowledge depending upon the philosophical needs of the moment. But once we have noticed, Molina's doctrine loses its appeal.

In the end, we cannot accept Molina's exposition as it stands. It depends on an equivocation in his account of what middle knowledge is. And we cannot accept Molina's unofficial, covert, inferential account of middle knowledge, for it does not successfully reconcile divine foreknowledge with absolute human autonomy. We are left, then, with Molina's official account. His doctrine, therefore, reduces to nothing more than a dogmatic assertion that divine middle knowledge is a reality and that its possibility is a divine mystery. I am not motivated to embrace Molina's views, given that this is what they amount to. I am not much attracted to what is no more than a dogmatic assertion that divine foreknowledge is possible even though human choices are absolutely autonomous.

Only on the assumption of divine determinism is the divine foreknowledge of freewill choices a rationally plausible doctrine. (This is one of the primary reasons that I embrace divine determinism.) Implicitly, therefore, Molina is urging me to abandon my rationally satisfying understanding of divine foreknowledge (based on the assumption of divine determinism) and join him in a dogmatic commitment to an incomprehensible mystery. Why should I do that? What assurance has Molina given me that middle knowledge under his conception of it—that is, middle knowledge of *autonomous* human choices—is a coherent concept? Until I am persuaded that the simultaneous affirmation of both divine middle knowledge and the absolute autonomy of human choice is not a blatant contradiction, Molina's attempt to bring Calvinism and Arminianism together is unpersuasive.

Human Freedom: Can Calvinism Do It Justice?

In the article to which I am responding, Craig invites us to join together in embracing Molina's views. If Molina's views are as unpersuasive as I have suggested, why would Craig venture to make such an appeal? Obviously, Craig considers Molina's views to be more compelling than I do. What accounts for the difference in our assessment?

Craig makes an unwarranted assumption, one that leads him to see Molina's arguments as more compelling than they really are. Craig assumes, with Molina, that Calvinistic divine determinism cannot do justice to the reality of human freedom. If doing justice to the reality of human freedom is genuinely a shortcoming of divine determinism, and if Molina's views have successfully preserved the truth of genuine human freedom where divine determinism has failed, and if he has done so without discarding or compromising the *de fide* doctrines of divine sovereignty, then surely his views would be attractive to even the most obdurate Calvinist. To gain such a rich philosophical payoff, even a hard-headed divine determinist might be willing to tolerate an appeal to the realm of divine mystery and accept as dogma the possibility of middle knowledge.

Surely, whatever risk of incoherence it entails is a small price to pay for the benefit of simultaneously embracing a *de fide* notion of divine sovereignty and an uncompromised notion of human freedom.

THE UNDERLYING REASONING BEHIND CRAIG'S APPEAL

We can formalize the underlying reasoning behind Craig's appeal:

Given the following three convictions, it is utterly reasonable to embrace Molina's doctrines :

1. absolute human autonomy is a vital biblical notion which is required to provide a foundation for human freedom and responsibility;

2. the *de fide* doctrines of divine sovereignty are thoroughly biblical notions; and

3. Molina's views of middle knowledge and divine foreknowledge are the only way to reconcile beliefs in divine sovereignty and human autonomy.

Craig would maintain, I think, that the risk that middle knowledge may not be a coherent concept is not a sufficient deterrent to embracing Molina's views in the light of 1–3.[226] I think Craig is right about this. If I were committed to 1–3, I too would find it reasonable to follow Molina.

But this is exactly why Craig's appeal is not compelling to someone like me. The Calvinistic divine determinist does not share Craig's commitment to 1–3. Most notably, the divine determinist does not accept 1; correspondingly, he does not accept 3. Even though he does not affirm the absolute autonomy of the human will, he feels no inadequacy in his concepts of human freedom and responsibility; and he feels no lack of compatibility between human freedom and divine sovereignty—at least, not to the degree that Craig thinks he should.

---

226. Craig and I undoubtedly assess the risks of middle knowledge being an incoherent notion quite differently. Craig, it would seem, is quite satisfied that middle knowledge is a coherent notion and sees little or no risk that he is embracing nonsense. I am quite certain that it is an utterly incoherent notion and am virtually certain that, were I to embrace it, I would be embracing nonsense. Craig fails to understand why the Calvinist will not embrace Molina's doctrines in part because he fails to see how certain the divine determinist is that divine middle knowledge makes no sense.

To conclude my discussion, therefore, I shall explore this important issue: does the divine determinist's concept of human freedom fail to do justice to the reality of human freedom (as Craig and Molina assume)? If so, then Craig can reasonably argue that he should welcome Molina's solution. But if not, it makes no sense for the divine determinist to trade in his theory of divine determinism, whatever problems its critics may think it has, for the theories of Molina; for, to the divine determinist, these theories are more clearly problematic than his own.

THE ALLEGED INADEQUACY IN THE CALVINIST'S VIEW OF HUMAN FREEDOM

What inadequacy does Craig see in the divine determinist's concept of human freedom? Why does Craig think that nothing short of the absolute autonomy of the human will can adequately capture the true nature of human freedom?

For a human choice to be truly free, Craig thinks, it must be possible for that choice to have been other than it was. The divine determinist, by the very nature of his position, must say that at any given time no one can ever choose or act contrary to what God has willed. Clearly, then, the divine determinist does not believe that a human is free to do differently from what he did; he is constrained by the governing will of God. If the divine determinist espouses human freedom, it must be freedom in a qualified and limited sense (specifically, in the weaker sense known as the "liberty of spontaneity"). The divine determinist, so long as he sees one's actions constrained by the will of God, cannot espouse human freedom in an unqualified sense (specifically, not in the strong sense known as the "liberty of indifference").227

---

227. Craig alludes to these two specialized terms : "the liberty of spontaneity" and "the liberty of indifference." I first encountered these terms in the philosophy of David Hume. One exercises the liberty of spontaneity when what he does is done in accordance with his own will and desires. One exercises the liberty of indifference when what he does is such that he could have done otherwise. Hence, a person passing time in a room reading and enjoying himself and fully wanting to be there because of the pleasantness of his surroundings is exercising the freedom or liberty of spontaneity. He is exercising the liberty of spontaneity even if, unbeknownst to him, the room is locked from the outside and he would be unable to leave the room even if he wanted to. His being in this same room would involve the liberty of indifference only if the room is unlocked and he is free to leave it whenever he should so choose. In the Reformers' view of sovereignty, argues Craig, a person does not exercise the liberty of indifference because he cannot do other than God wills. He does however exercise the liberty of spontaneity insofar as what he chooses, determined though it is by God, is nonetheless a result of his own voluntary choice and is fully in accord with his own wants and desires.

The essence of Craig's sentiments can be seen in the following:

> Here it must be admitted that Molina's perception of their [the Reformers'] teaching was clear-sighted: the principal Reformers did deny to man significant freedom, at least in his dealings with God. Luther and Calvin were prepared to grant to man only spontaneity of choice and voluntariness of will, not the ability to choose otherwise in the circumstances in which an agent finds himself.[228]

And again,

> His [Calvin's] view of freedom is in the end the same as Luther's: the liberty of spontaneity. God's complete sovereignty excludes any genuine possibility of man's choosing in any circumstances other than as he does choose.
>
> Thus, according to the Protestant Reformers, in virtue of God's prescience [foreknowledge] and providence, everything that occurs in the world does so necessarily. Human choice is voluntary and spontaneous, but the will is not free to choose other than as it does. Now to Molina, such a doctrine was quite simply heretical. He could not see how mere spontaneity of choice sufficed to make a human being a responsible moral agent nor how the Reformers' view would not lead to making God the cause of man's sinful acts and, hence, the author of evil. He was therefore deeply exercised to formulate a strong doctrine of divine prescience [foreknowledge], providence, and predestination that would be wholly compatible with genuine human freedom, and he believed that in *scientia media* [middle knowledge] he had found the key.[229]

But there is something entirely disingenuous about Molina's charge against Calvin and Luther that, under their view of human freedom, "the will is not free to choose other than as it does." For the same thing is clearly true under Molina's covert account of middle knowledge—the account upon which he ultimately relies to bring credibility to his doctrinal position (as we saw).[230]

---

228. Craig, "Middle Knowledge," 142.

229. Ibid., 144.

230. It is true that Molina's official account would allow him in good faith to contend that his position, unlike that of Luther and Calvin, gives an account of freedom wherein a person is free

Molina argued that middle knowledge is possible because, given the depth and infinite thoroughness of God's knowledge of a particular will, he knows what that will shall choose in any particular set of circumstances. That makes it possible for God to have an accurate and detailed picture of every possible world. But does this not entail (if his doctrine is to be coherent) that the particular choice one makes in situation S was made necessary by the will of the human person who made it? If not, then God, his knowledge of the person's will notwithstanding, cannot foreknow what that choice will be. According to Molina, if he is to be consistent, Peter's own will *necessitated* that he deny Jesus when he did. That being so, what complaint does Molina have against Calvin and Luther? Calvin and Luther assert that the human will is free, but then acknowledge a constraint on it—the outcome of its choices are necessitated by the will of God. Molina asserts that the human will is free, but then he too must logically acknowledge a constraint on it—the outcome of its choices are necessitated by its own nature or character.

It is clearly not just, then, to condemn Luther's and Calvin's views of human freedom as inadequate on the grounds that, under their views, the human "will is not free to choose other than as it does." The same charge could be leveled against Molina.[231] If not being able to choose otherwise makes the Reformers' view of human freedom inadequate, then it renders Molina's view inadequate as well. Conversely, if Molina's view of human freedom is adequate even while acknowledging the reality of a necessitating constraint, then the Reformers' view is no less adequate. My point is this: whereas Craig, Molina, and other nondeterminists seem to argue that any sort of constraint on the human will whatsoever is completely incompatible with genuine human freedom, yet they too must acknowledge some kind of constraint on the human will. It is disingenuous, therefore, to argue that the Reformers' view of human freedom is inadequate because it posits a constraint on that freedom. If they are going to reject the Reformers' views while maintaining their own, they must produce a more compelling reason why their view portrays the realities of human freedom more accurately than does the Reformers'.

---

to do other than he does. But Molina's official account, as we have seen, is nothing more than a dogmatic assertion that God, in the mystery of his greatness, can have foreknowledge of an autonomous choice that could be other than it will be. But the problem with this official account, as we have seen, is that there is no basis upon which to accept such a notion of divine foreknowledge as a coherent and plausible doctrine.

231. With reference to his unofficial view, not his official one. In his official view, he clearly and explicitly asserts that the human will is capable of choosing other than it does.

Undoubtedly, Molina would want to say that the constraint imposed by a particular will's own inherent nature and character is a radically different sort of constraint than that imposed externally, as it were, by God. It is reasonable to see the latter (God's external constraint) as inconsistent with human freedom while the former (the internal constraint of the character of one's own will) is not.

I offer two responses to this objection.

FIRST RESPONSE

On Molina's view, how does he propose to have Peter's actions necessitated by the intrinsic nature of Peter's own will without having them ultimately necessitated (and imposed on him externally) by the divine will? God is ultimately the author and designer of Peter's will. It functions in accordance with an intrinsic nature that God himself determined; hence, ultimately, Peter's actions have been directly determined by the God who created him.

We confront once again the philosophical schizophrenia of Molina's view. On the one hand, Molina wants to insist that Peter and Peter alone (through the spontaneous resolution of his own will), apart from any divine determination, determines his choice to deny Jesus. But, on the other hand, in order to explain how God can foreknow what Peter is going to do, he must implicitly suggest that something other than the spontaneous resolution of Peter's will determines that Peter will deny Jesus. A definitive and knowable something determines how the spontaneous resolution of Peter's will shall come out. Namely, it is the intrinsic nature or character of Peter's will. But once Molina has allowed for that, one of two things must follow:

- the very problematic suggestion that Peter's will is not created by God (i.e., it is either uncreated or self-creating),

    or

- it is ultimately created and designed by God.

From the standpoint of a serious biblical philosophy, the first case (Peter's will is not created by God) is altogether unacceptable. In the latter case (if Peter's will is created by God), then Molina must acknowledge that Peter's choice to deny Jesus was ultimately determined by God. This is the very thing he has set out to deny.

SECOND RESPONSE

I will concede that Molina's hypothetical objection is indeed under-standable. It is plausible for one to think that the external constraints imposed by the divine will are inconsistent with human freedom while the internal constraints imposed by the inherent nature of one's own will are not. But while I concede that this is plausible and understandable, whether it is ultimately "reasonable" is the crux of the debate between the divine determinist and the human autonomist.

To the divine determinist, the constraints imposed on our voluntary choices by the will of the transcendent creator God are ultimately of no more consequence than those imposed by the inherent natures of our own wills. Both are universal and necessary principles that, because of their uni-versality and necessity, fail to have any import for questions of freedom, responsibility, and the character and nature of evil.

God is, to the divine determinist, the transcendent author of all that is. He is the one "in whom we live, and move, and have our being."[232] He is the one who wills all that exists into existence. Apart from him, nothing that exists could exist. Nothing—good or bad, evil or righteous, voluntary or involuntary, coerced or uncoerced, free or not—could exist were its existence not willed by the divine author of all things. That being so, then the fact that God has willed something to occur cannot in any way be rel-evant or meaningful to the important distinctions we make between what is freely chosen and what is not, or between what is evil and what is good, or between what involves my culpability and what does not. It is not as if God wills what is not free and does not will what is free. That cannot be right, for God wills everything whatsoever. It is not as if God wills what is good and not what is evil; for, again, God wills everything whatsoever. In other words, to say that God has willed X (no matter what X is) is, for the purposes of defining human freedom, utterly trivial and philosophically useless.

Meaningful differences between them must define the difference between choices that are free and those that are not. It will be some impor-tant difference between a voluntary and involuntary action that will be philosophically useful and will distinguish the voluntary action as free. Being "willed by God," therefore, is philosophically useless with respect to defining human freedom, for it does not describe a difference between dif-ferent kinds of human action. "Being determined by God" can neither

---

232. Acts 17:28. In this passage, Paul quotes with approval the words of Epimenides, a Cretan poet.

make an action free nor preclude it from being free, for all actions, voluntary and involuntary, are determined by God.

What if, in a fit of absurdity, I were to suggest that the difference between voluntary and involuntary actions lay in part in the fact that voluntary actions do not really exist while involuntary actions do. Under such a suggestion, any adequate notion of true freedom would hold that voluntary actions are those that do not truly exist! (Remember, I'm being absurd.) Could I then reasonably charge the Reformers' with having an inadequate notion of true freedom—by analogy to Molina's charge—in that the Reformers' concept of voluntary actions requires that such actions actually do exist? This, of course, would be ridiculous. How can something that must of necessity be universally true of all human actions in order for them to be human actions at all (namely, existence) be something that distinguishes between two kinds of human action? That makes no sense.

From the Reformers' point of view, Molina's charge against them is equally absurd. The Reformers, following the biblical authors, view the divine determinism of real human actions as a universal and necessary feature of any human action whatsoever. It cannot therefore serve to distinguish between two different kinds of action, voluntary and involuntary. How could it? Whatever it means for an action to be free, it cannot mean that it is free from the determinative will of God any more than it can mean that it is free from existence in the real world. Nothing can be free from what must necessarily and universally be true of every thing that is in order for it to even be a thing.

So the fact that my actions and choices are ultimately determined by the will of him who is the author of everything cannot reasonably be understood to nullify human freedom any more than the fact that my actions are ultimately determined by the intrinsic nature or character of my own will nullifies human freedom. My choices are determined by the intrinsic nature of my own will, for everything whatsoever is determined by the intrinsic character of what it is. That goes without saying. Likewise, my choices are determined by the divine will, for everything whatsoever is determined by the divine will. That too goes without saying. Therefore, to charge that divine determinism does not allow for truly free human actions because it will not assert that they are free from the determining will of God is a hollow condemnation. It has about as much substance as charging that the Reformers' view of freedom is not compatible with genuine freedom because it does not allow for human actions to be truly free from existence. Or, because it does not allow for human actions to be truly free from the will of the person performing them. These latter two criticisms would not likely have caused the Reformers to lose any sleep. And neither, I submit, would the former.

Whereas all actions whatsoever are consistent with the nature of that which produces them, and whereas all whatsoever are consistent with the will of the divine being who brings all things to pass, nevertheless, some we know to be free, voluntary actions while others are not. The crucial question is this: what, then, is the difference? If the difference cannot lie in whether it has been determined by God, where then? What is the divine determinist's concept of a free choice?

Divine determinism holds that a free human choice is a choice that has in no way been determined by any other created reality. A free choice is one that has not been necessitated by any other thing, event, or cause that exists in and as a part of the created cosmos. Under this definition, being determined or caused by the transcendent Creator does not disqualify a choice as free. Only being determined or caused by some other *created* reality will do so. This is a completely adequate representation of genuine human freedom. Indeed, it is adequate in a way in which Molina's view is not!

Molina (at least in his covert account) replaces the determining will of God with the determining nature of a person's own will. In doing so, Molina has made human choice dependent upon another part of created reality. I choose what I do because something about the nature of me makes me do what I do. What exactly makes me do what I do? "The nature of my will," says Molina. But what is that? My genes? Then we have genetic determinism. The impact of my environment? Then we have a Skinnerian determinism. What is it about me (my will) that causes me to choose what I do? No matter what Molina answers, we appear to have some sort of natural determinism—some aspect of created nature is the necessitating cause of human choice and action. But is this not the sort of inadequate view of human freedom that Molina and Craig insist we must avoid? How can we be responsible for our actions if all our actions are necessitated by something in the created order?

The only way to avoid natural determinism and still have some sort of reasonable theory of human action is to embrace divine determinism. God can only foreknow what has been predetermined. What has been predetermined has either been predetermined by God (divine determinism) or has been predetermined by some other aspect of the cosmos (natural determinism). If it is the latter, then all of our intuitions tell us that our actions are not truly free.[233] My choices have been caused by something outside

233. Not everyone would concur with this, but I am committed to a concept of human freedom that precludes natural necessity. If our actions are necessitated by brain states, brain chemistry, genes, or even more vaguely, the impact of our environment on us, then I have to agree

of me and my control. But if it is the former, then (unless we draw a faulty analogy to the case of natural determinism) our intuitions tell us no such thing. No intuition tells me that a divinely determined action cannot be a free action.[234] As we noted, what else is an action supposed to be—free or not—if not divinely determined?

CONCLUSION: CALVINISM'S INADEQUATE VIEW OF HUMAN FREEDOM IS AN ILLUSION

From the divine determinist's perspective, he has no problem with the compatibility of divine sovereignty and human freedom. Contrary to Craig's expectations, he is not itching for a solution to this problem. Hence, he is not eager to accept Molina's solution, heedless of the philosophical problems it entails. Craig is confident that divine determinism is fraught with philosophical problems of its own—namely, that it cannot adequately account for human freedom. But this is a problem the divine determinist does not feel or acknowledge. Human freedom is no real difficulty to his theory. It looks like a problem only to one who has created an artificial, arbitrary, and unrealistic criterion by which to judge true freedom—namely, that a truly free act will not be determined by anything whatsoever, including God. The divine determinist sees no reason to accept such an arbitrary and naive criterion. An act can be a truly free act

---

with B. F. Skinner: the freedom and dignity of our actions is but an illusion. Since it is utterly unbiblical to view the freedom of our actions as illusory, I am forced by my own assumptions to reject natural determinism. If one could successfully argue for a naturally determined action being a truly free action for which the agent is fully responsible, however, then I would have no further reason to dismiss natural determinism as a possibility. The possibility that even natural determinism may not preclude human freedom and responsibility does not affect the argument of this essay, however. Surely one can have no problem with divine determinism coexisting with human freedom if he is willing to concede that natural determinism can coexist with human freedom.

234. Many people would try to maintain that it is intuitively obvious that a divinely determined action is thereby not a free action. It is outside the scope of this essay to defend my contention—specifically, that it is not intuitively obvious that a divinely determined action is not free. I have tried to argue elsewhere, in a series of lectures delivered at McKenzie Study Center in Eugene, Oregon, in 1987, that we have no such rational intuitions. Two things combine to leave us with the impression that divinely determined actions cannot be truly free: a cultural assumption that we rarely if ever examine; and an unexamined argument by analogy to a naturally determined action. The latter involves something like this fallacious argument to support it: Naturally determined actions are not free actions. It follows therefore that no determined action is a free action. Divinely determined actions are determined actions. Therefore, divinely determined actions are not free actions.

only if it has not been determined by him who determines all that is? That would be absurd! It is not the Calvinist who holds the inadequate view of human freedom! It is the Arminian whose view is inadequate.

Summary

Molina's attempt to reconcile the *de fide* doctrines of divine sovereignty with a belief in the absolute autonomy of the human will has an initial appeal, an initial plausibility. On closer scrutiny, we find that it contains a fatal tension that undermines it. The fatal tension—indeed, contradiction—lies between two conflicting conceptions of divine middle knowledge to which Molina alternatingly appeals. When we fail to notice the shift from one conception of middle knowledge to the other, Molina's reconciliation seems plausible. Its plausibility disappears when, recognizing the equivocation in his concept of middle knowledge, we see that his two different accounts of middle knowledge lead to contradictory results. If Molina's official conception of middle knowledge is right, then absolute human autonomy is salvaged. But if Molina's covert conception of middle knowledge is right, then absolute human autonomy is refuted. And yet, as we saw, the only way for him to render the notion of divine middle knowledge intelligible is by conceiving of it along the lines of his covert account—that is, by conceiving of it in a way that refutes absolute human autonomy.

Like a master illusionist, Molina prompts me to keep my eyes fixed on his first, official conception of divine middle knowledge when he wants to convince me that his views do fully and uncompromisingly embrace absolute human autonomy. Then he prompts me to keep my eyes fixed on his second, covert conception of divine middle knowledge when he wants to convince me that divine middle knowledge is a viable concept. What he never prompts me to do is to notice that the second, covert account of divine middle knowledge entails the denial of the concept of absolute human autonomy that is assumed and advanced by the first.

Molina's views fail to persuade a divine determinist like me. If I ignore Molina's covert conception of middle knowledge and consider only his official account, then, although it is true that I could embrace the *de fide* doctrines of divine sovereignty at the same time that I affirm absolute human autonomy, Molina asks me to affirm a doctrine that is philosophically problematic to me (namely, direct and intuitive middle knowledge in the context of absolute human autonomy). At the same time, he asks me to reject the doctrine of divine determinism, which is not philosophically problematic to me. If I ignore his official account of middle knowledge and consider his covert account, then Molina asks me to leave one theory of divine determinism for a different theory of divine determinism. The one he wants me to leave is a countertheory to natural determinism and as such is biblically and philosophically viable. The one he wants me to embrace is biblically and philosophically problematic, for it entails a form of natural determinism. Molina's views do not solve any problems; they simply create new and greater ones.

APPENDIX J
UNDERSTANDING THE SECOND COMMANDMENT

The following has been adapted from a portion of a lecture delivered in the fall of 1994 as a part of the curriculum of Gutenberg College. An article, substantially identical to this, was published in McKenzie Study Center's newsletter News & Views *in the spring of 1995 under this same title.*

This reprinted article contributes two things of note to the arguments of this book:

1. *It provides the requisite background to my claim in chapter 4 that the Babylonian god Marduk was sovereign without being transcendent. My point there was that, to have an adequately biblical concept of God, it is not sufficient to understand God as sovereign. While God is sovereign, he is more than that. He is transcendent. This is what God commanded Israel in the second commandment: "Do not conceive of me as merely sovereign such that you could capture the essence of my power and authority in a single image. Conceive of me as the transcendent author of all that occurs in reality. Nothing in the created order can adequately capture the essence of my power and authority, because my power and authority is reflected in everything that is."*

2. *It shows how the second of the ten commandments required a paradigm shift in Israel's conception of God. This same paradigm shift is required again of us modern Christians. The modern conception of God is more like that which an ancient polytheist would hold than it is like the conception of God that God himself commanded of Israel. I have been arguing that to conceive of God as the transcendent author of all reality is a valid philosophical option, and the one that most coincides with the biblical worldview. But, ultimately, this paradigm shift is not just a philosophical option. It is a* moral requirement. *It is commanded by the second commandment delivered on Mt. Sinai to Moses.*

The Problem with the Second Commandment

The second of the ten commandments presents the thoughtful Christian with a difficulty. He cannot help but be bothered by it:

You shall not make for yourself any graven image, or any likeness of what is in heaven above or on the earth beneath or in the water under the earth. You shall not worship them or serve them [i.e., the graven images]; for I, Yahweh your God, am a jealous God, visiting the iniquity of the fathers on the children, on the third and the fourth generations of those who hate Me, but showing lovingkindness to thousands, to those who love Me and keep My commandments.

(Deuteronomy 20:4-6, adapted from the NASV)

This commandment seems to forbid Israel from representing Yahweh with a symbol. Is God serious? Isn't that just a wee bit unreasonable? Humans rely on symbolism. It is an inherent aspect of our abilities to reason and to use language. What can possibly be so wrong about symbolizing Yahweh?

After all, am I not making a symbol of Yahweh—a graven image—every time I write the word, G-O-D? But if, somehow, it is not inappropriate to represent God symbolically with a word, G-O-D, then why not with something else? What could possibly be so inappropriate about inventing a pictogram, an image, or anything else to simply symbolize the living God? What could God possibly be thinking when he commands Israel as he does in this second commandment? It is difficult to understand how this commandment is not just petty and trivial.

It is tempting to solve this difficulty by understanding the second commandment—like the first one—to be a prohibition against idolatry. Under this interpretation, the second commandment was not forbidding them to symbolize Yahweh. Rather, it was forbidding them to worship *other* gods. It was graven images representing *other* gods that they were commanded not to worship, not graven images of Yahweh.

But in Deuteronomy, Moses makes it clear that God's commandment was intended to forbid them from making graven images of Yahweh himself.

So watch yourselves carefully, since you did not see any form on the day Yahweh spoke to you at Horeb [i.e., Mt. Sinai] from the midst of the fire; lest you act corruptly and make a graven image for yourselves in the form of any figure, the likeness of male or female, the likeness of any animal that is on the earth, the likeness of any winged bird that flies in the sky, the likeness of anything that creeps on the ground, the likeness of any fish that is in the water below the earth.

(Deut. 4: 15-18, adapted from NASV)

Moses links the prohibition to make a graven image to the fact that God, at Sinai, did not show himself to them in any form. This makes it clear, I think, that Moses understands the prohibition to forbid their making any graven image of Yahweh himself. So the difficulty remains. Why is God so insistent on prohibiting what, on the surface, would appear to be a very trivial matter—representing God by means of a symbol?

My Analysis of the Philosophical Worldview of Ancient Polytheism

To solve this difficulty, we must better understand the nature and structure of ancient near-eastern polytheism, for polytheism was the religious context into which God spoke the ten commandments.

I do not pretend to be an expert on ancient near-eastern religions. I do not have a serious scholar's grasp of the details of polytheistic beliefs and practices. But I think I have enough knowledge to attempt a reasonable analysis of the philosophical worldview and the philosophical assumptions upon which polytheistic beliefs and practices were founded. Perhaps an expert scholar on the subject could present evidence that would force me to modify or abandon this analysis, but short of presenting me with a philosophical essay written by an ancient Egyptian priest that offers an analysis of the philosophical underpinnings of his religion that is different from mine, it is hard to imagine what possible piece of contrary evidence a scholar could present. Either the following analysis makes sense, or it does not. I think it is as simple as that.

Life is full of events that are mysterious and are inexplicable in terms of those forces and realities that we can see. If two people with virtually identical resumes apply for a job, one gets chosen, the other does not. Why? How do we explain the outcome? We cannot reasonably explain the outcome in terms of their qualifications, experience, personality, or any other manifest reality, for we stipulated that they were virtually identical. How, then, do we explain the outcome? If I roll a die, it turns up one number rather than another. Why? Nothing I can see or know can explain the outcome. So how do I explain the outcome? I attribute the result to a god—the god *Chance*.

The philosophy behind ancient polytheism begins with this insight: nothing that occurs in our lives is explainable simply in terms of those realities are known to us. How, then, can we explain the events of human experience and understand them so as to control them? Ancient polytheism has its roots in an attempt to answer this question from the standpoint of a philosophical theory.

The philosophical theory that ancient polytheism advanced was based on two important distinctions:

First, it posited that there were both visible and invisible causes. Not only are there visible causes that one can readily observe, but there are also invisible forces that one cannot readily observe.

Secondly, polytheism distinguished between natural causes and personal causes. Most certainly the ancients understood (if they did not articulate) the concept of natural law. Ancients knew that water was essential to plant life, that water ran downhill, and that day followed night. It was simply in the nature of things. At a commonsensical level, the ancient near-eastern world believed in natural laws just as surely as anyone who came after them. Natural laws were automatic and predictable. You could count on them. If you dropped an object, it would predictably drop to the ground. If you withheld water from a plant, it would predictably die.

But natural causes are not the only forces that shape our reality. Human beings, what we might call *personal* causes, are also major players in the events of our lives. The actions of other humans are very significant in determining the outcome of events. Other humans can kill me, steal from me, lie to me…. Indeed, people are perhaps more important determiners of the events of my life than anything in impersonal nature.

Now personal causes are very different from natural causes. People are not orderly, predictable, and mechanical. They are quixotic, full of surprises, and hard to control. One minute they may like you, the next minute they do not. One day they may lie to you, the next day they tell the truth. They are driven by varied and conflicting desires that seem to roam free through their souls, not subject to any orderly or rational pattern. Unlike a natural cause, one cannot readily predict what a person is going to do.

It is not that we can't exercise any control over people. We can try to stay in their good favors and can expect, thereby, to be treated with kindness rather than harm. But it is so much more difficult to understand and control the behavior of a person than it is to know and control the behavior of any inanimate, impersonal object.

With these distinctions in mind, the philosophical worldview of ancient polytheism comes to this:

There exist two separate and distinct realms. There is the visible realm. In it lie all those forces that I can observe. In it I find both impersonal objects (natural causes whose nature I can come to know and whose behavior I can come to predict) and personal causes (humans), whose behavior is much more difficult to predict and whose actions are wild, free, and not altogether controllable. But there is also an invisible realm. In it lie all those forces that I cannot see. Now what sort of forces exist in the invisible realm? Are they natural forces, analogous to the impersonal objects in the visible realm? Or are they personal forces, analogous to the free and unshackled choices of human beings?

The distinctive character of the ancient near-eastern worldview is founded on this: the ancient polytheist believed that the invisible realm is "peopled" by personal forces—forces which are analogous to the free choices of human personalities. The invisible forces of the invisible realm are fundamentally more like people than they are like water, fire, air, earth, or plants. The forces in the invisible realm are wild, free, and ultimately unpredictable rather than forces that slavishly obey their simple nature like the parts of a machine.[235]

What better way to represent such forces, then, than to represent them as personal beings—i.e., as anthropomorphic "gods." Often their gods were represented as humans. But even when they were not represented as humans—as, for example, when they were represented as bulls, or dragons, or lions—they were nonetheless understood to be persons with very human-like motives, thoughts, intents, desires, etc.

Why assume the invisible realm to be peopled by personal causes rather than natural causes? Sometimes the rain comes in the spring, sometimes it does not. We cannot seem to predict when it will and when it will not rain, when there will be drought and when there will not. Accordingly, are the forces that dictate whether the rain will come more like natural laws that operate mechanically to produce an outcome, or are they more like personal forces that act as if they were free-will persons? Surely, one can understand how reasonable the latter answer would be.

So, in the ancient worldview, the coming of the rain is determined by personal forces, i.e., "gods," who operate invisibly in a wholly other realm of reality that is beyond my knowledge and who act freely—and largely (but not wholly) unpredictably—to try to bring about whatever they want to bring about in our realm.

For our purposes in this article, the crucial thing to understand about polytheism is this: There were many such "gods" whose actions impinged upon the lives of these ancient people. Each of them was limited and

---

235. This is where pre-Socratic philosophy made a decisive break with ancient polytheism. The pre-Socratic Greek philosophers answered, instead, that the invisible forces in the invisible realm were fundamentally more like water, fire, earth, and air (i.e., they were forces that mechanically obeyed the laws of their nature) than they were like people who acted out of a will that was fundamentally free.

finite, and they were all working at cross-purposes to one another. The society of the gods was conceived by analogy to human society. It was a community of roughly equal beings each of whom had his own purposes. Accordingly, the purpose of one god may work at cross-purposes to that of another. Some gods were stronger, some weaker. But all were seeking to bring their own will and purpose to fruition. The outcome in human affairs was the net result of all the activities of all these gods seeking to accomplish their purposes in this visible realm. Such an outcome, therefore, was hopelessly unpredictable. All that a human being could do was try to remain in the favor of as many of the most powerful gods as he could, so that they might be more disposed to do him good rather than harm.

For our purposes, the important point is this: a "god" in polytheism is nothing more and nothing less than a powerful force in the invisible realm of reality that potentially affects the outcome of human affairs. It is *not* invincible. It can be defeated or canceled out by the purposes of other "gods" and it can even be outmaneuvered by human ingenuity. Furthermore, it is not above and outside the cosmos, it is part of the cosmos—just one part among many.

But didn't the Egyptians worship the sun? That is where we grossly misunderstand polytheism. How are we to understand the Egyptians' claim that the sun is Ammon-Re? It is unthinkable that Ammon-Re, who is represented in all of their mythology as a personal being with a mind and will of his own, is nothing more and nothing less than the impersonal celestial object we call the sun. They do not mean to suggest that Ammon-Re just is the sun. Rather, they mean to suggest that Ammon-Re, like all the other gods, is visibly represented in this realm by a particular token. The sun is his token. The sun is not personal and is not in the least capable of doing the things attributed to Ammon-Re. The Egyptians surely knew that. They were not fools. But Ammon-Re is not the sun *per se*. Rather Ammon-Re is that invisible force working invisibly behind the scenes, out of our sight, in a wholly other realm. The sun is but a visible token of him that he has put in our realm. And it is an apt token, for the sun's nature and character accurately represent to us something of the personality and nature of Ammon-Re himself. Ammon-Re is finite. He is not represented by everything. He is like one thing and not like another. He is like the sun, not the dew. When the Egyptians worshipped the sun, therefore, they were not worshipping the celestial object *per se*. They were worshipping the supremely powerful personal force in the invisible realm of cosmic reality—Ammon-Re—who put the sun in the sky as his token.

Much more could be said about the philosophy of ancient polytheism, but enough has been said to make sense out of the second commandment.

The Meaning of the Second Commandment

When God commands Israel not to make and worship a graven image of himself, what is he forbidding them? Here, I think, is what he is commanding:

Do not conceive of me in the same way the rest of the nations conceive of their supreme god. They conceive of their supreme god as the most powerful of all the invisible forces to be reckoned with, but they conceive of him as finite, limited, and as just one of many influences in their lives. Their god can be aptly represented by just one aspect of the visible order, because his nature is so limited and finite. Do not think of me in such a way. I am not limited and finite. I am not one of many influences in your life. I am the one and only influence there is. When seen in the light of my all-controlling will, nothing else is a cause at all. There is nothing I cannot do. Nothing can thwart me in my purpose. There exist no other forces in reality that are even relevant compared to me. I determine everything, control everything, create everything, cause everything. Furthermore, nothing in the visible realm can adequately capture who I am and what I am like. In one sense, every visible thing reflects my nature and wisdom, for all of it is my handiwork. And in another sense, nothing in the visible realm is like me. Nothing can adequately represent who I am. I am too big to be understood in terms of any finite thing in the natural order.

Do not, therefore, conceive of me as a God who can be represented in terms of just one finite image. If you do so, then it will not be me, Yahweh, you worship. It will be some other god of your own imagination. I am a jealous God. I, Yahweh, the all-powerful, transcendent God that I am—I am the one you must worship. You must not worship the shrunken deity of your own imagination.

The purpose of the commandment, therefore, is not to command Israel with regard to *how* they must represent God—forbidding them to use symbols to represent him. Rather, it is to instruct them with regard to whom they are to worship and serve. In the context of Moses' day—when polytheism was the philosophy of the day—God was commanding Israel to have a radically different conception of God. They were to know and love a wholly transcendent God who was the only cause of anything and everything that happens. God could care less *how* they represented him to themselves. (Surely they could use a symbol to represent him. Indeed, how could they represent him any other way.) His concern was simply that they worship him in accordance with who he truly is—the wholly transcendent author of all that is and all that happens.

If our symbol represents the author of all that is, then we are not in violation of the second commandment when we worship him by means of that symbol. But if we forego symbols entirely, yet we worship and serve a shrunken god, then—for all our supercilious observance of the second commandment—we are, in fact, in violation of it.

The Contemporary Import of the Second Commandment

Does the second commandment have any relevance today? Indeed it does. Modern Christian culture has largely shifted its allegiance away from the God of Sinai. Far too often we worship an imaginary shrunken deity. He is the supreme being, the most powerful force in reality. But he is not the transcendent cause of everything. He can be thwarted. Satan, demons, human free will—any or all of these realities can do substantial work at cross-purposes to this god. To the extent that we conceive of God in this way, to just that extent we have made ourselves polytheists and have failed to obey the second commandment.

As it did to Israel, the second commandment is commanding us to radically alter our conception of God. If we do not come to see him in the full light of his transcendence and his utterly unchallengable sovereignty, then we worship a false god and must heed the warning attached to the commandment: "...I, Yahweh your God, am a jealous God, visiting the iniquity of the fathers on the children, on the third and fourth generations of those who hate Me, but showing lovingkindness to thousands, to those who love Me and keep my commandments." Implicit in this warning is a very frightening suggestion: to fail to acknowledge the unchallengable sovereignty of the God who is really there is tantamount to hating him; and hating God is something we dare not do.

APPENDIX K
DEFINING RATIONALITY

Critics and proponents of the reliability of reason often talk past each other, for they have very different conceptions of what reason is. Before he can profitably discuss whether reason is a reliable guide to truth, one must be clear about what he means by REASON. I will define what I mean by REASON and related terms as I use them in this book. I use these terms in a significantly broader sense than many do.

> **REASON (RATIONALITY)**—*that set of divinely created laws, principles, and processes, innate within human intelligence, whereby a human being formulates true beliefs about reality from the data of experience* {**A**}.

All the different processes that function within human intelligence to lead us to a knowledge of the objective reality outside ourselves are included within the scope of what I am calling reason. Reason is not limited to a particular kind of logical analysis or deduction. Reason includes *all* the various processes that transpire within human intelligence. It includes guessing, hunches, direct perception, imagination, aesthetic experience, athletic skill—anything and everything that human intelligence does in order to come to a true understanding and perception of reality and to act within and upon it.

Sometimes reason is used as a synonym for REASONING. This is the source of much confusion and misunderstanding. I discuss this later.

> **LOGIC**—*that set of divinely created laws or principles, innate within human intelligence, that serve as a guide in the formation of valid beliefs. As we formulate our beliefs about objective reality, logic either warrants or disallows those beliefs* {**B**}.

The principles of logic serve as the validity criteria for our beliefs. As one reflects on his experience, he instinctively seeks to formulate true beliefs about reality. The laws of logic are those principles in conformity to which one instinctively seeks to construct those beliefs.

It is these principles that any formal system of logic is trying to capture within a formal system. No formal system of logic has successfully captured the whole scope of what constitutes human logic. Hence, I do not use the term LOGIC to refer to any particular formal theory of logic.

Rather, I use it to refer to the innate principles themselves—those principles that we use everyday to evaluate the validity of possible beliefs about reality. Logic does not constitute a way of thinking. It is the guide and template for all our thinking; it is the very substructure of intelligence itself—an essential attribute of reason.

> **REASONING**—the act of constructing beliefs about objective reality from the data of life experience {C}.

There is no guarantee that the beliefs formed as a result of reasoning will successfully conform to the laws of logic. If we define successful reasoning in terms of its conformity to the principles of logic, then reasoning may be more or less successful. Reasoning can readily result in illogical and irrational beliefs.

The term REASON can be and often is used as a synonym for reasoning. This engenders a great deal of confusion. They are not synonymous. Reasoning, as I am defining it, is the activity of belief formation using human intelligence. Reason is that set of innate laws, principles, and intellectual procedures by which reasoning can be judged sound or unsound. Consider the following proposition: "Reason is a reliable guide to truth." This proposition is often mistaken for a second proposition: "Human reasoning is a reliable guide to truth." The latter proposition is obviously false. Human reasoning *per se* is not a reliable guide to truth, and that is not my contention in chapter 3. My contention is a very different claim. Namely, that REASON is a reliable guide to truth. In other words, while human reasoning is fallible and can quite frequently result in false beliefs, reason—the innate set of standards by which reasoning is to be judged as sound or unsound—is not fallible and never leads to false beliefs. If reason judges an instance of human reasoning to be sound, then necessarily that instance of human reasoning has led to a true belief. And if reason judges an instance of human reasoning to be unsound, then necessarily that instance of human reasoning has led to a false belief. That is what I mean when I claim that REASON is a reliable guide to truth.

RATIONAL has several different meanings. Its meaning varies as it is used to describe different things:

> **RATIONAL** (describing a being or person)—*a being (a person) is rational if he has reason as a part of his nature. To be rational is to have the ability to formulate beliefs about reality that are generated by the*

mental processes innate to God-given intelligence and that conform to
the principles of logic (reason) {**D.1**}.

By this definition, animals—as well as humans—are rational in some measure. The difference between humans and animals is not that humans are rational (in this sense) while animals are not. Humans differ from animals in the nature and extent of their rationality. Human rationality reflects divine rationality in a way that animal rationality does not. Most importantly, human rationality includes moral judgment while animal rationality does not.

'Rational' is sometimes used to distinguish one sort of person from another. For example, "Paul is quite rational; John is not." When used in this way, 'rational' is being used to describe a person in one of two ways: either (1) he is particularly skilled at reaching logical beliefs {**D.1a**}, or (2) he is particularly self-conscious of his rational processes and engages in them methodically and systematically rather than intuitively {**D.1b**}. For my purposes in the arguments of chapter 3, neither of these senses of 'rational' is in view. All human beings are equally rational in the sense in which I mean 'rational' in that chapter. No style of employing reason is more rational than any other.

> **RATIONAL** *(describing a sequence of reasoning or an argument)—an*
> *argument or some sequence of thinking or reasoning is rational if it con-*
> *forms to the principles of logic and results in beliefs that conform to the*
> *principles of logic* {**D.2a**}.

Thinking that is rational is opposed to thinking that is irrational—that is, thinking that fails to conform to the principles of logic and reason. Occasionally, a person might refer to 'rational thinking' or 'rational thought' when all they mean by the term is thinking that transpires in the mind of a rational being. In this sense, the opposite of rational thinking is behavior that is non-rational because it does not involve thought at all— that is, activity that is not the attribute of a rational being. Hence, there is another useful sense of 'rational'—

> **RATIONAL** *(describing a sequence of reasoning, an argument)—an*
> *argument or some sequence of thinking or reasoning is rational if it is*
> *something that an intelligent, rational being would engage in (as*
> *opposed to some being who is, by nature, incapable of intelligent,*
> *rational thought)* {**D.2b**}.

RATIONAL *(describing a belief)—a belief is rational if it conforms to and has been formulated in accordance with the principles of logic* {**D.3**}.

While humans are capable of irrational beliefs, we permit irrational beliefs relatively rarely and selectively. Most of our beliefs are rational. We have a built-in sense of obligation to hold rational beliefs and reject irrational ones. We instinctively feel shame when our beliefs are criticized for being irrational or illogical.

Sometimes we describe a belief as rational in the sense that it is formulated by a rational being {D.3a}. This sense would be related to D.1 and D.2b above. And sometimes we describe a belief as rational in the sense that it is the result of a conscious, deliberate process rather than the result of an intuitive hunch {D.3b}. This sense would be related to D.1b above. But neither of these is what I typically mean when I describe a belief as RATIONAL in the course of chapter 3.

RATIONAL (describing a thing)—*a thing is rational if it has the earmarks of having been fashioned, designed, created, conceived, or accomplished by a rational being and is, therefore, capable of being known or understood by another rational being* {**D.4**}.

One of the consequences of something having been designed by a rational being is that it can be known by another rational being. I discuss this more fully in chapter 3. Accordingly, if a rational being formulates rational beliefs about a rational thing, it follows that those beliefs will be true and will constitute knowledge of that thing. The beliefs will correspond to what the thing actually is. This is such an inevitable consequence of a thing's being rational that it is at the heart of what we mean by calling a thing 'rational'. A thing is rational if it is knowable to a rational being through normal rational processes.

LOGICAL has various meanings as well. Its meaning differs as it is employed to describe different things:

LOGICAL (describing a being or person)—*a being (a person) is logical if he tends to form beliefs that succeed in conforming to the principles of logic. In other words, a person is logical if he tends to be successful in formulating rational (logical) beliefs* {**E.1**}.

A common meaning for 'logical' will not be relevant to the arguments and claims of chapter 3. 'Logical' can be used to describe a person who tends to be self-conscious, deliberate, methodical, and/or analytical in the way he goes about formulating his beliefs {E.1a}. The opposite of being logical in this sense is to be intuitive. A person who relies on intuitive hunches employs his reason differently from the person who formulates his beliefs deliberately, step-by-step. Often the latter is called 'logical' in contradistinction to the former. While this is a common and acceptable sense of the term 'logical,' it has no bearing on the claims in chapter 3. Relative to my claims there, the intuitive reasoner is no less logical than the deliberate, self-conscious reasoner. What makes a person logical is that—in the end, however he gets there—he embraces beliefs that conform to the principles of logic. What style of reasoning he uses to come to those beliefs (whether intuitive or methodical) is not relevant to what is at stake in that chapter.

> **LOGICAL** (describing a sequence of reasoning or an argument)— *an argument or some sequence of thinking or reasoning is logical if it conforms to the principles of logic and results in beliefs that conform to those principles* {**E.2**}.

This is synonymous with 'rational' in sense D.2a above. Not infrequently, an argument or sequence of reasoning could be described as 'logical' in a sense that parallels E.1a above. Namely, 'logical' can describe an argument that is deliberate, self-conscious, methodical, and analytical {E.2a}. But, as above, this is not a sense of 'logical' that affects anything I assert in chapter 3.

> **LOGICAL** (describing a belief)—*a belief is logical if it conforms to and has been formulated in accordance with the principles of logic* {**E.3**}.

This is synonymous with 'rational' in the sense of D.3 above.

No sense of 'logical' corresponds to 'rational' in sense D.4. We do not typically employ 'logical' to describe a thing. Only people, arguments, or beliefs are commonly characterized as logical.

APPENDIX L

ARMINITAS: A DIALOGUE

JACRATES: So, as I think you can see from my arguments, it follows that God can foreknow and predict the future infallibly precisely because he is the one who controls and determines exactly what will transpire in the future and can predict it ahead of time because he knows what he purposes to do. So, the fact that he can predict the future is evidence that God determines even the very choices we make.

ARMINITAS: But, Jacrates, that is just the point. What makes you so sure that God could not accomplish his purposes and do so without fail and still have men make choices that he did not determine? That seems very reasonable to me.

JACRATES: Ah, yes, I see your point. Perhaps you could help me see it a little better though. How could God infallibly accomplish his purposes and yet not determine the choices of men? Could you help me see more clearly how that could be?

ARMINITAS: Most certainly!

JACRATES: Great! I am eager for you to proceed.

ARMINITAS: Do you not agree that God is very wise and skillful?

JACRATES: Oh yes! I do indeed.

ARMINITAS: And do you not agree that God does control and direct the physical environment around us?

JACRATES: Yes, I most certainly do.

ARMINITAS: And, in fact, if what I shall prove is so, he controls the actions of other people toward us as well?

JACRATES: Yes, certainly! We agree on that. How he does so seems to be the point at issue between us.

ARMINITAS: Then God controls and directs every influence that comes into our life and experience?

JACRATES: Yes, I agree that that is so.

ARMINITAS: Do you also agree that God understands us better than anyone else? Even better than we understand ourselves?

JACRATES: Yes, I agree with that.

ARMINITAS: And do you agree that God understands us well enough that he could predict with great precision how we will react to a certain situation and all of its influences?

JACRATES: Yes, I do. I agree with that.

ARMINITAS: Then, Jacrates, can you not see? God could quite easily accomplish everything that he purposes by simply bringing exactly those influences to bear on us that will compel us to choose whatever he wants us to choose. Now the choice is fully ours. God did not create the choice, as you suggest, nor determine it in the way that you have been saying. Rather, our choice is made in complete independence from God. But yet we are put in a position by God, who totally controls our environment, where God knows that we will make exactly that choice he wants us to make. In just such a way, by controlling the influences at work on us, God is able to control what our choices will be, but without actually creating or determining those choices for us. Do you see what I am saying, Jacrates?

JACRATES: Yes, Arminitas, I think I do.

ARMINITAS: Then, you can see how futile and unnecessary and ridiculous all your ramblings about divine determinism are?

JACRATES: Well, Arminitas, as for knowing how ridiculous my ramblings are, I have always known that. But I still do not find divine determinism ridiculous. It still seems much more reasonable than what you have suggested.

ARMINITAS: What, Jacrates, are you out of your mind?

JACRATES: Probably.

ARMINITAS: Why can you not see the logic in what I am saying? Where do you not find it compelling?

JACRATES: I can see the logic in what you are saying just fine. But your assumptions are what give me great trouble.

ARMINITAS: Please explain.

JACRATES: On the one hand, Arminitas, you assume that our choices are totally determined by something other than a person himself and you assume this in order to prove that God could control our choices by creating the network of influences at work on us. But then, after you have finished your proof, you tell me that "of course our choices are not determined at all" and that we make them "in total independence from God."

ARMINITAS: But I never did assume that our choices were totally determined by something other than ourselves.

JACRATES: In that case, Arminitas, I must take serious exception to your proof.

ARMINITAS: Why is that?

JACRATES: Arminitas, did you not ask me to agree that God understands us well enough that he could predict with great precision how we will react to a certain situation and all of its influences?

ARMINITAS: Yes, I did.

JACRATES: And did I not agree with you?

ARMINITAS: You most certainly did.

JACRATES: But you did not tell me that I was to agree with you without assuming that our choices were totally determined.

ARMINITAS: No, not explicitly; but I was assuming you would understand that.

JACRATES: Well, Arminitas, I don't see how I can agree with you any longer if you will not allow me to believe first that my choices are determined.

ARMINITAS: Why is that Jacrates?

JACRATES: Arminitas, do you think it possible that God could predict with great precision choices that were random?

ARMINITAS: No, most certainly not.

JACRATES: Then, you agree that God could not predict with great precision choices that were uncaused and undetermined?

ARMINITAS: Yes, I agree.

JACRATES: So you are assuming that our choices are determined and caused by someone or something?

ARMINITAS: Most definitely, by ourselves!

JACRATES: Now you don't mean that our choices cause themselves, do you?

ARMINITAS: No, of course not. We cause our choices, our choices don't cause themselves. That would be absurd.

JACRATES: So our choices are neither uncaused nor are they self-caused? They are neither undetermined nor self-determined?

ARMINITAS: That is correct.

JACRATES: So they must be determined by someone or something else?

ARMINITAS: Yes, that is what I have been saying all along. We cause our choices.

JACRATES: We are in agreement then that we cause our choices?

ARMINITAS: Yes, certainly! I do hope this argument of yours is going somewhere.

JACRATES: Now, can we agree, Arminitas, that our will is what causes our choices?

ARMINITAS: Yes, I think that is accurate.

JACRATES: Now, what do we know about the will? Is the will itself uncaused? Is it eternal and without any creator?

ARMINITAS: No! Most definitely not.

JACRATES: And did the will create itself out of nothing? Did it cause itself?

ARMINITAS: No, of course not.

JACRATES: So the will is caused by something other than itself.

ARMINITAS: Yes, that is true.

JACRATES: And is that something God? Did God cause our wills to be?

ARMINITAS: Yes, of course. God created our wills.

JACRATES: Now, Arminitas, does it make any difference in your answers just now that we have not defined precisely what our will is? Do we need to define it precisely? Or can we proceed on the assumption that however it is to be defined our answers just now would remain just the same?

ARMINITAS: We can proceed. I don't think I would change my answers no matter how we might define the will so long as it is anywhere close to a reasonable definition.

JACRATES: Good. And do you agree that it would be impossible for God to cause our wills to exist—that is, to create them—without thereby determining the principles by which they would operate in making our choices.

ARMINITAS: Yes, that seems reasonable.

JACRATES: So, do you agree that any choice we make has been deter-mined by our own will that has, in turn, been determined by God, who created it? And, hence, that every choice we make has been ultimately determined by God?

ARMINITAS: Yes, I believe I must if I am to be logical.

JACRATES: So do you see why I could agree with you that God under-stands us well enough to know how we will respond to particular influ-ences? I could agree with you if God is the one who has determined the way we will respond. But if God is not the one who determines the way we will respond, then I don't see how he could know. If God has not deter-mined the way we will respond, then no one has. If no one has, then our choices are undetermined. But if our choices are undetermined, then God could not know how we would respond in a given situation, for our choic-es would be random. So, Arminitas, if I agree with your assumption, then I must believe that God has determined our choices. But if I do not believe that God has determined our choices, then I cannot agree with your assumption. No matter how well God knows us, if the choices we make are random and uncaused, then not even he could predict what choices we would make.

ARMINITAS: If all this is true, Jacrates, then why does what I argued still make sense to me?

JACRATES: I think the problem is that you weren't altogether honest with me. You agreed with me that it would be impossible for God to cause our wills to exist—that is, to create them—without thereby determining the principles by which they would operate in making our choices. Now, on the one hand, you do believe that; but, on the other hand, you don't accept it at all. You apparently have some sort of notion that both are true at the same time. On the one hand, God created our wills and everything about them and determined the principles by which they would operate. But, on the other hand, you clearly want to believe that there is something about the way the will functions in making choices that is not determined by God, but is self-determining. That way you can eat your cake and have it to. God is the creator of our will, but God does not ultimately determine the function of the will that is decisive in dictating what my choices will be.

ARMINITAS: Yes, I believe you are right. That is exactly what I am thinking. I was too hasty then to grant you that if God created the will, he necessarily determines how it will function. I do not agree with that. He has, certainly, determined the general principles by which our wills operate. But the more specific principles that are decisive in determining our specific choices, God does not determine those. God has deliberately and purposely created them to be free of his control.

JACRATES: Good. Now we are beginning to get somewhere, Arminitas. You almost have me convinced. However, I need your help in seeing just one more thing..

ARMINITAS: What's that?

JACRATES: I just need for you to tell me, then—if God does not determine the more specific principles that are decisive in determining what our specific choices are, then who or what does? Is it perhaps our genetic code? Do our genes then finally determine our choices by creating the specific principles whereby our wills function?

ARMINITAS: Heavens, no! Our wills would certainly not be free wills if that were the case. B. F. [Skinner] is right about that. There's no sense talking about freedom and dignity if everything is determined by genes or chemistry or physics or what have you. But we all know that we have free wills! That's just plain common sense. No, its not genes.

JACRATES: What then?

ARMINITAS: Well, it's our personalities. My personality is what gives rise to the specific principles that determine decisively what my will chooses.

JACRATES: I see. And where did my personality come from? Did not God create it and determine exactly what it would be?

ARMINITAS: Yes, of course.

JACRATES: Then, you are just having fun with me, Arminitas. If God created my personality and determined exactly what it will be and if my personality determined what those specific principles are that determine exactly how my will will function in making specific choices, then God is the one who ultimately determines each and every one of my specific choices after all.

ARMINITAS: Well, no, I guess my personality is not what determines how my will functions.

JACRATES: Well, what then?

ARMINITAS: Nothing, I guess nothing determines it.

JACRATES: Nothing! You mean nothing causes those specific principles to exist that determine exactly how my will functions? Are those principles eternal then. Have they always existed right alongside God himself. Is there some part of God's creation that he did not create?

ARMINITAS: No, of course not...

JACRATES: Then these principles created themselves out of nothing all by themselves. This sounds like evolution! Is that what you are saying?

ARMINITAS: No, of course not. You are just beginning to rattle me a little, Jacrates. I spoke too hastily. I didn't really mean that nothing determines them. I just meant that I don't know what to name that thing that determines those principles. It is just some aspect of the will itself that God does not control.

JACRATES: Oh, all right. Let's give this "we-know-not-what-its-name-is" a name then. Can we call this aspect of the will, the 'brumpf'?

ARMINITAS: Sure, why not?

JACRATES: O.K. And where did my brumpf come from? Did not God create it and determine exactly what it would be?

ARMINITAS: No, you won't trap me this time. No! God did not determine exactly what it would be. That's the whole point.

JACRATES: Is it created, Arminitas? Or have our brumpfs always existed from before the foundation of the world?

ARMINITAS: No, my brumpf had to have been created.

JACRATES: And who created it?

ARMINITAS: It had to be God.

JACRATES: Are you not playing with me again, Arminitas? Tell me if this doesn't make sense: If God created my brumpf and determined exactly what it will be and if my brumpf determined what those specific principles are that determine exactly how my will will function in making specific choices, then God is the one who ultimately determines each and every one of my specific choices after all. Isn't that right?

ARMINITAS: It would be, Jacrates, except I think God created my brumpf without determining exactly what it will be.

JACRATES: My! God can work miracles. But I don't see how he could possibly do that. Well, let's suppose you are right. If not God, then who or what did determine what our brumpf would be, even though not he but God created it?

ARMINITAS: Well, I don't know the name of it.

JACRATES: Since we have shown ourselves so good at names shall we invent another? How about 'rottle'? Our rottle is what determines exactly what our brumpf will be that then determines what those specific principles are that dictate our specific choices. Now, is our rottle also created by God without being determined by God? And should we find yet another name for that thing that does determine what exactly our rottle will be even though God and not that thing created our rottle? And shall we keep on this way until we run out of names, Arminitas? Or shall we sooner or later find some part of our will that is either eternal and uncreated like God or is capable of creating itself out of nothing all by itself or is both created and determined by the same thing?

ARMINITAS: Yes, I think sooner or later we shall.

JACRATES: And which shall we find?

ARMINITAS: I think we shall find something that is both created and determined by the same thing.

JACRATES: Oh good! I was getting very tired thinking about it. And what will that same thing be that both creates and determines this aspect of our wills?

ARMINITAS: It must be God, of course.

JACRATES: And so God does finally determine those very specific principles that dictate what choices our wills will make after all?

ARMINITAS: Yes, I think he must. What do you think Allophon? Should we concede Jacrates his point? Are you convinced that divine determinism is the only way to explain how God can so totally control the affairs of history?

ALLOPHON: No, I'm afraid not. I must confess that I do not immediately see what is wrong with Jacrates' reasonings, but surely something is wrong. Your explanation, Arminitas, makes much more sense to me than Jacrates'.

JACRATES: Allophon, let us assume then for a moment that Arminitas was right in his explanation as you are quite confident is the case. Tell me, then, do you believe in free will?

ALLOPHON: Certainly. That is why I am so sure that you are wrong, Jacrates.

JACRATES: And what is 'free will,' Allophon?

ALLOPHON: Well, I'm not sure I have defined it for myself carefully enough, but I guess I would say it is something like man's ability to make choices that have not been decisively determined by anything or anyone other than the man himself.

JACRATES: Alright, that sounds like a good enough definition for a start. Would you say, then, that a machine has a free will? I mean, some machine that has artificial intelligence, for example?

ALLOPHON: No! Certainly not.

JACRATES: Why not? Is it because the laws of physics that direct the operations of the machine and the particular physical state of the machine's environment at any given time are decisive in dictating what that machine's choices or decisions will be at that time?

ALLOPHON: Yes, exactly!

JACRATES: Now what about this theory that Arminitas has offered to the effect that God can infallibly control men's actions without actually determining their choices? Help me understand it a little better. Do you understand Arminitas to be saying that God can so skillfully control a man's physical environment that he can compel him to make exactly that choice that he wants him to make?

ALLOPHON: Yes, that is how I understand it.

JACRATES: Now, we have already agreed that God knows the future infallibly, and that the only way that that can be so is if he has infallible control over the choices of men. Isn't that so?

ALLOPHON: Yes, we are agreed on that.

JACRATES: So you are suggesting then that God is able to have infallible control over the choices of mankind through skillful manipulation of their physical environment?

ALLOPHON: Yes, that's what I would say.

JACRATES: Now if God is capable of infallible control of men's choices through their physical environment, then does it not follow that a man's physical environment must have inexorable control over what a man decides? Otherwise, no matter what physical environment a man found himself in, there would always exist the possibility that the man would choose something other than what his environment was influencing him toward. Isn't that so?

ALLOPHON: That doesn't sound quite right. Explain what you mean some more.

JACRATES: Look at it this way. Let's make a distinction. Let's call an "influence" something in my physical environment that creates pressure on my will to choose in one direction rather than another. But although an influence creates pressure on the will to choose in a certain direction, it does not actually dictate that the will must necessarily choose that direction. It is always possible, by our definition, to choose something contrary to what an influence is pushing us toward. But let's call a "cause" something in my physical environment that makes it physically impossible for me to choose other than what the cause is dictating that I choose. Do you understand my distinction?

ALLOPHON: Yes. Clearly.

JACRATES: Alright then, how is it that God uses our physical environment to control our choices? Does he use it as a very compelling influence, or does he use it as a cause?

ALLOPHON: I'm not sure what difference it makes.

JACRATES: Well, let me ask you this: is it your belief that God controls the affairs of man absolutely with no margin for error. What I mean is this— is there any possibility of God somehow not succeeding to control a man's choices the way he wants?

ALLOPHON: No, I don't think there is any possibility of that.

JACRATES: So you really literally did mean that God controlled a man's choices infallibly.

ALLOPHON: Yes. I believe that is literally true.

JACRATES: Now, according to our definition, it is always possible for a man to make a choice contrary to what an influence is pushing him toward. So, if it is impossible for a man to make a choice contrary to what God is pushing him toward through his manipulation of the environment, then it must be the case, by our definitions, that God uses the environment to *cause* us to choose the way we do. He doesn't merely use the environment to *influence* our decision. He actually uses it to *cause* it.

ALLOPHON: Yes, that would seem to follow.

JACRATES: Now, let's return to our artificially intelligent machine for a moment. Would you agree that the choices the machine makes are caused by its physical environment? Or do you think that the physical environment is only an influence?

ALLOPHON: Certainly the physical environment causes the machine's choices.

JACRATES: And did we not agree earlier that the reason our machine does not have free will is because the laws of physics and its environment actually cause, by our definition, the choices the machine makes?

ALLOPHON: Yes, I suppose we did.

JACRATES: And did we not just now say that the physical environment causes us to make the choices we make?

ALLOPHON: Yes, we did.

JACRATES: Should I conclude then that you don't believe we have free will after all, Allophon? Or is there some difference between me and the machine that I have failed to notice?

ALLOPHON: Well, I think there is a difference. The machine doesn't choose how it will respond, it just does what the laws of physics make it do. But people choose what they shall do.

JACRATES: And what do you mean by that exactly? Do you mean that whereas the machine has to do what it does because it is simply responding to its physical environment, people don't have to do what they do in response to their physical environment and could actually do exactly the opposite?

ALLOPHON: Yes, that's right.

JACRATES: But Allophon, my friend, I thought you told me you believed that God controlled our choices infallibly; and, hence, that our environment *caused* our choices such that we do what we do out of necessity? Didn't we decide that must be the case if it is true that God infallibly controlled human choice?

ALLOPHON: Yes, I seem to recall that we did.

JACRATES: Then am I to take it that you do not believe that man has free will? Are we just like the machine? Or should we assume that Arminitas' theory is wrong? Perhaps we should reject Arminitas' theory that God can control human choices through skillful manipulation of his environment because the only way God could do that is if man does not have free will.

ALLOPHON: Well, I do believe in free will. That is precisely why I did not feel comfortable with your theory that God causes our choices. It has seemed to me that your theory is incompatible with free will. But if you're right and Arminitas' theory is incompatible with free will, then I don't like it either.

JACRATES: Shall we make that our conclusion then?

ALLOPHON: No. Not so fast. Perhaps Arminitas' theory is still sound. Perhaps rather we were wrong to assume that God was infallible in his ability to control our choices. Perhaps God is just very, very successful. Maybe 99.9999% successful. We still have free will and it is our free will that is the deciding factor in what we will do, but God is simply very good at exerting just the right influences to induce us to choose what he wants us to choose.

JACRATES: So Allophon, am I to understand that God's prophetic predictions are not infallible either? Are they only 99.9999% reliable? "Thus says the Lord, I'm 99.9999% sure that ...."?

ALLOPHON: Well, I don't know. That doesn't sound exactly right does it? But maybe. Well, why not?

JACRATES: Well, it's possible I guess. I'm just glad that I don't have to be the prophet when God misses. Seems to me there's another problem though. I understand why our machine's choices are controlled by its environment. There's a physical and mechanical relationship between what happens to the machine and what the machine does. But you are denying that kind of connection in people aren't you?

ALLOPHON: Yes, I am. I think that's one of the things that makes people different from machines.

JACRATES: Then, how is it that the physical environment could actually control what one chooses?

ALLOPHON: Well I don't know *how* exactly. I mean, I don't know the mechanics of it. But you surely know yourself that when you are very hungry and there is something to eat, you will eat it. Well, if you are hungry enough and God puts something desirable enough in front of you, he can pretty much guarantee that you will eat it. I think that must be how it works.

JACRATES: To the tune of 99.9999%?

ALLOPHON: Yeah.

JACRATES: Well, remember when God put Jesus in the wilderness and got him very hungry and then had Satan suggest that he use his supernatural powers to turn stones into bread. Was God trying to get Jesus to turn the stones into bread and eat them, but yet Jesus didn't do it? Is that an example of where God actually failed to control Jesus' choices? Is that one of the .0001%?

ALLOPHON: No, God didn't want Jesus to turn the stones to bread. That was a test and Jesus had the strength of character to resist the temptation.

JACRATES: But isn't that the same as saying Jesus had the strength of character to resist the influences on him? Like hunger?

ALLOPHON: Yes.

JACRATES: But what do you think? Did God not make normal human beings to have the strength to resist influences on their choices? Or is that how God can control us—because we always give in to the things that influence us? And if so, is it true that God wouldn't blame us for giving in to those kind of influences on our choices, since we don't really have the ability to resist them?

ALLOPHON: No, we're supposed to be able to resist too.

JACRATES: But you can't have it both ways, Allophon. Either we can't effectively resist influences (in which case it makes sense that God could be 99.9999% successful in controlling our choices) or we can resist and are expected to resist the influences on our choices. In fact, we are expected to freely choose what is right against whatever pressure of influences exists. If the latter, then I don't see how God, no matter how skillful he is, could rate as high as 99.9999%. Furthermore, doesn't it seem strange that we would applaud God for something we find so reprehensible in one another?

ALLOPHON: What's that?

JACRATES: Manipulation. We don't find it particularly noble when people try to manipulate others, exploiting their weaknesses to get them to do what they want them to. We find that rather wicked of them. Why would 99.9999% successful manipulation not be at least as wicked?

ALLOPHON: I suppose you have a point there.

JACRATES: I think divine determinism makes a lot more sense. Arminitas' theory gets us into all kinds of trouble.

ALLOPHON: Perhaps you are right.

J. A. "JACK" CRABTREE currently lives in Eugene, Oregon where he is a tutor at Gutenberg College and the Director of McKenzie Study Center. Gutenberg College is a Great-Books curriculum college offering a B.A. degree in Liberal Arts. McKenzie Study Center is an institute of Gutenberg College dedicated to understanding the teaching of the Bible and promoting biblical understanding.

Jack graduated with honors and was elected to Phi Beta Kappa when he earned his A.B. in philosophy from Stanford University in 1971. Jack has studied and taught the Bible for the past 35 years, first at Peninsula Bible Church in Palo Alto, California and then at McKenzie Study Center in Eugene, Oregon. In the 1980's Jack returned to graduate school, earning his Ph.D. in philosophy from the University of Oregon in 1992.

Jack's main interest and focus over the past 30 years has been his study of the New Testament, seeking a clear and accurate grasp of the apostolic gospel and apostolic teachings.

Jack and his wife Jody have four grown children.

Other books available from
GUTENBERG COLLEGE PRESS

Almost everyone assumes that sound science is the best hope for saving Pacific Northwest salmonids. But what is sound science? From his unique perspective, Dr. Charley Dewberry examines the background, assumptions, and inconsistencies behind the common view of science and he prescribes the remedies for saving science.

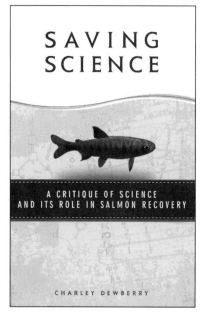

Charley began a Ph.D. program in stream ecology at Oregon State University but ended up completing a Ph.D. in philosophy of science at the University of Oregon in 1995, motivated largely by many of the issues raised in this book. He currently is a tutor at Gutenberg College in Eugene, Oregon.

Charley is among the most experienced field workers in the Pacific Northwest. He is also the chief architect of the Knowles Creek restoration project, one of the major science efforts within the Siuslaw partnership, which won the 2004 Thiess Riverprize, among the most prestigious international river prizes for river restoration.

For more information on ordering directly from the publishers, please visit our web site or contact us via e-mail:

www.gutenberg.edu
office@gutenberg.edu

 **GUTENBERG COLLEGE**

The Author is a tutor at Gutenberg College,
1883 University Street, Eugene, Oregon 97401.

Gutenberg College is committed to the idea that there is an objective truth that can be known, rooted in the nature of God and His creation. Truth does not vary from person to person, but is a fixed reality with which each person must come to terms. The process of wrestling with truth, however, is very personal and subjective, Gutenberg College seeks to recognize both the objective nature of truth and the subjective nature of learning. Over the course of four years, students are exposed to the fundamental questions of life and the answers, good and bad, offered by our cultural heritage. Ultimately, however, students must formulate answers to these questions for themselves. In the process, the Gutenberg College faculty encourage students to pursue truth and reason wherever they might lead.

"It is difficult to write of my school—to pin it like a butterfly on velvet and say this is the species of my education. The difficulty is that Gutenberg has been so much more than a school to me and so defies description as such. Gutenberg has been an invasion of my life, an event that has colored my soul. The piece of paper with two certain initials (B.A.) on it will mean so little to me in comparison with the "sea-change" that the cast of my life has taken. Gutenberg is not about the mind, but rather the soul. Thus, education is but a springboard to life, and Gutenberg seems to embrace this truth with a unique force."

–**AXON KIRK**, *Gutenberg graduate*